Advance Praise for Character

"Considerations of personal character have largely disappeared from modern public discourse and policy debates. Deborah Rhode wants them to occupy a more central role in 21st century society. As she defines it character includes moral traits such as honesty and integrity and performance traits such as perseverance and grit. Her wide ranging analysis considers how character develops and the impact it has on people's thoughts, feelings and behavior. Her thoughtful review amasses a formidable range of scholarship, including compelling profiles of exemplary individuals, to make a strong case for resurrecting character as a pivotal concern in our examination of legal, political and other societal leaders."

—**Tom Tyler**, Macklin Fleming Professor of Law
and Professor of Psychology, Yale University

"In this inspiring and hopeful book, Deborah Rhode shows how misconceptions about character and its assessment prevent our legal, criminal justice, and political systems from achieving even their own espoused aims, let alone the country's highest ideals. Drawing on a deep understanding of the psychology of character and its often surprising relationships to public policy, Rhode conveys and then cuts through the issues' complexity and offers sensible, humane guidance toward the change that is so urgently needed."

—**Anne Colby**, Consulting Professor, Center
on Adolescence, Stanford University

"Everyone agrees that character is important. Public and private schools are busy developing character education initiatives, the idea of good character is used and misused in occupational licensing, citizenship determinations, and the criminal justice system, and of course we argue vociferously about the character of politicians. But few concepts are as difficult to pin down. Drawing from the work of philosophers, psychologists, sociologists, educators, and lawyers, Deborah Rhode carefully distinguishes a meaningful concept of character from the platitudes, nostalgia, and thinly-veiled ideological arguments that are depressingly familiar. She does so not with dry academic definitions, but with engaging profiles of people who exhibit complex but admirable characters."

—**W. Bradley Wendel**, Associate Dean for Academic Affairs
and Professor of Law, Cornell Law School

"Deborah Rhode patiently and powerfully details why we need to pay more attention to character—and provides a roadmap for how to do so."

—**James Forman, Jr.**, Pulitzer-prize winning author
of *Locking Up Our Own*

Character

What It Means and Why It Matters

DEBORAH L. RHODE

OXFORD

UNIVERSITY PRESS

OXFORD
UNIVERSITY PRESS

Oxford University Press is a department of the University of Oxford. It furthers the University's objective of excellence in research, scholarship, and education by publishing worldwide. Oxford is a registered trade mark of Oxford University Press in the UK and certain other countries.

Published in the United States of America by Oxford University Press
198 Madison Avenue, New York, NY 10016, United States of America.

© Oxford University Press 2019

Library of Congress Cataloging-in-Publication Data
Names: Rhode, Deborah L., author.
Title: Character : what it means and why it matters / Deborah L. Rhode.
Description: 1st Edition. | New York : Oxford University Press, [2019]
Identifiers: LCCN 2018058188 | ISBN 9780190919870 (hardcover : alk. paper) |
ISBN 9780190919894 (electronic publication)
Subjects: LCSH: Character.
Classification: LCC BF818.R486 2019 | DDC 155.2—dc23
LC record available at https://lccn.loc.gov/2018058188

1 3 5 7 9 8 6 4 2

Printed by Sheridan Books, Inc., United States of America

For Thurgood Marshall

FIGURE 0.1 Thurgood Marshall. Photo by Deborah L. Rhode, United Supreme
Court, 1978.

Table of Contents

Acknowledgments

ACKNOWLEDGMENTS ARE A daunting craft. It seems impossible to express in any adequate way my appreciation to those who have done so much to make this work possible. I am deeply grateful to David McBride at Oxford University Press, who supported this project from the outset and made it immeasurably better. Many colleagues shared invaluable insights on earlier versions of the manuscript: Greg Ablavsky, Megan Denver, George Fisher, Robert Gordon, Lucas Guttentag, Robert MacCoun, Joan Petersilia, David Sklansky, Jaysahri Srkiantiah, Robert Weisberg, and Bradley Wendel. Lawrence Friedman gave the kind of close and thoughtful read to the entire draft that exemplifies what character means in academic life. The staff of the Stanford Law library offered superb reference assistance. Special thanks go to Leizel Ching, Sean Kaneshiro, Marion Miller, Sonia Moss, Katie Ott, Rich Porter, Sarah Reis, Kevin Rothenberg, Sergio Stone, Beth Williams, George Wilson, and Alex Zhang, I also owe enormous debts to the research and manuscript assistance of Gemma Donafrio and Eun Sze. My deepest gratitude goes to my husband, Ralph Cavanagh, whose support and insight has sustained my work for almost four decades.

The book is dedicated to Supreme Court Justice Thurgood Marshall, for whom I had the good fortune to clerk. His example gave me a personal glimpse of the kind of character that this book seeks to inspire.

Character

I

What Is Character

ANYONE WRITING ABOUT character should proceed with caution. It is a humbling task, and self-reflective authors may be uncomfortably reminded how often their own characters fall short. Moreover, this is a subject that, as one researcher noted, can "easily veer into vacuity."[1] British novelist H. G. Wells chided eighteenth- and nineteenth-century commentators for "all that cant about a character," and there is much in contemporary literature that might inspire similar criticisms.[2] Yet the concept is one that no civilized society can afford to ignore. Recognition of its importance dates back two thousand years to the classical Greek philosophers. In the United States, the founding fathers saw moral character as a foundation for the new republic. According to John Adams, a loss of principles would be more dangerous "than the whole force of the common enemy."[3]

Growing numbers of Americans are coming to share that view. After decades of decline, discussion of character has seen somewhat of a revival. Character curricula have become increasingly common in elementary and secondary schools. Philosophers have become more interested in "virtue ethics," with its emphasis on character as a foundation for moral conduct. And in a contemporary poll, 90 percent of Americans agreed that "democracy is only as strong as the virtue of its citizens."[4]

This book seeks a better understanding about what we mean by character and why it matters. How have philosophers, psychologists, judges, and the public generally thought about the concept? How is character developed? What role should it play in education, politics, and law? Whose lives best exemplify it? "Within the character of the citizen lies the welfare of the nation," said Cicero, and the discussion that follows suggests why.

Overview

I begin in this chapter with definitions of character. What has it meant to philosophers, psychologists, and the public generally? What can we learn from contemporary research about the significance and stability of traits associated with character and how they interact with situational influences in shaping behavior? I conclude by exploring key character traits, which cluster in two categories: *performance traits*, such as perseverance and "grit," and *moral traits*, such as honesty, integrity, and empathy. That overview lays the foundation for the chapters that follow.

Chapter 2 focuses on how such traits develop and our need to be more informed and proactive in shaping the process. I begin where character education begins: in the family. Analysis then turns to religious, sport, and youth organizations that seek to inculcate virtue. The second part of the chapter focuses on what schools are doing, and should be doing, to develop character.

Discussion then turns to law, where character plays a larger role than commonly assumed. Chapter 3 focuses on character requirements that determine who can receive occupational and professional licenses or lawful immigration and citizenship status. The law decides who has "good moral character" and often uses a single criminal conviction to exclude individuals from a vast range of jobs, including everything from florist and fortune tellers, to frog farmers and junk dealers. These obstacles to employment, regardless of how long ago the offense occurred or its relevance to the occupation at issue, are a significant barrier to rehabilitation. Minor or long-past criminal conduct has similarly obstructed the path to legal immigration and citizenship. Such character requirements are out of step with psychological research. Character is not defined by a single "bad act"; moral behavior can evolve, and a sensible legal framework should reward individuals' efforts to turn their lives around.

Chapter 4 addresses questions of character in criminal justice. What role should evidence about prior "bad character" play in criminal trials, punishment, and parole? How have assumptions about the character of defendants contributed to prosecutorial practices and mass incarceration? How have class and racial biases skewed judgments about character and culpability? What reforms might increase fairness and cost effectiveness in the criminal justice system?

Chapter 5 looks at politics, where the public stake in choosing individuals of character is greatest. Through examples drawn from modern presidents, I explore the role of honesty, temperament, ambition, and integrity. Although Americans generally say that character is important in politicians, they do not vote accordingly. For that, they pay a tremendous price. The 2016 election is only the most recent example of what can go awry when character is not a key factor in selecting political leaders.

Analysis then turns to the kind of character we should want in those who occupy positions of influence, and profiles individuals whose lives inspire our highest aspirations. That shift to narrative makes sense because, as novelist Henry Fielding noted, "examples work more forcibly on the mind than precepts" in demonstrating what is "praiseworthy."[5] A wide array of research makes clear that role models play a crucial role in character development.[6] To that end, chapter 6 focuses on three individuals who led exemplary lives of service and who also encouraged service by others: Jane Addams, Albert Schweitzer, and Mother Teresa. Chapter 7 focuses on social justice activists: Ida Wells, Mahatma Gandhi, Thurgood Marshall, and Nelson Mandela. Taken together, these individuals reflect a diversity of backgrounds and commitments. None were without flaws, but all had character traits that made them worthy of admiration: courage, integrity, persistence, and a deep commitment to the common good.

Chapter 8 concludes the discussion by reviewing the book's major themes and situating them against a broader cultural backdrop. Effective character development faces substantial challenges in a society increasingly preoccupied with wealth and status rather than moral values. What does it say about our national priorities that less than a fifth of Americans have a great deal of confidence of leaders in politics, business, and the professions, or think that their president is a person of integrity?[7] We urgently need more focus on character and a better understanding of how we can nurture and sustain it.

Definitions

Character is a contested concept. It has meant different things to different audiences, and its definition has changed over time and across culture. The dominant current understanding, as reflected in the *Oxford English Dictionary*, is that character is "the sum of the moral and mental qualities which distinguish an individual or a people."[8] Psychologists view character as patterns of thought, emotion, and behavior.[9] In conventional usage, character sometimes seems synonymous with personality, but experts note two important distinctions. First, character has a moral resonance that personality does not. Personality traits such as introversion carry none of the ethical connotations associated with character traits such as integrity.[10] Second, researchers generally have found a stronger genetic basis for personality than for character; moral qualities appear to develop largely through education and experience.[11] However, recent work in neuroscience suggests that variation in brain structure and functioning may also have some influence on ethical reasoning, motivation, and behavior.[12]

Studies of popular usage find that "character seems to be a catchall for everything—for anything—commendable."[13] Calling someone a person of character generally implies that he or she is virtuous. Good character is thought to involve "knowing the good, desiring the good, and doing the good—habits of the mind, habits of the heart, and habits of behavior."[14] Such sweeping moral labels can, however, be misleading because most of us possess some positive traits associated with good character but lack others, and often have "mixed traits," such as loyalty, which have ethical consequences that vary depending on the situation.[15] Suicide bombers may have loyalty, along with courage and steadfast adherence to principle, but we would not ordinarily speak of them as persons of character.[16]

In recognition of these complexities, contemporary experts often distinguish between the moral dimensions of character, including qualities such as honesty and integrity, and the performance dimensions of character, including qualities such as self-control, diligence, perseverance, and "grit."[17] Many performance traits are relatively stable over time, and are associated with various measures of achievement and well-being.[18] In one well-known study on self-control, Stanford professor Walter Mischel offered four-year-olds a marshmallow that they could eat immediately, but promised an extra one if they could wait until an experimenter returned. When the toddlers were evaluated decades later, those who had been able to delay gratification were more successful both academically and socially.[19] A ten-year study of more than a thousand young people in New Zealand similarly found that the degree of self-control in childhood correlated with a wide array of outcomes in adults, including health, addiction, credit rating, and criminal record.[20]

Performance traits are related to moral traits. Without self-discipline, and resoluteness, we could not be consistently honest or courageous.[21] For that reason, philosophers have long recognized the ethical importance of what Adam Smith labeled "self command."[22] Society has a stake in developing both dimensions of character. Without performance traits, individuals lack the capacity to follow through on good intentions. But without a moral compass, individuals may use their performance strengths in the service of unethical or self-interested ends.

Moral character is partly a function of moral identity—the belief that morality is important to our sense of self.[23] Moral identity is, in turn, associated with altruism, and associated behaviors such as volunteer service and charitable donations.[24] Nurturing moral identity should be a crucial aim of character development.[25] Considerable research suggests that the "centrality of morality" to our sense of self is what drives us to translate moral judgements into moral conduct.[26]

Historical Background

In Western thought, Plato's *The Republic* was the first major elaboration of the virtues that constitute character. With Socrates as his mouthpiece, Plato proposed wisdom, courage, justice, and temperance (i.e., self-restraint) as the four core virtues of the ideal society. In his view, character reflecting those virtues was the defining qualification of the ruling class. Leaders with character were the individuals "most likely to devote their lives to doing what they judge to be in the interest of the community."[27] Social disintegration was inevitable if rulers failed in this regard. As Plato put it, "the community suffers nothing very terrible if its cobblers are bad and become degenerate and pretentious; but if the Guardians of the laws and state, who alone have the opportunity to bring it good governance and prosperity become a mere sham, then clearly it is completely ruined."[28]

Plato's leading student, Aristotle, argued that virtuous character comes through practice. His *Nicomachean Ethics* maintained that virtues were the mean between two extremes. For example, courage was the mean between cowardice and rashness. Aristotle's list of virtues included the original Platonic four (courage, justice, temperance, and wisdom), but added others such as friendliness, truthfulness, and greatness of soul.[29] Habit was the key to acquiring virtues. Aristotle analogized the process to learning a craft: "by building, we become builders, by playing the lyre, lyre players. And so too we become just by doing just actions, and temperate by doing temperate actions.... [S]tates of character are formed out of corresponding acts."[30] Teachers are also critical, because "playing the lyre produces both good and bad lyre players" and teachers can identify the difference.[31]

Early Christian theologians also stressed virtues, but not character. Nor did most moral philosophers focus on character until relatively recently.[32] Rather than asking "what qualities make a good person?," philosophers asked, "what is the right thing to do?" They developed theories such as deontology and utilitarianism that stressed not moral character but moral action.

In the United States, character first attracted attention in the nineteenth century. The concept came to signify a group of traits that carried both social and moral significance. Hundreds of books, pamphlets, and articles provided advice about character development that would lead to worldly success. A representative example was Orison Swett Marden's 1899 volume, *Character, The Grandest Thing in the World.* Through historical examples, the book emphasized the moral traits and high ideals that ensured fulfillment and constituted a "true Christian gentleman." Character was "power," which supplied "a sure and easy way to wealth, honor, and happiness."[33] This "culture of character" was well suited to a society that thrived on hard work and a deep sense of duty.[34] Such understandings were also part of a broader trend that historian Gertrude Himmelfarb has described as the "democratization of virtue."[35] Qualities of moral worth were increasingly seen as available to anyone, regardless of birth or class.

In the early decades of the twentieth century, the attention to character began to decline. Growing economic abundance encouraged more emphasis on material pleasures and individual preferences. This new sense of self was captured by the term "personality," which first emerged in the late eighteenth century but only gained wide currency in the early twentieth. The adjectives associated with personality suggested a very different set of traits than those associated with character. The new focus was on being attractive, masterful, and dominant, rather than honest and virtuous.[36] Most advice manuals concerning personality offered somewhat inconsistent counsel: individuals should both "be themselves" and "eliminate the little personal whims, habits, and traits that that make people dislike you."[37] By 1921, Marden had shifted his focus from character to poise, wardrobe, and conversation. His publication *Masterful Personality* emphasized charm and other traits that make someone likeable. After all, he noted, "so much of our success in life depends on what others think of us."[38]

This shift in popular culture was mirrored in the social sciences. In their 1950 bestseller, *The Lonely Crowd*, sociologists David Riesman, Nathan Glazer, and Reuel Denney chronicled Americans' shift from being "inner directed" to "other directed," influenced less by internalized value and more by peers and media.[39] Around the same time, leading psychologists pushed the discipline to abandon character in favor of the less morally freighted language of personality.[40] According to Gordon Allport, character was "personality evaluated" and character study belonged to "social ethics" rather than to a social science such as psychology.[41]

Contemporary Understandings

Usage of terms such as "character" and "virtue" declined over the later part of the twentieth century, as did other measures of ethical concern.[42] In 1966, 80 percent of college freshman said that they were strongly motivated to develop a meaningful philosophy of life, and only 42 percent said that becoming rich was an important life goal. In more recent surveys, those values have reversed. Three-quarters of college students want to become rich and fewer than half care strongly about developing a philosophy of life.[43] A study of young adults age eighteen to twenty-three found that their horizons were dispiritingly parochial. Most had few aspirations beyond having a good job, a nice family, and an ability to buy what they wanted. Nothing "more meaningful, more transcendent, [or] more shared" were high priorities.[44] So too, as *New York Times* columnist David Brooks has noted, "intellectual prestige" has drifted away from theologians and philosophers ... [leaving] less moral conversation in the public square. ... There are fewer places in public where people are talking about the things that matter most."[45] Economist Robert Reich notes a similar decline: "Americans are "talking less about the common good and more about self-aggrandizement."[46] The public generally agrees. Almost two-thirds believe that Americans have less character now than fifty years ago.[47]

Yet there are also counter trends. As chapter 2 notes, the last quarter century has seen a growing interest in character education in the schools. So too, an increasing number of contemporary moral philosophers have redirected attention to virtue.[48] Some focus on its importance for individuals, others on its importance for society.[49] In both contexts, character is central. For virtue ethics, the key question is not "What ought I to *do*?" but rather "what sort of person ought I to *be*?"[50]

There are, however, certain difficulties with virtue ethics as a theory, which suggest corresponding difficulties with character as a concept. One is that people expect ethics to provide guidance on what they ought to do, and virtue ethics is structurally unsuited for this. Many moral dilemmas involve competing values and virtues.[51] Much ink has been spilled in attempting to enumerate master virtues, such as wisdom, courage, and kindness, which take precedence over the others, but there is no consensus among moral philosophers or the general public about which virtues should take priority, and answers may vary depending on the context.[52] Nor is it always self-evident how the hypothetically virtuous person of character would resolve actual ethical dilemmas. The vice of virtue ethics is that its "oughts are frequently too vague ... to be of great use in applied ethics."[53] Moreover, virtues, or positive character traits such as courage, loyalty, persistence, and self-control, can serve unethical as well as ethical objectives.[54] Terrorists may have all of those qualities. As noted previously, similar points can be made about character traits more generally: they are necessary but not sufficient for moral conduct. For these reasons, some philosophers believe that virtue ethics should focus more on the ethical qualities of conduct than of persons. As Gilbert Harman argues, "there is more reason to believe that there are virtuous and vicious acts than to believe that people have [consistently] virtuous or vicious characters.[55]

Psychological Underpinnings

From a psychological standpoint, the definition of character raises a number of questions. One long-standing debate is whether people possess character traits that are relatively consistent across time and circumstances. Among psychologists in the early half of the twentieth century, the prevailing view was that individuals had stable internal traits that could predict their conduct in varying situations.[56] As Walter Mischel explains, "the initial assumptions of the trait-state theory were logical, inherently plausible, and also consistent with common sense and intuitive impressions about personality. Their real limitation turned out to be empirical— they simply have not been supported adequately."[57] By the late 1960s, multiple studies had cast doubt on this trait theory of character.[58] A new model of behavior known as "situationism" emerged. This school of thought has argued that situational factors are often better predictors of behavior than personal traits.[59] Situationists see our tendency to attribute behavior to a person's stable character as a "fundamental attribution error."[60]

Situationists point to a broad array of research. The most famous example involves Stanley Milgram's obedience experiments, replicated many times in this and other countries.[61] These experiments showed that about two-thirds of participants were willing to deliver apparently dangerous electric shocks to a subject when instructed to do so.[62] Yet when such experiments were described to ordinary Americans, they predicted that at most one person in a thousand would follow those instructions. No one believed that he or she personally would do so.[63] Variations on the original experimental design further underscored the importance of situational influences. In one variation, participants were part of a team with a confederate who was working with experimenters. When the confederate uncomplainingly obeyed instructions to continue the shocks, 90 percent of the participants went along. When the confederate refused to administer high-level shocks and walked away from the experiment, only 10 percent of the participants complied, again demonstrating the importance of situational influences.[64] In another obedience study, Stanford professor Philip Zimbardo and colleagues simulated conditions of an American prison in the psychology department's basement. Students were randomly assigned the role of prisoner or guard. They so thoroughly embraced their roles, and the guards became so sadistic, that the experiment had to be terminated after just six days.[65]

Studies of helping behavior similarly document the influence of situational factors. In a Columbia University study, participants were filling out a questionnaire when they heard a loud crash and a woman's cries of pain in the next room. Seventy percent of participants offered help when they were working alone. When they were working with a confederate who ignored the cries, only 7 percent intervened.[66] John Darley and Daniel Batson's study of students at Princeton's Theological Seminary found that if they were in a hurry, 90 percent walked by someone slumped in a doorway ostensibly experiencing distress. If they were not in a hurry, almost two-thirds helped. When they were under time pressure, even seminary students about to give a lecture on the Good Samaritan were no more likely to behave like one and offer assistance than other classmates.

In fact, on several occasions, a student about to give his talk on helping behavior literally stepped over the victim as he hurried on his way.[67] Taken together, these findings call into question the stability of character across different contexts.[68]

Although such research has sometimes seemed to pit situational forces against character traits, most contemporary experts see the two as "intricately related."[69] The current mainstream view, sometimes labeled "interactionism," understands behavior to be a function of the interaction between situation and traits.[70] Some traits have a genetic component, and researchers can find stable and distinctive patterns underlying what seems to be variability in behavior.[71] For example, by probing for the reasons why an individual might cheat in one situation but not another, researchers can frequently identify such patterns of conduct.[72] But a considerable amount of information about past actions is often necessary to make accurate predictions of future ethical behavior.[73] And given the large variability in character-related conduct in response to situational cues, it is much easier to predict behavioral trends than single acts.[74] A person might act impulsively in one context and with self-control in another, but his average degree of self-control tends to be stable over time.[75] And the tendency to be impulsive in one domain (such as finances) has some correlation with tendencies to be impulsive in others (such as substance abuse).[76]

However, the stability observable in patterns of conduct may often result less from the stability of character than from the stability of the social circumstances that affect such behavior.[77] Major changes in those circumstances can dramatically alter qualities that we associate with character. These qualities are not static even in adults. Some individuals become wiser and more giving over time; others become more selfish.[78] Moral character can be cultivated, and its potential for change should make us wary about permanent pronouncements that individuals have it or they don't.[79]

One extensively researched interrelationship between traits and situation involves altruism. Altruistic behavior refers to intrinsically motivated actions that are primarily intended to benefit others. Studies of genetic twins suggest that anywhere from a quarter to over a half of our propensity for caring and giving is inherited.[80] For the remainder, the main motivations are sympathy, internalized values or principles, and strong moral identity.[81] As chapter 2 indicates, these motivations can be developed and nurtured in childhood and later life. Surveys of altruistic activists point to "roots of participation that are anchored in one's sense of self as a moral being inextricably connected to others."[82] As a lawyer who started a legal clinic for the homeless explained, "There's a feeling that their quality of life and their suffering is also connected to yours."[83] A growing body of research suggests a genetic component in empathy, and some stability in empathetic and other prosocial behaviors across lifetimes.[84] People with a "prosocial personality" are more likely to engage in altruistic actions ranging from volunteer work to heroic acts of rescue.[85] Findings from a study of electronically recorded daily behavior found considerable stability in compassionate behavior over time.[86] That is not to deny the role of situational influences, including mood, role models, and peer behavior in influencing such actions.[87] But it is to suggest that character matters: that some individuals have a persistent disposition to act altruistically across a wide range of circumstances.

A second psychological insight concerning character involves the link between moral reasoning and moral behavior. Popular understandings of character generally assume that people make reasoned decisions about whether to act ethically, and that persons of "character" are more likely to choose the moral course of action.[88] Yet recent neuroscience and cognitive theory suggest that most moral judgments are made without deliberation; they are governed by preconscious automatic processes, and then reasoning serves to justify or question the judgment after the fact.[89] People rely on rational deliberation to make ethical decisions only when initial intuitions are weak or in conflict, when the stakes are high, or when their judgments are contested.[90] In many mundane circumstances, cognitive moral development (namely, capacity for moral reasoning) does not accurately predict moral behavior.[91] However in more complex situations, intelligence and moral reasoning capabilities do predict ethical conduct, such as willingness to challenge and to resist unethical commands.[92] And, as evidence summarized in chapter 2 shows, ethics education appears to have some positive influence on behavior.

Although commentary on character generally ignores these complexities and the relative importance of intuitions over reasoning, the concept seems broad enough to take them into account. We could say that people with good moral character are those whose education and habits have inculcated sound moral intuitions and habits of reasoning. These intuitions, in turn, generally yield sound ethical judgments, and when they do not, ethical reasoning kicks in to counter inappropriate intuitive responses. By contrast, we could describe a person of weak character as someone whose intuitions lead him or her astray and who lacks the capacity or will to act otherwise.

Character Traits

Psychologists who focus on character traits have employed two methods of identifying those that are most valued. The first is to ask the public what qualities they associate with moral character. Recent research finds some consensus but also some variability across cultures.[93] One comparative study found that "honest" was a central moral trait in all four surveyed countries, followed by "friendly," "good," and "just," which were central in three. Culturally idiosyncratic traits included "obedient" in Germany, "sociable" in Brazil, "trustworthy" in New Zealand, and "well-mannered" in the Philippines.[94] Other research on moral traits finds that those ranking highest are honesty, loyalty, and justness.[95] Yet such popular rankings are of limited value, given that people give priority to flatly inconsistent qualities. From 81 to 95 percent of Americans agree that each of the following traits is an important attribute of good character: "obeying those in positions of authority, following your own conscience, sacrificing your own interests for the good of others, [and]protecting your own interests."[96]

Another method of identifying key character traits draws on philosophical, cultural, and religious traditions.[97] The most systematic effort is by psychologists Christopher Peterson and Martin Seligman. They consulted experts from multiple disciplines; reviewed relevant literatures from psychiatry, philosophy, psychology, education, and history; surveyed "virtue relevant messages in popular culture (greeting cards, bumper stickers, song lyrics, and personal ads)"; and examined codes of conduct ranging from a prominent medieval code of chivalry to the oath of contemporary Boy Scouts.[98] This method identified six virtues: wisdom, courage, humanity, justice, temperance, and transcendence. Peterson and Seligman argued that these virtues are universal, perhaps partly grounded in biology, and selected through an evolutionary process. In their view, a person needed all of these qualities to be considered someone of good character.

Peterson and Seligman also identified twenty-four "character strengths"—the psychological processes that give rise to virtues. The strengths that Peterson and Seligman associate with their six core virtues include:

1. *Wisdom and knowledge:* creativity, curiosity, open-mindedness, love of learning, perspective.
2. *Courage:* bravery, persistence, perseverance, industriousness, integrity, vitality.
3. *Humanity:* love, kindness, social intelligence.
4. *Justice:* citizenship, fairness, leadership.
5. *Temperance:* forgiveness and mercy, humility/modesty, prudence, self-regulation.
6. *Transcendence:* appreciation of beauty and excellence, gratitude, hope, optimism, future orientation, humor, spirituality.[99]

In societies such as the United States, however, it is by no means clear that common usage of "character" would include transcendence. Nor is it included in the virtues typically singled out in character education programs.

What are we to make of these varied lists? One insight is that the classic four Greek virtues—wisdom, courage, justice, and temperance—still command substantial respect. However, modern notions of good character often include integrity, which figures in many surveys and serves as a synonym for moral character in popular usage.[100] The qualities that Western society associates with someone of good character are the same qualities associated with integrity, such as honesty, benevolence, and dependability.[101] Compared with other individuals, people who score higher in integrity have more demanding ethical standards, are more likely to display empathy and helping behavior, attach more importance to being principled, and reportedly behave more consistently with their principles.[102] Those higher in integrity also demonstrate a stronger sense of personal responsibility for doing the right thing, and less tolerance of self-serving rationalizations of misconduct.[103]

Other insights emerging from this research on character traits is their potential for change, their susceptibility to situational influences, and their impact on overall character assessments. Traits can evolve and be cultivated; even Mischel's four-year-olds could learn mental imaging strategies that increased their self-control.[104] Character-related qualities can also manifest themselves differently in different contexts depending on situational incentives, pressures, and sanctions. As #MeToo reminds us, people can exercise considerable self-control in most of their professional lives but shockingly little in sexual behavior. Moreover, a negative moral trait has a stronger impact on our impression of character than does a positive moral trait.[105] We are more likely to assume that someone with a bad quality has a bad character than that someone with a good quality has a good character. In effect, character is often judged by its weakest link, and a large number of exemplary traits are necessary to overturn an initial impression of immorality.[106] Given these evaluative biases, as well as individuals' potential for change over time and circumstance, we should be cautious about making broad categorical claims about their innate moral character.[107]

The celebrated French commentator Michel de Montaigne put forth a similar argument over three centuries ago. In his essay "The Inconsistency of Our Actions," he noted:

The man whom you saw so adventurous yesterday, do not think it strange to find him just as cowardly today; either anger, or necessity, or wine, or the sound of a trumpet, had put his heart in his belly. His was a courage formed not by reason, but by one of these circumstances; it is no wonder if he has now been made different by other, contrary circumstances. . . . To judge a man, we must follow his traces long and carefully. In view of this, a sound intellect will refuse to judge men simply by their outward actions; we must probe the inside and discover what springs set men in motion. But since this is an arduous and hazardous undertaking, I wish fewer people would meddle with it.[108]

The point is not that character labels should always be avoided. As noted previously, individuals vary in their predispositions and in their susceptibility to situational pressures. Character can be a shorthand to describe those tendencies.[109] But as subsequent chapters note, it is often unjust to overgeneralize from single bad acts to bad character, and to use that label to deny fundamental rights and benefits.

Finally, it bears emphasis that not all qualities associated with character are inevitably indicative of virtue. Loyalty, courage, and commitment can all serve ignoble ends. Angela Duckworth's research on grit, which she defines as passion and perseverance, acknowledges the role of "gritty" villains: Joseph Stalin and Adolph Hitler are obvious examples.[110] The challenge for all societies is to develop not just character but moral character—individuals with strong ethical commitments and the capabilities necessary to realize them.

2

Character Development

To enter on a discussion about character and even more, about character education is to enter a minefield of conflicting definition and ideology.[1]

JAMES ARTHUR

EVERY FAMILY AND every society engages in character education. The only difference is how intentional and effective their efforts are. Two thousand years ago, Plato raised the question "What is the best way to teach the virtues?"[2] We are still searching for the answer, and the past half century has witnessed increasing calls to deal with "the hole in the moral ozone" of American youth.[3] Social critics and social scientists have identified a crisis in character education.[4] Philosopher Alisdair MacIntyre has warned that we may be raising a generation of moral stutterers.[5] Senator Ben Sasse has chronicled the declining focus on self-discipline, self-reliance, and the work ethic.[6] Other commentators have pointed to unacceptable levels of youth violence, cheating, lying, bullying, and harassment, as well as declining levels of civic concern.[7] At the turn of the twenty-first century, when asked about the most important problem facing today's youth, Americans identified "not learning values."[8] Although recent events have seen more positive trends in public engagement, particularly around issues of gun violence, there are also less encouraging counter trends. The Making Caring Common project at Harvard asked ten thousand middle and high school students to rank the values most important to them. Over 80 percent picked high achievement or personal happiness. Just 20 percent picked caring for others, and students ranked self-interest above fairness.[9] Those who gave caring a low priority were less likely to report interest in volunteer work and were at greater risk for harmful behaviors, including dishonesty and cruelty.[10] Such results are consistent with the studies of college students summarized in chapter 1, which made clear the priority of personal self-interest and financial well-being over other more selfless concerns.

Of course, handwringing over the state of adolescent character is nothing new. As James Hunter notes in *The Death of Character,* virtually every generation for the past two centuries has perceived a moral crisis among its youth.[11] Part of the reason, Hunter suggests, is that debates about the moral character of children are stand-ins for broader ideological disputes:

> Children have become a code for speaking about ourselves; a linguistic devise through which we talk about our own desires, commitments and ideals, and the world we wish to create. Young people thus get caught in a tug of war between adults who have contending ideas about "what is really in their best interest." When this happens, they become one more ideological weapon used on behalf of competing visions of America's future direction; a tool with which competing parties and interest groups leverage political power. In claiming to put children first, we often place them last—or at least subordinate to ideology.[12]

The stakes in this debate are substantial. At issue is the culture we wish to pass on to succeeding generations. This chapter explores the debate, and what we know and need to know, about how to develop character, particularly moral character, and associated prosocial behavior.

A threshold question is the extent to which biological factors influence the developmental process. Although self-help literature often claims that "character is completely within your control," most experts believe otherwise.[13] For example, identical twins are much more alike in their criminality and altruism than fraternal twins. Adopted children have criminal records more like those of their biological parents than like those of the parents who actually raised them.[14] Genes, hormones, enzymes, fetal drug syndrome, low birthweight, and toxins all may affect character development.[15]

However, education and experience also play a critical part. Child development literature suggests that moral character is acquired in three primary ways. One is through observing the actions and attitudes of trusted role models. Another is through engaging in moral activities, such as service to others. A third way is through reflective dialogue about the complexities of moral issues.[16]

My discussion here explores these processes in three settings. I begin where character development begins: in the family. I then turn to organizations that seek to shore up that development: Sunday schools, youth groups, and sports programs. Their limitations have led to increasing involvement of schools. In the third part of the chapter, I trace the evolution of formal character initiatives in educational institutions and identify strategies for improvement.

Families

Despite other disputes, experts agree that the family lays the foundations for moral character on which other social institutions build.[17] The home can also supply the secure attachments that help children acquire "performance character" traits such as resilience and perseverance.[18]

During America's early years, the conventional wisdom on child rearing stressed "less sentimentality and more spanking."[19] In the Colonial period, disobedient children could even be sentenced to a public whipping.[20] Character, not just obedience, attracted intermittent attention, and became an explicit focus by the end of the twentieth century.[21] A famous "wallet test" underscored the influence of upbringing on moral behavior. Researchers "lost" more than eleven hundred wallets in countries around the world to see how many would be returned, and what motivated individuals who returned them. Each wallet contained $50 in local currency and the name and phone number of the owner. The most honest behavior occurred in Norway and Denmark, where all of the wallets were returned. The United States placed in the middle range; about two-thirds of the wallets came back. Most people who made efforts to return the wallets credited their parents with instilling the desire to do the right thing.[22]

Experts describe three styles of parenting that influence character development: authoritarian, permissive, and authoritative. Authoritarian parents use commands, threats, and physical punishment but little reasoning. Permissive parents are high on affection but low on expectations and rules. Authoritative parents combine clearly defined limits and expectations with reasoning, fairness, and love. Research suggests that authoritative styles are most effective in promoting positive character development.[23] Other styles lead to more negative outcomes including delinquency, substance abuse, and bullying.[24] Physical discipline is particularly likely to prove counterproductive and to provoke aggression.[25] One study of some twenty thousand adolescents found that teens with authoritative parents were most persevering, academically successful, and least likely to abuse drugs or alcohol.[26] Another review of hundreds of studies concluded that the best way for parents to raise morally responsible teens was to have "warm and involved relationships with [them], to set clear expectations, and to monitor their activities in age-appropriate ways."[27] Involving children in charitable activities and encouraging their helping behavior promotes such altruism in adulthood.[28]

Individuals who engage in morally exemplary conduct often attribute it to childhood experiences. Samuel and Pearl Oliner's study of Europeans who rescued Jews from the Holocaust found that parents of rescuers had modeled caring behavior and values. As one rescuer explained, his mother taught him to be "responsible, honest, . . . to respect all people. . . . " His father taught him to "love my neighbor—to consider him my equal whatever his nationality or religion. He taught me especially to be tolerant."[29] Another rescuer had a mother who "always said to remember to do good for someone at least once a day."[30] Interviews with American crisis counseling volunteers and participants in early civil rights struggles found that those who were most dedicated had parents who modeled altruism and political activism.[31] One remembered being carried to a protest on his father's shoulders.[32] Other studies of "morally exemplary" individuals also document the influence of parental examples.[33] In all of this research, the most significant distinguishing feature of those with strong moral character was coming from families that modeled empathy, altruism, and integrity.[34] Children imitate the moral behavior of parents, and the influence is long-lasting.[35]

Biographies of American leaders reveal countless examples. Barack Obama credits his mother with conveying the message that "he was expected to do good."[36] Martin Luther King Jr. watched his father challenge racial discrimination and champion the registration of black voters. One day a white police officer pulled King's father over for a minor traffic offense and referred to him as "boy." King pointed to his son and said, "that's a boy there. I'm a man."[37]

Yet although parents generally recognize that they teach by example, they often lose sight of the unintended lessons that they reinforce.[38] Stanford psychologist William Damon gives an illustration of a mother whose daughter had watched a documentary on human trafficking and felt she just "had to do something about it." Her mother suggested starting a school awareness program and a fundraising drive to support anti-trafficking efforts. These would be great ideas, the mother suggested, because her daughter could describe them in her college application. The daughter responded with "some disappointment, not to mention cynicism, 'That's right, Mom, it's all about me, isn't it?' "[39] Parents who want to send a different message should model appropriate behavior and help children find volunteer projects that ignite their passions and sustain their moral commitment.[40]

The exact opposite message is sent by efforts such as those revealed in a 2019 college admissions scandal that broke as this book went to press. There, wealthy parents worked through a consultant to bribe test proctors and athletic coaches, and to fabricate childrens' achievements. Families should instead be reasoning with children about appropriate ethical decisions and setting high moral expectations.[41] Because such expectations demonstrate a faith in children's ethical capabilities, their sense of responsibility increases.[42] Similarly, it is better to praise or admonish young children for their character than for their behavior.[43] If you complement children for being helpers, or urge them not to be cheaters, they are more likely to comply because their morality has been tied to their identity.

Helping and cheating are isolated actions, which can be evaluated in cost-benefit terms. But being called a cheater or a helper evokes a sense of self, and invites children to consider the kind of person they want to be.[44] So too, because children imitate the altruistic behavior of adults, parents who volunteer and treat others with empathy and compassion increase the likelihood that their children will do so as well.[45] Directing children's attention to the consequences of their actions on others, rather than simply moralizing, lecturing, bribing, or punishing, also encourages prosocial behavior.[46] Helping children learn to take the perspective of victims of injustice can be a similarly important catalyst to moral development.[47]

Managing the moral environment is equally critical. Parents should monitor and guide their children's choice of peers, television, music, video games, and internet usage.[48] The American Academy of Pediatrics encourages families to develop a media plan.[49] Experts advise all caregivers to set limits, suggest quality media, talk about the messages conveyed, build critical viewing skills, and teach the importance of civility and respect for privacy.[50] Parents can also help their children use social media to seek credible information and find supportive communities, which can be especially important for LGBTQ teens or those with other special challenges.[51] Families should also look for ways of encouraging children to exercise moral judgment and to play a constructive role in family decision-making.[52] Alfie Kohn makes a point that is obvious in principle but often ignored in practice: "if we want children to take responsibility for their own behavior we must first give them responsibility."[53]

Perhaps hardest of all is what parents should refrain from doing. They should avoid excessive reliance on extrinsic motivators such as rewards and punishments. These often produce only short-term compliance and erode the intrinsic motivations necessary for long-term change.[54] Rewards may just motivate children to get more rewards and to cut ethical corners in the process.[55] Praising positive actions, and reinforcing effort, not simply performance, is more likely to encourage honesty, learning, and personal growth.[56] Rather than simply punishing undesirable behavior, parents should engage in the harder task of trying to understand and address its underlying causes.[57]

Experts also counsel families not to "give kids too much and ask too little of them," or shield them from the risks of failure and consequences of bad choices.[58] Learning from mistakes and responding with grace and resilience is a critical life skill and a crucial step in moral development.[59] Dan Kindlon, in his book about "raising children of character in an indulgent age," explores what not to do. An example is the effort of an affluent couple to reverse a disciplinary sanction against their sixteen-year- old son. His expensive private school had suspended him for three days for plagiarizing a paper off the Internet, and had given him a failing grade on the assignment, as well as on the quiz he would miss during his suspension. His parents objected, out of concern that this would jeopardize his chances for admission to a prestigious college, which was their main motivation for sending him to the school in the first place.[60] The message their son took from the incident was that his parents agreed that he hadn't really done anything wrong. In his view, "I'm not the only one in class who did it. So why should I take the rap? It was a stupid assignment. The paper I bought taught me more than the professor."[61] What no one forced the boy to consider was the effect of his conduct on "all the kids who didn't cheat," or the fact that such rationalizations for cheating "could get him into real trouble later in life." As Kindlon concludes, "he's myopic and self centered," and his parents, despite the best of intentions, had enabled him to avoid moral responsibility for his conduct. In *How Children Succeed*, Paul Tough similarly describes a paradox of privilege. Children from affluent backgrounds are too often insulated from the experiences of adversity that build character.[62]

Parents should also avoid projecting their own desires for vicarious achievement onto children who may not share those aspirations. Former Yale professor William Deresiewicz notes that for many couples, "When your kids get into a prestigious college, it's as if you got an A in being a parent. And nothing less than that, of course, will do. Nor is college the end of it, needless to say."[63] This vicarious ambition has fueled increasing efforts to "game the system" with SAT tutors, college application-essay "advisors" (i.e., ghostwriters), resume-ready public service experiences, strategic alumni donations, and fabricated learning disabilities to get students extra time on exams.[64] Children are victims as well as beneficiaries of this pressure to succeed, and all the accompanying course loads, extracurricular activities, tutoring, and test prep designed to "wring the last bit of performance out of them."[65] Such pressures do not generally produce higher achievement.[66] What they produce instead is disproportionately high rates of depression, substance abuse, suicide, and anxiety disorders in even the most affluent communities.[67] These symptoms are particularly pronounced in children who think their parents value success over character traits such as kindness and respect.[68]

Moreover, many parents may be overestimating the value of high grades and elite institutions in children's futures. Adam Grant, summarizing a wide range of evidence, concludes that "academic excellence is not a strong predictor of career excellence."[69] Children often thrive by leaving their comfort zones and risking setbacks that build resilience. They can also benefit from opportunities to excel that are available in less competitive and less elite educational environments. A Gallup-Purdue Index survey of more than thirty thousand college graduates found that attending a highly selective or top-ranked college did not affect any of the study's measures of well-being: individuals' health, satisfaction with what they were doing, sense of financial security, or connection to other people and

their communities.[70] *New York Times* columnist Frank Bruni's indictment of the
college admission mania, *Where You Go Is Not Who You'll Be*, looked up the undergraduate backgrounds of American business and political leaders. Less than a
third of US senators and CEOs of Fortune 100 corporations, and only a quarter
of governors, had attended elite institutions.[71] A larger study of leaders in both
the profit and nonprofit sectors found the same pattern.[72] As the director of
Georgetown's Center on Education and the Workforce put it, families should
focus less on where their children go to college, and more on what they're going
to do when they get there.[73] Parents need to support the child they have, not the
child they wish they had, and keep their own ambitions in check.[74]

While children from affluent backgrounds are too often shielded from adverse consequences, children from impoverished backgrounds have the opposite
problem, and have far too few resources to cope with disadvantages not of their
own making. Exposure to economic deprivation, violence, neglect, and inadequate schools can all undermine character development; these forces can impair
reasoning, self-discipline, perseverance, and resilience.[75] How best to address
child poverty and associated social ills is, of course, a complicated social and political question, and one beyond the scope of this book. But we cannot forget that
socioeconomic differences in the development of character strengths "are both a
cause and consequence of inequality" that demand societal responses.[76] Without
additional resources and policy interventions, millions of impoverished children
will lack adequate foundations for character development.[77]

Religious Institutions, Youth Organizations, and Sports Programs

Families have never been the only source of character education, and many rely on
religious institutions, youth organizations, and sports programs to share responsibility.[78] Yet all too often, the effectiveness of these partners is open to question.

Religious Institutions

Development of moral character has long been part of the mission of churches,
synagogues, temples, mosques, and other centers of religious life. Discussion here
centers on Sunday schools, which have reached the greatest number of American
youth and have served many faiths. Even religions that do not observe Sunday as
a holy day have run Sunday programs that seek to develop students' moral character as well as spiritual identities.[79]

Christian Sunday schools first emerged in Great Britain in the late eighteenth century to address disruptive behavior by unsupervised adolescents on their day off from work. The movement spread, and in 1785, the first such schools opened in America.[80] Although their mission was religiously oriented, the schools had lay teachers, were generally not affiliated with churches, and offered basic education as well as religious instruction. By teaching students to read the Bible, these schools aimed to provide a foundation on which youths could construct moral lives.[81] Such efforts gained greater prominence and a more religious focus during the Second Great Awakening in the early nineteenth century. Teachers who had experienced religious conversions themselves were interested in sharing their faith and ensuring the salvation of students.[82] By the 1830s, Sunday schools had become increasingly affiliated with churches and were often taught by ministers.[83]

During the twentieth century, the Christian Sunday school curriculum became more secularized in response to broader social trends.[84] Yet enrollments declined, and by 1986, over a quarter of adults reported having no such instruction.[85] After the turn of the twenty-first century, the decline continued, due to the increasing secularization of society, the growing proliferation of other youth activities, and scandals of child sexual abuse by Catholic priests.[86] Still, Sunday schools remain a force in many communities; estimates suggest that at least 22 million Christian youths participate, and many also attend religiously affiliated schools.[87] Millions more participate in programs in synagogues, temples, mosques, and other religiously affiliated schools, community centers, and related institutions.[88]

What isn't clear is how much effect this religious instruction has on character development. Only 40 percent of young Americans consider religion very important in their lives.[89] And almost no research has assessed the influence of religiously affiliated institutions on moral character. In one of the only studies on point, the most that could be said was that youth involved in faith-based activities self-reported higher rates of prosocial norms than youth involved in nonreligious activities such as sports and fine arts.[90] But that difference could reflect who self-selects for such activities rather than their influence on character.

Youth Organizations

Research is similarly lacking about other youth organizations that seek to develop character. The earliest such organization is the Young Men's Christian Association (YMCA), founded in London in 1844. Its objective was the "building . . . of Christian character," and the same goal gave rise to the Young Women's Christian Association (YWCA).[91] Although originally devoted to "building a Christian society," the YMCA and YWCA have since embraced a more inclusive mission that encompasses leadership in "values education."[92]

Similar objectives have inspired the Boy and Girl Scouts. They began in Great Britain shortly after the turn of the twentieth century. Their aim was to provide youth with leaders of "a strong and healthy character."[93] According to Robert Baden-Powell, the founder of the Boy Scouts, schools gave only "book instruction" not "character education," and scouting could fill the gap.[94] Juliet Low, founder of the Girl Scouts of America, similarly wrote in 1919 that its purpose was to "promote the virtues of womanhood . . . and to guide [girls] in ways conducive to personal honor and the public good."[95] More than half of the early troops were church-sponsored, and nearly a third of the first scoutmasters were ministers.[96] With the growing secularization of society, these religious ties grew more attenuated. Many Girl Scout troops focused on preparation for traditional gender roles, with badges available for homemaking and folk dancing.[97] Service in uncontroversial causes such as bond drives during World War I sought to nurture a sense of social responsibility, but commitments were not extensive. One estimate suggested that such service averaged less than a day per year.[98] Controversies also plagued the organizations over the moral message sent by its early policies on sexual orientation. Not until 2013 did the Boy Scouts lift its ban on openly gay scouts, and it took until 2017 to welcome transgender members.[99]

Scouting continues to play an influential role for some American youth, but its impact on character development is unclear. The Boy Scouts report 2.3 million members and the Girl Scouts claim 1.8.[100] In 2017, in the face of declining enrollments, the Boy Scouts announced a decision to admit girls, and it is unclear how that decision will affect both groups.[101] The official mission of the Boy Scouts is "to prepare young people to make ethical and moral choices over their lifetime," and Scout Law specifies obligations to be trustworthy, loyal, helpful, friendly, courteous, kind, obedient, cheerful, thrifty, brave, clean, and reverent. The Girl Scout mission is to develop girls of "courage, confidence and character, who make the world a better place." No systematic research has assessed the success of scouting in reinforcing these qualities.[102]

Nor is there significant evidence for some six hundred other major youth organizations across the nation.[103] One of the few efforts to measure impact surveyed youth delegates to a Kentucky 4-H conference. 4-H organizations, which began over a century ago in farming communities, seek to develop "head, heart, hands, and health" by focusing on leadership, responsibility, and life skills. Over 75 percent of surveyed youth said that their 4-H involvement had made them a better person, citizen, friend, or leader, and 90 percent said that they had gained character knowledge.[104] But such self-reports are hardly an adequate measure of influence. Although other studies suggest that well-designed youth development programs can help reduce problem behaviors and enhance social competence, researchers have not generally demonstrated comparable gains along other character-related dimensions.[105]

In short, millions of youth participate in organizations that aim to build character but offer "virtually no empirical checks on their effectiveness."[106] It may, however, be reasonable to hope that such programs have some positive impact. They engage youth in prosocial activities under the supervision of responsible adult mentors. And studies of morally exemplary individuals make clear that role models other than parents can play a positive role in character development.[107] But families across the nation would benefit from systematic efforts to assess the role of youth organizations in cultivating character and to identify strategies that might enhance their effectiveness.

Sports

We do, however, have a substantial body of data about adult-supervised extracurricular sports programs, which involve nearly 41 million youth.[108] And from a character standpoint, the results are not entirely encouraging. These programs began in earnest for boys in the 1950s, with the creation of Little League baseball, and expanded several decades later for girls after passage of antidiscrimination laws.[109] Advocates often claim that sports are a positive force in character development by reinforcing values such as honesty, fairness, self-discipline, loyalty, resilience, courage, and perseverance. Coaches can serve as important role models in that effort. But how often these programs realize their potential is dubious. Scholars have found no systematic evidence that athletic competition builds character.[110] In fact, some research finds a negative correlation between participation in many sports (especially team sports) and maturity in moral reasoning.[111] The title of a widely circulated *Psychology Today* article put it bluntly: "Sport: If You Want to Build Character, Try Something Else."[112]

There is, however, enough variation in research findings to counsel against lumping all sports together. Different forms of competition produce different norms and pressures. The dynamics of football are not the same as those of golf, and each sport and each team develops its own ethical culture.[113] But despite such qualifications, it is clear that too many athletic programs fall short in promoting positive character development. One problem arises from programs that indiscriminately reward participation. As psychologists note, "Real life . . . does not operate on the 'trophies for all' policy. . . . [Children need to] learn how to fail with grace and resilience" and to build the skills needed to actually deserve a trophy.[114] The opposite problem arises from overly professionalized programs that stress winning over pleasure and sportsmanship.[115] In one study of fifth through eighth grade athletes, 9 percent acknowledged cheating in the past season, 13 percent had tried to hurt an opponent, and 27 percent had acted like a "bad sport." Over a quarter reported that their coaches angrily argued with a referee, berated opponents, or encouraged their team members to retaliate.[116]

Cheating by adult role models, both parents and coaches, is also far too common. A textbook case was the 2015 scandal involving Chicago's Jackie Robinson West Little League team, which lost its US Championship title in the World Series games because it included players who did not live or attend school in the district the team represented.[117] Violations of age restrictions are similarly frequent. The father of a winning pitcher for the Little League World Series was indicted for fraud after he entered his fourteen-year-old son in a competition restricted to children who were nine to twelve years old.[118] The son pitched a perfect game, and received considerable acclaim until it was revealed that his father had falsified the boy's Dominican Republic birth certificate.[119] In another celebrated case, a high school principal changed the math grade of a football player to prevent him from failing and becoming ineligible to participate in the state playoffs.[120] In too many programs, good sportsmanship is a platitude trotted out at annual banquets but sidelined in actual competitions.

If we are serious about wanting sports to develop character, we need better training, mentoring, and oversight for coaches, parents, and program leaders. Organizations such as the Positive Coaching Alliance can help in supporting character education initiatives. Players with coaches who receive such support and training perceive their teams as putting a greater emphasis on fairness and moral values than players who lack such coaches.[121] As one expert notes, "we will never greatly improve students' moral development . . . without taking on the complex task of developing adults' . . . ethical capacities."[122]

Schools
The Historical Backdrop

Character education in early American schools had religious foundations. In elementary schools, the teacher's role was to reinforce habits of piety and obedience. Nineteenth-century New York public schools had students recite a catechism that denounced lying, stealing, and disobedience, and concluded with a reminder that "God knows all you do."[123] College faculty also sought to shape their students' moral character through compulsory chapel and required courses in ethics. The capstone of the curriculum was often a course in moral philosophy, which sought to provide a framework for students' entire course of study and future life.[124] The first president of Johns Hopkins summarized common views in claiming that "the object of the university is to develop character—to make men."[125]

By the end of the nineteenth century, character education began to lose its religious foundation and its toehold in colleges.[126] How to replace it attracted increasing attention. Some religions formed their own schools, but for most American youth, secularized character development in the elementary and secondary schools became the answer.[127] During the early twentieth century, state legislatures and local boards of education called for curricula to reflect ideals of character and citizenship. The result was a mix of moral, civic, and character education.[128] By 1921, *The McGuffey Reader,* a widely used text, had the largest circulation of any book except the Bible. Contents included excerpts from Aesop, Shakespeare, and the scriptures, as well as biographical readings about George Washington and William Wilberforce, the English activist who campaigned against the slave trade.[129] Many schools adopted a "Children's Morality Code," which emphasized "ten laws of right living," including self-control, kindness, sportsmanship, duty, reliability, truth, and teamwork.[130] Articles asking "Can Virtue Be Taught?" attracted widespread debate.[131]

The answers were not always encouraging, as was clear from a landmark 1929 study by Yale researchers Hugh Hartshorne and Mark May. They surveyed nearly eleven thousand children between the ages of eight and sixteen across the nation. One of their findings was that "the discussion of standards and ideals of honesty . . . has no necessary relation to the control of conduct."[132] So too, "efforts to train children in forms of charitable and cooperative behavior . . . have very little, if any effect."[133] Hartshorne and May found no evidence of any unitary "character."[134] Moral conduct, they concluded, was situation specific, and could not be cultivated by any single educational technique.[135] A recent re-examination of the original Hartshorne and May data shows greater cross-situational consistency in honesty than they identified. [136] But at the time, the study undermined the concept of character. Psychologists began to use instead the more morally neutral term "personality."[137] Emphasis shifted from virtues associated with strong moral character (such as honesty and integrity) to those associated with psychological well-being (such as self-confidence and social adjustment).[138]

Higher education also lost interest in character education until relatively recently. Throughout most of the twentieth century, only a few institutions required courses in ethics, and most philosophy departments gave little attention to applied ethical issues.[139] A 1964 survey found that at one representative university with twelve thousand students, ethics enrollments averaged eleven students per year.[140] Another survey found that college curricula had little effect on student values.[141] Philosophers were talking largely to each other and relatively few students were listening.[142] In business and professional schools, a 1980 Hastings

Center Report noted that "those attempting to introduce courses of ethics can expect considerable disinterest or resistance."[143] Only a minority of business schools even offered courses in ethics, and fewer still made them mandatory. Not until the late 1970s, in the aftermath of Watergate, did most law schools require ethics, and the newly instituted courses were typically viewed as the "dogs of the law school [curriculum] . . . often presented to vacant seats or vacant minds."[144]

Early Character Education Initiatives

However, sporadic efforts to strengthen the character curriculum persisted. The prominent educator John Dewey led one such initiative in the early twentieth century. According to Dewey, character developed through habits, and through reflecting on experience.[145] Too many school programs assumed that "if you can only teach a child moral rules and distinctions enough, you have somehow furthered his moral being."[146] According to Dewey, this approach conceived ethics in too abstract and "too goody-goody a way."[147] He believed that preparation for moral life in a democracy required students to participate in ethical decision-making in their schools and communities.[148] In 1915, Dewey and his daughter wrote *Schools of Tomorrow* to highlight how cities including Gary and Indianapolis had embraced such a progressive educational philosophy. In Gary, students acquired civic and ethical responsibility by "helping to take care of their own school building, by making the rules for their own conduct in the halls and on the playgrounds," and by doing charitable work in the neighborhood. In effect, they were "learning citizenship by being good citizens."[149]

Dewey's experiential approach to moral education was most influential in the period between the two world wars.[150] Later, during the Cold War era, rivalry with Russia pressured schools to focus more on core academic subjects, and the growing importance of science and technology pushed in similar directions.[151] In the late 1960s, however, a wave of social justice activism prompted renewed concerns about moral education.[152] Jerome Bruner, a leading psychologist, called on the schools to help "bring society back to its sense of values and priorities in life."[153] By the mid-1970s, more than two-thirds of Americans believed that schools should take some responsibility for the moral development of students.[154]

To respond to those concerns but minimize conflict over content, many educators avoided teaching values directly and engaged instead in "value clarification." This approach got its start in 1966 with the publication of *Values and Teaching* by Louis Raths, Merrill Harmin, and Sidney Simon.[155] In their view, schools should not be telling students to "stand a dreary watch over ancient values." Rather, youth should learn the "grim but bracing truth" that they must "recreate those values continuously in their own time."[156] Teachers should avoid "sermonizing or moralizing" but instead make students aware of their own beliefs and values.[157] If the teacher, "no matter how subtly—were to make judgments or provide standards . . . he would be implying that students cannot do their own thinking."[158]

For example, in a citizenship class, fifth and sixth graders were asked to complete statements such as:

- The bad thing about cheating is
- The good thing about cheating is
- Is it ever OK to cheat? When?[159]

Virtue was simply one option among many.

Values clarification quickly attracted widespread criticism. As opponents noted, the approach was intended to be value neutral, but in practice it reinforced relativism, and conditioned students to view values as matters of personal preference. Such relativism ran contrary to the views of most contemporary ethicists, as well as the accumulated wisdom of several thousand years of civilization. According to philosophy professor Christina Hoff Sommers,

> To pretend we know nothing about basic decency, about human rights, about vice and virtue, is fatuous and disingenuous. Of course we know that gratuitous cruelty and political repression are wrong, that kindness and political freedom are right and good. Why should we be the first society in history that finds itself hamstrung in the vital task of passing along its moral tradition to the next generation? . . . It is perversely misleading to suggest that helping children to develop habits of truth telling or fair play threatens their ability to make reasoned choices. Quite the contrary: Good moral habits enhance one's capacity for rational judgments.[160]

In *Why Johnny Can't Tell Right from Wrong*, William Kilpatrick similarly argued that values clarification had

> turned classroom discussion into "bull sessions" where opinions go back and forth but conclusions are never reached. It has resulted in classrooms where teachers act like talk show hosts. . . . For students, it has created a generation of moral illiterates; students who know their own feelings but don't know their culture. . . . [or] the Ten Commandments.[161]

Such moral agnosticism, critics argued, had compromised the entire educational process by leaving teachers powerless when students disputed basic norms of conduct. An often-cited example was a Massachusetts teacher, schooled in values clarification, who discovered that her class of sixth graders wanted to be free to cheat on their tests. The teacher's solution was to tell the students that they could not because it was her class and she was opposed to cheating. But, she added, "In other areas of your life, you may have more freedom to be dishonest."[162] Critics of values clarification also cited research indicating that it had no positive impact on students' values.[163] Nor did values clarification promote other prosocial opinions and behaviors.[164]

A different technique, pioneered by Harvard psychologist Lawrence Kohlberg, looked like an attractive alternative. His approach sought to bring students to higher stages of moral reasoning through Socratic dialogue, based on ethical dilemmas. Like the prominent French psychologist Jean Piaget, Kohlberg defined moral life more in terms of the process than the content of moral judgment. In his view, the goal of ethics education should be to increase students' capacity to reason at higher stages, based on universal principles, rather than at lower stages, based on avoiding punishment or gaining rewards. At the highest level, individuals should be applying principles such as Kant's categorical imperative, which demands that individuals act as they would want others to act. Unlike values clarification, Kohlberg's approach was not relativistic. It asked students for moral reasons, on the assumption that some reasons were more adequate than others. But it also asked teachers to avoid imposing their own views.[165]

Kohlberg's approach also attracted criticism. Some researchers claimed that it was culturally specific, not universal.[166] Feminists including Carol Gilligan claimed that it was gender biased and that it privileged abstract rights and responsibilities at the expense of concrete values of care and connection traditionally associated with women.[167] Other critics objected that Kohlberg's hypothetical dilemmas were too far removed from a child's moral life. One example involved pioneers trapped by snow who must choose between starvation or cannibalism.[168] Students often responded to these abstract dilemmas using a different stage of reasoning than they used to respond to personally relevant dilemmas.[169] Critics also charged that Kohlberg overestimated the importance of moral reasoning; research indicated that moving a child to a more sophisticated stage of ethical reasoning did not necessarily increase ethical conduct.[170] As one expert noted, Kohlberg's approach

obscures the fact that relatively few of our moral failings are attributable to inept reasoning about dilemmas. Many more arise from moral indifference, disregard for other people, weakness of will and bad or self-indulgent habits. The hard part of morality, in short, is not about *knowing* what is

right but *doing* it. And if this is so, the remedy lies not in forming opinions
but in forming good habits.[171]

Many commentators also believed that the dilemma approach, however
useful for upper-level high school or college students, was for younger students
"woefully inadequate. It involves young people in repeatedly questioning values
that may never have taken hold for them in the first place."[172] Even Kohlberg himself came to share this view. In his later life, he believed that "concerns guiding
moral education must be partly indoctrinative. This is true, by necessity, in a
world in which children engage in stealing, cheating, and aggression, and in a
context where one cannot wait until children reach . . . [higher stages of moral
reasoning] to deal directly with moral behavior." The educator therefore needed
to be a "socializer teaching value content," not simply a "process facilitator of
development."[173]

Despite these controversies over how to teach values, surveys at the close of
the twentieth century found that about 85 percent of parents wanted schools
to make the effort. Most Americans also thought there were broad values that
people shared and schools weren't doing enough to teach them.[174] About 90 percent of those surveyed agreed on an American Core of desirable character traits,
including persistence, compassion, fairness, and respect for others.[175] In response
to this consensus, public schools in all states, like those in many other nations,
implemented character education.[176] States commonly called on local school
boards to mandate a comprehensive K–12 program, with at least ten minutes of
instruction per day.

The federal government lent further support to such initiatives. In 1995,
Congress declared a national "Character Counts!" week, and followed up
three years later with legislation to "support and encourage character building
initiatives in schools across America," and to urge colleges and universities "to
affirm that the development of character is one of the primary goals of higher
education."[177] Presidents Clinton and Bush made character education a focus.[178]
Between 1995 and 2005, thirty-six states and the District of Columbia received
seed money through the Department of Education's Partnerships in Character
Education Pilot Projects.[179]

A "Character Counts!" coalition sought to give this growing movement
greater coherence. The effort began in 1992, when the Josephson Institute of
Ethics convened a group of religious, civic, and political leaders. Their Aspen
Declaration affirmed "core ethical values rooted in democratic society" that
"transcend cultural, religious and socioeconomic differences." These pillars
of character were respect, responsibility, trustworthiness, justice and fairness,
caring, civic virtue, and citizenship. To support these values, the Character

Counts! coalition brought together church groups, teachers' and principals' unions, youth organizations, charities, and foundations.[180] Character.org formed to provide support and resources for school and community-based character education programs.[181]

In implementing character mandates, state education boards usually convene a diverse group of stakeholders who identify values that schools should promote.[182] For example, public schools in Baltimore County, Maryland, teach a common core of twenty-four values; in Nashville Tennessee, they offer a curricula covering eighteen "universal virtues"; and in Saint Louis, school districts list fifty desired qualities.[183] Nonprofit groups have also developed model programs. For example, the Jefferson Center for Character Education offers materials on "How to Be Successful in Less than Ten Minutes a Day" for middle school children.[184] The program emphasizes a dozen or so directives, such as: be friendly, be polite, be responsible, be a goal setter, be confident, be on time, and be a tough worker.[185]

What such generalities accomplish, is, however, open to question. Moreover, recent educational budget cuts, together with increasing pressure on public schools to improve students' academic test performance, have squeezed out other curricular initiatives, including character education.[186]

The Rationale for Character Education

The case for focusing on character in schools rests on three claims. The first involves the centrality of such education for individuals and society. Moral character is necessary to realize our full potential, to foster flourishing democratic institutions, and to raise the next generation of responsible citizens.[187] Even in our ethically pluralist society, there is wide consensus about the importance of certain basic qualities such as honesty, fairness, compassion, and respect for others.[188] Democracies have a particular stake in fostering moral character because the people themselves are responsible for ensuring a free and just social order. Schools can foster the qualities essential for well-functioning political systems. A study of some ninety thousand adolescents across twenty-eight countries found that open classroom climates that enabled discussion of key issues led to greater tolerance, civic knowledge and engagement, and support for human rights.[189] Students themselves acknowledge the importance of character development. In a survey of twenty-three thousand students, 99 percent agreed that "It's important for me to be a person with good character."[190]

The second rationale for character education is that schools are more effective when they are "communities of character," where values such as diligence, honesty, and respect are "expected, taught, celebrated, and continually practiced."[191]

Without a basic commitment to core values, cheating, bullying, harassment, and violence can compromise the educational process.

The third rationale for a character curriculum is that schools cannot avoid teaching values; the only question is how intentional and effective they will be in doing so.[192] There is no such thing as "value free" education. Even if "questions of right and wrong are never discussed in classrooms, that, too, teaches a lesson about how much morality matters. In short, the relevant issue is never 'should schools teach values' but rather 'which values will they teach.'"[193] Children spend more than twelve thousand hours in classrooms before they graduate from high school. That leaves an inevitable and indelible imprint on their developing characters, which imposes corresponding responsibilities on educators.[194]

Although the case for character education attracts wide support, there is no corresponding consensus on how or what to teach. Controversy continues to center on the meaning of character, the strategies best suited for its development, and the priority it should assume in contemporary classrooms.

The Focus of Character Education

A threshold question is how educators should define character. As chapter 1 noted, experts distinguish between traits of moral character, such as honesty and integrity, and traits of performance character such as perseverance and self-discipline.[195] Educators have varied in their definitions but most programs have focused primarily on ethics.[196] But performance qualities are also crucial because they promote schools' central academic mission.[197] Self-discipline, drive, and persistence, which underpin good work habits, are at least as important as talent and cognitive skills in predicting high achievement.[198] Angela Lee Duckworth's research on grit, which she defines as passion and perseverance, finds that this quality is a reliable predictor not only of achievement but also of motivation "to seek a meaningful life that matters to society."[199] And that quality is more a matter of cultivation than genetic endowment.[200] Persistence is a value that 90 percent of Americans think that schools should teach, and a growing number of educators are trying to do so.[201]

They are also putting increased efforts into prevention of morally troubling conduct including harassment and bullying. Although estimates of the frequency of such behaviors vary, most studies suggest that somewhere between 30 to 50 percent of students report being harassed, bullied, or cyberbullied.[202] The problem is increasing. In a Human Rights Campaign survey of over fifty thousand adolescents, 70 percent of young people reported witnessing bullying or hate incidents since the 2016 election.[203] In a 2017 Southern Poverty Law Center survey of ten thousand K–12 educators, four in ten had witnessed hate incidents based on race, religion, gender, or sexual orientation, and four in ten also did not believe that their schools had action plans to respond to such incidents.[204] Racist epithets, displays of swastikas or Confederate flags, and threats of deportation are depressingly common.[205]

Such abuse impairs learning and mental health, and fosters attitudes that perpetuate abuse. Perpetrators are more likely to commit such actions as adults, and their victims sometimes become perpetrators as well.[206] Bullying is a major cause of school violence, and in one study of school shooters, two-thirds had been bullied.[207] In another study of youths age eight to fifteen, bullying ranked as more of a problem in their lives than discrimination, racism, or violence.[208] Character programs, along with counseling and treatment initiatives, have an important part to play in addressing these issues. These programs can employ personal narratives, role-playing exercises, conflict resolution techniques, and bystander intervention training to give students a clearer sense of the harms of abusive behavior and their ability to prevent it.[209]

Many character education initiatives also encompass civic, or citizenship, education. Growing numbers of educators see moral and civic responsibility as inextricably linked, and maintain that schools should promote values necessary for democracies, such as tolerance, respect, fairness, and concern for others and for community well-being.[210] Robert Reich's *The Common Good* argues that civics education should inform students of the "gap between how our system *should* work and how it *actually* works, and why we all have an obligation to seek to bridge that gap."[211] Service learning that combines assisting others with classroom reflection is particularly effective in nurturing civic as well as moral values.[212] By giving back to their communities, students can develop what De Tocqueville called "habits of the heart." Public service is also a valuable way of enabling young people to move out of their comfort zones and engage with those of diverse backgrounds and perspectives.[213] Such experiences can teach students how to listen and how to learn from difference.

Other curricular strategies vary widely. Some involve symbolic appeals on banners, posters, and bulletin boards.[214] Many focus on social learning and coping skills.[215] Stories featuring real or fictional role models draw on a long tradition of using narrative to convey the importance of ethical values and traits such as perseverance and resilience.[216] The difficulty lies in deciding which stories to use. Shortly after conservative commentator William Bennett published a widely used text, *The Book of Virtues*, Colin Greer and Herbert Kohl released what they believed was a more progressive and inclusive collection, *A Call to Character*, and Steven Barboza edited *The African-American Book of Values*.[217] These books all have similar aims but draw on quite different narratives.

The Effectiveness of Current Programs

A common challenge in developing effective character education arises from the inadequacy of evaluation and accountability. Findings about the impact of character initiatives is mixed, and many programs as currently conceived fall short. With the exception of service learning, which has well-documented benefits discussed later, there is little evidence of long-term behavioral changes resulting from character education.[218] And short-term progress is not always sustained.[219] One Brookings overview concluded that "over the past fifty years, attempts at character education as a distinct pursuit have not been particularly successful—in some cases, student behavior is not affected, or changes in beliefs and behaviors don't last."[220] Several studies have found no differences in prosocial conduct between students who participated in character education programs and those who did not.[221] For example, one evaluation by the National Center for Education Research identified "no significant impact on student behavior, academic achievement, or school culture."[222] However, other research summaries by Marvin Berkowitz and colleagues have reported more positive findings along those dimensions.[223] Their conclusion is that "quality character education works," but they also acknowledge that too many educators lack adequate preparation and resources to ensure quality.[224]

Part of the problem is the shallow symbolism and cheap fixes that too often pass for character education. Per pupil expenditures of under a dollar a year is unlikely to "buy a lot of practical virtue."[225] Nor does ten minutes a day on the "virtue of the week." Educational expert Alfie Kohn parodies this approach as "If It's Tuesday, This Must Be Honesty." In these programs, "one value after another is targeted with each assigned its own day, week or month. This seriatim approach is unlikely to result in a lasting commitment to any of these values."[226] Equally problematic, according to other critics, are "programs that . . . call themselves 'character education' [but] are aimed mostly at promoting good manners and compliance with rules, not developing students of strong independent character."[227] There is, experts note, "little evidence that moralizing to children or giving them direct instruction in moral principles has much effect."[228] Critics also worry that the focus on individuals' ethical reasoning will divert attention from the structural causes of misconduct.[229]

Challenges also arise from some teachers' lack of inclination or expertise to undertake character education. Some are wary of controversy. Underlying society's broad consensus on certain virtues is considerable disagreement over definitions. As Lawrence Kohlberg notes, "What is one person's 'integrity' is another person's 'stubbornness,' what is one person's honesty in 'expressing your true feelings' is another person's 'insensitivity to the feelings of others.'"[230] To some teachers, the prospect of engagement on divisive issues "seems like asking for trouble."[231] Others, particularly at the high school level, see themselves as specialists in substantive areas, and resist spending time on discussions that appear peripheral to their specialty.[232] Moreover, many teachers who are willing to undertake character education lack preparation to do so.[233] Many teachers report wanting more training in how to develop children's social and emotional skills and values such as empathy. In one study, 90 percent of deans and department chairs of teacher education programs said that schools should teach core values, but fewer than 25 percent indicated that their own programs highly emphasized character education. Only 13 percent were satisfied with their character education efforts.[234]

The results of this inattention emerged clearly in *Lost in Transition,* a 2011 study of young American adults, age eighteen to twenty-three years.[235] What was most dispiriting about its findings was how unwilling and ill-equipped most of these individuals were to reason about ethical issues. Sixty percent viewed right and wrong as "essentially matters of individual opinion."[236] Common responses were:

- Whatever works for an individual is fine with me as long as it's not affecting me in any way.
- Who am I to judge?
- I don't want to be an ideologue. I'm essentially trying not to impose my views on other people.[237]

This tolerance extended to cheating. One Ivy League student saw it as "a decision everyone is entitled to make for themselves. I'm sort of a proponent of not telling other people what to do."[238] Others saw nothing wrong with cheating because "everyone does it, whether it's with your girlfriend, or a test or your taxes."[239] Another agreed. "People cheat. That's how a lot of people have gotten ahead in life especially in this country. It's like a cutthroat world out there. . . . I will do what I can to get ahead."[240] Some young adults similarly rationalized shoplifting from large businesses on the theory that "they have money." If it's "not hurting an individual, it's not really wrong." Companies "have funds that cover them."[241] One-third acknowledged that they would "do something they thought was morally wrong if they could get away with it."[242] Another third did not know what made anything right or wrong; they "didn't have a clue, didn't understand the question, or said that it was not something they thought about."[243]

Equally disturbing was the low level of civic engagement. Most felt no significant societal responsibilities.[244] Their conception of the good life was highly self-centered and materialist: "Get a good job, become financially secure, have a nice family, buy what you want. . . . Nothing bigger, higher, more meaningful, more transcendent, more shared."[245] Similar priorities emerged from the Harvard

Making Caring Common Project, in which students overwhelmingly prioritized personal achievement and happiness over other values. As one explained, "moral goodness" was only important if it "make[s] me happy."[246] The priorities that youth develop help account for Americans' relatively low civic engagement as adults and voter turnouts that lag well behind most other comparable nations. In one recent survey, the United States ranked 139 in voter participation of 172 democracies around the world.[247]

Since publication of the *Lost in Transition* study, however, student activism has increased, sparked by school shootings and national political elections. And as noted in the next section, some states, including California, have enhanced their civic learning and engagement efforts. But among young adults, voter turnout remains dispiritingly low and materialism dispiritingly high. The *Lost in Transition* study aptly summarized our continued challenges:

> families, schools, religious communities, sports teams and other voluntary organizations of civil society are failing to provide many young people with the kind of moral education and training needed. . . . We are failing to teach our youth about life purposes and goals that matter more than the accumulation of material possessions and material comfort and security. . . . And we are failing to teach our youth the importance of civic engagement and political participation . . . how to think about and live for the common good.[248]

Strategies

For an approach to character education, Aldous Huxley's phrase comes to mind: "nothing short of everything will really do."[249] There is some truth to the proverb that "it takes a village to raise a child." But then "what does it take to raise a village?"[250] How do we ensure that children get consistent messages from parents, coaches, youth group workers, religious leaders, and teachers? Broad public engagement is one strategy.[251] For example, in Hamburg, New York, four hundred community members brainstormed in town hall meetings for ways to support character development, including mandatory community service and greater outreach to at-risk students.[252] The lesson of these initiatives is the more coordination and collaboration the better. Character.org's Principles of Effective Character Education emphasize that programs "must include all stakeholders in a school community and must permeate school climate and curriculum."[253] And because character education continues into early adulthood, colleges and universities must also play an active role.

Each school should have a plan for character education that community members can help shape, support, and assess.[254] Many school districts have committees or councils, composed of staff, students, parents, and youth leaders, that assume responsibility for implementing character initiatives.[255] Well-designed plans integrate character education into curricular and extracurricular activities, service and civic learning, and school governance and disciplinary procedures.[256] Students should have a role in addressing ethical issues that arise throughout their educational experience. Curricula should draw on a diverse array of materials including literature and biography, and clearinghouses should be available to offer examples and best practices.[257] Schools should regularly communicate with parents, coaches, and leaders of youth organizations and involve them in character initiatives. All of these individuals need to model the values that they are seeking to inspire. The hidden curriculum is as important as the formal curriculum in the messages it sends, and schools need to lead the way in creating an ethical climate in all interactions with students.[258]

The creation and enforcement of disciplinary rules should be opportunities to foster moral reasoning and moral habits.[259] Anonymous reporting channels should be available and complainants should be protected from retaliation. Schools should step up efforts to address bullying and harassment.[260] In responding to misconduct, teachers should engage students in helping to define the problem and devise a solution.[261] Caring classrooms that model concern, fairness, honesty, empathy, and mutual respect are a key strategy in fostering prosocial development.[262] Students who describe their schools and classrooms as caring communities show greater empathy and concern for others, stronger motivations to be kind and helpful, and greater ability to resolve conflicts fairly.[263]

To develop performance character, teachers should work with students to set goals, monitor progress, and encourage perseverance in the face of difficulties.[264] Seeking help from a friend or tutor can often provide a path forward. In *How Children Succeed*, Paul Tough emphasizes the power of positive imaging; children should envision the desired outcome, the obstacles standing in the way, and the strategies that will overcome them.[265] Struggling students can benefit from studying narratives of resilience: Michael Jordan once lost a spot on his high school's basketball team, Henry Ford went bankrupt five times, Walt Disney was at times so poor that he resorted to eating dog food while his cartoon ideas were stolen and rejected, and Dr. Seuss was rejected twenty-three times before one publisher took a chance on *Green Eggs and Ham*.[266]

Teachers can also help motivate students through feedback that combines constructive criticism, high expectations, and confidence that the student can meet them.[267] KIPP Charter Schools gives character report cards that evaluate progress on traits such as perseverance.[268] KIPP schools further reinforce those traits in ways large and small. Students even receive shirts with the slogan "Don't Eat the Marshmallow," a reference to the famous experiments on self-control among four-year-olds discussed in chapter 1.[269] But students sometimes need help in throwing the brakes on unattainable goals, particularly those fueled by parental ambitions that they do not share. Persistence in these cases can mainly produce depression, stress, and frustration, and forging a different path may be the best alternative.[270]

The California Child Development Project has institutionalized a number of these character education strategies. They include student participation in problem-solving, use of literature and classroom incidents to develop respect and understanding, and student involvement in helping behaviors.[271] A comparison of experimental and control schools showed that these strategies significantly enhanced the development of prosocial behaviors involving altruism and concern for others.[272] However, not all positive effects persisted over time, which underscores the need for sustained initiatives and longitudinal studies to evaluate program impacts.[273] Assessment is particularly needed concerning efforts to develop performance character and civic engagement.[274] Some strategies, such as character report cards, have yet to be studied. Educators have worried that that these grading strategies might give rise to "test prep" and metrics that "could then be gamed."[275]

Another strategy worthy of greater experimentation and assessment is experiential education. Examples include raising funds for famine relief, writing letters on behalf of prisoners of conscience, and participating in the Giraffe project, which honors people who stick their necks out for the common good.[276] Students can undertake their own search for giraffes and for service learning projects that will be meaningful for them.

Examples of youth activism can also provide inspiring role models. A case history involves a twelve-year-old Canadian boy, Craig Kielburger, who read that another twelve-year-boy was murdered in the mid-1990s while riding a bike in his hometown in Pakistan. [277] The boy was executed for speaking out against child labor, which he had experienced from an early age. Kielburger told his seventh grade classmates about the murder and enlisted volunteers to join him in working on the issue. But the nonprofits that they contacted with offers of assistance told them that they were too young to make a difference. So the twelve-year-olds began raising money for a new organization that they called Free the Children. Kielburger himself financed a trip to Pakistan, and while there, he learned that a Canadian trade delegation, headed by the prime minister, was in town. Kielburger arranged an impromptu press conference at which two child slave laborers told their stories. The result was widespread press coverage and a large increase in donations. To address the economic roots of the problem, the group developed a community-based approach called "Adopt a Village." It has focused on education, healthcare, employment, clean water, and sanitation. Over the last two decades, Free the Children has worked in forty-five countries around the world, and has benefited some 2.3 million children.[278] Such examples can inspire students to find causes that ignite their own passions.

Civic and service learning opportunities can also be a way of enhancing engagement and a sense of social responsibility, and some studies suggest that they are the most effective character development strategy.[279] By the turn of the twenty-first century, a majority of Americans supported school-sponsored service, and about two-thirds of all public schools offered such opportunities. But far fewer schools provided service learning courses that linked students' volunteer activities with classroom discussion.[280] And many failed to follow other best practices, which call for a good fit with students' interests and a sufficient duration and frequency of service to build relationships of trust and understanding.[281]

These are critical oversights. Well-designed service learning courses give students an invaluable opportunity to reflect on their experience and to put it in a broader social and ethical context. These opportunities can enhance character development in several ways. Students can "witness the commitments of community leaders . . ., experience social issues both cognitively and emotionally, [and encounter] . . . world views and perspectives of others . . . unlike themselves." [282] Empathy increases when "students develop personal connections with those who have experienced hardship or injustice." And by working closely with inspiring role models, students can "internalize images of what they want to be like."[283] A large body of research finds that middle and high school students who take such courses make significant gains on multiple measures of social responsibility.[284] Service learning enhances civic engagement, tolerance, trust, empathy, social responsibility, moral reasoning, and commitment to equal opportunity and cultural diversity.[285] Students can be "empowered by their successes [and] educated by their failures."[286] California's recently launched civic learning initiatives build similar capacities by involving youth in partnerships with community organizations and governance bodies.[287]

The impact of such programs can be long-lasting. One in-depth study followed middle class high school students who worked at a soup kitchen as part of a course on social justice.[288] Most of these students registered significant positive changes that persisted years later. Participants emerged with a deeper understanding of the harsh realities of poverty, and the complexity of strategies designed to address it. As one student observed, "I don't think anyone leaves the class unchanged." Of the students who had not done such volunteer work in high school, only 29 percent volunteered after graduation, compared with 68 percent of those who had participated in service projects such as the soup kitchen.[289]

College students experience similar benefits. In one study of twelve thousand college alumni, those who had taken undergraduate service learning courses were more likely five years after graduation to engage in civic activities and to help others in difficulty.[290] Of course, that result may at least be partly attributable to self-selection among the students who took such courses. But other research suggests that the experience itself may have been transformative, particularly for students who worked with communities unlike their own. One study that randomly assigned some students to community service sections of a course on contemporary political issues found that they showed greater gains than other students on measures including tolerance, a commitment to helping others, and an intention to do volunteer work in the future.[291] In other research on adults who demonstrated a long-term commitment to the common good, the single most important factor was their previous engagement with a person significantly different from themselves, which enabled them to recognize a shared humanity.[292]

In addition to providing service learning opportunities, colleges need to explore more ways of fostering character development. Relatively few campuses do so.[293] Yet as psychologist Ann Colby puts it, "education is not complete until students have not only acquired knowledge, but can use that knowledge to act responsibly in the world."[294] Colleges inevitably influence a student's moral identity; they need to be more intentional about that process. To that end, a Hastings Center Report recommended that all undergraduates should take a course in ethics that would enhance moral reasoning skills and a sense of social responsibility.[295]

In designing new programs, colleges could learn from military academies, which make development of "leaders of character" a core priority.[296] For example, West Point has an extensive Character Development Strategy to ensure that all graduates internalize ideals of duty, honor, and country.[297] An ethics center is responsible for periodic assessment of the academy's overall program as well as the character development of individual cadets.[298] To be sure, these efforts have not shielded West Point from ethical challenges that face other campuses, particularly those involving sexual assault and honor code violations.[299] But the Academy's commitment to identifying and addressing the problems, and its investment in intentional strategies of character development, hold valuable lessons for higher education generally.

One of those lessons is the importance of integrating issues of ethics and values into the core curricula. These issues arise in a wide array of substantive contexts, and failure to address them there sends a message that no single ethics course can counteract.[300] Extracurricular programming, speakers, and counseling can similarly channel students' attention toward strategies for crafting a well-lived life.[301] All of these efforts require more long-term assessment.

We know that significant changes occur during early adulthood in people's strategies for dealing with moral issues.[302] We need to know more about how higher education can best aid that process.[303] If we are truly committed to nurturing moral character in our youth, then adults will need to show more responsibility in making that a priority.

3

Character in Law

AMERICAN LAW CARES about character. "Good moral character" requirements play an important role in determining who can work in licensed professions and occupations, who can pass employers' background checks, who can immigrate to the United States, and who can become a citizen.[1] As chapter 4 indicates, character assumes comparable significance in the criminal justice system. Yet all too often, legal norms and requirements are inconsistent with psychological research and social justice. As a consequence, the law's concept of character undermines the values it seeks to express.

It is not just lawyers who should care about these issues. Prevailing legal definitions of virtue speak volumes about our cultural values and policy priorities. Character standards determine whether a criminal offense should forever bar someone from becoming a florist or subject them to deportation. In an era of mass incarceration, and widespread racial bias in the criminal justice system, such character exclusions should be a matter of substantial public concern. Seventy million Americans, one in three adults, have a criminal record, and character-based employment and licensing requirements can be a substantial barrier to their economic livelihood and rehabilitation.[2]

An all too typical example is Quiana Williams, a single mother in her thirties who testified at a 2015 White House conference on criminal justice and incarceration. At age 19, she got a ticket for driving without a license in St. Louis. Because she could not afford to pay that ticket, she was subject to additional fines and fees, and when she couldn't pay them, warrants were issued for her arrest. Those warrants didn't specify that the original offense was a traffic violation. They only said "I'm a fugitive, I'm a wanted person."[3] That record dogged her for the next two decades.

> Not only was I unable to get a job, get adequate housing, I didn't see a way out, I didn't see a way to pay for those fines and fees. I thought maybe if

I just got an education, that I would be able to be in an earning income bracket that would help me to pay these fines and fees. And so I went to school. . . . And twelve credits away from getting my degree, I was arrested for traffic tickets.[4]

Because racial and ethnic minorities are disproportionately likely to have run-ins with the criminal law, they pay a special price for employment policies that use criminal records as a proxy for character deficiencies. So too, since the election of Donald Trump, increasing rates of deportation gives new urgency to questions about the definition of good moral character in immigration proceedings.

These issues should be matters of greater public concern and higher priorities for legal reform. Americans' stake in this debate is substantial. How the law treats character adversely affects the lives and livelihoods of millions of individuals. Change is long overdue.

Moral Character as an Occupational Credential

Moral character as an occupational credential has an extended history. For lawyers, the requirement dates back sixteen centuries, to a Roman code mandating that legal advocates be of "suitable character," with praiseworthy lives.[5] In the United States, moral character requirements have long been an integral part of occupational licensing laws and employer decision-making. These requirements serve several purposes. The first is public protection. Employers and occupational licensing authorities assume that the moral character required for a particular position is a stable attribute that they can predict with reasonably accuracy based on past conduct. An individual either has it or does not. Prior misconduct, particularly when it results in a criminal record, is seen as predictive of future dishonesty, theft, violence, breach of fiduciary obligations, and/or lack of a work ethic.[6] Employers also worry about their own liability for negligent hiring if third parties suffer.[7] Another concern is reputational. Requiring applicants to have an unblemished background expresses aspirational norms and enhances an organization's and an occupation's image. Licensed professionals want to believe, and want the public to believe, that they are certifiably ethical.

The research summarized in what follows casts doubt on the effectiveness of current character screening processes in serving these interests, and exposes the substantial social costs that the processes impose. Many character-related exclusions are arbitrary, overinclusive, and insufficiently justified by performance concerns. Some seem calculated less to enhance public protection than professional image. And from a societal standpoint, it makes little sense to allow such occupational self-interests to supersede values of fairness and rehabilitation for job applicants.

The adverse consequences are particularly great for individuals with criminal records. An estimated 20 million Americans, almost 9 percent of the adult population, and a third of the African American adult male population, have felony convictions.[8] Another fifty million more have a criminal record including misdemeanor convictions.[9] By some estimates, over a quarter of American adults have criminal histories that would require disclosure in typical job applications and interviews.[10] Because employers and licensing authorities typically use criminal involvement as a proxy for immoral character, ex-offenders often face insurmountable obstacles in their search for paid work. Unemployment is the single most important predictor of recidivism.[11] Nearly seven hundred thousand Americans leave prison each year, and half will return within three years without having found jobs.[12] Two-thirds of former inmates are unemployed or underemployed five years after release from prison.[13] The costs are particularly great for racial minorities, who, as chapter 4 notes, are treated more harshly than similarly situated white defendants, and also to suffer greater adverse employment consequences than white job applicants with similar criminal records.[14]

Character Requirements for Occupational Licenses

During America's first two centuries, formal standards for occupations were "few and loose."[15] Professions other than law and medicine were rarely subject to state oversight.[16] Then, toward the end of the nineteenth century, regulation increased in response to lobbying by the professions and occupations themselves, many of which saw strict licensing requirements as a way of preventing competition from non-licensed service providers.[17] By the mid-twentieth century, the United States had more than twelve hundred licensing laws, an average of twenty-five per state.[18] Regulation extended not only to established professions, but also to egg graders, guide-dog trainers, yacht salesmen, potato growers, beekeepers, septic tank cleaners, and tree surgeons.[19] Statutes typically required good moral character, which excluded those with felony convictions regardless of the nature of the felony or its relevance to the intended occupation.[20] As law professor Walter Gellhorn noted, a "blanket proscription of this sort seems more vindictively punitive than it does selectively preventive."[21] Was the public really safer if Vietnam protestors could not obtain licenses as watchmakers due to draft-related offenses?[22] And what justified requiring commercial photographers to pass a test for syphilis?[23] Equally problematic were Cold War requirements of loyalty oaths and inquiries concerning potentially "subversive" conduct for groups as diverse as professional boxers, pharmacists, and piano tuners. Veterinarians in some states could not "minister to an ailing cow or cat unless they [had] first signed a non-Communist oath, thus assuring that they ... [would] not indoctrinate their four legged patients."[24]

Although current licensing processes are no longer concerned with loyalty, they remain inconsistent, idiosyncratic, and overinclusive. And it matters. More than eleven hundred occupations are licensed in at least one state, and nearly 30 percent of the workforce is covered by licensing laws.[25] Almost all of these occupations require good moral character or the functional equivalent, although for many, the need for character screening is scarcely self-evident. Frog farmers, florists, fortune tellers, street artists, upholstery repairers, and massage therapists (even those for animals) are subject to licensing requirements in some states.[26]

In most cases, review is fairly cursory, and focuses on whether an applicant has been convicted of a felony or had a license revoked or suspended.[27] In some jurisdictions, however, the inquiry is more intrusive. For Texas mortgage brokers, licensing officials can consider factors including "emotional stability," "strong community ties," and "petty offenses."[28] In Iowa, the inquiry into good moral character extends not only to applicants for liquor licenses, but also to their spouses.[29] Other jurisdictions impose requirements that seem like mindless formalities. For example, the City of Santa Barbara requires massage therapists to provide affidavits of good moral character by five residents of Santa Barbara County.[30]

A few professions, particularly law and medicine, engage in much more searching scrutiny, but often focus on conduct that bears only a tangential relationship to professional practice. A case in point is the requirement that acupuncturists be current in child support obligations as a condition of receiving a license.[31] Of the twenty-two California chiropractors recently disciplined for criminal conduct, only four involved offenses related to chiropractic obligations.[32]

One major effect of character review is to exclude individuals with a criminal record. At least twenty-seven thousand statutes across the states restrict the employment of the 70 million Americans who have such a record.[33] In half the states, licenses can be denied due to any kind of criminal conviction, regardless of whether it is relevant to the employment, or how long ago it occurred.[34] A survey by the American Bar Association reported over twelve thousand disqualifications of individuals with any type of felony and over six thousand disqualifications based on misdemeanors. Most are permanent. Over eleven thousand are mandatory, which means that regulatory agencies lack discretion to grant a license based on mitigating circumstances or rehabilitation.[35] Even where no flat ban exists, many courts and licensing agencies have concluded that anyone who ever committed a crime necessarily lacks the requisite good character for a license.[36]

Such license denials are a significant contributor to unemployment, racial inequality, and recidivism.[37] And they often bear little relationship to the requirements of the occupation. Half the states deny a beautician license to former felons.[38] In Pennsylvania, a person who had been a health worker for thirty years attempted to change jobs and learned that a new law barred him from any healthcare position due to conviction for possession of marijuana three decades earlier.[39] In Wisconsin, a grandmother had her home day-care license revoked based on a thirty-year-old misdemeanor conviction for accepting an overpayment of public assistance.[40] In Texas, marijuana offenses can disqualify applicants from becoming mortgage brokers.[41] A case study in injustice involved a young New York drug offender who turned her life around in prison. After earning a college degree at Baruch College and a master's degree in social work at New York University, she began work helping other prisoners do the same. When she received a promotion to management that required a social degree license, New York authorities denied it because of her criminal record. After years of effort to transform her life and give back to society, the government told her that she lacked good moral character.[42]

Several thousand licensing restrictions exclude applicants convicted of crimes involving "moral turpitude," a term subject to varying definitions by the courts.[43] Moral turpitude also affects discipline and license revocation in ways that bear little relation to workplace conduct. Physicians have been subject to discipline including suspension for offenses such as shoplifting, possession of marijuana, and soliciting sex in a public restroom.[44] Disciplinary officials have often been more concerned with minor criminal offenses, which are easy to prove, than with negligent performance, which is not, but which is more relevant to patient care.[45] One sobering study found that criminal misconduct unrelated to job performance tended to be disciplined more severely than misconduct that had a closer connection to competent medical practice.[46]

In theory, civil rights law imposes some constraints on employment exclusions based on a criminal conviction if they have a racially disparate impact. Such discriminatory exclusions are justifiable only if they meet a business necessity.[47] In practice, however, licensing boards have found such a necessity even where there is only an attenuated connection between the offense and the job sought.[48] California bars ex-offenders from working in real estate or physical therapy. New York prevents ex-offenders from receiving a license as an auctioneer, junk dealer, dental hygienist, veterinarian, undertaker, fire suppression piping contractor, or bingo operator. Virginia denies licenses to ex-offenders in fields involving optometry, funeral homes, or pharmacology.[49]

Some licensing systems provide opportunities for applicants to appeal their denials. Little research is available concerning the frequency and outcomes of such review. One of the only studies on point examined cases in which offenders who were initially denied licenses to be unarmed security guards in New York appealed their denials to administrative law judges. More than three-quarters of those appellants were successful, suggesting that the initial denials rested on overly restrictive approaches.[50] Successful applicants were generally able to show either meaningful change and improvement since their criminal conviction, or that the behavior leading to the offense was aberrational and not representative of their general character. A typical rationale for granting the license was that the applicant, "having started life with the deck stacked against him, and "making one big mistake," has striven to improve himself and lead a productive life."[51] Such considerations should play a role for all applicants, not just those who are unreasonably denied a license and have the determination, resources, and capability to contest the injustice.

The inconsistencies in current state licensing structures point up their arbitrary underpinnings. If a good moral character requirement that bans ex-offenders was truly necessary to protect public health and safety in all of the thousands of occupations to which it currently applies, we would expect to see more consensus among the states about which jobs require screening.[52] We would also have more convincing evidence that the value of such protection is worth its costs. The studies on character summarized in chapter 1 and the studies of employee performance discussed below suggest otherwise, and counsel against sweeping exclusions of applicants with criminal records. That research makes clear that a single criminal act, committed many years earlier under vastly different circumstances, is not a good predictor of current threats to the public. The Wisconsin grandmother denied a license is a case in point. To conclude that she lacks character to run a home day-care after she has been doing so effectively for a decade, because she had accepted a $294 welfare overpayment thirty years earlier, defies basic fairness and common sense.[53] Rather, as subsequent discussion argues, we need fundamental regulatory reform, which requires character requirements to be job-related, and considers all relevant factors, including mitigation and rehabilitation.

Character Requirements for the Legal Profession: A Case Study

To provide a better sense of how character requirements function in practice, an in-depth exploration of lawyer admission and disciplinary practices is useful. As noted earlier, the American legal profession has long demanded "good moral character" in its members. However, until recently, the mobility of applicants and the absence of centralized records made character standards difficult to enforce.[54] What kept the system workable was that lawyers in the eighteenth and nineteenth century generally practiced within small professional communities where reputation was a matter of common knowledge and unethical practitioners could be shunned by clients and colleagues.

As the profession grew in size and diversity, this approach appeared increasingly inadequate. Much of the impetus for more stringent review rested on nativist, ethnic, and anti-Semitic prejudices, as well as anticompetitive concerns during the Depression.[55] With large numbers of lawyers desperate for business during the 1930s, bar organizations found character exclusions to be a convenient way to limit new entrants to the profession. Pennsylvania had perhaps the most rigorous screening system. Prospective candidates faced a character investigation both at the beginning of law school and when seeking admission to the state bar. The initial interview offered an opportunity to dissuade the "unworthy" from pursuing a legal career.[56] The definition of "unworthy" was quite elastic. Those rejected by one county board in 1929 included individuals deemed "dull," "colorless," "subnormal," "unprepossessing," "shifty," "smooth," "keen," "shrewd," "arrogant," "conceited," "surly," and "slovenly."[57] Examiners believed that they could tell from the interviews that candidates lacked "moral . . . stamina."[58] The extent to which comparable biases affected decisions in other states is unclear. However, the scant evidence available leaves no doubt that concerns with competition during the Depression influenced some bar committees. Examiners frequently argued that "with an overcrowded bar [and] an abundance of candidates who have unquestioned character," any doubts should be resolved against admission.[59] Among those raising doubts were political radicals, religious "fanatics," and fornicators.[60]

Moral character concerns also figured in bar disciplinary processes. Courts have traditionally asserted power to disbar, suspend, or otherwise sanction lawyers for conduct involving "moral turpitude." Application of that standard has been ambiguous, inconsistent, and idiosyncratic. The term is itself redundant: as one court noted, "turpitude" means moral wickedness or depravity, so moral turpitude "means little more than morally immoral."[61] A leading California decision unhelpfully concluded that "to hold that an act of a practitioner constitutes moral turpitude is to characterize him as unsuitable to practice law."[62] But what exactly made someone unsuitable has been subject to long-standing dispute. During the early part of the twentieth century, habitual drunkards, home brewers, fornicators, and radical political activists fared differently in different courts.[63] To a 1929 Missouri court, seduction by an unfulfilled promise to marry reflected "baseness and depravity" mandating disbarment.[64] By contrast, in the preceding year, a New Jersey court found fornication with a fifteen-year-old to warrant only a six-month suspension from the bar, in light of the victim's previously dissolute life and the attorney's reputation as an "upright and moral man."[65]

In the 1970s, although a Florida lawyer lost his license following a conviction for indecent exposure in a public lavatory, an Indiana practitioner received only a year's suspension for making sexual advances to clients and offering to exchange legal services for nude photographs of one of those clients and her daughter.[66] Inexplicably, it was the latter attorney whose activities were deemed "personal and unrelated" to professional practice.

Throughout the twentieth century, the moral character requirement placed a price on nonconformist political commitments. Conscientious objectors, suspected subversives, and student radicals were exhaustively investigated and occasionally denied admission.[67] Such inquiries had a chilling effect on free speech. In one survey in the mid-1970s, a third of law students reported refraining from activities such as attending political rallies or signing petitions because of impending character reviews.[68] In addition to its deterrent effect on constitutionally protected activities, the character oversight process sent a disturbing message about the kind of conformity that the bar valued.[69]

My own 1985 study offered an in-depth account of how the moral character inquiry operated in both admission and disciplinary processes.[70] Taken together, the data demonstrated what the Supreme Court once candidly acknowledged: character requirements are "unusually ambiguous. . . . [A]ny definition will necessarily reflect the attitudes, experiences, and prejudices of the definer."[71] Perhaps for that reason, the Court has largely avoided specifying what constitutes good moral character. Rather, it has rested with the general observation that any criteria of character must have a "rational connection with the applicant's fitness or capacity to practice law."[72] The difficulty is that examiners have had inconsistent and idiosyncratic views about what constitutes such a connection. Violation of a fishing license ten years earlier was sufficient to cause one local Michigan committee to deny admission. But in the same state, at about the same time, other examiners on the central board admitted applicants convicted of child molesting and conspiring to bomb a public building.[73] Convictions for marijuana possession were taken seriously in some jurisdictions and overlooked in others; much depended on whether the examiners had, as one put it, grown more "mellow" toward "kids smoking pot."[74] States divided evenly over whether they would investigate sexual matters, including cohabitation, sexual orientation, or "lifestyle."[75] Some questioned bar applicants about the details of their sex lives and living arrangements to see if they reflected a "contumacious attitude" toward laws on fornication.[76] Another official expressed relief that issues such as technically illegal cohabitation rarely arose: "Thank God we don't have much of that [in Missouri]."[77]

Although applicants' sex lives are now rarely of interest, courts and bar examiners continue to divide over the conduct that constitutes grounds for exclusion. Five states prohibit all felons from practicing law.[78] The remaining states consider a wide range of factors that yield inconsistent and idiosyncratic judgments.[79] Cases involving bankruptcy, marijuana, compulsive gambling, repeated traffic offenses, and driving without insurance have generated conflicting precedents.[80]

Opinions have also differed over the significance of rehabilitation. Some courts and committees have assumed, contrary to the psychological research summarized in chapter 1, that "a leopard never changes its spots"; neither good works nor "self-serving" statements of remorse are sufficient to justify admission.[81] For example, in 2014, the California Supreme Court declined to admit Steven Glass, a former reporter who had fabricated stories in the late 1990s while working for the *New Republic*. The hearing judge and state bar court had recommended admission, based on evidence including "his employment history, community service, character witnesses, progress in therapy, remorse, and acceptance of responsibility," all of which provided a "more accurate picture of his moral character than his misconduct of many years ago."[82] The California Supreme Court, however, was unimpressed, and even ignored the consensus of his psychiatrists, who were concededly "well regarded in their field" and "convinced that he has no remaining psychological flaws tending to cause him to act dishonestly."[83] By contrast, in another 2014 case, the Washington Supreme Court allowed Shon Hopwood, a man convicted of five bank robberies in 1997 and 1998, to take the bar exam, and, if he passed, to be admitted to practice. While in prison, Hopwood had drafted a pro se petition for a fellow inmate that led to a 9–0 victory in the Supreme Court. Hopwood's exemplary record since prison gained him a prestigious clerkship and a faculty position at Georgetown Law School. The judge who sentenced him to twelve years in prison observed that the case "proves that my sentencing instincts suck."[84]

That lesson however, apparently escaped Washington's bar examiners, who four years later denied Tara Simmons the right to sit for the bar exam. Simmons had a string of convictions resulting from activities to fund her drug addiction. However, after leaving prison and ending drug use, she graduated magna cum laude from law school and received a highly prestigious fellowship to work on prison re-entry issues. In denying her application to the bar, the state's Board of Character and Fitness reasoned that her almost six-year record of complete sobriety and exemplary achievement was not long enough. The Board was also troubled that that her attitude betrayed a sense of "entitlement," and that she had only used the word "sorry" once at her hearing.[85] The Washington Supreme Court unanimously reversed. It rejected "word counts" of repentance as an adequate basis for judgments about moral character and noted that over four-fifths of addicts who maintain sobriety for at least five years are able to continue doing so. In the Supreme Court's view, the bar should recognize that "one's past does not dictate one's future."[86] That is not, however, the view in other states, some of which have lifetime bans or heavy presumptions against admitting anyone with a felony conviction.[87]

Another inconsistency and injustice in character decision-making involves undocumented immigrants. Although most states do not require applicants to the bar to disclose their immigration or citizenship status, some do, and the applicants' eligibility to practice has been a matter of dispute.[88] The United States Justice Department has opposed admission, relying on a federal statute that prohibits state agencies from granting public benefits including professional licenses to undocumented individuals. An exception to that law exists where state statutes permit such licensure.[89] In 2014, the California Supreme Court relied on such a statute to determine that Sergio Garcia satisfied the good moral character standard although he was in the country without lawful immigration status.[90] Garcia's personal story is compelling. His parents, Mexican farmworkers, had brought him to the United States when he was seventeen months old. His father and most of his siblings are citizens, but Garcia had been waiting eighteen years, since age eighteen, for a lawful permanent resident visa. Despite the California Supreme Court decision admitting him to the bar, federal law prohibited employers from hiring Garcia because as an undocumented immigrant he lacked work authorization. Until he finally obtained a green card, he ran a solo practice, handling accident disputes and immigration matters for low- and moderate-income individuals. Half of his cases were pro bono, and when clients could not afford to pay the bill, they sometimes gave him fruit and vegetables.[91]

By contrast, Florida has denied admission to undocumented immigrants.[92] In response, three former American Bar Association presidents filed a brief with the Florida Supreme Court claiming, without success, that exclusion of undocumented immigrants is a "waste of exceptional talent for our profession."[93] Lawyers such as Garcia suggest that they are right.

Not only is the bar admission process inconsistent and idiosyncratic, it comes both too early and too late. Screening takes place before most applicants have faced situational pressures comparable to those in practice, yet after applicants have made such a significant investment in legal training that examiners are reluctant to deny admission. Estimates suggest that the bar refuses to certify fewer than 1 percent of applicants.[94] However some significant number of individuals are deterred from applying to law school or are refused admission by schools out of fears that they could not satisfy the moral character requirement. These individuals are disproportionately people of color.[95] A recent survey of one hundred formerly incarcerated college graduates who identified themselves as criminal justice leaders found that many wanted to go to law school but cited the moral character requirement as the primary reason that they were not applying.[96] The effect of current screening processes is to exclude those with reform agendas and impede the profession's efforts to become as diverse as the clients and country it serves.

The necessity for such restrictive exclusionary policies is unsupported by the research on character reviewed in chapter 1. As it reveals, ethical conduct reflects a complex interrelationship between traits and situations, and people can be ethical in some respects but not others. Regulators would need to know a considerable amount about why individuals acted the way they did in the past in order accurately to predict how they will act in particular circumstances in the future. Licensing authorities frequently lack that information. Even trained psychiatrists and psychologists have been notably unsuccessful in predicting future dishonesty based on the kind of limited information at issue in character proceedings.[97] Untrained bar examiners and judges can hardly do better. Decision-makers are frequently drawing inferences based on one or two prior acts committed under vastly different circumstances.

The inadequacies of this system emerged in a recent study that reviewed some thirteen hundred Connecticut bar applicants and their subsequent disciplinary records to determine whether anything at the admission stage predicted subsequent misconduct. The study found that although some factors increased the likelihood of discipline, even those factors were still poor predictors. As the authors explain, "even if some variable (e.g. having defaulted on a student loan) doubles the likelihood of subsequent disciplinary action—a very strong effect—the probability of subsequent discipline for an applicant with a student loan default is still only 5 percent."[98] Taking all the risk factors together, "only two individuals [of thirteen hundred] were predicted to have a better than even chance of being disciplined, a finding that casts serious doubt on the character and fitness inquiry as a useful way to prevent lawyer misconduct."[99]

A further problem in bar character requirements involves the double standard of admission and discipline. From the standpoint of protecting the public, the misconduct of someone already practicing law is more predictive of future offenses than the misconduct of someone not yet admitted. Yet the bar's admission and disciplinary processes have operated on precisely the opposite assumption. Much of the conduct that triggers character investigation of applicants, such as financial mismanagement, psychiatric treatment, minor drug offenses, and civil disobedience, almost never results in disciplinary investigations of practicing attorneys.[100]

Moreover, the same inconsistencies and idiosyncrasies that plague the interpretation of good moral character in the admission process arise in disciplinary proceedings. Every state has some version of the American Bar Association (ABA) Model Rules of Professional Conduct, which authorize discipline for a criminal act that reflects adversely on the lawyer's honesty, trustworthiness, or fitness.[101] ABA standards identify eleven aggravating circumstances and sixteen mitigating circumstances that can be relevant in determining sanctions, which permits wildly varying responses to similar offenses.[102]

A case history of arbitrary interpretations of moral character involves Laura Beth Lamb. She lost her license after taking the bar exam for her abusive husband. At the time of the exam, she was seven months pregnant. Her husband, who had previously failed two exams, had bouts of rage and depression during which he threw heavy objects and threatened to kill Lamb and her unborn child if she did not take the test in his place. She reluctantly agreed. After an anonymous tip alerted the state bar, she pleaded guilty to felony impersonation and deception. She received a fine, probation, and a requirement of two hundred hours of community service. On losing her job at the Securities and Exchange Commission, she took a position as a legal secretary. She also divorced her husband and received psychological treatment. Despite her therapist's conclusion that Lamb's "prognosis for the future is good provided she remains in therapy," and that she was unlikely to "do anything remotely like this again," the California Supreme Court imposed disbarment. In the court's view, the "legal, ethical, and moral pressures of daily practice come in many forms . . . [and] may include the sincere but misguided desire to please a persuasive or overbearing client."[103] Yet for the court to equate the pressure of an insistent client to that of an abusive, mentally unstable spouse suggests a profound insensitivity to the risks of battering for a pregnant woman.[104]

In most published disciplinary decisions involving conduct outside a lawyer-client relationship, courts do not even bother to consider the likelihood of its replication in a professional context. It is enough that the conduct threatens the reputation of the profession. A representative example involved Albert Boudreau, a Louisiana lawyer convicted of importing several magazines and a video displaying child pornography.[105] Boudreau purchased the items in the Netherlands, where the magazines were lawful and the models were of legal age to be photographed nude. They were, however, underage by American definitions. The Louisiana Supreme Court agreed with the disciplinary board that the actions constituted a "stain upon the legal profession," and clearly reflected on the lawyer's "moral fitness to practice law."[106] Despite the absence of any prior disciplinary record, or any relationship between personal and professional conduct, the court ordered disbarment.

Yet if the goal of such sanctions is to ensure public confidence, a better strategy would be to make the disciplinary process more responsive to professional misconduct, and less idiosyncratic in its responses to nonprofessional offenses. It can scarcely enhance respect for the process when lawyers guilty of such offenses receive wildly different treatment, and the focus is professional reputation rather than public protection. Sanctions for drug offenses, tax evasion, and domestic violence now range from reprimand to disbarment, and bear too little relationship to whether misconduct is likely to occur in a professional context.[107]

As currently implemented, the bar's character requirement trivializes the values it seeks to advance. It is inconsistent, intrusive, and ineffective. Unaccountable decision-makers render intuitive judgments, largely unconstrained by formal standards and uninformed by research that casts doubt on their assessments. A profession concerned about the legitimacy of its own regulation must do better.

Character Screening by Employers

Similar problems arise in workplaces other than licensed occupations. Surveys find that around 80 percent of employers ask about criminal records on job applications and around 70 percent conduct background checks.[108] In the past year, more than 30 million Americans were asked about criminal records on job applications.[109] The majority of employers report unwillingness to hire individuals convicted of a serious criminal offense.[110]

James Foreman's recent book, *Locking Up Our Own*, offers a wrenching example of how even a minor offense can upend a life. Police in Washington, DC, pulled over a young woman of color for a pretextual motor vehicle violation.[111] The officers found two small bags of marijuana in her car, which led to her arrest. Because she had no prior convictions, no charges were brought, but the arrest was enough to deny her permanent employment at a job where she had been performing well. "It's company policy," her supervisor regretfully explained.[112] In a similar case in a New York, police arrested a man after finding a pipe with marijuana residue in a car in which he was a passenger. He had no knowledge of the pipe, did not use marijuana, and had no prior criminal record. However, his employer fired him from his job as a bus driver, telling him he could be reinstated if he proved his innocence. It took five months to get the charges dismissed, and when the *New York Times* ran the story, he had yet to be rehired.[113]

Recognition of the overly harsh and racially disproportionate consequences of hiring bans based on criminal records has prompted some reform efforts. In 2012, the Equal Employment Opportunities Commission issued guidance that advises employers to limit criminal background checks to job-related convictions and to make individualized character assessments that include evidence of rehabilitation.[114] Over half the states and more than 150 cities have passed "ban the box" statutes that prevent employers, mainly those in the public sector, from asking about job applicants' criminal records and eliminating ex-offenders from

consideration before conducting individualized assessments.[115] A growing array
of research suggests that these statutes have unintended consequences. Employers
reluctant to hire ex-offenders often decline to consider those whom they suspect
of having a criminal record, particularly black and Hispanic males without a college degree.[116]

Yet many organizations may be overestimating the risks and understating
the benefits from giving these applicants a second chance. A growing number of
organizations have found that employing those with criminal histories is cost-
effective. The largest recent study on point compared the performance of over
a million ex-felons and other comparable enlistees in the military, the nation's
largest employer. It found that prior offenders who were allowed to enlist through
a "moral character waiver" screening process received promotions more rapidly
and to higher ranks than counterparts with no criminal histories. Ex-offenders
had no higher rate of attrition due to poor performance than non-offenders and
only a slightly higher rate of discharge for a legal offense (6.6 versus 5 percent).[117]
Although as the researchers noted, the military environment is different from
civilian workplaces in significant ways, its experience is consistent with that of
many corporate employers surveyed in a recent American Civil Liberties Union
Report, *Back to Business*.[118] These private sector organizations, including large
companies such as Walmart, have found that ex-offenders have lower rates of attrition than other employees with comparable credentials.[119] Some organizations
have cut their turnover rates in half by targeted recruitment of those with criminal records. Because such employees anticipate fewer job opportunities, they
have higher motivations to succeed and greater loyalty to employers who give
them a chance.[120]

Society as a whole would benefit from less punitive attitudes toward offenders
who are on a path to rehabilitation. Reducing their joblessness also reduces recidivism and the accompanying social costs of homelessness, crime, and incarceration. Pew Center research, as well as several other studies, show that states could
save billions by reducing re-offense rates through employment and related social
services.[121]

An Agenda for Reform

Moral character requirements for employment respond to legitimate concerns
but do so in a way that is idiosyncratic, unjust, and unsupported by psychological
research. As that research makes clear, character is not static.[122] Nor is it defined
by a criminal record, abstracted from situational factors, and individuals should
have the opportunity to demonstrate as much. They should also have incentives

for rehabilitation. Any sensible policy framework would reward peoples' efforts to turn their lives around. The vast majority of Americans agree. Nine out of ten believe that we should break down barriers that make it hard for ex-offenders to find work and support their families.[123]

One fundamental challenge in crafting a reform agenda is how to balance competing values: consistent treatment of similar conduct, and individualized consideration of all the situational factors that affect conduct and influence our character judgments. This trade-off between the consistency achieved through bright-line rules and the fairness achieved through discretionary standards is not unique to employment contexts, and decision-makers are likely to differ about how the precise balance should be struck. The following proposals seek to accommodate both concerns through rules that limit the kind of offenses that can be considered in character assessments, and standards that enable decision-makers to consider the full record, including evidence of rehabilitation and mitigation.

One way of addressing problems in moral character requirements for occupational licenses is to reduce the number of occupations subject to licensing. This strategy would have other benefits. As a recent Brookings Institute report concluded, "the literature provides little evidence that stricter licensing regimes lead to improved quality of services."[124] What the research does show is that such regimes lead to higher prices for consumers, unwarranted burdens for licensees seeking to move across state lines, and unjustified exclusions of those with criminal records. Society as a whole would benefit if states conducted cost-benefit analyses of the need for licensing in selected occupations and the advantages of less restrictive alternatives, such as registration or voluntary certification systems.[125] The federal government could jump-start this review process by providing financial incentives and establishing best practices.[126] A few states have begun moving in this direction. For example, Arizona recently removed licensing requirements for yoga teachers, geologists, and citrus fruit packers.[127] More states should follow suit.

They could also adopt the approach of jurisdictions that have abandoned the good moral character requirement altogether, and replaced it with a more narrowly tailored question asking whether applicants have "engaged in conduct warranting disciplinary action against a licensee."[128] This strategy should also be coupled with a review of disciplinary sanctions to ensure that they are available only for misconduct reasonably related to job performance.

A further strategy for occupational licensing authorities that retained the moral character requirement would be to eliminate categorical bans based on criminal records and to require individualized assessments. A model statute by the National Employment Law Project suggests that such assessments should consider:

- The nature and gravity of the offense;
- The nature of the job;
- The length of time that has passed since the offense;
- The circumstances surrounding the offense, including the age of the offender and contributing social conditions; and
- The evidence available concerning rehabilitation, including subsequent work history and character references.[129]

Under this statute, licensing authorities could not consider convictions unless they were job-related. That would entail an inquiry into whether the offenses were directly relevant to the responsibilities of the occupation and whether the occupation offered an opportunity to commit such offenses in the future.[130]

The same approach should guide reform of lawyer admission and disciplinary proceedings. Courts and bar authorities should require a direct and substantial relationship between legal practice and prior misconduct. In assessing that relationship, decision-makers should consider factors such as the remoteness and seriousness of the behaviors, their relationship to the specific duties of lawyers, evidence of rehabilitation, and any other mitigating circumstances. Under those criteria, bar examiners should not categorically exclude undocumented immigrants. Nor should bar admission and disciplinary decision-makers disregard psychological research and mental health testimony in proceedings such as those involving reporter Stephen Glass, and domestic violence survivor Laura Beth Lamb, where there is little likelihood of future misconduct. The process should also be more transparent, and should provide training to bar officials on rehabilitation and offer guidance or conditional decisions to would-be law school applicants about their prospects for admission.

Similar reforms are necessary for private employers, and a number of states as well as the EEOC, are pushing in that direction. For example, New York prohibits an employer from using criminal convictions to deny employment unless there is a "direct relationship" between the previous criminal offenses and the position sought, or the applicant's employment would involve an "unreasonable risk" to public safety or welfare.[131] Unlike laws in other states, this statute also sets forth specific criteria for determining the relationship between the job and the criminal offense. These criteria include the seriousness of the offense, the link between the job and the crime, the time that has elapsed since the offense, the applicant's age at the time of the offense, the rehabilitation of the applicant, and the state's interests in protecting the public and the business.[132] Accordingly, in one New York case, the court held that the city could not deny a custodial job to an individual convicted of manslaughter and drug offenses because the crimes were not related to the employment, and the applicant did not present an unreasonable risk to persons or property.[133]

In assessing risk, employers could also look to statistical data on the likelihood of recidivism. This was the approach suggested in a challenge to a Pennsylvania transportation authority's policy of excluding anyone ever convicted of a violent crime from working as a para-transit driver for disabled passengers.[134] Forty-seven years earlier, the plaintiff had been convicted of second degree murder arising from a gang-related fight when he was fifteen years old. He claimed that the employer's categorical ban had a disparate impact on racial minorities, and the EEOC agreed. The employer responded that the policy was justified by business necessity, relying on expert testimony suggesting that those convicted of violent offenses were somewhat more likely to re-offend. On a motion for summary judgment, the court accepted that justification and upheld the policy, but indicated that the result might have been different if the plaintiff had produced evidence demonstrating that after a certain period of time, convictions ceased to be reliable predictors.[135]

A growing body of research could supply such evidence. It shows that most detected recidivism occurs within three years of an arrest and almost always within five.[136] One large-scale study of eighty-eight thousand offenders found that it was possible to predict the point at which the likelihood of an arrest for someone with a prior offense would decline to the same rate as for the population generally. For burglary, it was 3.8 years; for aggravated assault, it was 4.3 years.[137] Such research should inform decision-making by employers, courts, legislatures, and licensing authorities in considering how long a prior conviction should have relevance. But as noted earlier, character determinations should also include other factors, such as the circumstances surrounding the offense, the age at which it was committed, its relationship to the job, and evidence of rehabilitation.

Other strategies are also available to reduce the adverse effects of criminal records. For applicants who meet specified criteria, states could expand and simplify options for expungement or sealing of records, and could issue certificates of recovery (sometimes called certificates of re-entry, relief, or employability), which serve as evidence of rehabilitation.[138] More occupations could also issue conditional licenses, which become permanent after a specified period (such as a year) in the absence of misconduct. Almost half of all bar admission authorities do so, without apparent ill effects.[139] So too, more states could provide significant tax credits for employers who hire ex-offenders and could pass legislation shielding these employers from liability for negligent hiring if they follow guidelines such as those set out above.[140]

The goal of all of these proposals is to make moral character inquiries in employment more consistent with what we know from research on moral character in practice. Character is not static, and conduct can vary in response to changes in situational pressures and constraints. Licensing and hiring practices need to reflect that reality, and promote not only public protection but also individual rehabilitation.

Character in Immigration Proceedings
Historical Background

Another legal context in which character plays a pivotal role involves immigration. Good character as a prerequisite for citizenship appeared in the country's first naturalization statute enacted in 1790. Congress extensively debated the requirement, and Georgia representative James Jackson introduced the idea of having prospective citizens produce testimonials of proper and decent behavior. His hope was that the title of "citizen of America" would become as "highly venerated and respected" as a citizen of ancient Rome.[141] In its initial form, the 1790 act required only "good" character. Five years later, Congress added the term "moral" after supporters of the amendment made clear that it had no reference to religious opinions.[142]

The absence of standards for this requirement led to inconsistent judicial opinions over how moral "moral character" should be.[143] Courts divided over whether the test was the average man's convictions or his conduct.[144] Until relatively recently, behavior that could be relevant in assessing the applicant's fitness for citizenship included adultery, sexual orientation, and traffic offenses.[145] In one adultery case, the court acknowledged evidence from the Kinsey Report suggesting that marital infidelity was widespread, but reasoned that the test is not "what a community does, but rather what the community feels."[146] In trying to make sense of competing case law, one commentator concluded that the most an applicant could learn from "anxious study of the law and relevant cases is that the judge is going to compare [the applicant's] behavior . . . with the requirements of the community's moral conventions; which conventions, the judge will freely admit, cannot be ascertained, so he will have to guess at them."[147] Another commentator agreed, with the "sorrowful admission that not many definite conclusions can be reached as to what good moral character is under the Nationality Act."[148]

The irrationalities of character standards attracted widespread attention during the 1970s, when the government sought to deport John Lennon. After the Beatles broke up, Lennon came to the United States on a temporary visa. Although he had once pleaded guilty to possession of a half ounce of hashish in Great Britain, US Immigration officials temporarily waived that potential ground for exclusion.[149] However, after Lennon began performing at rallies to protest the Vietnam War, President Nixon ordered his removal. The proceedings sparked a flood of letters from eminent musicians, writers, entertainers, and even the mayor of New York, attesting to the value that Lennon's continued presence would bring to the country's cultural heritage.[150] Lennon prevailed, but not because of the testimonials. He was saved by a legal technicality. The British statute that he had violated did not require his possession of the substance to be "knowing," as mandated by US drug law.[151] To many observers, the fact that Lennon could have been excluded but for this technicality underscored the problems with character standards.

Contemporary Law

Contemporary law includes a "good moral character requirement" for most immigration determinations.[152] As a manual by the Immigration Resources Center notes, this requirement is "increasingly complicated and . . . confusing" in part because there is no statutory definition.[153] The governing legislation does, however, specify certain offenses, including "aggravated felonies" and almost all drug crimes, that will bar a finding of good moral character for purposes of naturalization as a citizen.[154]

Related provisions of immigration law passed in the late 1980s and 1990s also make noncitizens convicted of "aggravated felonies" and other specified offenses subject to deportation.[155] Although these provisions are doctrinally separate from the moral character requirement, they rest on the same justifications and are subject to the same objections. They apply regardless of when the felony occurred, and even where there is overwhelming evidence of rehabilitation.[156] The term "aggravated felony" is misleading because Congress has expanded the list of deportable offenses to encompass crimes that are neither aggravated nor felonies. As currently interpreted, those crimes have included public urination, college drug offenses, and shoplifting of necessities totaling less than $30 dollars, including baby clothes and eye drops.[157] An alien convicted of turnstile jumping was placed in removal proceedings and detained for over three years before the government dropped the case.[158] A host of other misconduct also can justify deportation, including document fraud, minor drug offenses, and becoming a "public charge" by accepting government benefits.[159] With deportation comes a ban on return to the United States for a specified period, sometimes as much as twenty years, depending on the ground for exclusion.[160]

This expansive definition of deportable offenses is not justified by the common assumption that immigrants are driving up the crime rate: these individuals, including those who are undocumented, have lower crime and incarceration rates than native-born citizens.[161] Moreover, deportation carries life-shattering consequences, and not only for the individual deported. One estimate suggested that some eleven hundred families are separated every day and that in one ten-year period, one hundred thousand children lost a parent.[162] Even before the Trump administration crackdowns, Immigration and Customs Enforcement (ICE) were removing as many as thirty-one thousand immigrants a year who had at least one US-born child.[163]

Crimes of moral turpitude also prevent naturalization as citizens and constitute grounds for deportation if the crime was committed within five years of admission to the United States.[164] Again, this category has become expansive, and has included lewdness, minor drug offenses, and knowingly issuing a bad check.[165] In commenting on the idiosyncratic interpretations of moral turpitude, Supreme Court Justice Jackson concluded "there appears to be universal recognition that we have here an undefined and undefinable standard."[166] For purposes of naturalization, the good moral character requirement excludes a broad range of individuals, including those who violate marijuana laws, or have extramarital affairs that tend to destroy an existing marriage.[167] Worse still, some individuals have been penalized for seeking naturalization because the process reveals a prior offense that triggers deportation hearings. In one celebrated case, Quing Hong Wu applied for citizenship and revealed that he had been convicted of muggings at the age of fifteen. His subsequent behavior had been exemplary, and a dozen years after his conviction he had worked his way up from a data entry clerk to vice president for internet technology at a national company. But immigration officials not only denied his application for naturalization, they placed him in detention and began removal proceedings. Only after public outcry and a pardon from New York's governor did officials reverse their decision and grant his citizenship application.[168]

Wu is not an isolated case, and legal aid attorneys have reported that some clients are deterred from applying for naturalization due to concerns that old offenses could trigger deportation proceedings.[169] For example, a Dominican Republic émigré who has been a lawful permanent resident for forty years has been afraid to file for citizenship because of two criminal offenses more than a quarter century old: possession of a weapon in the fourth degree and disorderly conduct.[170]

The injustices of using minor criminal offenses as proxies for moral character were underscored by a 2016 New Yorker profile of Noemi Romero, who was brought to United States when she was three, by undocumented parents.[171] Although she wanted to apply for legal status through the Deferred Action for

Childhood Arrivals (DACA) program, she couldn't afford the $465 application fee. To help support herself and earn the necessary amount, she obtained a job at a local grocery store by borrowing her mother's social security card. Several months later, the store was raided. She was charged with aggravated identity theft and forgery. While she was held in jail for two months, her lawyer arranged a plea bargain to reduced charges. She accepted, not realizing that her felony conviction would make her permanently ineligible for DACA. Although she was not immediately deported, her life was in limbo: she "can't work and can't go to college, although she has lived virtually her whole life in the United States and has no reason to go back to Mexico and nowhere to live if she's sent there."[172] For undocumented individuals such as Romero, Trump administration policies are likely to make a bad situation worse.

Immigration and Character under the Trump Administration

Moral character issues have taken on a greater urgency under the Trump administration. As this book went to press, new problems were constantly emerging. In the 2015 announcement of his presidential candidacy, Trump characterized many Mexican immigrants as rapists, and promised that he would build a wall between the United States and Mexico.[173] Later that year, he called for a complete ban on Muslims entering the country.[174]

President Trump has attempted to follow through on both promises, and his actions reflect inaccurate assumptions regarding the character and productivity of immigrants. Less than a week after assuming office, Trump signed an executive order to hire five thousand additional Border Patrol agents and construct a wall along the US-Mexico border. "We are going to get the bad ones out," he told the press.[175] His view of "bad" is expansive. It reportedly includes immigrants from Haiti and Africa, which he reportedly described as "shithole" or "shithouse" countries, as well as those from Muslim-majority nations.[176] In 2017, he issued executive orders limiting citizens of those nations from entering the United States, based on deeply problematic assumptions about the link among religion, nationality, and moral character.[177] The national security concerns that Trump invoked ignore the fact that none of the recent mass shootings or terrorist attacks in America were perpetrated by individuals from the nations covered by his executive order.[178] In its original form, the executive order gave priorities for refugee claims to religious minorities, such as Christians, in predominantly Muslim countries on the apparent theory that only Muslims had terrorist tendencies. After federal courts temporarily enjoined the ban on the ground that it would likely be found unconstitutional after a full trial, the administration issued a revised version eliminating the priorities for religious minorities and creating a more extensive review process for determining which countries' immigrants posed a national security risk.[179] That revised order was upheld by a narrow 5–4 vote of the Supreme Court.[180] According to the order, the risk of even one person from these countries entering the United States is "unacceptably high."[181] But the costs of such a blanket ban were insufficiently acknowledged both by administration officials and the Supreme Court majority.

In another 2017 executive order, Trump also dramatically expanded the groups of undocumented immigrants who would be priorities for deportation. Those groups included anyone with a criminal conviction or criminal charges pending, and anyone who, "in the judgment of an immigration officer . . . pose[a risk to public safety or national security."[182] This order put at risk individuals convicted or even just accused of petty offenses, as well as those who merely seemed threatening to ICE authorities.

Once again, the assumption underlying this order appeared to be that any conviction or arrest was sufficient evidence of bad character to justify deportation. The result was that the number of immigration arrests rose more than 40 percent in Trump's first year in office, and even residents stopped for routine traffic violations were often handed over to ICE and placed at risk of deportation.[183] Arrests of undocumented immigrants with no criminal record have more than doubled since Obama's final year.[184] Those affected include individuals of exemplary character, including community leaders and gainfully employed parents whose children have disabilities that would put them at risk in home countries.[185] In a recent ICE raid in Oakland, authorities deported a woman who had lived in the United States for over two decades, working as an oncology nurse, paying taxes, committing no crimes, and sending children to college; she left behind other children with no clear means of support.[186] One reason for such deportations is that Trump administration policies have curtailed prosecutors' discretion to take positive character and compelling family concerns into account in enforcement decisions.[187]

The injustice was well illustrated in a case profiled by *New York Times* columnist Nicholas Kristof. Syed Jamal is a fifty-five-year-old Bangladeshi, who has been in the America for thirty years, after initially overstaying his student visa. He has been a chemistry professor at Kansas University, where he does research in cancer and genetics and has been actively involved in community service. He has no criminal record and is the sole support of his wife and three children, who are American citizens. After his arrest, sixty-six thousand individuals signed a petition on Change.org, protesting his deportation. As Kristof puts in his column title, "Mr. Trump, How Is This Man a Danger?"[188] The petition at least prompted a hearing that was pending as this book went to press.[189]

The administration also ramped up a "zero tolerance" immigration policy on the southwest border by separating children from their parents, even those who were legally seeking asylum, until widespread public outrage forced Trump to reverse the practice.[190] Administration officials had originally defended the order as a way to deter migrants, and Trump himself had falsely blamed the policy on Democrats. Yet research suggested that such punitive measures were unlikely to discourage asylum seekers, who are influenced more by violence in their home countries than by US border policies.[191] Research also showed, as the American Pediatrics Association concluded, that separating families and detaining unaccompanied children can cause psychological trauma, toxic stress, and long-term mental health risks. [192] Neither this evidence, nor condemnation of family separation as a serious human rights violation by the United Nations Human Rights Office, had any effect on administration policy.[193] It took heart-rending media coverage of children in cages, an adverse judicial ruling, overwhelming public outrage, and widespread bipartisan congressional opposition to cause Trump to issue an executive order banning the practice, something he had initially claimed he was powerless to do.[194]

Yet that reversal did nothing to address the broader problem of families seeking asylum, and the enormous collateral costs of punitive immigration policies.[195] One such cost is the decreased willingness of undocumented immigrants to approach authorities to apply for crucial benefits such as food stamps, Medicaid, and prenatal assistance.[196] Some undocumented parents are afraid to leave home for any nonessential reason, and have stopped taking children to parks, libraries, preschool programs, and even doctors' appointments.[197] The result is to deny millions of young Americans, the vast majority of whom are citizens, the resources they need for physical health and character development. Other toxic effects of Trump policies are the high levels of stress for children whose parents are at risk for deportation, and the unwillingness of immigrant victims of domestic violence to seek protection.[198] Exposure to such chronic stress and family violence can permanently impair children's cognitive, psychological, and character development.[199]

Of course, the concerns raised by recent immigration policies go well beyond the character-related issues that are the focus of this book. But the dramatic increase in deportations and climate of fear in immigrant communities underscores the importance of rethinking the role that character should play in national policies. There are irreversible and toxic consequences for character development if current problems remain unaddressed.

Reform Strategies

In the words of John F. Kennedy, "Immigration policy should be generous; it should be fair; it should be flexible."[200] By this standard, current policy falls far short. Although this is not the occasion for exploring all the necessary reforms, the preceding discussion has identified character-related concerns that urgently need attention. As a 2009 Human Rights Watch Report put it:

> We have to ask why . . . significant immigration enforcement funds are being spent on deporting legal residents who already have been punished for their crimes. Many of these people have lived in the country legally for decades, some have served in the military, others own businesses. And often, they are facing separation from family members, including children, who are citizens or legal residents.[201]

Although critics have argued that Congress should eliminate the moral character requirement entirely, that seems politically implausible.[202] But four other less sweeping reforms merit consideration. First, Congress should dramatically restrict the offenses that decision-makers can consider in citizenship and deportation contexts. Only truly serious crimes should matter. Second, Congress should restore discretion to individual judges to consider the full range of facts bearing on character before an individual is deported. These include the same factors relevant in employment contexts, such as the nature and circumstances of the offense, the time that has elapsed since the offense, the age at which it was committed, and evidence of mitigation and rehabilitation. The approach of other countries, such as the United Kingdom, is instructive; it specifies a time period for the relevance of offenses, after which they would no longer have adverse consequences if the applicant can demonstrate rehabilitation.[203] Third, either legislation or judicial rulings should establish clear norms for courts and immigration officials in making character determinations. The framework of the European Court of Human Rights in deportation contexts provides a useful model.[204] It specifies relevant considerations including the seriousness of the offense, the individuals' records since the offenses were committed, the amount of time the individuals have lived in the country, whether their family resides there, and the likelihood that they could successfully re-establish family life in another country.[205] Individuals whose lives and families are at risk deserve a holistic review of their entire records before they are deported or denied citizenship.

Conclusion

Good moral character is a cornerstone in American law, and its role leaves much to be desired. It is a requirement for occupations ranging from frog farmer to fortune teller, and a prerequisite for most immigration rights. Yet character judgments have been idiosyncratic, inconsistent, and ineffective in predicting future misconduct. They have also undermined rehabilitation. A preferable system would reduce the number of occupations subject to licensing requirements and eliminate categorical bans on ex-offenders. And it would not deny employment on character grounds unless there were a direct and substantial relationship between prior misconduct and occupational requirements. So too, in immigration contexts, a dated or minor criminal offense should not be grounds for deportation or a bar to citizenship. Immigration law should also encourage a more complete view of individuals' entire records as a way to promote basic fairness, reward rehabilitation, and offer a path to citizenship.

In his 2004 State of the Union address, President Bush declared America to be "the land of the second chance," and maintained that a criminal past should not prevent individuals from turning their lives around after they have completed their sentences.[206] Employment and immigration policies should recognize as much. Character is not a static state. Nor is a single bad act, taken out of context, an accurate predictor of future misconduct or an adequate measure of virtue. If moral character standards are to play a defensible role in American law, they must be better grounded in psychological research and fundamental fairness.

4

Character in Criminal Justice

THE ROLE OF character in the criminal justice system is complex and contested. In principle, American criminal law is committed to punishing conduct, not character. Our justice system aims to hold individuals accountable not for who they are but for what they have done. But in practice, views about character often influence decisions about guilt, punishment, and parole in ways that are unjust and counterproductive. Although the United States accounts for just 5 percent of the world's population, it houses over one-fifth of the world's prisoners.[1] According to the World Justice Project, the United States ranks twenty-third among thirty-one peer countries on a host of criminal law issues, including fairness for the accused and effectiveness of the correction and legal process.[2] Ideas about character, and how it affects punishment are at least part of the problem.

For the millions of Americans who pass through the criminal justice system, and whose families, neighborhoods, and racial groups are devastated by its injustices, our understandings of character have enormous significance. And all Americans have a stake in ensuring that the process by which we take away lives and liberties expresses our highest ideals. The discussion that follows explores ways in which the process falls short because of judgments about character. Character-related issues are, to be sure, only a small part of the problems plaguing our criminal justice system, but they are implicated in some of its most fundamental injustices, including mass incarceration, class and racial bias, and prosecutorial misconduct. Although a comprehensive discussion of criminal justice reform is beyond the scope of this book, a focus on character can inform that agenda.

To that end, this chapter explores the flawed conceptions of character that affect both the law of evidence and judgments about punishment by courts, prosecutors, and parole board members. The discussion concludes with some proposals to make the system less punitive and biased, and more rehabilitative, equitable, and cost-effective.

Character Evidence

When should the law permit evidence of character to prove conduct? The rules governing this question have generated what one scholar termed "illusion, illogic, and injustice in the courtroom."[3] In general, these evidentiary rules are designed to ensure that we convict based only on the offense charged. A central premise of the American criminal justice system is that bad character is neither a necessary nor sufficient condition of guilt. Good people can be accountable for illegal acts that are "out of character" and atypical of their normal behavior, just as morally despicable people can escape legal accountability if they are not guilty of the particular acts at issue.[4] But our understanding of criminal responsibility necessarily includes questions of character in gauging intent, assessing credibility, and predicting future dangerousness, all of which inform judgments of culpability. That tension between our reluctance to convict based on character and our recognition of its relevance has led to policies that are sometimes unjust in principle and unworkable in practice.

The General Ban on Character Evidence

A core principle in both federal and state courts is that "evidence of a person's character or character trait is not admissible to prove that on a particular occasion the person acted in accordance with the character or trait."[5] These rules of evidence do not define character, nor do most courts and commentators, but the leading treatises describe it as "disposition."[6] The rationale for banning such evidence rests on several concerns that deserve closer scrutiny.

The first justification for the ban is that jurors exposed to character evidence could decide to punish parties irrespective of guilt. This risk is sometimes labeled "nullification prejudice" because jurors who are swayed by this information may nullify the correct verdict out of a desire to penalize personal qualities or avenge misconduct apart from the offense on trial.[7] In effect, character evidence erodes the presumption of innocence. A wide array of psychological research suggests that we are particularly likely to attribute criminal responsibility to seemingly "bad people" who have acted with "bad motives" on other occasions.[8] For example, in one experiment, participants received an account of a skier who crashed into another skier on the slopes, causing his death. Participants who learned that the first skier was an irresponsible worker and a bad son perceived him as more reckless, more responsible for the accident, and more deserving of punishment.

That perception highlights what experimenters described as the "tension between the process of legal blame and the psychology of moral blame."[9] As Supreme Court Justice William Brennan noted, the concern is that the "jury may feel that the defendant should be punished for [extrinsic] . . . activity even if he is not guilty of the offense charged."[10] This result would run counter to a fundamental principle of American jurisprudence: a "defendant must be tried for what he did, not for who he is."[11] Although the concern about character evidence is strongest when the criminal defendant's character is at issue, similar reasoning underpins the rule against using the prior sexual conduct of rape complainants to impugn their character and undermine their credibility. Rape shield laws barring introduction of victims' sexual history were a response to the intimidating and demeaning use of character evidence to show that they were promiscuous or otherwise unworthy of belief and protection.[12]

The second justification for excluding character evidence is that jurors will overvalue its significance. People commonly make what psychologists term "the fundamental attribution error," described in chapter 1. We often mistakenly attribute conduct to stable character dispositions and ignore the extent to which it is influenced by circumstances.[13] Our decisions incorrectly "assume that a single sample of behavior is representative of what the actor ordinarily does."[14] A related problem is the "halo effect": people's tendency to judge someone on the basis of one outstanding quality.[15] Also troubling is their tendency to give greater weight to unfavorable than favorable character information.[16] Moreover, once decision-makers have formed a misperception based on an overemphasis of negative evidence, they are unlikely to change their views, and will interpret subsequent evidence in a skewed manner to confirm their prior belief. This "confirmation" bias leads people to assess information that is consistent with their prior beliefs as relevant and reliable, and to discount contrary information.[17]

The third concern with opening the door to character evidence is that it will also open the door to less relevant disputes over prior misdeeds that could demonstrate a fixed trait, such as aggression. For example, a trial for assault could degenerate into mini-trials of prior assaults, with competing evidence about whether the defendant was provoked or was acting in self-defense.[18] Courts worry that such trials within a trial could consume an excessive amount of judicial time and could obscure or confuse the central issue in the case.[19] At a time when most state courts face staggering caseloads, the diversion of scarce judicial resources to peripheral disputes is a significant concern.

Limitations on the Character Evidence Prohibition

The ban on character evidence is, however, subject to many limitations that significantly undermine its effectiveness. Federal and state rules permit evidence of prior crimes or misconduct for other purposes than to show character, such as "proving motive, opportunity, intent, preparation, plan, knowledge, identity, absence of mistake, or lack of accident."[20] Take for example, a store owner who is on trial for buying stolen property. If, on a previous occasion, he had purchased stolen diamonds at a fraction of their value, that fact might be admissible to show that he knew in the current case that the stones were stolen. The evidence could not, however, be used to prove that he had the character of a thief.[21] Yet as law professor Richard Uviller notes, "To the ordinary human mind, struggling through life without the benefit of a legal education . . . the division between the prescribed and the proscribed uses of the . . . [prior crime] may be a bit difficult to perceive."[22] The risk of unfair prejudice is particularly great in weak cases. In one study, introduction of the defendant's criminal record in such a case increased the probability of conviction from less than 20 percent to 50 percent.[23]

A similar problem arises from a second exception to the ban on character evidence. This exception gives courts discretion to allow proof of prior crimes or misconduct in order to bolster or impugn the credibility of witnesses including defendants who testify.[24] Under this exception, testimony can be impeached by misconduct that has nothing to do with truthfulness. Yet psychological research suggests that prior crimes that do not bear on honesty are unlikely to affect witnesses' likelihood of lying under oath.[25] Special concerns arise when prosecutors use prior misconduct to impeach, or threaten to impeach, testimony by defendants. Studies of decision-making both in actual trials and in experimental settings consistently finds that jurors use evidence of previous offenses to infer guilt, not just dishonesty.[26] Instructions to the jury do not prevent such inferences.[27] As Uviller observes, "No one in court believes that the jury will consider this evidence only as affecting [credibility], particularly if the crime on trial is similar to the prior offense."[28] Other commentators point out that this evidence will typically add nothing crucial to jurors' assessment of credibility, because they already assume that most defendants would lie to save themselves from conviction. Thus, any probative value of information about prior misconduct is dwarfed by its prejudicial impact in skewing perceptions of guilt and deterring defendants from testifying.[29]

When the threat of adverse character evidence prevents defendants' testimony, jurors lose exposure to exculpatory information that they can receive in no other way. And despite instructions to the contrary, many jurors are likely to infer guilt from a defendant's failure to take the stand.[30] Moreover, by discouraging defendants from exercising their right to be heard, the current rules on impeachment compromise procedural fairness and defendants' faith in the legitimacy of the process. Research suggests that defendant's confidence in the credibility of the justice system depends more on their sense of having an opportunity to be heard than on the trial outcome.[31]

Another limitation on the general ban on character evidence concerns sexual misconduct by defendants even if it has not resulted in a conviction. In 1994, Congress amended evidence rules to give federal courts discretion to admit proof of such misconduct in civil and criminal cases involving sexual assault and child molestation.[32] The amendments were a response to serious inconsistencies in the way that courts had previously handled such evidence, as well as a reaction to celebrated cases of seeming injustice. One involved the acquittal of William Kennedy Smith on charges of rape after the trial judge refused to allow evidence of his similar prior sexual assaults.[33]

Sponsors of the amended rules offered several justifications for treating sex offenses differently than other misconduct, which is inadmissible to show character. One is a probabilistic argument, sometimes referred to as the doctrine of chances.[34] As the sponsors explained, "It is inherently improbable that a person whose prior acts show that he is in fact a rapist or child molester would . . . fortuitously be subject to multiple false accusations by a number of different victims."[35] A second justification for treating sex offenses differently is that the severity of the crimes and the difficulties of proof suggest a greater need for evidence of prior misconduct. When Americans rate the seriousness of offenses, rape and child abuse rank second and third, just after murder.[36] Sex crimes are generally difficult to prove beyond a reasonable doubt because there are rarely any witnesses besides the accuser and accused, and cases will often come down to "he said /she said" disputes. Even if physical evidence of sex is present, the defendant can claim that an adult victim consented, and the frequent success of that defense distinguishes rape from other crimes.[37] Evidence of the defendant's prior sexual misconduct can lend crucial credibility to a complainant's testimony.

Opposition to allowing such evidence came from many experts in criminal law, as well as the American Bar Association and the United States Judicial Conference, and most states failed to follow the federal amendment.[38] As opponents argued, the potential for unfair prejudice is particularly great in cases involving sex offenses, given their often inflammatory nature. That risk of unjust prejudice is particularly great for defendants of color, because, as subsequent discussion notes, their "character" is especially likely to be associated with criminality.[39] Moreover, contrary to common assumptions, it is not clear that sex offenders have exceptionally high rates of recidivism.[40] Bureau of Justice data reveals that the percentage of rearrest rates within three years are about 3 percent for child molesters and rapists, and 34 percent for thieves.[41]

However, the methods for calculating recidivism have been subject to dispute, and research tracking sex offenders for longer periods finds higher rates of subsequent offenses.[42] One study that followed child molesters for an average of six years after their release from a maximum security psychiatric facility found that almost a third of those individuals committed a new sex crime.[43] And recidivism rates of sex offenders may be even higher than subsequent conviction records suggest because most research fails to account for the disproportionately large number of unreported sex crimes. One study found that convicted sex offenders acknowledged having committed five sex crimes for which they had never been arrested.[44]

Permitting evidence of serial abuse is often the only way to convict offenders, as the recent trial of entertainer Bill Cosby suggests. By 2018, some fifty women had accused him of sexual misconduct dating back decades, the vast majority barred by statutes of limitations.[45] He reached civil settlements with many complainants, and the only case that proceeded to criminal trial initially ended with a hung jury. Cosby's defense attorneys presented the complaining witness as a gold-digging "con artist," and because Pennsylvania does not have an exception to bans on character evidence for sexual misconduct, the court permitted only one other alleged victim to testify.[46] On retrial, the court permitted five other accusers to testify in order to show a pattern of behavior, and the jury convicted him on three counts of aggravated indecent assault.[47] Similar issues involving sexual history will undoubtedly surface in other celebrated cases of serial offenders exposed in the aftermath of #MeToo. As that movement makes clear, the presence of multiple victims is often what empowers other survivors to come forward. Multiple claimants can also provide the credibility for their evidence that is necessary to hold predators accountable.

Proposals for Reform

Experts generally agree that current character evidence rules make no sense, but disagree about how to fix them. My argument here is for an evidence-based approach to evidentiary reforms, grounded in the research summarized earlier about how juries actually use character information and the competing values at issue. That approach involves a "structured balancing" framework. Under this framework, courts would consider the frequency, similarity, and proximity of other misconduct in determining whether its probative value substantially outweighs its unfairly prejudicial potential.[48] Because decision-makers often overgeneralize from prior "bad acts," courts should start with a general presumption against admission of such evidence. This would reverse the current presumption favoring admissibility of prior misconduct for purposes other than to show character.[49] This framework would be more honest than the current rule, which lets in evidence of prior misconduct for limited purposes under the implausible assumption that jurors will consider it only for those purposes.

Under this structured balancing approach, character evidence would be less likely to be admitted in two contexts where the potential for unjust prejudice is substantial. One involves sexual misconduct that is not substantially similar to the offense charged. Given the often inflammatory nature of such evidence, courts should be wary of admission unless it demonstrates a reasonably recent common pattern of abuse, as was the case in Cosby's trial. This was the approach recommended by the Judicial Conference during debates over amending the federal rules, and it merits reconsideration now.[50] A second context in which character evidence should more commonly be excluded is impeachment of defendants' testimony. Only convictions for crimes involving dishonesty should be admissible to undermine the credibility of the accused. To allow evidence about other misconduct runs too great a risk of convicting the defendant for his character, and, licensing a "free ranging inquiry . . . into his moral worth."[51] Where life, liberty, and reputation hang in the balance, courts should exercise special caution to exclude prejudicial information. Character is relevant in the criminal justice system but it is not what is on trial.

Character and Punishment

Debates about the purposes of punishment are "as old as the idea of punishment" itself."[52] Courts, legislators, commentators, and the general public differ about what purposes are most important, what sentences will best serve those purposes in particular cases, and even how to think about those questions. Most Americans know little about the difficulties of assessing character-related factors such as genuine remorse and future dangerousness, and even less about the effectiveness of various crime control strategies. Only by better educating policymakers and the public can we begin to address the vast miscarriages of justice in our current legal system.

The Punitive Turn in Criminal Justice

American law builds on four primary purposes of punishment: retribution, deterrence, incapacitation, and rehabilitation. Character is relevant to all of these objectives but for different reasons. Retribution focuses on issues of desert. According to some philosophers, notably Immanuel Kant, punishment should be proportionate to the nature of the offense and the blameworthiness of the offender.[53] It should not be used as a means to promote some other good for the criminals themselves(such as rehabilitation) or for society generally (such as deterrence or incapacitation).[54] Character is central to retribution because it is how we gauge desert; punishment is appropriate only for acts that "stem from some . . . defect of character."[55] Character is relevant for different reasons to those who see deterrence as the primary goal of punishment. From the standpoint of specific deterrence—how to deter a particular offender—judgments about character are necessary to determine how stringent penalties must be to prevent future offenses. The unrepentant recidivist will require more severe punishment to ensure compliance than a defendant with an otherwise spotless record. From the standpoint of general deterrence—how to discourage other potential offenders—character is also relevant because the message society wants to send is that bad actors will receive harsh treatment.[56] For those concerned with incapacitation—how to prevent offenders from committing further crimes—assessments of character can help in determining how long people need to be imprisoned to protect society.[57] Similarly, if a primary goal is rehabilitation, then it is necessary to know the extent to which a defendant's character requires transformation.[58]

In recent polling, 85 percent of Americans agreed that the primary goal of our criminal justice system should be rehabilitation.[59] This consensus reflects a significant shift in attitudes. In earlier research on the purposes of punishment, Americans ranked not only rehabilitation but also specific deterrence and desert (i.e., retribution) as very important.[60] And when given specific fact patterns, the public traditionally has placed greatest importance on desert, measured by the seriousness of the offense.[61] Compared with other nationalities, Americans have favored more punitive responses to crime.[62]

Punitive attitudes were encouraged by a crime spike beginning in the 1960s and 1970s, and by the efforts of politicians to capitalize on the issue. Some characterized street offenses as a "reign of terror," and made the "war on drugs" a centerpiece of campaign rhetoric.[63] By the early 1990s, Americans ranked crime as their greatest social problem.[64] This concern was reinforced and amplified by powerful interest groups such as prosecutors, private prison companies, corrections officers, victims' rights organizations, and the National Rifle Association. They all united in support of lengthy prison sentences. Opponents, such as the criminal defense bar and prisoners' rights associations, lacked comparable resources and political leverage.[65] Legislative, judicial, and prosecutorial candidates promised to "get tough on crime," "lock up" the perpetrators, and "throw away the key."[66] State and federal legislators lengthened sentences, imposed mandatory minimums for many offenses, enacted "three-strikes" statutes that made life imprisonment more likely for repeat offenders, and reduced opportunities for parole. The greatest support for these policies came from white Americans who held the strongest negative racial stereotypes about criminals, leading some researchers to conclude that in many political campaigns, "the text may be crime," but the "subtext is race."[67]

This crackdown fundamentally changed enforcement practices. The percentage of felony offenders who received probation dropped from three-quarters in the 1970s to a quarter today, the rate of incarceration increased fivefold, and the average length of time in prison doubled.[68] Although the crime rate declined 45 percent between 1990 and 2012, prison populations continued to swell.[69] Once punitive policies were in place, politicians found it risky to reverse course and support alternatives.[70] Michael Dukakis's presidential campaign was torpedoed by ads profiling his support for the furlough program that enabled Willie Horton, a convicted murderer, to commit rape.[71] Yet this punitive turn in enforcement policies imposed enormous costs. Mandatory minimum sentences led to gross injustices, including life sentences for minor crimes.[72] One impoverished mother of four was convicted for accepting $47 to post a package for a stranger, which she did not know contained crack cocaine. The prosecutor argued that she was deliberately ignorant, and she landed in prison for ten years, a result that even the sentencing judge labeled "just crazy."[73] In another such case, the Supreme Court upheld a sentence of life imprisonment for a third offense involving a forged check for $88 dollars' worth of groceries.[74] These inequities were compounded by the absence of programs to treat the mental health and substance abuse problems that often drove criminal behavior.

The punitive turn in law enforcement also brought increased reliance on high levels of monetary bail, ostensibly to prevent flight risk and further offenses. Until quite recently, judges got little or no credit for releasing low-risk offenders, few if any penalties for incarcerating them, and considerable adverse attention if defendants committed further offenses while free before trial.[75] Such skewed incentives encouraged unaffordable bail requirements, which resulted in disproportionate pretrial detention of low-income and minority defendants. That, in turn, increased pressure to plead guilty, leading to higher rates of conviction and incarceration, and lower rates of employment after release.[76] About 60 percent of the Americans in jail have not been convicted, and they are there mostly because they cannot afford bail, a rate that has doubled over the last three decades.[77] This escalation in pretrial detention persisted despite mounting evidence that unaffordable bail is a major cause of job loss and homelessness, and is not a necessary, or even the most effective, way to prevent flight or to deter future offenses.[78]

As a result of this punitive turn in criminal justice policy, the US incarceration rate is about five times higher than the rest of world. This nation imprisons more people than any other country, and, compared with other developed nations, imposes longer sentences and provides fewer treatment programs and social services for disadvantaged populations.[79] The costs are staggering. Roughly 2.3 million people are incarcerated in American jails and prisons, a 500 percent increase over the last forty years, at a cost of about $80 billion a year.[80] The human suffering is incalculable, not only for offenders but also for their families and communities. And, as subsequent discussion notes, the price is disproportionately paid by people of color, who face harsher treatment at every level of law enforcement.[81]

Growing numbers of Americans recognize these problems, and are open to reforms. To assess which strategies make most sense, it is first necessary to understand the practices that have contributed to excessive and inequitable sentences, and the role that character considerations have played in that process.

Character in Sentencing

Federal and state criminal codes generally define the elements and severity of offenses and appropriate punishment. These codes reflect the perceived seriousness of the harm and culpability of the offender, and can take into account factors related to character that affect mitigating or aggravating circumstances. In some instances, the range for sentences is quite broad (zero to thirty years for computer fraud), while in other cases, judges' discretion is quite narrow due to mandatory minimum penalties.[82] The federal government and many states also have guidelines that clarify the criteria for sentencing decisions and that seek to promote transparency, proportionality, and consistency in those decisions. According to most experts, these guidelines have fallen well short of their intended purpose. All too often, punishments have been excessive, and morally similar cases have yielded substantially different sentences.[83] In 2005, the Supreme Court held that mandatory guidelines were unconstitutional because they infringed defendants' Sixth Amendment rights to have facts justifying a sentence decided by juries not judges. Guidelines could therefore be used only as a point of reference.[84] Judges now vary in how much deference they give to guidelines, and in how they exercise the considerable discretion that guidelines authorize. There is similar disagreement among legislatures, experts, and the general public on how to weigh considerations reflecting on character in criminal proceedings.

One dispute centers on the importance to attach to prior conduct, both bad and good, such as previous criminal activity, military service, charitable contributions, and volunteer work. Some courts and commentators see no principled basis for considering only certain kinds of conduct; by their logic, if bad acts can serve to enhance punishment, good deeds should be allowed to reduce it.[85] As one federal appellate court explained, "if Mother Teresa were accused of illegally attempting to buy a green card for one of her sisters, it would be proper for a court to consider her saintly deeds in mitigation of her sentence."[86] However, individuals with reputations for sainthood rarely end up in American criminal courts, and punishment criteria are not designed with such offenders in mind. Most sentencing guidelines specify more aggravating than mitigating circumstances, some state guidelines give no consideration to good acts, and federal guidelines provide that these acts "are not ordinarily relevant."[87] The Supreme Court has given no guidance about how to weigh aggravating and mitigating factors except in death penalty cases; there, unlike other cases, courts must consider anything that might reduce punishment.[88]

Authoritative guidance is often missing for state courts as well. As a result, their decisions vary considerably in how to prioritize various factors, and whether even to permit consideration of good acts.[89] State constitutions and legislatures typically leave broad scope for discretion. For example, under Alabama law and sentencing guidelines, courts may mitigate a sentence when "The defendant has been a person of good character or has a good reputation."[90] What factors establish goodness is unspecified. The Illinois Constitution includes a proportionate penalties clause, which courts have interpreted to require careful consideration of all aggravating and mitigating factors, including "general moral character."[91] According to the Illinois Supreme Court, this includes the offender's "mentality, his habits, his social environments, his abnormal or subnormal tendencies, his age, his natural inclination or aversion to commit crime, the stimuli which motivate his conduct . . . [and his] life, family, [and] occupation."[92] Such an approach, which lacks guidance about how courts should weigh these factors, opens the door to intrusive, inconsistent, and biased decision-making. Some commentators believe that for "courts to [attempt to] take into account a social accounting of all the defendants' good and bad acts is outside the judicial function and an invasion of privacy."[93] According to law professor Jeffrie Murphy, "Issues of deep character are matters about which the state is probably incompetent to judge—it cannot even deliver the mail very efficiently."[94]

Reported cases bear out such concerns. For example, one Texas state court invoked the defendant's good character to justify a lenient sentence for the murder of two gay men. The judge emphasized that the killer had no criminal record, was attending college, and came from a good home headed by a father in the police force. Moreover, in the court's view, the defendant may have been understandably provoked by the conduct of the victims, who would not have been killed "if they hadn't been cruising the streets picking up teenage-age boys."[95] An Indiana judge enhanced the sentence of a young woman whose character he considered "incorrigible" in part because she had been away from home without permission and had given birth to two children out of wedlock by the age of eighteen. An appellate court agreed.[96]

Class bias can also skew character assessments that underlie sentencing laws and decisions. Many studies reveal disturbing disparities between street criminals and "suite" criminals.[97] Defendants convicted of auto theft were four times more likely to receive a prison sentence than embezzlers, and their sentences were longer.[98] White collar defendants convicted of grand theft (by cheating Medicaid) were less than half as likely to be incarcerated as blue collar offenders. Yet the median financial losses from the white collar offenses were more than ten times the median losses from the blue-collar crimes.[99] A case study of leniency involved a clerk who looted a municipal retirement fund; she was placed in a probation program that permitted expungement of her criminal record once she paid restitution.[100] In one example so egregious that it was reversed on appeal, a federal trial judge sentenced a former chief executive who had been found guilty of conspiracy, fraud, and money laundering to just seven days in prison. The court justified its dramatic departure from sentencing guidelines on the grounds of the defendant's family and community involvement and his business expertise.[101] However, only 15 percent of surveyed Americans agree that such good acts prior to an offense should affect punishment, and those who were willing to consider these acts supported only a modest reduction in penalties (24–30 percent).[102]

Even more disturbing are overly punitive responses for defendants with prior criminal offenses. There is, of course, some basis for treating recidivists more harshly than first offenders. An otherwise law-abiding person who commits an "out of character" act is more deserving of a second chance than a repeat offender who continues to defy the law.[103] The recidivist clearly needs greater deterrence, or, failing that, incapacitation.[104] The difficulty lies in determining how much additional punishment is enough, and how to prevent prior history from leading to grossly disproportionate sanctions for similar offenses.[105] These difficulties are particularly likely with laws that impose draconian sentences for "habitual" or "three strikes" offenders. In one such case, the US Supreme Court declined to find a punishment of fifty years imprisonment "cruel or unusual" for petty theft with a prior conviction when it involved stealing only nine videotapes.[106] Yet the labels used to justify such sentences, including "super predator" and "persistent offender," are not accurate over extended periods.[107] As earlier chapters noted, character is not "fixed," and changes in life circumstances such as marriage, steady employment, or military service can redirect individuals to a life free of crime.[108]

Although courts can sometimes exercise discretion to avoid harsh results, concerns about their own reputations push in the opposite direction. Appearing "tough on crime" is generally the best way to ensure re-election, avoid a recall, and secure a promotion.[109] Research shows that courts impose more punitive sentences close to elections.[110] Judges are occasionally candid about the pressures they experience. An example involved a defendant convicted of burglary and drug possession when he was a young adult. He then had a clean record for twelve years, before being arrested for a third strike on marijuana possession. He was married, supporting a wife and son, and a lengthy imprisonment would destroy his family and economic livelihood. The judge was not insensitive to the equities, but, as he explained to a researcher, he had his own record to consider. If he gave a sentence of probation and the defendant committed another robbery, who would everyone blame? "They'll wonder what I was thinking."[111]

Such concerns are well founded. When a New York judge accepted a misdemeanor plea and conditional discharge for a defendant who became subsequently involved in a gang assault, the *New York Post* lambasted this "junk justice" from a "soft" judge.[112] In 2018, California voters recalled California judge Aaron Persky, after he gave an exceptionally lenient sentence to a Stanford athlete, Brock Turner. The student was discovered in the act of raping an unconscious woman behind a fraternity house dumpster. Persky sentenced him to six months in jail (which was reduced to three months with good behavior) and ordered him to register as a sex offender and participate in a sex offender rehabilitation program. Although the prosecutor had requested six years imprisonment, the judge followed the probation department's more lenient recommendation based on Turner's age (nineteen), his lack of a criminal record, the severe effect that long imprisonment would have, his expression of remorse, and his "lack of danger to others.[113] After the victim's statement went viral, activists launched a successful recall campaign that raised over a million dollars and removed Persky from office with 60 percent of the vote.[114] The initiative was opposed by a broad coalition of public defenders, law professors, and the local prosecutor, not because they agreed with the sentence (many did not), but rather because they worried about the effect on judicial independence and leniency in appropriate cases. As one local public defender wrote, "the recall would 'have a chilling effect on judicial courage and compassion' and 'deter other judges from extending mercy,' instead encouraging them to 'issue unfairly harsh sentences for fear of reprisal.'"[115] Even before the votes came in, local judges were reportedly worried about "getting Perskied."[116] The problem with the recall, argued one *Washington Post* op-ed, was not that supporters were wrong about the egregiousness of Persky's sentence. It was that "they aren't adequately accounting for the costs of avenging it."[117]

Deterrence and Incapacitation

What makes America's exceptionally harsh punishments even more problematic is the lack of evidence that they are effective in significantly reducing crime. Deterrence is, to be sure, notoriously hard to measure, and a vast literature yields many conflicting results. Crime rates reflect multiple factors and it is extremely difficult to isolate the impact of any single contributor, such as the severity of punishment. However, most researchers agree that long sentences are not an effective way of discouraging those with bad characters from engaging in criminal activity.[118] The certainty of punishment is more critical than severity.[119]

Part of the reason for the lack of deterrence is that most offenders lack accurate knowledge of the likelihood of apprehension, conviction, and length of imprisonment.[120] Nor do they generally think about uncertain or remote legal consequences before acting.[121] In one study of repetitive burglars, none said that they or other thieves they knew considered legal consequences. The vast majority did not think they would be caught or did not know what the punishment would likely be if they were.[122] Even more sophisticated offenders, such as white collar tax evaders, generally reported that the expected size of the penalty did not influence their decisions.[123] Many criminals are particularly susceptible to conditions that interfere with rational cost-benefit decision-making, such as substance abuse or poor impulse control. In one study of eighty largely middle-class sellers of cocaine, only two seemed to have stopped due to concerns about punishment, and a majority felt no criminal justice pressures at all.[124]

A final explanation for why harsh sentences yield such inadequate deterrence is that they do not affect the underlying risk factors that fuel crime and recidivism, factors that may have little do with character and everything to do with poverty, lack of education and employment, mental health difficulties, substance abuse, dysfunctional families, and antisocial peer influences.[125] As subsequent discussion indicates, programs targeted at these problems can be more cost-effective than extended incarceration in reducing recidivism.

Defenders of lengthy sentences often respond that even if the deterrent effect is weak, long sentences at least incapacitate "bad actors" for the period when they are likely to re-offend. But at what cost? International researchers generally agree that countries with high incarceration rates pay an enormous price in social as well as financial terms, including not only the often devastating effects on prisoners but also the disruption of family ties and the increase in poverty that occurs when primary earners are imprisoned and then denied employment after release.[126] And when it comes to the most violent crimes, America does not seem to reap additional protection from its "get tough" policies; its homicide rate is higher than most other economically developed countries, which have far lower rates of incarceration.[127]

Remorse

Another context in which conventional wisdom on character has led criminal justice policy astray involves attitudes toward remorse. The consensus among judges, jurors, parole commissioners, and the general public, is, as Professor Murphy notes, that "[t]he repentant person has a better character than the unrepentant person . . . [and] deserves less punishment."[128] People regard remorse "as a measure of whether the defendant's bad act is consistent with his general character or a deviation from it. Remorse suggests that a defendant will strive to avoid such aberrant behavior in the future rather than pose a continuing danger to society."[129]

Research consistently confirms the significance of repentance in criminal proceedings; it affects decisions about what offenses to charge, what punishments to recommend, and what sentences to impose.[130] Multiple studies find that offenders who express remorse receive less severe punishment.[131] If defendants in capital cases fail to seem repentant, 40 to 70 percent of jurors are more likely to vote for the death penalty.[132]

Sentencing guidelines for judges generally allow reduced sanctions for defendants who accept responsibility for their crimes, and failure to do so typically affects the length of punishment, sometimes by as much as a third.[133] In a study of five hundred federal judges, fewer than a fifth said that a defendant's statement at the sentencing hearing was not important; about a quarter considered the statement extremely or very important, and another half said it was somewhat important.[134] Some judges interpret an absence of remorse as indicative of "wanton cruelty," a "propensity to act in a similar fashion in the future," or a "continuing threat to society."[135] The prevailing assumption, as one federal appellate court put it, is that a "person who is conscious of having done wrong, and who feels genuine remorse for his wrong is on the way to developing those internal checks that would keep [someone] from committing [future] crimes."[136]

Despite the importance of remorse in criminal justice proceedings, decision-makers have reached no consensus about how to define or assess it.[137] Nor do they have any systematic evidence that outward displays of repentance accurately reflect character or predict a lower likelihood of further criminal conduct.[138] Although courts typically want to see not just a guilty plea, but also "authentic remorse," they vary greatly in what they consider "authentic."[139] Some judges focus on outward expressions of inner feelings, while others want to see acts of atonement.[140] Many acknowledge relying on "gut instinct" in determining whether defendants are sincere, and have different, sometimes contradictory, views of what genuine remorse looks like.[141] Judges vary in how to interpret offenders' silence or eye contact, and about whether to credit repentance expressed only years after the offense.[142] Other judges doubt that they can accurately ascertain remorse and, "as a matter of principle," do not consider it "terribly important."[143] Giving too much consideration to the issue could make them a "sitting duck . . . for sham protestations of remorse and breast beating."[144] Courts also differ on whether punishing defendants for professing innocence violates their constitutional privilege against self-incrimination.[145] In some jurisdictions, trial judges discourage defendants from speaking at all at their sentencing hearing, and leave heartfelt letters from offenders unopened and un-read at the bottom of their file folders.[146]

Such widely varied attitudes are problematic on several grounds. They lead to different treatment for similar offenses and similar evidence of contrition. And they rest on what one expert aptly described as "folk knowledge" that is "unsubstantiated or demonstrably wrong."[147] There is no evidence that facial ex-pression, body language, or other psychological markers can accurately identify genuine repentance.[148] As law professor Paul Lippke note, "most adults will long ago have learned how to mimic remorse," and once offenders realize that sentence reductions are available "if they feign remorse . . . they will be quick to do so."[149] It is "exceedingly difficult for anyone, let alone . . . [overworked] judges," to distin-guish genuine from fabricated remorse, and few make more than "casual efforts" in that direction.[150] Much of the repentance on display at sentencing hearings does little to realize its true potential, which would require genuine unscripted dialogue with victims and/or community members in an effort toward healing, rehabilitation, and reintegration.[151]

Moreover, factors such as age or disability may skew manifestations of remorse. Juvenile offenders often have difficulty grasping the gravity of their offenses until well after sentencing. And their true feelings may not be apparent from outward appearances. As one child psychiatrist put it, fourteen-year-old offenders "do not appear remorseful, almost categorically. They feel relatively powerless . . . and react by rebelliousness, and [adoption of] a tough front as a protective shell."[152] Mental illness, disability, or psychotropic drugs can also compromise defendants' ability to express remorse.[153] Yet some judges reason that if the offender's impair-ment is not severe enough to excuse his offense, it is also not severe enough to excuse his lack of repentance.[154]

Race or class bias may further distort decision-making. A study of cases in which courts reduced punishment based on remorse found that they viewed white defendants as more repentant than similarly situated defendants of color.[155] Wealthy offenders can also afford lawyers with the time and expertise to provide effective coaching. Extensive preparation can help defendants avoid body language or statements that are likely to irritate judges, such as those that blame others or seem "self indulgent," or "disingenuous."[156] Equally problematic are biases against offenders who are in fact innocent and unwilling to repent for crimes they did not commit.

Even if decision-makers were able to make more accurate and unbiased assessments of remorse, the result may not justify the effort. At the time of sentencing, it is too soon for accurate predictions about whether even sincerely repentant offenders will turn their lives around. As Lippke notes, some offenders who are "genuinely remorseful for their crimes may be weak-willed or irresolute, and prone to further offending." What we most need to know about defendants "is not how repentant they are immediately after their offenses are committed, but how successfully they will make use of their repentance to effect lasting changes in their lives."[157]

Prosecutorial Power

Many experts attribute part of the problems in criminal justice to the outsized role of prosecutors and the reward structures that drive their decision-making. The enormous discretion that prosecutors exercise, coupled with workplace cultures that reinforce winning, have suppressed character qualities of empathy and fairness on which a just system depends. The politicization of crime issues during the late twentieth century spurred increases in prosecutorial power that persisted well after the crime rate declined.[158] When legislatures lengthened sentences and authorized mandatory minimum sanctions and harsh penalties for habitual offenders, prosecutors gained additional leverage. By stacking charges through multiple counts for the same offense, prosecutors could threaten draconian penalties for defendants who refused to plead guilty.[159] The pressures to plead intensify for indigent defendants who cannot afford bail and are being detained for protracted periods in often inhumane conditions. Particularly if the crime is minor, many individuals, even if innocent, will accept convictions in exchange for modest sentences or time already served just to avoid serious disruption in jobs, housing, and family circumstances.[160] But the cost is that they now have a criminal record, which hampers employment and may subject them to harsh sanctions if they re-offend. Still, most poor defendants see no alternatives, particularly since their overburdened court-appointed attorneys lack resources to investigate and try the vast majority of cases. About 94 percent of state felony prosecutions, 97 percent of federal felony prosecutions, and an even greater proportion of misdemeanor prosecutions end in plea bargains.[161] Defendants' futures are generally decided outside of courtrooms with little investigation and few procedural protections, prompting comedian Lenny Bruce's famous observation that in the "halls of justice the only place you see the justice, is in the halls."[162]

Not only do prosecutors have enormous power over charging and plea bargaining decisions, they also have enormous discretion in how to exercise it.[163] Judicial review of such decisions, is, as Stanford Law School Professor David Sklansky notes, "virtually nonexistent."[164] Nor is there sufficient political accountability for office priorities and practices.[165] Of course, in theory, the public exercises some oversight. In all but five states, the district attorneys who head local offices are elected.[166] But in practice, the political checks are weak. Eighty percent of district attorneys run unopposed in both primaries and general races, and 95 percent of incumbents win.[167] Campaigns have traditionally focused on issues such as the number of cases processed and convictions secured, which says nothing about fairness, efficiency, or substantive priorities.[168] In the federal system, the president appoints US attorneys and the Justice Department sets broad policies, but local federal prosecutors have considerable day-to-day autonomy.

The problem is not simply the extent of prosecutorial power, but also the norms and values that guide its exercise. Although the vast majority of prosecutors appear motivated by a genuine desire to "do justice," their workplace culture often fosters an unduly punitive view of what justice looks like. The priority is winning, and there is insufficient incentive to unearth potentially exculpatory evidence, or to develop cost-effective alternatives to incarceration. Many ambitious prosecutors see the position as a stepping stone to higher office.[169] And as commentators note, "the one thing that can cripple a prosecutor's political ascent is a reputation, even if based on only a single case, for being too lenient. In short, our system has huge incentives for brutality, and no incentives for mercy."[170]

Such reward structures can have a corrosive effect on character. In reflecting on that fact, former prosecutor Paul Butler describes his evolution from a "progressive guy" intent on changing the system, to a gung ho advocate hell bent on winning. "I wanted to be well regarded by my peers, to be successful in my career, and to serve my country. And the way to do that, I learned on the job, was to send as many people to jail as I could."[171] Butler's office, like most others, prized "victory above all else, "and often defined victory as imposition of the maximum allowable sentence.[172] Rachel Van Cleve's study of the Cook County, Illinois, prosecutor's office documents the costs of this mindset. There, an office bulletin board celebrated every prosecutor's first win. Some placed their ties next to mug shots of defendants taken after the verdicts. In one photo, a young Latino girl was crying so hard that her mouth was frozen in grief. Underneath the picture, the prosecutor had written "not very happy with verdict," as if her suffering was something to be proud of.[173] Indifference to the hardships for offenders was common. One prosecutor put it this way; his job was to put "bad guy[s] away" for as long as possible to make sure that they "don't hurt others again or if they do, it will be other inmates."[174] Young prosecutors, who constitute about half of those working in state systems, are particularly likely to display a mindset they later describe as "hard ass," balls-to-the-wall," "lock them up."[175] They are out to "impress" others and themselves with their ability to "prosecute the hell out of everyone."[176]

Because "victory" on these terms generally requires close cooperative relationships with law enforcement officers, prosecutors have often maintained willful blindness toward police misconduct.[177] And because many prosecutors see themselves on the side of righteousness, doing "God's work on earth," they sometimes succumb to tunnel vision, and fail to acknowledge exculpatory evidence, or rationalize cutting ethical corners in order to obtain convictions.[178] That tendency is encouraged by the absence of serious sanctions for abuses. In one all-too-representative study of some almost 1,300 cases alleging prosecutorial misconduct, and 277 finding reversible error, none resulted in professional discipline.[179] In the nation generally, only one prosecutor has ever been imprisoned for misconduct resulting in a wrongful conviction. The sentence was eight days; the defendant he wrongfully convicted served twenty-five years.[180]

Even the most egregious ethical violations often go unaddressed. John Thompson spent fourteen years on death row for a murder he never committed. New Orleans prosecutors failed to disclose blood samples from the crime scene that failed to match Thompson's. The office had a history of failing to turn over exculpatory evidence and to train prosecutors in their obligations to do so. Because individual prosecutors have immunity from lawsuits, Thompson brought an action against the office for its oversight failures, and a jury awarded him $14 million in damages, $1 million for every year spent in prison.[181] However a divided Supreme Court reversed, on the theory that the government should not be liable for individual misconduct.[182] The result, as Thompson noted in a *New York Times* op-ed, was that none of the prosecutors involved in suppressing the evidence or covering up the misconduct faced criminal or ethics charges: "No one was fired," he reported, "and now, . . . no one can be sued. . . . A crime was definitely committed in this case, but not by me."[183] That needs to change.

Parole

Parole is yet another context in which arbitrary and ill-informed character decisions perpetuate injustice. Until the mid-1970s, every state as well as the federal government operated a parole system that permitted early release from prison for those who could show evidence of rehabilitation. At the high point of that system, nearly three-quarters of all departures from prison occurred early as a result of parole.[184] The process lost popularity in the late twentieth century in the wake of studies documenting widespread problems. Most parolees continued to offend or to violate the terms of their release, and parole decision-making was frequently idiosyncratic, inconsistent, and subject to racial and class biases.[185] According to prominent experts such as James Q. Wilson, the United States should abandon rehabilitation as a primary goal of corrections, and see its purpose as simply "to isolate and to punish." This, Wilson argued, was not cruel or barbaric, but rather "a frank admission that society does not really know how to do much else."[186] The public largely agreed. By 1995, only a quarter of Americans thought the primary purpose of prison should be rehabilitation, down from almost three-quarters in 1970.[187] By 2013, thirty-four states and the federal government had eliminated or restricted use of discretionary parole, and the number of state prisoners released early dropped to 30 percent.[188] In recent years, however, the spiraling financial and human costs of mass incarceration have prompted many jurisdictions to rethink their policies. And a growing body of research reveals a process in urgent need of reform.

The Injustice of Decision-Making

The parole systems currently in place vary considerably in the amount of discretion that they allow and in their procedures and criteria for decision-making. But certain common features and common problems are apparent. Surveys of parole boards find that the most important factors in determining eligibility for early release are the type and severity of crime, and the offender's criminal history.[189] The difficulty is that these factors, which a prisoner can never change, outweigh or overshadow the things that a prisoner can demonstrate as evidence of rehabilitation. This ranking system is inconsistent with evidence summarized in earlier chapters documenting the possibility of character development. And the result is needless suffering, despair, and expenses associated with imprisonment. All too often, decision-makers focus on retribution for past mistakes, not on future potential, and ignore evidence of how offenders have transformed their lives and what contributions they could make to their families and communities on release.

The injustices are particularly great for those who are wrongfully convicted and refuse to acknowledge guilt. David McCallum was one of those individuals. He was sixteen when sentenced for a murder that he did not commit. He spent thirty years in prison before his exoneration, and was repeatedly denied parole because of the severity of the offense and his insistence that he was innocent. His codefendant, also innocent, died in prison.[190]

Juvenile offenders are another group that pays a disproportionate price for our policy failures. A recent study by the American Civil Liberties Union found repeated examples of prisoners held for life for a single impetuous act in their youth, despite outstanding records of rehabilitation.[191] John Alexander, a fifty-four-year-old black man, is a case in point. He had been in prison since he was eighteen, when he had killed another youth during a night of drinking and gambling. For thirty-six years, Alexander compiled a near perfect record for work performance, completed multiple educational programs, tutored other prisoners, and served as a role model. The judge who sentenced him argued for his parole. Alexander also had a supportive family, housing, and a job waiting for him. Yet he was still denied parole six times.[192] A 2018 *New York Times* editorial described the similar case of Carlos Flores, who was seventeen when he and three accomplices tried to rob a bar. An off-duty police officer who intervened was shot and killed. Although Flores was not the shooter, he was convicted of second degree murder and sentenced to twenty-five years to life. He is now fifty-four and has served thirty-seven years behind bars, with an almost flawless disciplinary history. According to a recent assessment, his release would pose the lowest possible risk to the community. Yet for sixteen years he has been denied parole. In its most recent decision, the Parole Board gave only its standard boilerplate reason: "discretionary release at this time would not be compatible with the welfare of society and would tend to depreciate the seriousness of the instant offense and undermine respect for the law."[193] Whose respect?

These examples are depressingly common. Over eight thousand individuals in twelve surveyed states are serving sentences of life or forty years imprisonment for offenses committed as juveniles. Data on recidivism make clear that these individuals are unlikely to commit future crimes after their mid-twenties, which makes these extended sentences particularly unjust and unnecessary.[194] Under the current system, many juvenile offenders, if they are ever granted parole, will be released at such an advanced age that they will have little prospect of effectively rebuilding their lives, regardless of how much their character has been reformed.[195]

Inadequate Procedural Safeguards and Reentry Programs

The potential for unfairness is compounded by a lack of procedural protections, and the perfunctory nature of review in some state systems.[196] Applicants may have to wait as long as fifteen years between reviews, and if their original crimes are sufficiently serious, may never have a realistic chance for parole, no matter how much time passes and how exemplary their prison records.[197] In some states, parole approvals are so rare as to create false illusions of hope. During one surveyed period, Ohio granted parole to only 9 percent and Florida to less than 1 percent of individuals serving life sentences for offenses committed when they were juveniles.[198]

A final injustice involves the inadequacy of re-entry programs and support services for those who manage to achieve parole. Most inmates leave prison having had little education, job training, substance abuse assistance, or mental health treatment.[199] In-prison and post-prison programs are often poorly designed or funded. One nonprofit evaluation rated only 6 percent as very effective and 17 percent effective; 43 percent were judged not effective.[200] Such inadequate re-entry initiatives help explain why 60 percent of parolees return to custody within three years either for committing a new offense or for violating a condition of their release, such as failing a drug test, losing a job, or missing an appointment with their parole officers.[201] Subsequent discussion makes clear that many of these revocations could have been prevented if offenders had access to better treatment, training, and support services. But without such assistance in place, policymakers and parole boards often resist early release. Because it is impossible to prevent all former prisoners from re-offending, particularly if they lack support, it appears only a matter of time before some parolee's brutal crime causes public outrage and fixes blame on parole supporters or decision-makers. That turns the process into a kind of "political Russian roulette," which board members are often reluctant to play.[202] Overreaction to the possibility of one horrendous case can make for "good politics but bad policy."[203]

Race and Class Bias

Decades of research have revealed racial disparities at every level of the criminal justice system: searches, arrests, pretrial detention, charges, sentences, probation, and parole.[204] Blacks are incarcerated in state prisons at more than five times the rate of whites.[205] At current rates, one in three black men, and one in six Latino men, will go to prison at some point in their lives, compared with one of every seventeen whites.[206] Two-thirds of inmates of state prisons come from households with an annual income of less than half the poverty rate;[207] Part of the reason for these disparities involves differences in life circumstances. Poor people and people of color are disproportionately subject to conditions associated with the most serious crimes: lack of adequate education, jobs, housing, or hope.[208] They are also the most dependent on overworked and underfunded public defenders for legal representation, which can materially affect outcomes.[209] All too often, the character of the defendant is less critical than the quality of the defense lawyer in determining punishment. According to prominent experts such as Stephen Bright, former director of the Southern Center for Human Rights, and Brian Stevenson, director of the Equal Justice Initiative, in our criminal justice system, "it is better to be rich and guilty than poor and innocent."[210]

However, not all racial disparities in the criminal justice system can be explained by higher rates of criminal activity among impoverished people of color or inadequate defense representation. At every stage of the process, similarly situated individuals are treated differently on the basis of race and ethnicity. Most studies that compare similar offenders find that blacks and Hispanics are more likely than whites to be arrested, to be detained before trial, and to receive extended prison sentences.[211] Disparities are particularly great for petty crimes. For example, blacks are four times as likely as whites to be arrested for possession of marijuana, although rates of use are roughly the same.[212]

Racial profiling, whether or not intentional, has been common. One study using six years of the New York Police Department's own data found that people of color were nine times more likely than whites to be stopped and also were subject to greater force but were no more likely to have engaged in activity justifying arrest.[213] Racially targeted traffic stops have been so pervasive that the practice is known as DWB, "driving while black."[214] Just being in the wrong neighborhood with the wrong color skin can trigger an arrest. New York police have used vague justifications for stops such as "furtive movement," while Nashville police offered the explanation "Walking down the road around 1:30 a.m." with "no legitimate reason."[215]

Blacks are also more likely to receive a death sentence even when controlling for the severity of the crime and the characteristics of the victim.[216] White jurors are substantially more likely to convict black defendants than white defendants even where the evidence is similar.[217] The only exception to that pattern occurs when race is a prominent issue at trial, perhaps because this reminds jurors to be on guard against discriminatory decision-making.[218]

Experts attribute these racial disparities partly to implicit bias: that is, attitudes and stereotypes that function automatically without individual awareness. Techniques such as brain imaging and the Implicit Association Test (IAT) reveal these biases by measuring how quickly individuals can follow instructions to pair pictures and images that are consistent with stereotypes (a black face and weapon) compared with how quickly they can make inconsistent pairings (a white face and a weapon).[219] Decades of research finds that implicit bias measured by the IAT is a more reliable predictor of discrimination than explicit bias, measured by self-reports or other evidence.[220] Considerable evidence independent of that test suggests that implicit bias is pervasive, and affects judgments about character traits associated with criminal behavior, particularly violence, dangerousness, and lack of remorse.[221] These unconscious stereotypes help explain why prosecutors are more likely to charge African Americans under habitual offender laws than whites with similar histories, why judges are more likely to incarcerate or deny bail to offenders of color, and why jurors are more likely to impose the death penalty.[222] Individuals with dark skin tones and Afrocentric facial features are particularly likely to "activate automatic associations with negative . . . stereotypes . . . such as aggression, violence and criminality," and some consider bias based on these physical attributes the "next frontier" in the fight against racial discrimination.[223]

Racial disparities in criminal justice reflect not only negative stereotypes about the character of people of color but also positive stereotypes associated with whites. Some experts use the term "implicit white favoritism" to describe the disassociation of whites with violence, which helps account for why ambiguous evidence of criminal behavior is resolved in their favor, but against racial minorities.[224] Studies also reveal a racial empathy gap; people are less sensitive to the pain experienced by someone of a different racial group than by a member of their own group.[225] Empathy strongly influences judgments about guilt and punishment.[226] This helps explain why white judges who make allowances to protect white college students from the consequences of youthful mistakes do not extend the same protection to juveniles of color.[227] Race and class bias also help account for the irrationality of sentencing practices noted earlier that punish white "suite" criminals less strictly than nonviolent black or Hispanic "street" criminals even when the public harms from white collar offenders are greater. Such bias may also underlie certain differential treatment of drug offenses. For example, in the federal system, offenses involving small amounts of crack cocaine, a drug used primarily in communities of color, have led to far harsher punishments than offenses involving large amounts of powder cocaine, a drug used predominantly by whites.[228]

Racial and class bias is particularly hard to combat in contexts such as the criminal justice system, where excessive workloads, time pressures, and inadequate information require decision-makers to make quick, intuitive judgments.[229] Most lawyers and judges operate under conditions of triage; they make crucial determinations about which few cases deserve detailed inquiry and which defendants deserve a break, generally with little oversight or accountability.[230] Effective responses to implicit bias have also been elusive because so many individuals are unwilling to suspect it in their own behavior. In recent surveys, between 50 and 87 percent of judges and 96 percent of federal probation officers ranked themselves in the top quarter of their colleagues in their ability to avoid racial prejudice in decision-making.[231] Such self-confidence is particularly troubling because individuals who perceive themselves as free of bias are more likely to display it; they lack the motivation to monitor their own judgments.[232] As law professor Michelle Alexander argues, such "racial indifference and blindness," far more than racial hostility, is what perpetuates systemic injustice in criminal processes.[233]

Strategies for Reform

Reforming the criminal justice system is a mammoth undertaking, and a comprehensive overview is well beyond the scope of this chapter. Rather, the aim here is simply to identify improvements in how the system evaluates character, determines appropriate punishment, and enables character growth through parole and rehabilitation.

Character Assessment

One cluster of strategies should focus on flaws in character assessments. Training for judges and prosecutors, and explicit instructions for juries can try to reduce the importance that decision-makers attach to inaccurate signals of remorse.[234] Education about the misleading folk wisdom on repentance can reduce the penalties now paid by offenders who receive insufficient coaching or who maintain their innocence.[235] Training on implicit bias can alert decision-makers to unconscious racial, ethnic, and class stereotypes and ways to reduce their influence.[236] Studies of judges who have received such training show a modest reduction in bias, and such initiatives are also being adapted for juries.[237] The US Justice Department recently made bias training mandatory for federal prosecutors and law enforcement officials, and local jurisdictions should follow suit.[238]

More auditing of judicial, prosecutorial, and police decision-making for patterns of bias could also spur corrective action.[239] For example, the Vera Institute has evaluated tools for monitoring racial equity, and many local prosecutors' offices have undertaken their own internal reviews of potential bias.[240] Legislative, judicial, and executive branch officials could mandate data collection, and non-profit organizations could publicize the results in order to promote greater accountability and encourage reform efforts.[241] For example, prosecutors' offices might be required to record the factors that influenced charges in a specified cases, what plea bargains were offered, what alternatives to incarceration were considered and accepted or rejected, how the case was resolved, and the race or ethnicity of the offender and prosecutor.[242] Courts could also respond more effectively when patterns of racial bias emerge. At a time when the Black Lives Matter movement has raised increasing concerns about the fairness of law enforcement and criminal justice decision-making, we should not tolerate practices that compound distrust and undermine the legitimacy of legal processes.

Punishment

A second cluster of strategies should focus on making sanctions less punitive and more rehabilitative. Sentencing decisions should take greater account of research demonstrating the potential for positive change in character-related behaviors. The public is more open to such a reorientation than current punitive policies might suggest. One reason those policies have persisted is that Americans grossly underestimate the severity of current sanctions and the cost-effectiveness of alternatives. When judges have asked jurors about appropriate sentences in particular cases, they often suggest punishments far lower than the mandatory minimum. One study found that on average, jurors recommended sentences only about a fifth of the length of median federal guidelines.[243] A similar case history involved a defendant who was caught selling small amounts of marijuana to informants while in possession of a firearm. The jurors suggested an average prison term of fifteen to eighteen years; the judge was forced to impose fifty-five years.[244]

The documentary *Snitch* highlights the problem. It profiles Clarence Aaron, an Alabama man convicted of conspiracy for driving some friends with drugs across state boundaries. The movie ends with filmmakers asking one of the jurors in the case how much prison time he thought Aaron, a first-time offender, should have received. The juror responded, "I don't know, three to five years, maybe something like that." On learning that Aaron had received three life sentences, the juror looked visibly dismayed. The film closes with a picture of Aaron sitting in the cell that he will occupy for the rest of his life as the juror says, "I'm surprised at that, I really am, that harsh a sentence. He seemed to be a pretty promising boy."[245]

Such harsh sanctions are out of touch with evolving values. Between 2003 and 2016, the number of Americans who said that the justice system was not tough enough on crime dropped from 65 to 45 percent.[246] By a huge margin, 76 percent to 19 percent, the public preferred to spend tax dollars on prevention rather than prisons.[247] In other surveys, close to nine out of ten Americans opposed mandatory minimum penalties for nonviolent offenders, and over two-thirds supported rehabilitation efforts and alternatives to incarceration.[248] Almost three-quarters of the public favor reducing time in prison for nonviolent offenders posing little danger.[249] Even victims of crime are, on the whole, less interested in maximizing punishment than in creating opportunities for emotional healing, apologies, and restitution.[250] In the most comprehensive recent study of victims' concerns, 60 percent preferred shorter prison sentences and more spending on prevention and rehabilitation. By a margin of three to one, victims favored holding people accountable through options other than prison, such as mental health and drug treatment, community supervision, or community service.[251]

Experts overwhelmingly agree. There is broad consensus that the United States imprisons too many offenders for too long a period. Although research on the relationship between incarceration and recidivism varies somewhat in quality and outcomes, most studies find that imprisonment does not reduce the chances of reoffending and may even increase its likelihood.[252] The experience and conditions of confinement in the United States often impair offenders' character development and their ability to become productive, law-abiding citizens.[253] Defendants who have been incarcerated have higher risks of divorce and domestic violence, and lower rates of marriage, employment, effective parenting, and civic engagement.[254] In one of the most comprehensive recent surveys, serving time in prison was associated with a 40 percent reduction in earnings, and three-quarters of former inmates never rose out of the bottom fifth of earnings distributions.[255] For juveniles, incarceration reduces the chances of graduation from high school and increases the likelihood of criminal activity as an adult.[256] Of course, for obvious reasons, these studies generally lack control groups of similar offenders who were not incarcerated, so it is difficult to identify the extent to which imprisonment contributed to these outcomes. But most experts believe that incarceration plays some role; it can school them in criminal behaviors, disrupt family relationships, and make them less employable on release.

For many offenders, well-designed alternatives to prison would cost less and provide more likelihood of rehabilitation. Only slightly over half of state prison inmates are violent criminals; the rest are serving time mainly for property and drug offenses.[257] Estimates suggest that about two-thirds of prisoners have substance abuse problems and half have mental health challenges.[258] Many of these individuals would benefit more from treatment than incarceration. Researchers have estimated that as many as 30 to 40 percent of prisoners pose no significant threat to public safety based on the seriousness of their offenses and likelihood of recidivism.[259] Separating these individuals from jobs and families while exposing them to the toxic aspects of prison life is counterproductive.[260]

Experience with alternative sentencing strategies bears this out. Options include halfway houses, restitution, community service, house arrest, electronic monitoring, supervised job training, educational programs, and mental health treatment, including substance abuse and behavioral therapies. Since 2010, thirty-one states have decreased incarceration and experienced no increase in crime.[261] Some, such as New York, have expanded employment programs, social services, and treatment opportunities, and found that both prison and crime rates have gone down.[262] Therapeutic referrals for drug offenses saved New York taxpayers over $13,000 per offender compared with incarceration, a savings of over $300 for every dollar spent.[263] Drug courts focusing on treatment now operate in all fifty states, but reach only a small fraction of potential beneficiaries.[264] On average, these courts decrease nonviolent drug recidivism by 10 to 15 percent, and those that employ best practices have success rates that are considerably higher.[265] Other therapeutic interventions, as well as participation in educational programs, also show reductions in criminal behavior.[266] Alternatives to commercial bail bonds have proven more just and no less effective than pretrial detention in guaranteeing court attendance and preventing future crime.[267] Options include electronic monitoring, reminders of court dates, and participation in training or treatment programs.

Alternatives to incarceration are particularly important for juvenile offenders. Recent research makes clear that many delinquent behaviors are tied to inadequate development of brain regions involved in impulse control and evaluation of risks and rewards.[268] Almost all adolescents mature out of crime if left to develop cognitive skills and character strengths without criminal sanctions.[269] Prisons are a particularly toxic environment for young offenders due to inadequate rehabilitative services and protection from abuse, and inappropriate role models.[270] Severe punishment is especially likely to lead to increase in offending, while community treatment programs can reduce crime, typically by as much as 20–30 percent.[271] For violent juvenile offenders, intensive therapy involving family, school, and peer-based interventions over a four-month period can reduce future offenses by as much as 75 percent compared to matched control groups.[272]

Restorative justice initiatives are another promising alternative to traditional forms of punishment. These initiatives require offenders to accept responsibility for their conduct and make reparations. Through direct dialogue with victims, defendants gain a greater understanding of the consequences of their actions, which can encourage genuine remorse, empathy, and reconciliation, and can lower the risk of recidivism.[273] Restorative justice programs have been at least as effective in controlling crime as traditional methods; they also have reduced repeat offenses and given victims a greater sense of justice and closure.[274]

Sentencing should rest on evidence-based practices that focus on what will best enable offenders to become productive members of families, workplaces, and communities.[275] To that end, judges should look for the least restrictive punishment that can balance goals of rehabilitation, deterrence, and community protection.[276] This will require changes in sentencing statutes, guidelines, and practices. We need to repeal mandatory minimum and three-strike laws; judges should always have discretion to mitigate punishments and consider alternatives to extended incarceration.[277] Money now spent on jails and prisons should be diverted to treatment, training, and support programs that can enhance character development and coping strategies. The federal government has recently moved in this direction. The 2018 First Step Act shortens mandatory minimums for non-violent drug offenses, expands early release programs, and enables those convicted under harsh crack cocaine laws to petition for reevaluation of their sentences. Still, the legislation falls far short of what reformers have advocated and affects only federal prisoners, a small proportion of those subject to mass incarceration.[278]

Reforming punishment will also require reforming the culture, oversight, and reward structures of prosecutors' offices. The goal should be a commitment to justice that is broader than maximizing sentences and convictions.[279] To that end, a growing number of prosecutors' offices have established Conviction Integrity Units (CIUs) that investigate charges of wrongful convictions and propose structural reforms to enhance fairness.[280] However, despite their potential, relatively few prosecutors' offices have adopted them, so legislatures could should consider following the lead of other nations, such as Canada and the United Kingdom, which have mandated external government review bodies.[281] More efforts could also be made to educate voters about prosecutorial policies and performance. Almost nine of ten Americans say that it is important for prosecutors to work toward ending mass incarceration, and are more likely to support a prosecutor who believes in reducing racial bias in the criminal justice system.[282] Initiatives such as the Massachusetts ACLU's "What a Difference a DA Makes" have enabled voters to act on those policy preferences and elect a wave of progressive prosecutors who support less punitive, more rehabilitative approaches.[283]

Parole and Re-Entry

Reforms should also focus on making the parole and re-entry process more just and effective. A half century ago, experts who drafted the nation's Model Penal Code recommended a presumption that prisoners should be paroled the first time that they become eligible, unless there were strong reasons for delay.[284] That recommendation should now be implemented. Parole boards should operate with a presumption favoring release, rebuttable only by a showing of public risk that requires further time in prison. The process should include more procedural safeguards, including a hearing at which prisoners can contest adverse evidence. If parole is denied, they should receive goals for rehabilitation that can be met before the next review. Boards should include individuals with diverse experiences and should have sufficient resources, staff, and limits on caseloads in order to permit meaningful review. Risk assessment tools should be open to public scrutiny, and should be monitored and readjusted to reduce racial bias and promote greater accuracy in predicting recidivism. As experts note, the "devil is in the data" in far too many tools currently in use, which end up incorporating and therefore replicating the discrimination that they were designed to reduce.[285] Adequate re-entry services and treatment programs should also be available.[286] Legislatures should eliminate the collateral consequences of criminal records that have no demonstrated deterrent value and that subvert the character rehabilitation process. The Council of State Governments lists nearly nine thousand statutory consequences that accompany criminal convictions, including loss of welfare, public housing, student loans, and occupational licenses.[287] Such deprivations undermine ex-offenders' opportunities to find work, support their families, and avoid re-offending.[288]

Sister Helen Prejean, a nun who worked with death row inmates, reminded us that "people are more than the worst thing they have ever done in their lives."[289]

The parole and re-entry process should better reflect that insight and offer more individuals a realistic possibility of redemption.

A Commitment to Justice

By almost every measure, the American criminal justice system falls far short in its commitment to justice. The vast majority of the public recognizes as much. In popular opinion surveys, two-thirds to three-quarters of Americans agree that the system needs major improvement or a complete overhaul.[290] What is less commonly recognized is that laws and practices related to character are part of the problem; they undermine appropriate principles of evidence, punishment, and rehabilitation. It has been over a half century since Martin Luther King Jr. famously shared his dream that one day all Americans would be "judged not by the color of their skins but by the content of their character."[291] We remain a far distance from that ideal.

To make King's dream a reality will require a deeper commitment to social justice by those most responsible for current practices. We need individuals of character as judges, prosecutors, legislators, and parole board members who will put concerns about fairness and faith in character rehabilitation before politics and self-interest. That is not to impugn the good intentions of the vast majority of criminal justice decision-makers. But it is to suggest that too many have been in-sufficiently self-reflective about their own potential for bias, and insufficiently in-formed about the cost-effectiveness of incarceration and its alternatives. More of those leaders need to take responsibility for the failures of the current system and for the development of reforms. And the public needs to hold them accountable if they do not. "Equal Justice Under Law" is a slogan that we put on courthouse doors. It should better describe what goes on inside them.

5

Character in Politics

NOWHERE HAS THE concern for character been more frequently affirmed but more routinely ignored than in politics. The American presidency is no exception, and provides a useful case study for exploring the role character plays in political life. Never are the stakes higher, and when voters fail to consider candidates' integrity as well as policy, the consequences can be calamitous. Alexander Hamilton, in the *Federalist Papers*, argued that the commander in chief must be an individual "preeminent for ability and virtue."[1] Franklin Roosevelt similarly viewed the presidency as, above all else, "a place for moral leadership."[2] In principle, the public overwhelmingly agrees. Recent polls find that 95 percent of Americans think that a president's character is important; two-thirds agree that it is very important.[3] Yet somewhat paradoxically, a majority of the public (54 percent) believes that a politician can be effective despite deficiencies in character, and less than a third think that character is more important than policies.[4]

The 2016 presidential campaign was a textbook illustration of those views. During the campaign, two-thirds of Americans did not think Donald Trump had "strong moral character."[5] Only about a third thought he was trustworthy, and only about a quarter thought that he had the right temperament to be president or that he would be a good role model for children.[6] As he began his presidency, less than a fifth considered him honest and trustworthy.[7]

Trump is an extreme, but not an isolated case. As one researcher noted,

> Integrity has rarely been a trait that has been commonly associated with U.S. presidential candidates. . . . Since Eisenhower, it has been far more common for the losing candidate to be evaluated better on honesty than the winning candidate. In particular, incumbent presidents Johnson, Nixon, and Clinton all survived their reelection bids with negative scores on integrity.[8]

Until Trump, Clinton had the lowest personal character rating since polls began collecting that information, but also one of the highest job approval ratings.[9] Although Robert Dole sought to make the 1996 election a referendum on moral leadership, and Americans by a substantial margin thought he was more honest and more likely to stand by his convictions than Clinton, a majority voted for Clinton.[10] In recent elections, a declining number of voters, especially younger voters, are giving priority to personal qualities, and those qualities are more likely to be evaluated through a partisan lens.[11] Political leaders' standing on core traits of character now "depends a good bit on the political sensibilities of whoever is doing the judging."[12]

This chapter suggests why that is a worrisome trend. It begins by exploring what character means, and should mean, in American political life, and why it matters. Discussion then turns to the qualities that are most critical in national leaders, and what can be done to encourage them.

What Constitutes Character in Politics and Why It Matters

Concern with character in politics dates back to the earliest and most influential writing on the subject. As chapter 1 noted, classical philosophers such as Plato and Aristotle, as well as America's Founding Fathers, all emphasized the importance of virtue in governmental leaders. And while the public today generally agrees in theory, its views in practice are more complicated. Stanley Renshon, an expert on presidential leadership, notes that although the relevance of character is now "firmly established, the criteria by which candidates should be judged clearly are not."[13] No consensus has emerged concerning which of the cluster of characteristics described in chapter 1 are the most critical. Further complications can arise in assessing whether given politicians have desired traits. Candidates, Renshon noted, have a "vested interest in showing themselves as they would like to be seen, not necessarily as they are."[14] And observers are often biased by political ideology and information silos in their character evaluations. In America's climate of increasing polarization, partisans tend to see character flaws in the other party's candidates, not their own.[15]

To understand the stakes in this debate, it makes sense to begin by clarifying why exactly character matters in political life. For the most powerful public offices, and particularly the presidency, character is important for both practical and symbolic reasons. As a practical matter, it matters partly because of the uncertainties that arise in governance. Personal qualities may be more significant than policy positions because no one can predict all the situations that will confront a leader once in office. Given that "new and unforeseen crises may face the country . . . [it is most] important to select an individual who will apply a sound set of principles and values in unexpected circumstances."[16] Moreover, what a candidate says during a campaign may often reflect less what he truly believes than what "he thinks he needs to say in order to be elected."[17] And even the most sincere intentions may need to adapt to new information and constraints. People who think that policy matters more than character still want leaders to alter their views in light of changed circumstances, and qualities of character enable politicians to make appropriate adjustments.[18]

Presidential character also shapes the influence that the United States can exercise in global affairs. How people around the world view the American commander in chief can affect international security and economic performance. One worrisome consequence of Donald Trump's conduct is that the median approval of US leadership across 134 countries stands at a record Gallup low of 30 percent.[19] So too, when Pew researchers asked individuals around the world how much confidence they had in Trump to do the right thing regarding global affairs, three-quarters said they had no confidence, the lowest level of confidence since the poll has been conducted.[20] That lack of trust can seriously impair the United States' ability to secure alliances and promote international peace and prosperity.

Character is also crucial to ensuring accountability. William Bennett notes that "if the president's word cannot be trusted—an issue of character—voters cannot take seriously his election platform or his campaign promises—an issue of public duty."[21] Nor can voters who are denied an honest account of presidential actions make informed decisions about how to respond. As subsequent discussion notes, the lies that Lyndon Johnson and Richard Nixon told about military progress during the Vietnam War kept Congress and the public from exercising appropriate oversight.

So too, the president plays an important role as a symbolic leader who embodies the nation's values and aspirations.[22] As political theorists note, one way that people "reduce the complexity of political affairs to manageable proportions [is] by placing the president at the center of things. Keeping track of international and national events then reduces to the simpler task of keeping track of the President."[23] Contemporary politics is also psychodrama, and presidents have exemplary as well as executive moral duties.[24] They represent Americans by who they are as much as by what they do. They need a character fit for moral leadership that can serve as a role model for youth and a spokesperson for the nation. Peggy Noonan, a former presidential speechwriter, accordingly concludes that for the country's chief executive, "character is everything. A president . . . doesn't have to be clever; you can hire clever. . . . But you can't buy courage and decency; you can't rent a strong moral sense."[25]

Leaders who fail to embody those values erode confidence in public institutions. When pollsters have asked why Americans have lost confidence in government and politicians, one of the most common explanations, offered by almost two-thirds of those responding, is the lack of honesty and integrity among elected officials.[26] Three-quarters of Americans fault political leaders for being "more concerned with managing their images than with solving our nation's problems."[27] In a survey of young adults, a key reason for disengagement with politics was the belief that most politicians are untruthful and more concerned with their own interests than those of the public. As one survey participant put it, they "just tell you what you want to hear."[28]

As the scope of presidential power has increased, so too has the importance of presidential character.[29] As commander in chief, the occupant of the Oval Office is responsible for decisions that can risk millions of lives, threaten world peace, or cause a nuclear holocaust. That power calls for qualities of temperament that are sometimes loosely labeled "character issues." So, for example, In 1964, Democrats charged that Barry Goldwater was unsuited to have his finger on the nuclear button. A widely circulated survey of psychiatrists agreed with that assessment, although they were also widely criticized for evaluating someone that they had not treated.[30] Goldwater's successful libel lawsuit arising from the survey has helped deter similar polls, but concerns about temperament have continued to surface in presidential campaigns. In 1992, George Bush asked voters, "When that crisis call comes in to the White House in the middle of the night, who would you like to have answer the phone?"[31] In 2016, Hillary Clinton claimed that the nuclear code should not be given to Donald Trump, someone "you can bait with a tweet," and many psychiatrists publicly agreed.[32]

That campaign reignited debates over professional ethics rules barring experts from evaluating the mental health of politicians based on their public conduct.[33] After Trump's election, more than fifty thousand mental health professionals signed a petition concluding that he was "too seriously mentally ill to perform the duties of president and should be removed."[34] Whatever one thinks about the role that mental health experts should play in assessing presidential fitness, it is clear that candidates' self-discipline and temperament should be factors for voter consideration.[35]

Yet while few doubt that presidential character matters, there is no corresponding consensus about which qualities are most critical and how they rank in comparison to other leadership traits. Nor is there agreement about the role that private moral conduct should play in assessing fitness for public office. As the subsequent discussion indicates, we should be wary about narrowing the pool of politicians to those whose personal lives are entirely above reproach. We should also worry about the invasions of privacy and distortions of public debate that

would result if political campaigns became referenda on rectitude in private conduct. According to opinion polls, most Americans do not believe that presidents
should be held to higher moral standards in their personal lives than are ordinary
citizens.[36] But neither does the public think that all private conduct should get a
free pass. The critical question is what that conduct reveals about character traits
that are crucial to effectiveness in public office.

As earlier chapters noted, the qualities most often associated with character
have both a moral and performance dimension. That is equally true for politicians,
although the particular demands of their positions may call for a somewhat different ranking of qualities than is desirable for individuals generally. Philosophers
such as Reinhold Niebuhr have reminded us that what constitutes virtue depends
partly on context.[37] The quality of loyalty that we value in friends is not what we
value in politicians when they are filling key public offices. As a general matter,
studies of presidential leadership reviewed more fully in what follows suggest a
cluster of both moral and performance traits that are critical to effectiveness in
office. Key moral qualities include honesty, integrity, humanity, and a commitment to democratic principles. Key performance qualities include self-discipline
and diligence.

Integrity is a particularly important measure by which to judge politicians,
especially presidents.[38] Research summarized in chapter 1 makes clear that people
of integrity are more likely to be behave consistently with their principles in the
face of social pressure to do otherwise, and are more likely to display empathy
and helping behavior.[39] Those higher in integrity display a stronger sense of personal responsibility for doing the right thing, and less tolerance of self-serving
rationalizations of misconduct.[40] This quality is particularly important for
politicians because, as philosopher Bernard Williams notes, a

> predictable and probable hazard of political life is that there will be
> situations in which something morally disagreeable is clearly required. . . .
> [O]nly those who are reluctant and disinclined to do the morally disa-
> greeable when it is really necessary have much chance of not doing it when
> it is not necessary. . . . A habit of reluctance is an essential obstacle against
> the happy acceptance of the intolerable.[41]

Equally important are virtues that underpin democratic governance. They entail a commitment to act, and to motivate others to act, according to principles
central to a well-functioning democracy. These include honesty; tolerance of opposing views; respect for due process, individual rights, and a free press; and a
commitment to put public above personal interests.[42]

Yet crucial though these qualities may be to a politician's effectiveness in governing, they appear less crucial in winning, as the polls cited earlier made clear. A century ago, Lord James Bryce wrote a book on American politics including a chapter titled "Why Great Men Are Not Chosen Presidents." One reason, Bryce suggested, was that the nominating process "places more value on getting a candidate who can win than one who can govern" and that the American voter likes his candidate to be "above all, what he calls 'magnetic.'"[43] In contemporary politics, the electorate tends to value performance traits such as competence and strength as more important than trust.[44] The result, as Americans themselves acknowledge, is that moral character is not what they get in politicians. Four-fifths believe that most politicians are more interested in winning elections than in doing what is right.[45] Three-quarters believe that most elected officials put their own interests ahead of the country's.[46] Half believe that politicians have less character than the average American.[47] And only 7 percent have "a great deal of trust and confidence" in politicians.[48]

This erosion in public confidence reflects not only character deficiencies in elected leaders but also campaign practices that degrade and deter ethical candidates. As one commentator noted, the way that you "get to be a public official in this country is by screaming louder or more expensively about what a bum your opponent is.... Over these years of more and more negative ... advertising, and more and more 'character issues,' politicians have done a very very effective job in destroying their own credibility."[49] Equally to the point, the nastiness of recent political campaigns discourages many individuals with high principles from running for office. That is particularly true for women, who are disproportionately targeted for sexually violent threats and disproportionately put off by negative campaigning.[50] If, as most experts agree, integrity is critical for effectiveness in public office, the public needs to make that quality a priority and to demand campaigns that reflect it.[51]

The discussion that follows explores the qualities that matter most through the lens of the American presidency. Performance in that office reflects a complex interplay between context and character.[52] Character both shapes and is shaped by circumstance, and is neither static nor entirely consistent.[53] One of Lyndon Johnson's cabinet members and close advisors described him as "brave and brutal, compassionate and cruel, incredibly intelligent and infuriatingly insensitive.... He could be altruistic and petty, caring and crude, generous and petulant, bluntly honest and calculatingly devious—all within the same few minutes."[54] A *New York Times* profile of Bill Clinton described an equally complex figure. According to one of his aides, "it's almost impossible not be charmed by him, and it's almost impossible not to be disappointed by him." One of the "most talented, articulate, intelligent, open, colorful characters ever to inhabit the Oval

Office can also be an undisciplined, fumbling, obtuse, defensive, self-justifying rogue. . . . Most of the traits that make him appealing can make him appalling in the flash of an eye."[55]

Given these complexities, the discussion that follows avoids assessments of particular presidents' overall characters. Rather, the focus is on the qualities that are most effective or most toxic in public office, and the implications for voting behavior and structural reforms.

Honesty

The Renaissance philosopher Michel de Montaigne argued that "lying is an ugly vice" that undermines the trust on which societies are founded.[56] Deception by politicians is particularly corrosive because democratic institutions depend on citizens having accurate information. Lies by political leaders are "great betrayals of trust in democratic societies; they thwart or subvert the will of the populace."[57] James Madison observed that "a people who mean to be their own governors . . . must arm themselves with the power knowledge gives."[58] That knowledge is possible only if leaders share truthful information. Its absence enables corruption, conceals errors, preempts dissent, prevents accountability, and distorts the decision-making process.[59] For that reason, the presumption against dishonesty should be very strong.

Yet politicians and political theorists have long recognized a role for what Plato called "noble lies," which benefit the governed.[60] Over five hundred years ago, Niccolò Machiavelli argued in *The Prince* that leaders "who have accomplished great deeds are those who . . . have known how cunningly to manipulate men's minds; and in the end they have surpassed those who have laid their foundations upon sincerity."[61] Of course, Machiavelli was writing in a historical context that lacked democratic governance institutions. But modern politicians have made similar claims. Richard Nixon, long before Watergate, warned a friend that "If you can't lie, you'll never go anywhere."[62] In his autobiography, Nixon elaborated:

> [A] leader has to deal with people and nations as they are, not as they should be. . . . Guile, vanity, dissembling—in other circumstances these might be unattractive habits, but to the leader they can be essential. . . . Roosevelt talked of keeping America out of war while maneuvering to bring it into war.[63]

However, as Nixon's own sorry experience makes clear, some presidents have found it all too easy to justify deception by equating their own interests with those of the country. Princeton historian Sean Wilentz notes that "Richard Nixon lied because he was trying to save his presidency, which was imperiled by his misdeeds. Franklin Delano Roosevelt misled the country . . . in order to advance a policy he thought would save the world, but which he knew would be difficult to sell politically. . . . What the public has to judge is whether [presidents] are lying for the good of the country—or for their own good."[64]

To aid that evaluation, Harvard political theorist Dennis Thompson has proposed the following framework:

> To be justified, official deception must satisfy stringent conditions. It should be in the service of a goal that is widely acceptable (not merely in the political interest of the president and his party). There should be no reasonable alternative means of achieving the goal (such as saying only no comment). It should be an isolated incident rather than part of a permanent practice. . . . [Presidential character should] tilt toward candor.[65]

Or, as other commentators have suggested, the only justifiable lies are those that the public itself would agree are justified, such as those necessary to protect lives or security operations in support of a legitimate policy.[66] A review of the most famous examples of presidential deception over the past century reveal almost none that meet this standard.

Lies to Promote National Security

One of the only lies that does seem justifiable is the one Nixon invoked: Franklin Roosevelt's deception about America's initial involvement in World War II. In 1940, Franklin Roosevelt was seeking an unprecedented third term as president. Public opinion was strongly opposed to entanglement in the European conflict, and he ran as a peace candidate. Roosevelt told voters: "I have said this before, but I shall say it again and again and again: your boys are not going to be sent into any foreign wars."[67] In fact, while professing peace, he was secretly meeting with Winston Churchill to provide Great Britain with urgently needed arms, and strategizing about how to justify increased American assistance.[68] According to Churchill, "The President . . . said he would wage war but not declare it . . . and that he would become more and more provocative. . . . Everything was to be done to force an 'incident' that could lead to war."[69] In 1941, Roosevelt succeeded. When, under presidential orders, an American ship followed a German submarine and signaled its location to the British Navy, the sub attacked. In describing that incident to the public, FDR claimed that the German sub was the aggressor, and failed to disclose what had provoked its action. Rather, he stated, "We have sought no shooting war with Hitler. We do not seek it now."[70] That deception helped secure the support he needed to move America closer to war. Although historians have generally supported Roosevelt's actions, they were not without cost. In 1971, Senator William Fulbright argued that "FDR's deviousness in a good cause, made it much easier for [Lyndon Johnson] to practice the same kind of deviousness in a bad cause": the escalation of the war in Vietnam.[71]

Another lie with a still less convincing national security justification involved Cold War espionage activity. In 1960, in the run-up to a nuclear test ban summit, Premier Nikita Khrushchev announced that the Soviets had shot down an American spy plane engaged in "aggressive provocation."[72] On the assumption that the pilot was dead and the plane destroyed, President Dwight D. Eisenhower approved a false statement that the mission had involved weather research rather than espionage. When Khrushchev then announced that he had rescued the pilot and analyzed wreckage from the plane, Eisenhower was forced to admit the truth. That effectively prevented a productive summit. Ironically, the deception served no significant purpose. The flights were no secret to the Soviets or to the United States' European allies. The lie was aimed only at the American public, and it undermined Eisenhower's most important assets—his reputation for honesty and the people's trust in government.[73] He later recognized as much. "I didn't realize how high a price we were going to have to pay for that lie," Eisenhower told a reporter. "And if I had to do it all over again, we would have kept our mouths shut."[74]

A final example of a deception often justified on national security grounds involves John F. Kennedy's secret agreement to remove American missiles in Turkey in exchange for Khrushchev's removal of Soviet missiles from Cuba. In 1962, the public story of the Cuban missile crisis was that Kennedy courageously stood up to foreign aggression and demanded unilateral withdrawal of the warheads. According to the administration: "we were eyeball to eyeball; the other guy just blinked."[75] Kennedy's national security advisor appeared on national television and stated unequivocally that the public knew "the whole deal" and that no secret negotiations had taken place.[76] The facts were otherwise. In 1982, on the twentieth anniversary of the crisis, six top Kennedy advisors joined a statement published in *Time* magazine that revealed the truth. The president, they explained, was willing to remove the Turkish missiles because they were of no significant strategic value, but was unwilling to reveal that fact because it "would have been misread as an unwilling concession granted in fear at the expense of an ally."[77] Yet Kennedy's motivations were not entirely selfless. If he had been forthcoming, he would have handed Republicans a political issue. Because he lied, he was hailed as a bipartisan hero.[78]

Yet as in other cases of presidential deception, the Cuba lie had long-term costs. Motivated partly out of a desire to save face, the Soviet Union embarked on a massive arms buildup, which encouraged the United States to do the same.[79] Moreover, "these lies begat other lies."[80] What Kennedy's Assistant Secretary of Defense Arthur Sylvester called the government's "right to lie" became firmly established as part of the president's "arsenal"; management of the news became seen as "one of the power factors in our quiver."[81] Some historians believe that this view was reinforced by the failure to expose the missile crisis deception for so many years after the need for secrecy had elapsed.[82]

Moreover, the personal interests that often drive presidents' policy deceptions have had disastrous consequences. The Vietnam war is a tragic example. In 1964, Lyndon Johnson assured the American public that "we are not about to send American boys nine or ten thousand miles away from home to do what Asian boys ought to be doing for themselves."[83] When asked whether the United States was preparing to move the Vietnam war into the North, he denied any such preparations, although his secretary of defense had previously briefed congressional committees on plans to do just that.[84] Escalating the war seemed the less politically risky choice. It would defang Johnson's hawkish opponents (Nixon and Goldwater), and leave doves with nowhere else to go.[85] As Johnson told one of his biographers, if "I . . . let the Communists take over South Vietnam, then I would be seen as a coward and my nation would be seen as an appeaser and we would both find it impossible to accomplish anything for anybody anywhere on the entire globe."[86] To him, withdrawal without victory would be personally humiliating, and could jeopardize his Great Society domestic agenda.[87] As LBJ put it, "if I don't go in now, they won't be talking about my civil rights bill or education or beautification. No sir, They'll push Vietnam right up my ass every time. Vietnam, Vietnam. Vietnam. Right up my ass."[88]

But of course that is exactly what opponents ultimately did and Johnson gave them ammunition by refusing to allow a candid debate about the prospects for military success. In May of 1964, LBJ told his national security advisor that "I don't see what we can ever hope to get out this, and I don't think we can get out."[89] But a month later, he misled Congress into giving him a blank check for escalation of hostilities. In June 1964, confusion arose over whether the North Vietnamese had opened fire on a US ship patrolling the Gulf of Tonkin. Although the ship's chief officer reported a torpedo attack, neither pilots flying overhead nor sonar experts from a nearby destroyer could detect any such weapons. Rather than wait for confirmation, as a key advisor suggested, Johnson called for retaliation. He also sought the Gulf of Tonkin Resolution from Congress, which would authorize "all necessary measures to repel any armed attacks against the armed forces of the United States and to prevent further aggression.[90] In arguing for the Resolution, the Johnson administration told Congress about the attack but not about the basis for doubting it.[91] Johnson himself later admitted that "for all I know, our Navy was shooting at whales out there."[92] But he was afraid that unless he responded forcefully and suppressed doubts, hawkish opponents including Nixon and Goldwater would accuse him of "vacillating or being an indecisive leader."[93]

Following his success in "misleading Congress and the country about the war's origins, Johnson proceeded to operate on the same model with regard to its escalation."[94] He did his best to conceal the extent and cost of US involvement out of concerns that disclosing the full amount would undercut financial support for his Great Society Program.[95] Yet his deceptions were so transparent that a joke circulated in Washington: "How do you know when Johnson is lying? "When his lips are moving."[96] In evaluating Johnson's performance, presidential historian Michael Beschloss points out that LBJ had inherited the military commitment from Kennedy, had resisted expanding the war through invasion of Cambodia or tactical nuclear weapons, and may have prevented a North Vietnamese expansion that granted other Southeast Asians nations time to strengthen and thus preserve their own democracies.[97] But Johnson also demonized critics, underestimated his enemy's resolve, and overestimated Americans' tolerance for an unprovoked war and a South Vietnam regime that was corrupt and unpopular among its own people. Most important, Johnson "did not fulfill one of the most basic responsibilities of a wartime President, which is to level with the American people when their sons and daughters are being asked to risk their lives."[98] Ultimately, the high price of war, in lives as a well as dollars, cost Johnson his presidency. His decision not to run again in 1968 paved the way for the election of Richard Nixon, who learned shockingly little from his predecessor's mistakes.

Like Johnson, Richard Nixon campaigned on a peace platform but ended up escalating the hostilities and lying about it.[99] In 1969 and 1970, his administration authorized the secret bombing of Cambodia to reach North Vietnamese operations there.[100] Secrecy was necessary, Nixon later admitted, to avoid "domestic antiwar protest. My administration was only two months old and I wanted to provoke as little public outcry as possible at the outset."[101] Nixon also misled the public about his interest in peace negotiations. Although he maintained at the time that "I would never do anything to encourage [South Vietnam] not to come to the table," notes discovered later revealed that he had ordered his closest aide to do just that.[102] His concern was that the prospect of peace could give his opponent, former vice president Hubert Humphrey, an edge in the 1968 election. For years, Nixon also misrepresented the success of American bombing campaigns. For example, in 1972, he maintained on CBS News that the campaigns had been "very very effective." Yet the next day he wrote to then national security advisor Henry Kissinger: "We have had 10 years of total control of the air in Laos and Vietnam. The result = Zilch. There is something wrong with the strategy or the Air Force."[103]

In another foreign policy debacle, the Iran Contra affair, the facts surrounding Ronald Reagan's misstatements are less clear. The scandal arose in 1984, when Shiite Muslims closely connected to leaders of Iran kidnapped seven US hostages. Iran was at war with Iraq, and willing to trade hostages for desperately needed military equipment. The administration, however, had a policy of not making concessions to terrorists, and was pressuring US allies not to sell arms to either Iran or Iraq. For the United States to sell such military equipment would also violate the Arms Export Control Act and the National Security Act. Reagan was chafing not only under these prohibitions but also under legislation that he had signed prohibiting the United States from assisting the Nicaraguan Contras who were fighting the Sandinista government. Oliver North, of the National Security Council, proposed using the money from a covert Iran arms sale to support the Contras.[104]

The plan was a disaster. When details were exposed, Congress held hearings and Reagan appointed an independent Commission to investigate the matter. The hearings concluded that the bargain had not improved relations with Iran or lessened terrorist threats. Although three hostages were released, three more were captured. The scandal also undermined American credibility abroad and relations between Congress and the president at home.[105]

How much Reagan knew about the debacle was contested. In 1986, after claims about the trade became public, Reagan initially maintained that they were "utterly false. . . . Our government has a firm policy not to capitulate to terrorist demands. . . . We did not —repeat—did not trade weapons or anything else for hostages."[106] Many historians believe that although he may not have known about the diversion of funds from Iran to the Contras, his discussions with aides encouraged it, and he almost certainly knew about the exchange of arms for hostages.[107] Yet he persisted in his denials, even after his secretary of state George Shultz told him that they were "factually wrong."[108] The Independent Counsel determined not to charge Reagan with wrongdoing despite "his hopelessly conflicting statements to the Commission" because it would be impossible to prove beyond a reasonable doubt that his misstatements were intentional or willful.[109] Reagan himself came to an uncomfortable conclusion. In an address to the nation, he acknowledged: "A few months ago, I told the American people I did not trade arms for hostages. My heart and my best intentions still tell me that's true, but the facts and the evidence tell me it's not."[110] Still, Reagan could not quite manage an apology for lying; he simply claimed that "I asked so many questions about the hostages welfare that I didn't ask enough about the specifics of the Iran plan."[111]

Reagan's vice president, George Herbert Walker Bush, similarly refused to acknowledge complicity. In the run-up to his campaign for the presidency, Bush claimed in his autobiography that he had been "deliberately excluded from key meetings involving details of the Iran Contra Operations."[112] In an interview with the *Washington Post,* he again denied that he was "in the loop" in discussions when Secretary of State George Shultz and Secretary of Defense Cap Weinberger had objected to the project.[113] But notes of the meeting indicate otherwise, and Shultz in his memoir reported being "astonished to read [Bush's] claim."[114] Moreover, Bush's decision to pardon six Iran Contra coconspirators effectively ended the Independent Counsel's investigation and compounded public mistrust.[115]

Decades later, statements by his son, George W. Bush, about the rationale for the war in Iraq also raised concerns about policy deception. In the aftermath of 9/11, President Bush made multiple statements about Iraq's nuclear capability that were subsequently found to be false.[116] He also claimed a level of certainty that, according to many historians, he knew or should have known was false as well. For example, in 2002, Bush told the Veterans of Foreign Wars that "there is no doubt that Saddam Hussein now has weapons of mass destruction. There is no doubt that he is amassing them to use against our friends, against our allies, and against us."[117] In a 2003 address to the nation, Bush similarly asserted that "intelligence gathered by this and other governments leaves no doubt that the Iraq regime continues to possess and conceal some of the most lethal weapons ever devised."[118] In Bush's view, to wait for confirmation by United Nations' weapons inspectors would have been a pointless and perilous delay: "time is not on our side."[119] Two months into the invasion, Bush proclaimed, "we have the weapons of mass destruction." In fact, no evidence of a functioning nuclear weapons program ever emerged.[120]

Bush and his administration officials also implied a link between Iraq and al-Qaeda, which helped a majority of Americans to believe, erroneously, that Saddam Hussein was personally involved in the 9/11 attack, and that Iraqis had been among those responsible.[121] According to the 9/11 Commission Report on the circumstances surrounding the attack, there was "no evidence" of a collaborative relationship between Iraq and al-Qaeda in developing any assaults on the United States.[122] Yet the drumbeat of Bush administration misstatements left an indelible imprint, and 42 percent of Americans continued to believed that that Saddam Hussein's government had been "directly involved" in the 2001 attacks.[123]

Although it is clear that Bush's statements misled the American public about the justifications for invading Iraq, it is less clear how much of the deception was attributable to faulty intelligence and how much to selective perception or willful blindness. In his memoir, Bush claimed "Nobody was lying. We were all wrong."[124] Critics, however, emphasize the reasons why they were wrong. In their view, Bush was looking for an excuse for war and some intelligence officers felt pressure to supply it.[125] Although a bipartisan Senate Intelligence Committee report found no evidence that the intelligence community deliberately distorted evidence regarding weapons of mass destruction, some members of that community recalled a climate that was by no means objective.[126] According to one intelligence department chief, any skepticism about such weapons was greeted with a suggestion to "think it over again."[127] Bush advisors reportedly believed that a quick victory would yield political payoffs, and worried that after all of the president's saber rattling following 9/11, a failure to bring down Hussein would lead to a "collapse of confidence."[128] As former *New York Times* columnist Frank Rich put it, "Bush was in a box of his own making."[129] One way out was to project a false certainty about enemy capabilities that came back to haunt him. In commenting on a series of Bush's false statements justifying the Iraq invasion, the best response one press aide could manage was "The President of the United States is not a fact checker."[130]

But he employed those who were. And according to many analysts, Bush displayed a "willful disregard for the truth" and did no "due diligence with the facts."[131] Nor did he correct himself when proven wrong. In 2003, when pressed by ABC's Diane Sawyer about his misstatements regarding weapons of mass destruction, Bush evaded the question and responded simply that "Saddam was a danger. And the world is better off because we got rid of him. . . . I made the right decision for America."[132] But the issue was not simply whether Saddam Hussein was a threat. It was also whether the regime change was worth the cost, now estimated at over $800 billion and hundreds of thousands of lives lost. And at a more fundamental level, the issue was whether the president should have made that decision without an informed public and congressional debate.[133] Most Americans thought not. By 2005, only a third approved of his handling of the war in Iraq and a majority believed that the administration had intentionally misled the nation into combat.[134] As the public now recognizes, a country that so fervently advocated democratic governance for Iraq should have displayed more faith in democratic processes at home.

Cover-Ups

The conventional wisdom in modern American politics has been that it is less the wrongdoing than the cover-up that will wreak havoc. That is surely the lesson of the Watergate scandal, but whether it still holds true may be tested by the scale of deception in the Trump administration.

In his acceptance speech at the 1968 Republican National Convention, presidential candidate Richard Nixon stated: "let us begin by committing our-selves to the truth—to see it like it is, and to tell it like it is—to find the truth and to live the truth."[135] Yet that speech preceded one of the most sustained cover-ups in American political history. In 1971, in an effort to stem politically embarrassing leaks and to obtain intelligence on opponents, Nixon author-ized creation of a team of operatives later known as the "plumbers." The fol-lowing year, five of the plumbers were caught breaking into the Democratic National Committee headquarters in the Watergate complex in order to repair a wiretap that they had previously placed. They were arrested and eventually traced to the White House.[136] Nixon issued a categorical denial: "I had no part in, nor was I aware of, subsequent efforts that may have been made to cover up Watergate."[137]

In fact, Nixon was directly involved in the effort, and his participation was recorded on a secret White House taping system. When a special prosecutor and Senate committee investigating the break-in demanded the tapes, Nixon provided altered transcripts. The Supreme Court then required Nixon to turn over the tapes. They revealed Nixon ordering an aide to instruct the CIA di-rector to call the director of the FBI and tell him to halt the Watergate in-vestigation because it might reveal classified information.[138] That, along with other evidence of obstruction of justice, led to articles of impeachment by the House Judiciary Committee and Nixon's resignation. He brought many others down with him. Twenty lawyers, including two attorney generals, were convicted of crimes involving perjury, fraud, obstruction of justice, burglary, and conspiracy.[139]

Nixon devoted much of his later years to claiming that what he did was "normal for the presidency . . . [and] that others had bugged, lied and covered up, perhaps even more than he."[140] In one of his memoirs, he characterized his denial of a cover-up as an "error of recollection" and claimed that he was the victim of a "political vendetta."[141] On French television in Paris in 1978, he even maintained, "I was not lying. I said things that later on seemed to be untrue."[142] In the end, it was Nixon's self-deception that created a climate in which public deception seemed normal.

Policy Deception

Nikita Khrushchev is credited with claiming that "politicians are the same all over. They promise to build a bridge even where there is no river." American presidents are no exception. It is, however, important to distinguish between broken promises and knowing deception. Almost all candidates make claims that turn out to be exaggerated or imprudent in light of new information or changed circumstances. George H. W. Bush famously told the American public, "Read my lips. No new taxes."[143] He reneged. In 2003, his son stood under the now infamous "MISSION ACCOMPLISHED" banner and claimed that "Iraq is free," and that "major combat operations in Iraq have ended."[144] Barack Obama, in pushing for the Affordable Care Act, promised "If you like your doctor or health care plan you can keep it." When the new legislation went into effect in 2013, millions of Americans received cancellation notices.[145] Obama later apologized: "I am sorry that they . . . are finding themselves in this situation based on assurances they got from me."[146] Donald Trump promised during the campaign that his replacement for the Affordable Care Act would be "much less expensive" and "everybody's going to get covered." It would be "better health care, much better, for less money."[147] However the Congressional Budget Office estimated that the Republican substitute would leave 24 million Americans without coverage by 2026 and would dramatically increase costs for older Americans of limited means.[148] After congressional passage of tax reform legislation that the administration had promised, Trump repeated over fifty times the falsehood that it constituted the largest cut in history; Treasury Department data showed that it ranked eighth.[149] Although voters expect a certain level of puffing in political campaigns, they lose trust in the political process when critical pledges routinely go unfulfilled or accomplishments are grossly exaggerated.

Of similar concern are false but politically expedient policy-related claims. For example, Ronald Reagan justified major welfare cuts based on a mythical Chicago "welfare queen" who used eighty names, thirty addresses, and twelve social security cards to bilk the government out of $150,000. The actual woman on which the story was based used two aliases to collect $8,000. Reagan continued to use his version of the story even after the press pointed out the actual facts of the case.[150] When a speechwriter balked at including an apocryphal story that he knew was untrue, Reagan refused to take it out. The writer told him, " 'It will diminish your speech when it comes out that this is false.' Reagan reportedly shook his head and said, 'It's too good a story.' "[151] When a reporter exposed another of his false claims, Reagan responded that he didn't remember making it but if he did, he had probably just "read something from a piece of paper that had been placed in front of

him."[152] David Gergen, one of Reagan's communication aides, labeled these un-
founded claims "parables."[153] But these parables can do substantial damage when
they shape public perceptions and drive policy agendas. The myth of the welfare
queen served to justify punitive welfare programs for decades.[154]

Donald Trump's claims about immigrants do similar damage. During his
presidential campaign, Trump asserted that Mexicans crossing the border were
"bringing drugs, they're bringing crime, they're rapists."[155] He maintained,
without factual support, that "thousands and thousands" of Muslims in New
Jersey cheered the 9/11 attack, and when challenged, he repeated the claim and
mocked the disabled reporter who disputed it.[156] He justified his punitive deportation policies with false claims about immigrants' disproportionate criminal
activities. In fact, those individuals, including undocumented residents, have
lower crime and incarceration rates than native-born citizens.[157] Trump insisted
that a border wall was necessary to deal with a national security crisis involving
terrorists, crime, and drugs. Yet when he made those claims, the number of people
apprehended was near a forty-five-year low, there was not a single known case of
terrorists sneaking into the United States along unfenced areas, and virtually all
illegal drugs came through legal points of entry.[158]

Such assertions were part of a broader pattern of dishonesty, unprecedented
in scope. *PolitiFact* calculated that only 2 percent of Trump's campaign claims
were true and only 7 percent were mostly true. Of the remainder, 42 percent were
false, another 15 percent were mostly false, and 18 percent were "pants on fire"
false; the dishonesty rate was a stunning 75 percent.[159] In March 2016, when three
Politico reporters fact-checked Trump's statements for a week, they found that he
had made "roughly one misstatement every five minutes."[160] The *Huffington Post*
chronicled seventy-one inaccuracies in single hour-long town hall session—more
than one a minute.[161] A *Washington Post* review of his first year in office found
over two thousand false claims, an average of more than five a day. Seventy claims
were repeated three or more times, even in the face of repeated corrections.[162]
A *New York Times* overview, using a slightly stricter standard of "demonstrably
and substantially false statements," concluded that Trump told three times as
many falsehoods during his first ten months in office than Obama did during his
entire eight-year presidency.[163]

What is even more worrisome is Trump's lack of concern about his dishonesty. As a *Media Matters* editorial put it, Trump is a "remorseless liar," and "there's
no indication that he . . . even cares if he gets caught. . . . He cannot not tell lies. In
other words, it's not a political strategy. It's a character defect."[164] It is one that is
long-standing. A 1990 *Vanity Fair* profile quoted his lawyer as saying, "Donald is
a believer in the big lie theory. If you say something again and again, people will
believe you."[165] Trump's typical response to exposure has been to double down on

a falsehood and lie about lying. He denies that he said it, or blames "fake news," "incompetent dishonest" reporters, the "failing" *New York Times,* or the "pathetic" CNN for getting the story wrong.[166]

Alternatively, he maintains that he was simply repeating what others had said. For example, in the first month of his presidency, Trump claimed without substantiation that President Obama and the British intelligence service had wiretapped him in Trump Tower.[167] When challenged, Trump refused to apologize and maintained that his statement about British surveillance had just repeated an assertion made by a Fox News commentator. Fox disavowed the assertion.[168] A leader of Britain's Liberal Democrat party called the Trump administration's refusal to back down "shameful," and added that the president was "compromising the vital UK-US security relationship to cover his own embarrassment."[169] In another discomfiting instance, Trump faced evidence that he had falsely denied helping to draft a misrepresentation about one of his son's Russia meetings. Trump responded simply that his lie was "irrelevant" because it was "not a statement to a high tribunal of judges." It was only a statement "to the phony New York Times."[170]

Trump has also appeared untroubled by inconsistency or flat out fabrication. After he fired FBI Director James Comey, Trump's aides dutifully if implausibly maintained that the action "has nothing to do with Russia." Then just two days later, Trump himself admitted on national television that the firing was driven by Comey's refusal to clear him of the "the Russia thing."[171] In some instances, Trump seemed almost to delight in deception.[172] When recounting a conversation with the Canadian prime minister Justin Trudeau, Trump recalled challenging Trudeau's assertion that the United States had no trade deficit with Canada. According to Trump's account, "I said, 'Wrong, Justin you do.'" But "I didn't even know. . . . I had no idea."[173] Four months into his administration, a *New York Times* editorial concluded that "any relationship between White House statements and accuracy seems coincidental."[174] Or, in the words of former FBI director James Comey, Trump is simply "untethered to truth."[175]

Trump's lies do serious damage, particularly since they are repeated in the news and retweeted on social media more often than his other statements.[176] What his aide Kellyanne Conway labeled "alternative facts" divert media attention and distort public understanding. As one commentator noted, "President Trump's lies alone have become their own beat, forcing publications to devote precious resources to invalidating the many outrageous claims he makes daily, sometimes within a single interview."[177] Moreover, Trump is setting a worrisome example among colleagues. In what is becoming the new political normal, Obama observes, "we see the utter loss of shame among political leaders where they're caught in a lie and they just double down and they lie some more."[178]

Although we like to assume that the corrective for false speech is more speech, that remedy is often fruitless. As psychologists have found, "when we are overwhelmed with false or potentially false, statements, our brains pretty quickly become so overworked that we stop trying to sift through everything."[179] In the face of such cognitive overload, "it doesn't matter how implausible the statements are . . . people will inevitably absorb some."[180] And when such lies are consistent with preconceptions or politically preferred views, then attempts at correction can backfire, and plant the misinformation even more firmly in peoples' minds.[181] Such research helps explain why 78 percent of Trump supporters thought that the news media regularly produced false stories, but only 17 percent thought that the Trump administration did so.[182]

Yet Trump appears utterly unconcerned with the corrosive effects of repeated misstatements. In his view, as he explained in *The Art of the Comeback,* "a little hyperbole never hurts."[183] When pressed on this issue by a *Time* reporter, he responded simply "I can't be doing so badly, because I'm President and you're not."[184]

The Personal and the Political

Most lies in everyday life serve self-interests, such as the desire to avoid embarrassment, to enhance our reputation, or to gain some other personal or financial advantage.[185] Politicians are no exception. A celebrated account of such misstatements involves Huey Long's first race for governor in Louisiana. Before an audience including a large number of Catholic as well as Baptist voters, Long recounted a story from his youth: "When I was a boy, I would get up six o'clock in the morning on Sunday, and I would hitch our old horse up to the buggy and I would take my Catholic grandparents to mass. I would bring them home, and at ten o'clock I would hitch the old horse up again and I would take my Baptist grandparents to church." The anecdote was effective, and later that evening, a local political leader said admiringly, "Why, Huey, you've been holding out on us. I didn't know you had any Catholic grandparents." "Don't be a damn fool," Long responded. "We didn't even have a horse."[186]

For modern American presidents, the prevalence of fact checkers has made such deception more costly, but the urge to embellish or evade persists. Some relatively harmless examples of lies about personal matters include:

- John Kennedy told *Time* magazine he could read twelve hundred words a minute (a figure pulled out of thin air);
- Lyndon Johnson told troops that his great great grandfather "died at the Alamo" (he didn't);

- Bill Clinton claimed that he had heard about the Iowa caucuses since he was a little boy (they started when he was in graduate school);
- Nixon told a French audience that he had majored in French (he majored in history),
- Donald Trump repeatedly inflated the size of his inaugural crowds and asked the National Park Service to release more flattering photographs that would reflect a larger audience.[187]

Of greater concern are presidents' false or misleading statements about prior misconduct. George W. Bush claimed that he concealed a youthful drunk driving arrest not for political reasons but in order to avoid being "a bad role model" for his teenage daughters. [188] The failure to be forthright eroded support among his base, and his memoir characterized the decision as "the single costliest political mistake I ever made."[189] Bill Clinton earned the nickname "Slick Willie" for false or misleading answers to a variety of questions including draft avoidance during the Vietnam war, extramarital affairs, and marijuana use in which he "didn't inhale."[190] His first response to claims of financial misconduct and conflicts of interest arising from a "Whitewater" Arkansas investment was to "brush [them] aside, promise full cooperation, and then frustrate every inquiry."[191] He followed up with "evasions, half-truths, and misstatements."[192]

Other troubling issues involve presidents' dishonesty about their health. Woodrow Wilson made transparency a campaign issue in 1912, but after suffering a debilitating stroke, he kept his condition secret.[193] Franklin Roosevelt, with the cooperation of the press, misled the public about disabilities resulting from polio; few Americans realized he spent most of his presidency in a wheelchair, and could not stand erect without support or walk more than a few yards.[194] Although he was the most photographed American of his era, only one photograph of him in a wheelchair was seen publicly in his lifetime.[195] Of course, given Americans' prejudices concerning disabilities at the time, FDR's caution was understandable. But he also deceived voters about his other health issues. At the height of World War II, the commander in chief was working at most four hours a day and sometimes as little as one or two, due to medical conditions including hypertensive heart disease, cardiac failure, and acute bronchitis.[196]

So too, when a reporter asked John Kennedy if he had Addison's disease, a malfunction of the adrenal gland that could be fatal, he falsely responded: "I never had Addison's disease . . . and my health is excellent."[197] Although he cultivated an image of vitality, Kennedy had multiple ailments and was in chronic pain from a back injury stemming from football at Harvard and compounded during the war.[198] Some historians doubt that he would have been nominated or elected if his medical problems had been known.[199] But there was also an admirable side to his stoicism and his willingness to perform presidential duties without complaint, feigning a vigor that he rarely had.[200]

Sex

Politicians also lie about sex. A lot.[201] Eighteen American presidents had known sexual affairs, almost all involving adultery.[202] Many were not required to lie about them, at least publicly, because the press traditionally observed a gentlemen's agreement to remain silent. John Kennedy was a chronic philanderer, and Lyndon Johnson wanted to equal if not surpass that record. He claimed to have had "more women by accident than Kennedy had on purpose."[203] And he was explicit about expecting the media to remain discrete. He reportedly told a group of journalists, "You may see me coming in and out of a few women's bedrooms while I am in the White House, but just remember, that is none of your business."[204]

The mainstream media's willingness to engage in such self-censorship broke down during the presidential campaign of 1988, when the reckless infidelity of front-runner Gary Hart goaded reporters into coverage. He invited them to "put a tail on me," and predicted, "they'll be bored."[205] They did, and they weren't. His brazen lies about promiscuity ended his campaign. When Bill Clinton ran for president in 1992, claims about what one aid called his "bimbo eruptions" made front page news.[206] His tendency was to "spin [his] way out of it" and to view dissembling as justified under the circumstance.[207] As he once famously claimed, "Nearly everyone will lie to you, given the right circumstances."[208] And he believed that he had such circumstances. During his first presidential campaign, he appeared on national television denying an affair with Gennifer Flowers but acknowledging having caused "pain in my marriage."[209] That was enough to put the matter temporarily to rest. Yet although he was elected, it was with the lowest personal character rating since polls had been taken.[210] In 1994 surveys, only a third of Americans rated Clinton good on ethical values and only half thought he had the honesty and integrity to serve effectively as president.[211]

Matters got worse. The difficulties stemmed from a sexual harassment suit brought by Paula Jones, an Arkansas state employee. She claimed that while Clinton was governor, he unzipped his fly, dropped his pants, and invited her to offer oral sex. When she refused, he reportedly suggested that they keep this "between ourselves."[212] She didn't. She sued. When Clinton denied the charges, Jones's lawyers named many other women as potential trial witnesses. The ostensible point was to establish that Clinton had a habit of soliciting sex with other government employees, but the aim was also to embarrass the president. One of those potential witnesses was Monica Lewinsky. She was a twenty-two-year-old White House intern who had angled for Clinton's attention in 1995 and received it. Lewinsky could not resist sharing details of their sexual relationship with a colleague at the Pentagon, who taped their phone conversations and tipped off Jones's lawyers. They turned the tapes over to Independent Counsel Kenneth Starr, who was investigating the Clintons' involvement in Whitewater land deals.[213] Starr then broadened his inquiry to include possible perjury and obstruction of justice in connection with the *Jones* case.

After reviewing some poll numbers, Clinton did what they suggested was politically expedient.[214] On national television he claimed, "I did not have sexual relations with that woman, Miss Lewinsky."[215] His lawyer made a similar denial in the *Jones* case. Unfortunately for Clinton, Starr had physical evidence as well as sworn testimony from Lewinsky indicating otherwise. He brought Clinton before a grand jury, and forced him to acknowledge "inappropriate intimate physical contact" with Lewinsky. Clinton was, however, inexplicably evasive about whether he and Lewinsky had ever been alone, responding that "it depends on how you define alone."[216] On eighty-four occasions during his grand jury testimony, he replied to a question by claiming that he couldn't remember. To most observers, this inability to recall facts such as whether he and Lewinsky were alone during oral sex seemed like an exercise in "optional amnesia."[217] As *New York Times* columnist Maureen Dowd noted, "he is like the cursed girl in the fairy tale: every time he opens his mouth, a toad jumps out."[218]

According to the Republican prosecutor in the House Impeachment proceedings, Clinton ultimately had "no one left to lie to."[219] Following his grand jury testimony, in a nationally televised address, he acknowledged his infidelity. Sounding combative as well as contrite, he admitted engaging in a relationship that was "not appropriate. In fact it was wrong. It constituted a critical lapse in judgment and a personal failure on my part for which I am solely and completely responsible."[220] However, he also reminded viewers that the questions had been asked in a "politically inspired lawsuit," and insisted that the Whitewater investigation had "gone on too long, cost too much and hurt too many innocent people. . . . Even presidents have private lives. It is time to stop the pursuit of personal destruction and the prying into private lives and get on with our national life."[221]

The public largely agreed. Two-thirds of Americans thought that the matter was private and had nothing to do with his performance as president.[222] After the Republican-controlled House of Representatives voted to impeach Clinton for perjury and obstruction of justice, the Democratic-controlled Senate acquitted him. About 60 percent of the public continued to approve of his performance in office, although close to that number also thought that he was not a "man of character."[223] When asked how the country could avoid scandals like Clinton's, 34 percent of Americans said by electing presidents with high moral character;

60 percent said by making sure a president's life stays private.[224] Yet when it comes to privacy, what the public says it wants is not what its behavior rewards. Television news ratings soared during the Clinton-Lewinsky scandal, and several programs recorded their highest ever audiences.[225] For many Americans, there is "something secretly gratifying about nabbing so many national leaders with their pants—and their contradictions—around their ankles."[226] Sex sells, and in a world of intense media competition with a 24-7 news cycle to fill, it is hard for journalists to resist.

With Trump, there was no pretense of resistance, partly because so little of his problematic conduct required real investigation. Trump's extramarital affairs were well known before his run for president, and in *The Art of the Comeback*, he even bragged about his adultery with "seemingly very happily married and important women."[227] He was also caught on tape bragging about how "when you're a star," women are fine if you "Grab 'em by the pussy."[228] At the time this book went to press, at least nineteen women had publicly claimed that they had extramarital affairs with Trump or accused him of sexual misconduct.[229] Details had also surfaced about both a Playboy model and a porn star whom his lawyers had paid for silence about their sexual relationships with Trump.[230] Yet none of this seemed to undermine Trump's support among his base, including even evangelical voters. When pollsters asked in 2016 whether Americans thought elected officials "who commit immoral acts in their private life can still behave ethically and fulfill their duties in their public and professional life," 61 percent said yes, up from 44 percent in 2011. Among evangelicals, 72 percent said yes, up from 30 percent just five years earlier.[231] And in a 2018 Gallup poll, three-quarters of Republicans rated Trump either very strong (22 percent) or somewhat strong (55 percent) in moral leadership.[232]

Yet at the same time that much of the public gave Trump a pass on his sexual behavior, this permissiveness did not carry over to other politicians. The #MeToo movement signaled a renewed concern about sexually abusive or exploitative behavior by public figures. In 2017 and 2018, a record number of prominent male political leaders were forced to resign over sexual misconduct, some far less damning than Trump's. It is by no means clear that his experience signals the irrelevance of sex lives for politicians in general or future presidential candidates in particular.

How much we should care about such conduct is another matter. Certainly society pays a price when its choices for leadership narrow to those willing to put their entire sexual histories on public display.[233] And the disproportionate attention that the media gives to personal sexual conduct can divert attention from issues of policy and performance. But particularly for offices such as president, where the politician serves as a moral role model for the nation, private behavior matters. How much depends on the seriousness of the misconduct and the attitudes toward women and truth that it reflects. As journalist Matt Bai points out, American history is full of examples of men who were "crappy husbands . . . but great stewards of the state, just as we had thoroughly decent men who couldn't summon the executive skills to run a bake sale."[234] Some presidents, including Clinton, who were reckless in personal choices involving sex, were generally prudent in matters of state. And some male leaders who exploited women in private supported women's issues in public. Many feminists rallied around Bill Clinton for precisely that reason. However Trump has no such record. And the views toward women and sexual assault that he has exhibited in his public statements, policy priorities, and support for government officials and candidates accused of sexual misconduct suggests that for him, the personal and political are inextricably linked.[235]

Temperament

For any leadership position, but especially one with the stresses and responsibilities of president, individuals need those qualities of character that we loosely describe as "temperament." These include self-discipline, self-control, self-awareness, empathy, emotional intelligence, and a willingness to accept criticism and personal responsibility. Stanley Renshon, a psychoanalyst and political scientist, notes that temperament is integral to character and critical for presidential effectiveness.[236] Supreme Court Justice Oliver Wendell Holmes Jr. famously said of President Franklin Roosevelt that he had "a second-class intellect but a first class temperament."[237] And it is temperament that is most essential for governance. Political leaders can draw on the intelligence of advisors, but they need the qualities of character that enable them to listen to such advice and to unite others in pursuit of societal interests. In 2016, a letter by fifty Republicans who had served in senior national security and foreign policy positions identified the character attributes that were most important for a commander in chief. This person "must encourage consideration of conflicting views; and must acknowledge errors and learn from them . . . [President] must be disciplined, control emotions, and act only after reflection and careful deliberation."[238]

Self-Awareness

Of all these qualities, self-awareness is among the most important. Presidents who have some appreciation of their failings and fallibility are best able to prevent and correct misjudgments. This capacity includes a willingness to learn from criticism and mistakes. A distinguishing characteristic of successful leaders is their openness to challenge and critique.[239] For example, President Kennedy learned from his administration's failed "Bay of Pigs" invasion of Cuba that he needed to encourage uninhibited debate and dissenting views. His willingness to do just that helped him defuse the Cuban missile crisis.[240]

Barack Obama has a mixed history along these lines. Some aides and biographers have credited him with exceptional self-awareness and "openness in engaging people with whom he disagrees."[241] In 2008, when asked about his national security team, which included his former opponent, Hillary Clinton, Obama responded:

> I am a strong believer in strong personalities and strong opinions. I think this is how the best decisions are made. One of the dangers in a White House based on my reading of history is that you get wrapped up in group think and everybody agrees with everything and there is no dissenting view. So I am going to be welcoming a vigorous debate inside the White House.[242]

Subsequent reports indicated that Obama did, in fact, initially develop a "culture of debate" on major foreign policy decisions that invited disagreement and pushback.[243] But as his administration wore on, many insiders and commentators faulted his isolation, and insularity. Seldom did he reach for advice beyond a tight circle of the White House, and too often heard only what he wanted to hear.[244]

Obama did, however, try to respond to criticisms that he had a "tendency to talk over or down to people."[245] Although by all accounts Obama remained "supremely confident in his intellect," he also acknowledged that he "might be wrong," and he remained aware of the risks of arrogance.[246] In *The Audacity of Hope*, he recalled how in a *Time* magazine piece he had compared his own struggles to those of Lincoln, and then was rightly called out by Peggy Noonan. She wrote, "This week comes the previously careful Sen. Barack Obama, flapping his wings in *Time* magazine and explaining that he's a lot like Abraham Lincoln only sort of better." Obama's response was a rueful "Ouch."[247]

By contrast, other presidents suffered from a lack of self-awareness and inability to tolerate dissent. Richard Nixon was famously hostile toward critics, and his administration drew up an "enemies list" of individuals who deserved retaliation.[248] Lyndon Johnson was similarly unwilling to accept criticism or to hear doubts about his decisions.[249] He interpreted dissent as disloyalty, "and to him loyalty was all."[250] When Vice President Humphrey expressed concerns about attacking North Vietnam, Johnson was furious and excluded him from meetings of the National Security Council for months.[251]

Donald Trump's hypersensitivity to criticism is equally apparent and equally corrosive.[252] He is notoriously "thin skinned and combative," and intolerant of dissent, no matter how legitimate.[253] He dismisses opponents as "losers," and media critics as "enem[ies] of the people" and mouthpieces for "fake news."[254] His assaults on the justice system sacrifice "public safety and national security on the altar of his own ego."[255] When confronted by critics, he stews in self-pity, complaining that "No politician in history has been treated worse, more un-fairly."[256] To avoid challenge, he once went for over a year without a press confer-ence, compared with Obama, who held eleven in his first year.[257] He repeatedly dismissed an investigation into his campaign's ties with Russia as a "witch hunt," and denounced his former FBI director as a "slimeball."[258] During rallies, he encouraged supporters to rough up protestors—and confessed that he would like to punch one of them in the face.[259] Even his friends and advisors complained that Trump "has these yes-men around him, and now he's living in a parallel world," a kind of "fortress Trump."[260] His long-time secretary once confessed that "I've kept my job this long by knowing I must never bring him bad news."[261] Trump's campaign staff similarly found that the best way to keep Trump's inflammatory tweets under control was to feed him a steady stream of praise. And when they failed to find enough praise, they drummed some up from friendly outlets and made sure it landed on Trump's desk.[262]

Trump's friends and aides are reportedly reluctant to give him "negative feed-back" and have stressed the importance of showing him deference, flattery, and a change of subject if he nurses a grudge.[263] As Trump famously acknowledged in one of his autobiographies, "I love getting even," and the way he manages it is seldom pretty.[264] He humiliates top officials with his public dismissals; FBI Director James Comey learned about his on television. Staff have also have warned against leaving him alone too long.[265] Their descriptions evoke a portrait of a petulant toddler, not a responsible leader of the free world.

Inside accounts of the White House reveal a decision-making style that is im-pulsive, erratic, and ill informed. When cabinet secretaries present facts that un-dercut his instincts, such as those on trade and tariffs, his response is "I don't want to hear that. It's all bullshit."[266] Rex Tillerson, then secretary of state, reportedly complained that the president "can't make a decision. He doesn't know how to make a decision. He won't make a decision. He makes a decision then changes his mind a couple of days later."[267] To derail what they believe are Trump's "most impulsive and dangerous orders," some top members of his administration re-portedly have worked together to delay or obstruct his demands, sometimes even removing draft orders from his desk before he can sign them.[268] Experts note that Trump would be unable to pass the test for "personal reliability" required of any Air Force officer with connections to nuclear weapons. It includes thirty-seven questions about physical and psychological health designed to screen out individuals with Trump's emotional volatility.[269]

What makes that trait even more worrisome is its combination with arrogance, a quality that three-quarters of citizens around the world use to describe Trump.[270] His self-aggrandizing self-image and intolerance of criticism discourages any reflection about his own limitations or mistakes. As he explained to one of his biographers, "I don't like to analyze myself because I might not like what I see."[271] Even if meant as self-deprecating wit, the portrait is all too accurate. Trump is incapable of acknowledging error. Former economic advisor Gary Cohn noted, "He's never been wrong yet. . . . He's not going to admit he's wrong, ever."[272] In the wake of widely unpopular administration policies, such as separating immigrant families at the border, or cuts in healthcare coverage, Trump blames Democrats.[273] He also berates the press because its accounts "do not sync up with t[his] glossy, self-regarding image."[274] His belief in his own infallibility is particularly alarming, given his lack of experience in politics and international relations. Yet when asked during the campaign whom he consulted on foreign policy, he said "my primary consultant is myself," and when accepting the Republican nomination, he claimed, "nobody knows the system better than me, which is why I alone can fix it."[275] After taking office, when a reporter asked what he was thankful for at Thanksgiving, Trump said "himself" because he had made a "tremendous difference in this country."[276] Such "self-aggrandizement untethered to fact" has shielded him from the self-corrections necessary for effective governance.[277]

Although Trump and his Twitter tirades set a new low for presidential temperament, the tendency to shift blame, deflect responsibility, and lose control hobbled other contemporary leaders as well. Nixon attributed the failures in Vietnam to Kennedy and Johnson. "They got us in. I didn't," he told David Frost in a celebrated interview.[278] And he blamed biased media coverage for his early unsuccessful campaigns for the presidency and the California governorship. Following his California concession speech, he famously told the press that they had distorted stories about him for sixteen years, and now "You won't have Nixon to kick around anymore." To his aghast aide, he added, "These guys deserved it," a position he defended in his memoir.[279] His feelings of persecution frequently erupted in rage.[280] He once even slapped a Democratic Party worker during a political rally.[281]

Bill Clinton also had an explosive temper, which erupted when anyone or anything reminded him that his performance had failed to match his promises.[282] According to top aide George Stephanopoulos, Clinton had a "morning roar," a "night cap" tirade, and a prolonged "slow boil," prompted by something that he couldn't control or a mistake that he didn't want to admit.[283] Another close advisor noted that "everything that went wrong was somebody else's fault. Never his."[284]

According to biographers, Clinton tended "to see himself as victim. He . . . not only lashes out at his staff, but also demonizes his opponents."[285] When an aide's mistake kept supporters from a campaign event, Clinton exploded: "I want him dead, dead. . . . I want him horsewhipped."[286] He blamed his failure to end sexual orientation discrimination in the military on his opponents, and falsely claimed that they had forced the issue.[287] The press was also a target. He told one *Rolling Stone* reporter: "I have fought more damn battles here for more things than any President in the last twenty years . . . and have not gotten one damn bit of credit for it from the knee-jerk liberal press, and I am sick and tired of it and you can put that in the damn article."[288]

Work Ethic

Another character attribute that is critical to effectiveness involves a work ethic, and the perseverance required for addressing complex problems. Lyndon Johnson was able to push through an ambitious domestic policy agenda in part because he "interacted with senators and representatives on a daily and even hourly basis." He became "personally familiar with the details of the more than one thousand major bills Congress considered during this period . . . and got to know its members 'even better than they [knew] themselves.' "[289] Clinton also had a prodigious capacity for work, but the downside was his inability to set limits for either himself or his staff. He held meetings at all hours on evenings and weekends, with almost ruinous effects on the lives of his aides and the quality of his work.[290] As one advisor put it, "there are only twenty four hours in the day and you should sleep a few of them." If you try to be in control of everything, "you can't be effective on anything."[291] Hillary Clinton would buttonhole aides to try to get them to force her husband to take a break, and aides would buttonhole Hillary to ask her to do the same.[292]

Ronald Reagan was entirely different. He was notoriously uninformed and uninterested in policy. He was also not particularly worried about being uninformed.[293] Rather than preparing for a crucial presidential debate, Reagan left his briefing book unopened and spent eight hours with advisors watching old movies, most of them his.[294] Once elected, Reagan generally made decisions based on options that aides presented, without questioning or seeking to shape those choices.[295] "Tell me what you want me to say," he would instruct his staff.[296] He kept bankers hours and sometimes fell asleep during cabinet meetings.[297] When accused of being lazy, he responded, "I know hard work never killed anyone but I figure, why take a chance."[298]

Barack Obama had a mixed record. He was impressively diligent on matters of policy. He reportedly slept only four hours at night and routinely worked until midnight.[299] But he was also faulted for inattention to detail, inadequate management, and unwillingness to cultivate relationships with lawmakers.[300] In his first term, he took thirteen vacations, and played over a hundred rounds of golf, almost always with close friends or aides.[301] His "approach to social engagement with lawmakers" was, by all accounts, "almost nonexistent."[302]

Donald Trump, however, is in a league of his own. He has displayed a stunning unwillingness to become informed and a similar lack of concern about his ignorance. As one *Time* magazine profile noted during his presidential campaign, Trump "not only doesn't sweat the details of policy, he sometimes won't even give them a glance."[303] He told a *Time* reporter, "I come from these rallies and get in here, and they want me to look at documents. I can't do it."[304] On even the most important policy issues, such as healthcare, Trump displayed stunning ignorance about the contents of his own proposals.[305] Shortly after he took office, Trump met with governors to discuss his promised repeal of Obamacare. He emerged and acknowledged "It's an unbelievably complex subject. Nobody knew that health care could be so complicated."[306] Everyone knew.

In the run-up to the presidency, Trump repeatedly criticized Barack Obama for spending too much time on the golf course and too little time on the nation's business, and promised to do otherwise himself.[307] In one representative tweet, Trump asked, "Can you believe that, with all the problems and difficulties facing the US, President Obama spent the day playing golf."[308] During the campaign, and after the election, he repeatedly reassured voters, "I'm going to be working for you; I'm not going to have time to go play golf."[309] Yet in his first year, he spent more than ninety days at a golf club, almost as much as Obama spent his entire first term.[310] And that comparison is based only on Trump's known games; staff members have been so embarrassed that they have gone to considerable pains to avoid disclosing how much time he spends golfing.[311] Two less visible costs of the president's leisure life is the price imposed on taxpayers and the symbolic message it sends from the national role model. According to the Government Accounting Office, each trip to Mar-a-Lago costs about $3.6 million, largely due to security.[312] And who can take seriously the president's suggestion that Americans should observe Martin Luther King Day through acts of civic work and community service, while he played golf at his private course?[313]

The problem is not just the amount of time Trump declines to spend on governance obligations; it is also that he lacks the attention span necessary to master policy choices. The ghostwriter on his book *The Art of the Deal* summarized widespread views that Trump "can't keep focused on anything other than his own self aggrandizement."[314] One of his first decisions after his election victory was to dispense with the tradition of daily intelligence briefings, which he found boring and redundant. "I'm like a smart person," he explained, "I get it when I need it."[315] In the run-up to his summit with North Korean leader Kim Jong Un, Trump told the press, "I don't think I have to prepare very much. It's about the attitude. It's about willingness to get things done."[316] The intelligence community worries that if a crisis or emergency arises, and the president has to make an immediate decision, he may lack the background knowledge necessary for an informed judgment.

Aides also have expressed concern about the constraints that Trump has put on the memos that he will at least look at. "I want it short," and "I like as little as possible," he has told staff and the media.[317] Rather than spend time on boring briefings or memos, Trump spends hours every day in front of a television, flipping channels looking for news about himself. And when he doesn't like what he sees, he tweets his frustrations.[318] In an effort to encourage the president to read their memos, National Security council officials have inserted Trump's name in as many paragraphs as possible because, as one explained, "he keeps reading if he's mentioned."[319] Some intelligence officials have reported warnings not to give the President any assessments that contradict his public stance.[320] Other staff have been instructed to keep memos to a single page, to provide only three in daily briefings, and to include only facts supporting the main position, not dissenting views.[321] As a result, Trump gets only a quarter as much information as Obama received, and nothing that might challenge the party line.[322] Trump is the first president without any political or military experience, and even his own cabinet members and prominent Republican Congressional leaders are reportedly "rattled" by his lack of understanding of complex policy issues.[323]

Not only does Trump avoid any heavy lifting on substantive matters, he also disdains the kind of serious reading that helped his predecessors learn from past experience: history, biography, and social criticism. Rather, as Trump explained in a series of media interviews, he did not need to read extensively because he reaches the right decisions "with very little knowledge other than the knowledge I [already had] . . . because I have a lot of common sense and I have a lot of business ability."[324] Nor did he need to accept common wisdom among scientific experts on climate change because he had an uncle who was an MIT professor, and though the two did not discuss the issue, Trump himself had a "natural instinct for science."[325] That combination of arrogance and ignorance, along with Trump's total lack of political experience, could become truly toxic in crisis situations. The problem is compounded by Trump's willingness to appoint key advisors and even cabinet secretaries with almost no relevant expertise because they share his policy preferences and give him unqualified loyalty. Betsy DeVos as Secretary of Education and Ben Carson as head of Housing and Urban Development are only the most notorious examples.[326] Trump explained to James Comey, "I need loyalty. I expect loyalty."[327] He gets it or subordinates are gone.

During the first 2016 presidential debate, Trump claimed that "my strongest asset—maybe by far—is my temperament. I have a winning temperament. I know how to win."[328] A *New York Times*/CBS Poll around the same time found that less than a third of Americans agreed that Trump had the kind of temperament necessary to be a good president.[329] That so many individuals voted for him anyway speaks volumes about the lack of priority that the public places on character issues.

Ambition and Integrity

Other qualities that matter in politics are ambition and integrity, and how a candidate resolves tensions between them. Of course, no one campaigns for president without a strong desire for power and achievement.[330] Barack Obama once wryly noted that "you could argue that if you're too well adjusted, you don't end up running for president."[331] But he also stressed the need for candidates to recognize and impose some checks on their ambition: "If you don't have enough self-awareness to see the element of megalomania involved in thinking you should be President, then you probably shouldn't be President."[332] A focus on ensuring recognition of one's personal legacy can get in the way of achieving it. Presidents who hoard power, status, and credit have difficulty enlisting others in their mission. There is, as leadership experts note, a distinction between "making a difference" and "making 'my' difference and making sure everyone knows it."[333]

In short, ambition in a leader is clearly necessary but also clearly hazardous; its consequences depend on what and whom it serves.[334] Renshon notes that presidents who lack a strong desire to achieve can drift, while presidents who have too much may "take ethical short cuts . . . or circumvent other centers of power such as the press and the Congress."[335] What is needed, Renshon argues, is ambition guided by a sense of personal ideals and public values.[336] Ambition needs to serve principles, not the other way around. Particularly for our highest political office, we want individuals with integrity, who pursue public interests, not just personal achievement.[337] *New York Times* columnist David Brooks has similarly underscored the importance of ethics as a check on ambition.

> It is a paradox of politics that the people who set out obsessively to succeed in it usually end up sabotaging themselves. . . . They lose any honest internal voice. After a while they can't accurately perceive themselves or their situation. . . . [I]f candidates don't acquire a moral compass outside of politics, they're not going to get it in the White House, and they won't be effective there.[338]

Of course, as political theorists have noted for centuries, virtually all politicians rationalize their pursuit of power in terms of societal interests.[339] In the process, many come to conflate the two, and assume that whatever serves their own objectives in gaining and retaining political leadership also advances the nation's interests. What distinguishes America's greatest presidents is their ability to recognize that danger and to maintain an overarching commitment to the public's welfare. William Herndon described Abraham Lincoln's ambition as "a little engine that knew no rest."[340] But it was in the service of broader ideals. He wanted "to link his name with something that would redound to the interest of his fellow man."[341] Another commentator similarly observed that Lincoln "liked to get on in the world, of course, but the way he got on was by thinking about his job, not by thinking about himself."[342]

Barack Obama shared that aspiration. As he noted toward the end of his presidency, youthful ambition

> [V]ery much has to do with making your mark in the world. . . . [But for effective leaders] there's a point where the vanity burns away. . . . And then you are really focused on: What am I going to get done with this strange privilege that's been granted to me? How do I make myself worthy of it? And if you don't go through that, then you start getting into trouble, because then you're just . . . clinging to the prerogatives and the power and the attention.[343]

At an earlier point in his career, before his election as president, Obama elaborated on that danger:

> There's a vanity aspect to politics, and then there's a substantive part of politics. . . . I think it's easy to get swept up in the vanity side of it, the desire to be liked and recognized and important. It's important to me throughout the day to measure and to take stock and to say, now, am I doing this business because I think it's advantageous to me politically, or because I think it's the right thing to do. Am I doing this to get my name in the papers, or am I doing this because it's necessary to accomplish my motives?[344]

At times during his presidency, Obama also commented on the trade-off between personal versus public objectives. Critics would ask, " 'Why is he doing that? That doesn't poll well.' Well I've got my own polls. I know it doesn't poll well. But it's the right thing to do for America."[345]

Yet on some matters, Obama was criticized for exactly the expedience he deplored. His initial opposition to gay marriage and his inadequate agenda on

racial justice attracted widespread criticism.[346] As Harvard Law School professor
Randall Kennedy put it, "Obama is a professional politician first and last. For the
sake of attaining and retaining power, he is willing to adopt, jettison or manipulate positions as evolving circumstances require."[347] A former girlfriend similarly
cited his "deep seated need to be loved and admired" as diverting him from truly
serving the nation's long-term interests.[348] Still, compared with other contemporary presidents, Obama appeared far more self-aware of the dangers of confusing
personal and public objectives. And even critics who found him too often "dis-
dainful, aloof . . . and insular" acknowledged that he also embodied "an ethic
of integrity [and] humanity" that was missing in other occupants of the Oval
Office.[349]

Take Nixon. A prominent biographer observed that what drove Nixon was
less a concern about national policy than "a controlled and consuming [personal]
ambition, which occupied the better part of his working life."[350] And the same
drive for self-aggrandizement that propelled him to the White House sabotaged
his performance once he got there. Nixon himself later acknowledged that "in
view of the 30 percent lead I had in the polls it made no sense to take such a risk"
in burglarizing the Democrats' Watergate headquarters; their likely presidential
candidate, Senator George McGovern, "stood virtually no chance of winning."[351]
But as one of his aides explained, Nixon and his administration "wanted a cor-
onation," not just a victory.[352] Ironically, that same ambition also sabotaged his
efforts at a cover-up. Nixon created a taping system for the Oval Office to assist
him in writing memoirs that would secure his place in the pantheon of great presidents. Yet it was the material on those tapes, including his instructions to halt the
FBI's Watergate investigation, that forced his resignation and marred his legacy.

Bill Clinton was another president with seemingly limitless ambition who
cut some legal and ethical corners in its pursuit. According to critics, Clinton's
"chief political principle has been his own political advancement . . . he has never
deviated from that single obsessive goal."[353] If so, he seems to have come to that
goal early. His high school principal recalled limiting the number of organizations that a student could join, because otherwise, "Bill would have been president of them all."[354] Clinton himself reports that at age sixteen "I knew I could
be great in public service."[355] By age thirty-two, he was governor of Arkansas, and
after one loss, he was re-elected four times.

Even Clinton himself acknowledged his exceptional urgency, which he
attributed to his father's death six months before he was born:

> For a long time I thought I would have to live for both of us in some
> ways. . . . I think that's one reason I was in such a hurry when I was younger.
> I used to be criticized by people who said, "Well, he's too ambitious," but

to me, because I grew up sort of subconsciously on his timetable, I never knew how much time I would have. . . . It gave me an urgent sense to do everything I could in life as quickly as I could.[356]

In his memoir, Clinton elaborated, "The knowledge that I too, could die young drove me both to try to drain the most out of every moment of life and to get on with the next big challenge. Even when I wasn't sure where I was going, I was always in a hurry."[357]

That desire for achievement was coupled with an equally powerful need for approval. Clinton was intent on pleasing those around him, and being "liked, appreciated, and respected" by everyone.[358] As one close advisor put it, he "wanted to be all things to all people."[359] He needed the "crowds, the cheers," the constant reinforcement.[360] Clinton's incessant search for admiration had its downside. He was often willing to sacrifice principles for popularity. Part of what earned him the nickname "Slick Willie" was his tendency to tell people what they wanted to hear.[361] Aides noted his willingness to take different positions before different audiences, all with seemingly genuine sincerity.[362] This inconsistency eroded trust.[363] As one congressman put it, "I think most of us learned some time ago, if you don't like the President's position on a particular issue, you simply need to wait a few weeks."[364]

A related problem was Clinton's willingness to advance his political career by letting polls drive policies. He had learned the importance of popular opinion the hard way, after failing to win re-election following his first term as governor of Arkansas. According to his chief of staff, voters saw Clinton as "an arrogant young man who was going to impose his ideas on Arkansas people whether they were ready for them or not."[365] That defeat taught Clinton never to get too far in front of popular opinion. In his first term as president, Clinton had consultants constantly assessing his ratings and polling how particular decisions would play with the public.[366] The results often dictated his choices, including his disastrous decision to lie on national television about his affair with Monica Lewinsky after his leading pollster told him that the truth would not sit well with most Americans.[367]

Ironically enough, Richard Nixon is the president who has been most explicit about the downsides of polling. As he put it in *Leaders*,

Too many politicians today ride toward destiny "at full Gallup." The candidate who slavishly follows the polls may be elected, but he will not be a great leader or even a good one. Polls can be useful in identifying those areas where particular persuasion is needed. But if he sets his course by them, he abdicates his role as a leader.[368]

Clinton's problem, however, was not just his excessive deference to public opinion; it was also his willingness to disregard that opinion when it no longer served his political ambitions. In his final days as president, he made a number of troubling pardon decisions. The most questionable involved Marc Rich, an international financier who had fled the country to escape charges of tax evasion. What earned attention to his case was his wife's contribution of $1.5 million dollars to Clinton and the Democratic party.[369] This pardon fit with Clinton's long-standing history of trading political for financial favors.[370] It is a telling comment on his candor and character that Clinton defended the pardon in his memoir without mentioning the contribution.[371]

A final downside of Clinton's drive for self-aggrandizement was his overextended agenda. His unrealistic pace of policy initiatives, without adequate deliberation and public outreach, sabotaged their chances. During his first term as president, Clinton proposed legislation in virtually every area of public policy, including some extremely controversial measures with almost no likelihood of passage.[372] His hastily conceived healthcare initiative was the most notorious casualty.[373] According to Clinton' s deputy chief of staff, "every day we are throwing a ball in the air. . . . [Now] they're all in the air. . . . That's what terrifies me."[374] A more effective approach would have been to "do less and explain more."[375] Yet when asked how he would respond if Congress resisted his agenda, Clinton's reply was simply "just keep going at 'em 'til they tire."[376]

Barack Obama sometimes suffered from a similar excess of ambition. As he acknowledged, "There are many times when I want to do everything and be everything. . . . And that can sometimes get me into trouble. That's historically been one of my biggest faults."[377] One example he offered was from his early days in Chicago, when he was simultaneously trying to do grass-roots organizing, write a book, work for a law firm, and teach part-time at the University of Chicago law school.[378] Some commentators criticized his presidency on similar grounds. Renshon asks "how this smart, very knowledgeable, and at least at first, engaging president so misjudged the relationship between his ambitions and the public's appetite for them. Part of the answer surely has to do with Obama's enormous confidence and investment in his own ideas."[379] Obama himself acknowledged that the public may have "started feeling some sticker shock" at the scope of his agenda.[380] Yet rather than rethink his strategy, Obama acknowledged a "perverse pride . . . that we were going to do the right thing, even if short term it was unpopular."[381]

Obama did, of course confront enormous policy obstacles, including a Republican congressional bloc hell-bent on obstruction. But his resistance to compromise and occasional appearance of arrogance made matters worse. In one memorable exchange with Republican Eric Cantor over tax policy, Obama simply dismissed his opponents' position with the observation that "elections have consequences and I won."[382] That was true, but unhelpful. And after the 2010 midterm elections, when Democrats lost control of the House, Obama had to grapple with those very "consequences" in a climate hostile to collaboration and alienated by his seemingly "condescending and arrogant" attitude.[383]

By contrast, although Lyndon Johnson had the same kind of grand policy ambitions as Obama, he was much more adept at building the bipartisan support necessary to realize them. As a college student, Johnson wrote of the "restless, energetic, purposeful . . . ambition that makes of the creature a real man. . . . If one wishes to make something of his life, he must have steadfast purpose, subordinate all other hopes to its accomplishment, and adhere to it through all trials and reverses."[384] Like Obama, he recognized the distinction between ambition in the service of vanity and ambition in the service of social transformation. He told his biographer Doris Kearns Goodwin,

> Some men want power simply to strut around the world and to hear the tune of "Hail to the Chief." Others want it simply to build prestige. . . . Well I wanted power to give things to people—all sorts of things to all sorts of people, especially the poor and the black.[385]

Growing up in Texas, Johnson had witnessed firsthand the ravages of poverty and racism. Empathy, along with ambition, drove his agenda. He made the 1964 Civil Rights bill a priority despite warnings by Democratic leaders that it would "cost you the South and cost you the election."[386] Even civil rights leaders such as Andrew Young agreed that it was not "politically expedient" for Johnson to back the bill.[387] Johnson himself acknowledged as much. After signing the legislation, he told his aide Bill Moyers "I think we just delivered the South to the Republican party for a long time to come."[388]

Johnson's willingness to make such sacrifices, together with his legendary coalition-building skills, was responsible for one of the most far-reaching progressive agendas in American history, including aid to education, public housing, food stamps, environmental protection, and healthcare for the poor and elderly.[389] Of course, Johnson did not confront the kind of monolithic obstructionism that Obama did. But Johnson's ambition had its downside. As noted previously, his escalation of the war in Southeast Asia seemed less driven by a conviction that the South Vietnamese could and should be free than by a fear of looking weak and suffering the short-term political consequences.[390] Yet the long-term consequences were far more significant both for him and for the country. Johnson's "fear of failure . . . made it impossible to succeed," and his reputation will always be tarnished by his unwillingness to exhibit the same adherence to principle in foreign affairs that he showed on domestic policy.[391]

Yet of all the recent American presidents, Donald Trump is again in a category of his own in hunger for affirmation, applause, and self-aggrandizement.[392] A *New York Times* profile of Trump's governing principles ran under the title "Me, Me, Me, Me, Me." As columnist Frank Bruni put it, "There's no topic that Trump can't bring back around to himself, no cause as compelling as his own."[393] For example, at what was billed as a "listening session" to celebrate Black History Month, he did little actual listening. Rather, a *Washington Post* account notes that "in the entirety of his opening remarks, Trump said absolutely nothing that didn't tie directly back to him in some way, shape or form. His election results. His views on the media, His election results again."[394] He even bragged about his success with black voters although he got only 8 percent of the black vote.[395] The effect was to transform "Black History Month into Trump Appreciation Day."[396] So too, at a national Prayer Breakfast, he recommended prayers for Arnold Schwarzenegger, as a way to "remind everyone—yet again—that his own ratings on 'The Apprentice' were much higher."[397]

What is distinctive about Trump's bragging is his utter lack of awareness of how pathetic his need for adulation appears. In talking to a *New Yorker* reporter about his forthcoming profile in *Time,* he commented, "I just learned that they're doing yet another cover on Trump—I love that. . . . [W]ho ever thought you'd be on the cover of *Time* magazine? Especially so much?"[398] Yet even those covers proved insufficiently fawning, so Trump fabricated his own. Featured prominently in at least eight of his golf resorts was literally fake news: a fabricated *Time* magazine with himself on the cover and quotes such as "The Apprentice is a television smash."[399] In Bruni's metaphor, Trump is like a "Russian nesting doll of self-infatuation. Boast within boast within boast."[400]

Worse still, that narcissism has seemed untethered to any broader commitment to moral values. Historian William Leuchtenburg, who worked on a study of presidential misconduct, concludes that none matched the Trump presidency "in its malfeasance, and in the depth of his failure as President."[401] By Trump's own account, politicians are "mostly driven by ego," and to some lesser extent, greed.[402] In his own case, those motivations appear unmatched by any less self-interested concerns. In *It's Even Worse than You Think*, David Cay Johnstone sums up the Trump presidency as "all about Trump. Period. Full Stop. He says so himself all the time." His tweets and rallies offer a steady stream of assertions about "how great he is."[403] As one commentator concluded, "What bothers me most of all about Donald Trump is that he seems to lack a moral compass. He does not appear to have any sort of core principles or underlying philosophical beliefs to guide his decisions. His only consistent guiding objective, it seems, is maximizing his personal wealth, pleasure, and notoriety by any and all means."[404]

Those priorities have taken a predictable ethical toll. Many experts regard the Trump administration as the "most corrupt in American history."[405] From the outset, Trump, his family, and his top officials displayed a pattern of ethical indifference and improprieties, large and small. A full examination of just his first two years in office would require a book itself. In 2017, the *New York Times* ran an editorial under the title "Pick Your Favorite Ethical Offender in Trumpland," which concluded that the administration was offering the country a "graduate-level course in the selling of the presidency."[406] The most obvious abuse involved Trump's failure to put his own assets in a truly blind trust and to avoid personal profits from his presidency, such as through his hotel's revenues from foreign dignitaries or business deals with foreign governments.[407] Other examples of moral myopia included his circumvention of rules on nepotism and conflicts of interest in making high-level appointments.[408]

As in any leadership context, the tone at the top is critical, and Trump's indifference to integrity radiates outward. By 2019, six cabinet secretaries had been investigated for unethical expenses. Housing secretary Ben Carson spent $31,000 on a dining set for his HUD office after running a presidential campaign targeted at excessive federal spending. EPA Administrator Scott Pruitt accepted under-market housing from the wife of an EPA lobbyist, used aides to do personal errands, and exploited his public office to help his wife's business career.[409] The Secretary of the Interior Ryan Zinke resigned under a cloud of ethics inquiries.[410] As the *New York Times* concluded, the message to Trump officials is that "if you're avoiding the appearance of impropriety, you're not pushing the boundaries hard enough. Government ethics officials say dealing with this administration is an exhausting game of whack-a-mole: go after one potential violation, and two others crop up."[411] Conservative commentator David Frum sums it up this way: "Trump has enriched himself in government in a way that disheartens every honest public official, and invites dishonest ones to imitate him."[412] As this book went to press, the report by Special Counsel Robert Mueller had yet to become public. But many knowledgeable sources made clear that evidence of further ethical violations was likely to emerge.

Also troubling is the stoking of xenophobia and racial animosity to serve his political ambitions. This is a charge Trump has denied so often that CNN has compiled excerpts from speeches in which the president says he's "the least racist person I know."[413] It's hard to believe that even Trump himself can believe that. But on the off chance that he or anyone else does, Vox put together a collection of what it titled "Donald Trump's Long History of Racism, From the 1970s to 2018."[414] Recent examples from a target-rich environment include:

- his presidential campaign launch, in which he called Mexican immigrants rapists and criminals;
- his travel ban targeting Muslims;
- his call for a judge of Mexican heritage to recuse himself on grounds of bias from a lawsuit involving Trump University;
- his retweet of messages from white supremacists and neo-Nazis;
- his claim following the violent 2017 white supremacist rally in Charlottesville that "some very fine people" were on both sides of the protest;
- his characterization of Haiti and African nations as "shithole" or "shithouse" countries.[415]

The problem is not simply what this conduct reveals about Trump's character. It is also how Trump's racial and religious biases have inflamed and legitimated racial hostility among the general public. Whatever else they believe about Donald Trump, most Americans think that the way he talks appeals to bigotry, and research bears this out.[416] Since his election, hate crimes, discrimination, and harassment in schools have spiked, particularly against racial and religious minorities.[417] Following an incident where a Trump supporter mailed bombs to his opponents, the president characteristically placed responsibility on the "Fake News Media, the True Enemy of the People" rather than his own incendiary rhetoric.[418] Most experts on hate speech thought otherwise, and almost four-fifths of Americans were very or somewhat concerned that the negative tone and lack of civility in Washington was leading to acts of violence.[419] This nation's greatest presidents have inspired Americans to live up to what Abraham Lincoln called "the better angels of our nature."[420] Trump does the opposite, and incites bigotry, nativism, and xenophobia. Only about a third of Americans have found Trump to be someone they admired.[421]

Finally, and perhaps most worrisome, is Trump's assault on fundamental democratic institutions. In their book *How Democracies Die*, Steven Levitsky and Daniel Ziblatt note that these deaths do not typically result from some catastrophic event, such as a military junta.[422] Rather, democracies falter through the rise of autocrats who exploit perceived emergencies, and the gradual weakening of core institutions such as the judiciary and the press.[423] These are precisely the institutions that Trump has demeaned and denigrated. When he has disagreed with a court's ruling, such as the one that initially struck down his travel ban, Trump has lambasted the "so-called judge."[424] He has also challenged courts' fairness, as when he accused a judge of Mexican descent of being unable to objectively decide a case involving Trump University. Such disrespect is part of a long-standing pattern. He walked out of a settlement conference during his divorce proceedings with Ivana Trump, telling the judge: "you are full of shit. I am leaving."[425]

Trump has displayed the same contempt for journalists, whom he groups among "the most dishonest beings on earth."[426] In his view, "network news has become so partisan, distorted and fake that licenses must be challenged, and if appropriate, revoked," and libel laws should be changed to permit damages for false articles. "It's frankly disgusting the way the press is able to write whatever they want to write."[427] To Trump, a free press is "the enemy of the American people."[428] Yet what he demands from the media is not facts but favoritism, "more bias not less . . . not objectivity but complicity."[429]

Sadly, his strategies work. An ABC News/*Washington Post* poll found that 78 percent of Trump supporters thought that news media regularly produce false stories but only 17 percent thought the same of the Trump administration.[430] In the nation as a whole, confidence in the press is at a historic low. Only about a third of Americans trust the media to report the news accurately and fairly, down from almost three-quarters in 1976.[431] Another third of the public has very little or no confidence in the press.[432] This lack of trust in mainstream journalism, coupled with the internet's ability to target the delivery of information, has shielded much of the public from facts that might challenge partisan messages and preconceived views. Today's "bubbles, filters, and echo chambers" preempt the kind of marketplace of ideas that is necessary to hold governments accountable.[433] The media has sometimes compounded the problem by its efforts to provide "balance" by neutral reporting of unsupported views, and by falsely equating character concerns that are on different orders of magnitude. A report by the Shorenstein Center on Media, Politics and Public Policy found that stories about Hillary Clinton's and Donald Trump's fitness for office gave them equal proportions of negative coverage.[434]

The greatest danger is that this climate will become the new normal. The public is becoming so inured to Trump's misconduct and misrepresentations that the administration feels able simply to shrug off challenges. A senior presidential aide, who could not explain one of Trump's repeated and demonstrably false claims, finally responded that the president was "just, you know, doing his thing."[435] But that "thing" is not in fact normal. Although presidential fabrications and ethical lapses are nothing new, prior administrations have generally felt some need to respond and remedy such conduct when publicly exposed. Walter Shaub, who resigned in 2018 as director of the Office of Government Ethics, noted that the Trump administration's utter indifference to the Office's objections to his policies made it unlike that of any other presidency in the last four decades.[436]

Trump's repeated assaults on democratic institutions reflect and reinforce broader global trends. Many Western nations are experiencing an erosion of commitment to core democratic values, particularly among younger citizens. Less than a third of American millennials believe that it is essential to live in a democracy or to have civil rights that protect people's liberty.[437] Americans urgently need a president who can challenge those views and reaffirm the importance of judicial independence, a free press, and governmental accountability. Over two centuries ago, John Adams gave us some good advice. The people, he said, "ought to consider the president's office as the indispensable guardian of their rights. The people cannot be too careful in the choice of their president."[438]

Making Character Count

In a 1972 *New Yorker* cartoon featuring two men at a bar, one observes, "Look, Nixon's no dope; if the people really wanted moral leadership, he'd give them moral leadership."[439] A similar cartoon could run today. Americans may *say* they *want* a president "to reflect the best in us," but their voting behavior generally reflects other priorities.[440] If recent presidents too often fall short in qualities of character, the fault lies not just with them but with their supporters. In commenting on the loyalty of his base, Donald Trump once joked that "I could stand in the middle of Fifth Avenue and shoot somebody and I wouldn't lose any voters."[441] Polling data from the first two years of his presidency suggest that his confidence was not far off. His approval ratings among Republicans remained at 90 percent even after repeated ethical scandals and policies widely perceived as immoral, such as separating immigrant children from their families.[442]

The point of this chapter is not to suggest that character (or its lack) is at the root of all that ails American presidential politics. There are significant substantive problems beyond the scope of this book, including campaign finance, polarization, social media, the Electoral College, foreign influence, and the structure of the office itself. In *The Impossible Presidency*, Jeremy Suri argues that our commanders in chief may hold the most powerful position in the world, but they are

> [S]et up to fail. . . . Today power elicits demands, at home and abroad, that exceed capabilities. Power pulls the presidents into mounting commitments, exaggerated promises, and widening distractions. . . . Despite their dominance, modern presidents have . . . consistently overcommitted, overpromised, and overreached.[443]

Electing presidents of character cannot solve those problems. Nor can it reshape the social, economic, and global dynamics that encourage bigotry, nativism, and a focus on short-term economic interests at the expense of broader values. Still, there is much to be said for thinking more carefully about the character of leaders who will confront these challenges. To at least some extent, "we make our own history," as Eleanor Roosevelt put it.[444] And our choice of political leaders is one of our most important ways of doing so. Just as we demand more of those leaders, we must demand more of our media and ourselves. We need to get out of our information silos, look for better coverage of character issues, and educate ourselves and our children about how to be wiser consumers of the news. And we need to place more emphasis on ethical integrity and a commitment to core democratic values when casting ballots. Less than a third of Americans now have a great deal of confidence in the presidency.[445] To restore such trust, we need to change our priorities when choosing who will occupy that office.

6

Profiles in Character

LIVES OF SERVICE

ONE CRUCIAL WAY that we develop character is by observing others. At all stages of life, we draw inspiration from those who model the virtues described earlier, such as wisdom, courage, fairness, integrity, and self-discipline. What makes some individuals particularly worthy of respect is not only these qualities but also their personal sacrifices for the common good. This chapter profiles three individuals who made such sacrifices in the service of others: Jane Addams, Albert Schweitzer, and Mother Teresa. Chapter 7 explores the lives of individuals who made comparable sacrifices in pursuit of social justice. None were without flaws or above criticism. But all were figures of exceptional commitment, whose examples have inspired millions. As discussion in chapter 2 indicated, role models who exemplify integrity and altruism play a crucial role in character development.[1]

In profiling "moral exemplars," psychologists Ann Colby and William Damon noted that what distinguishes them is not only "selfless goals," but also the "timeless, universal, yet still elusive notion of character— . . . [a] word that implies personal integrity in word and deed."[2] These individuals are prepared to sacrifice their own interests and comfort to assist and inspire others. Such examples of sustained moral commitment help shape our understandings of character and the difference that it can make in the world.

Jane Addams

Jane Addams was born in 1860 into a prosperous Illinois family. In dedicating her life to help the poor, she gave up wealth and social position. When she was two her mother died, and when she was four she contacted a spinal disease that caused a curvature and lifelong health problems. Most of what we know about

Addams's childhood comes from her autobiography, *Twenty Years at Hull House.* By her own account, her father drew her into the "moral concerns of life."[3] He was a businessman, politician, and civic leader who also organized his community's first public school and assisted the local underground railway for runaway slaves.[4] Although an abolitionist, he was not without racial and ethnic prejudices, and his daughter initially shared his disdain for immigrants. She wrote in college about their "low grade of intelligence" that made them a likely source of "vice," a view that she would later come to abhor.[5]

Her ambition and idealism led her to dream of serving the poor as a physician. At a time when few women entered college, she earned an undergraduate degree and began medical school. But health problems, depression fueled by her father's sudden death, and then a nervous breakdown, prompted her withdrawal. She floundered in her twenties as she led the life expected of a well-to-do young woman—visiting family, traveling in Europe, and pursuing cultural interests.[6] She suffered on and off from depression and a sense of uselessness. In the winter of 1885–1886, she wrote a college friend, Ellen Starr, "I am filled with shame that with all my leisure I do nothing at all."[7]

In 1887, Addams read two publications that changed her life. The first was Tolstoy's *What to Do.* It described his encounter with urban poverty and his conclusion that a Christian living in comfort was an economic parasite who had a responsibility to help address problems of the poor. The second publication was an article on Toynbee Hall, a new settlement house in a working-class London neighborhood, in which privileged youths lived among the poor and offered clubs and classes.[8] On her next trip to Europe, Addams visited Toynbee Hall, and in 1889 she decided to establish a similar settlement house in Chicago.[9] Her plan modified the British model in two respects. First, the Chicago residence would include immigrants. In Chicago, 78 percent of the population was either foreign-born or had parents who were. Second, women would play a special role in her settlement house.[10] It would take educated young women away from their "undernourished" lives and into "the great opportunities for helpfulness" through engagement with life's "starvation struggle."[11] Women with leisure and resources would become civic housekeepers.

In 1889, Addams and Starr founded Hull House. Bought and repaired with Addams's inheritance, the settlement house at its height housed about twenty-five women and served two thousand people per week.[12] Located between a saloon and a funeral home, it provided particularly crucial aid and education to immigrants and African Americans.[13] Among its famous former residents were the first head of the National Consumers League, the nation's first woman cabinet member, and the key author of the Social Security Act of 1935.[14] Hull House's guiding philosophy incorporated three principles: teach by example, practice cooperation, and embody social democracy through egalitarian relations across class lines.[15] To that end, Hull House offered kindergartens, clubs, medical services, cultural events, vocational training, a library, a gymnasium, and an employment bureau. It also provided the city's first college extension courses to the working class. A Working People's Social Science Club hosted weekly lectures on topics such as strikes, socialism, trade unionism, unemployment, and race relations.[16] Residents offered social services and child support for women whose husbands had deserted them, helped collect damages for injured employees, and launched investigations into social problems.[17] Topics included overcrowding, truancy, infant mortality, and typhoid fever. To finance these efforts, Addams raised money from Chicago's wealthy families and paid for budget shortfalls out of her own pocket.[18] By the mid-1890s, she had given away almost all of her wealth. For the rest of her life, from her mid-thirties on, she lived off her income from lecturing and writing.[19]

A visit to Tolstoy's Russian estate in 1896 cautioned against complacency. Tolstoy was not impressed by her willingness to give up a life of privilege to live in an urban slum. He approached Addams dressed in work clothes, dirty from the hayfields where he had been toiling with peasants. Why was she dressed in such finery, he wanted to know. As one historian recounted the visit, Tolstoy noted that

> a whole dress for a peasant girl could be made from the cloth [of her sleeves] . . . He was horrified that she did not eat porridge, . . . horrified that she had a servant to prepare her meals. Jane Addams was mortified. . . . Tolstoy was right. She cared for . . . [the poor] but she had not made herself their equal. She had tried to help, but had not truly identified with their suffering.[20]

Addams also discovered that individual philanthropy could only go so far. Improving the conditions of poor people in Chicago would take interventions by the municipal and federal governments. With the help of labor unions, social reform organizations, and other activists, she successfully campaigned for juvenile-court laws, the first "mother's pension" legislation, tenement-house regulations, an eight-hour workday law for women, factory-inspection statutes, and workers' compensation.[21] The public, she believed, had "a duty toward the weak and defenseless members of the community."[22] For Addams herself, no task was too ignoble or unfeminine. In 1894, she was appointed as Chicago's first female sanitary inspector. With the help of the Hull-House Women's Club, she identified over a thousand health law violations within a year, which helped reduce deaths and disease.[23]

Addams's education in labor conditions began at the settlement house's first Christmas party, when a group of little girls turned down candy because they could "not bear the sight of it."[24] The children had been working fourteen-hour days in a candy factory during the Christmas rush. It was not only children whose labor conditions were oppressive, and it was not only during the holidays. Addams helped sponsor a sweatshop bill, and turned down a large gift for Hull House that was conditioned on dropping support of the legislation. Yet instead of feeling self-righteous about rejecting the bribe, she felt shame that she had received one.[25]

In 1893, when the nation was in the throes of a depression, Addams delivered a celebrated speech on unemployment. Her argument was that "We ought to come together and regard it as a common trouble, and we should consider not what shall *we* do for the unemployed but what shall we and the unemployed do together."[26] In the context of devastating economic hardship, Addams came to view Hull House's cultural programs as "futile and superficial."[27] So she set up a free health clinic, homeless shelter, sewing workshop, and relief bureau to help the poor obtain charitable assistance.[28] Addams's frustrations in political reform efforts also led her to speak out on women's suffrage and to promote other movements for social justice. She joined the board of the newly created National Association for the Advancement of Colored People and was a prominent supporter of challenges to racial discrimination.[29]

Addams's activism and publications won her substantial acclaim. By the turn of the twentieth century, she was commonly regarded as the nation's preeminent female public intellectual.[30] The *Ladies Home Journal* in 1908 declared her the Foremost American Woman, and Yale University awarded her the first honorary degree that it ever gave to a woman.[31] Her career redefined the role of women in a way that was acceptable to both sexes.[32] In 1910, one journalist wrote, "Jane Addams is a blend of the saint and the statesman. She has the purity of life and character and immense capacity for self-sacrifice of the one, combined with the . . . knack of securing results of the other."[33]

This acclaim faded, however, in response to her principled pacifism during World War I. Her opposition to the war effort cost Hull House donors and decreased her own income from lectures and magazine articles. She was publicly booed, her speeches were canceled, and the Daughters of the American Revolution expelled her from membership. As she told one group, "In America at the present day none is more detested than the pacifist."[34] Her membership on the board of the National Civil Liberties Union and its successor, the American Civil Liberties Union, added to her unpopularity. The Women's Peace Party, of which she was national chair, was also reviled.[35] After the war was over, she worked to feed starving German children.[36] When she was called unpatriotic, unfeminine, and subversive, she responded: "I cannot change my convictions."[37]

Her steadfast pacifism did not, however, go wholly unrewarded. Her efforts helped influence the shape of the United Nations. In 1931, she became the first American woman to win the Nobel Peace Prize. With her characteristic generosity, she donated the prize money to the Women's International League for Peace and Freedom, which she had served as president.[38] When she died in 1935, a *New York Times* obituary noted that "she was, perhaps, the world's best-known and best-loved woman.[39] Her own assessment was more modest. She claimed simply that that "Hull House had made her, not that she had made Hull House."[40]

Albert Schweitzer

Albert Schweitzer was born in 1875 in Kayserberg, Germany, in a province recently annexed from France. His father was a Lutheran pastor, who began teaching him to play the organ at age eight, when his feet barely touched the pedals.[41] He pursued his interests in music while earning doctorates from the University of Strasbourg, first in philosophy and then in theology. After finishing his studies, Schweitzer became a curate and a professor at the Theological College of Saint Thomas.[42] He also gave organ concerts and published a major book on Bach as well as a widely acclaimed history of the life of Jesus.[43] He was, however, conflicted about his career choices, and at age twenty-one, pledged that at the age of thirty, he would devote himself to service.[44]

In 1904, shortly before his thirtieth birthday, Schweitzer stumbled on an article about the need for missionaries in the Congo. Then, as he put it in his autobiography, "my search was over."[45] From what he knew about the missionary society, he doubted that his views on Christianity would be orthodox enough to earn its sponsorship for any religious position. But, as he noted, "a doctor was, according to the missionary reports, the most urgent of all its needs."[46] To Schweitzer, the life of a medical missionary seemed ideal. The work would be "active, practical, merciful."[47] The problem was that he knew nothing of medicine and the prospect of starting his career over at age thirty was daunting. His friends and family were appalled by the prospect. He would be throwing his talents away in the jungle.[48]

Schweitzer persevered. To finance his medical studies, he maintained a grueling pace. He continued to work as a curate and to give organ concerts in addition to taking classes in medicine. He also published a book on the apostle Paul.[49] In what he described as "a continuous struggle with fatigue," he worked late into the night while soaking his feet in a bucket of cold water to keep himself awake.[50] After finishing what was now his third doctorate, this one in medicine, he married Helene Bresslau. She trained as a nurse in order to assist him in Africa. They spent the first months of their married life purchasing and packing medical supplies.[51] To raise money for his work abroad, he also "begged his way around the cities" of Paris and Strasbourg.[52]

He then needed approval from the Paris Missionary Society. As Schweitzer had feared, at least one member of the screening committee found his views unacceptably unorthodox. That man "knew clearly what a Christian was and Schweitzer was not one of them."[53] Only by promising to be as "dumb as a carp" on the subject of religion did Schweitzer gain the required approval.[54]

In 1913, he and Helene set off to establish a hospital at the mission in Lambarene, in what is now Gabon, Africa. Conditions were challenging. The climate is one of the world's worst, with "fiercely hot days, clammy nights and seasonal torrents of rain."[55] In addition to all the usual diseases, natives suffered from dysentery, malaria, yellow fever, and leprosy. From the moment of his arrival, before he had even unpacked his drugs and instruments, Schweitzer was "besieged by sick people."[56] His first operations were in a refurbished chicken hut.[57] The Paris Missionary Society had provided funds for the construction of a hospital, but it was difficult to find laborers or to keep them working. Schweitzer pitched in himself, but found it irritating to be wielding a shovel while the African foreman "lay in the shade of a tree and occasionally threw us an encouraging word."[58] No task was too menial for Schweitzer. In addition to his medical duties, he "mended fences, dug drains, improvised outhouses, and tended the livestock."[59] In his first nine months, Schweitzer and his barebones staff treated nearly two thousand patients while building a hospital.[60] Until his death at age ninety, Schweitzer served not only as a doctor for his Lambarene hospital, "but also [as] its pharmacist, purchasing agent, architect, construction foreman, builder, lumberman, gardener and plumber. . . . He simply could not avoid any work that he saw needed doing."[61]

When World War I broke out in 1914, the Schweitzers, who were German citizens in a French colony, were placed under house arrest. But the absurdity of having a doctor remain isolated and idle while the sick went untended led to widespread protests. That prompted the local district commandant to allow Schweitzer to resume seeing patients. However, he was cut off from his funding sources in Germany, and his debts mounted while food and medical supplies ran short. To cope with the shortages, the Schweitzers reluctantly trained themselves to eat monkeys.[62] In 1917, they were sent to internment in Europe. There, Schweitzer suffered from dysentery, and his wife from tuberculosis. Never did she recover sufficiently to join him again in Africa.[63]

During and after the war years, Schweitzer worked on two volumes, *The Decay and Restoration of Civilization*, and *Civilization and Ethics*. In the latter volume,

Schweitzer elaborated on the "reverence for life," which became his guiding philosophy. He believed that respect for the life of others must be individuals' highest principle and defining purpose. "How can ethics become the basis for a world philosophy?," Schweitzer asked. "It does that only if it shows how we are linked with all living things."[64] In Schweitzer's view, "A man is ethical only when life, as such, is sacred to him," including plants and animals, and "when he devotes himself helpfully to all life that is in need of help."[65]

This principle implied a strong commitment to altruism:

> It does not allow the scholar to live for science alone, even if he is very useful to the community in so doing. It does not permit the artist to exist only for his art, even if it gives the inspiration to many by its means. It refuses to let the businessman imagine that he fulfills all legitimate demands in the course of his business activity. It demands from all that they should sacrifice a portion of their own lives for others.[66]

From the time children start school, Schweitzer believed, they "must be imbued with the idea of reverence for all living things. Then we will be able to develop a spirit based on ethical responsibility and one that will stir many."[67] As he told an American radio commentator, "Seek always to do some good somewhere. Every man has to seek in his own way to make his own self more noble. . . . You must give something to your fellow man . . . something for which you get no pay but the privilege of doing it."[68]

The remainder of Schweitzer's life exemplified these principles of service. After the war, despite the lingering effects of his dysentery and his wife's tuberculosis, Schweitzer was determined to return to Africa. To raise money for the hospital, he gave lectures and organ concerts and published a widely acclaimed account of Lambarene, *On the Edge of the Primeval Forest*. When he returned to Africa in 1924, he found that the buildings were in decay and needed rebuilding. After the reconstruction, outbreaks of famine and dysentery created new problems, and convinced Schweitzer to rebuild again at a better site upriver. In 1927, he returned to Europe to see his wife and daughter and do more fundraising for the hospital. Two years later he came back to Africa, and he continued this travel pattern until his wife died in 1957. Then he stayed at Lambarene until his death at age ninety.

His lifestyle was simple, because "anything I spend on myself, I can't spend on my Africans."[69] He once told an American woman that his tie, worn on ceremonial occasions, was a hand-me-down from his father. The woman responded "I know men who have a hundred ties!" "Really?," asked Schweitzer, "For one neck?"[70]

Schweitzer's work attracted increasing notice. While on fundraising tours, he collected awards. Organizations and cities were "competing in offering him honorary citizenships, honorary memberships, honorary whatever they could think of."[71] This temporarily halted when World War II broke out, and drugs and equipment stopped coming. Schweitzer, now a French citizen, was not at risk, but the hospital had to refuse all but the most serious cases.[72] It survived only through assistance from supporters in Great Britain and America.[73] Even after the war, money remained an urgent problem. Costs were rising, and European benefactors had grown poorer. In 1946, Schweitzer wrote about his patients, "My great and continued concern is how to feed them all."[74]

Publicity helped. In the late 1940s, *Time* magazine gave him a front cover and *Life* magazine ran a major article titled "The Greatest Man in the World—That Is What Some People Call Albert Schweitzer, Jungle Philosopher."[75] His seventieth birthday did not go unnoticed. One British newspaper wrote, "If sainthood consists in making the good life attractive, Albert Schweitzer is a saint of our century.... He ennobles us.... His story is a living sermon on the brotherhood of man."[76] In 1953, he received the Nobel Peace Prize. He used the funds to build a leper village, and accepted the award in absentia because he felt too involved in the construction to get away.[77] One celebrated profile called Schweitzer the "only man in this century who has become famous by being good."[78]

In 1963, on the fiftieth anniversary of the hospital's founding, it had grown to five hundred patients and seventy-two buildings. Since its inception, it had treated 6,500 patients and performed 950 operations, with a mortality rate lower than 1.2 percent (which was below the European average).[79] Its example inspired other hospitals in Haiti, Mexico, Korea, and Brazil.[80] An Albert Schweitzer Fellowship supported the hospital and sponsored medical students working in impoverished communities.[81]

In his later years, Schweitzer used his reputation to inspire opposition to nuclear weapons. When he received the Nobel Peace Prize, he sent to Oslo a series of radio addresses that were broadcast in 1958, and published in book form under the title *Peace or Atomic War?* It argued that the renunciation of nuclear weapons was vital to peace.[82]

Schweitzer was, however, not without flaws. He was often arrogant, autocratic, and intolerant of criticism.[83] The noted journalist John Gunther famously portrayed him as "august and good ... but cranky on occasion, dictatorial, prejudiced ... irascible and somewhat vain."[84] Critics charged that he refused to incorporate the latest life-sustaining therapies because he did not personally understand them.[85] But the most searing criticism was that he was racist: patronizing, demeaning, and sometimes abusive toward the natives he served. Schweitzer found it difficult to motivate his African construction staff, to persuade patients to take their medications at the right time in the right order, to dissuade them from cooling their open sores in the infected river, and to prevent them from cutting down fruit trees for firewood.[86] He found that everything had to be supervised, locked, and checked; he became a "walking bunch of keys" because anything left unlocked was liable to "take a walk."[87] Schweitzer often responded with anger and frustration. He shouted at natives, called them "monkeys," and occasionally even hit them.[88]

Schweitzer's experiences left him with little respect for nationalist movements. When asked if natives could ever "develop responsibility without us," he answered "no they cannot.... Democracy is meaningless to children."[89] In 1963, he claimed that "[a]t this stage, Africans have little need for advanced training. They need very elementary schools run along the old missionary plan, with the Africans going to school for a few hours every day and then going back to the fields. Agriculture, not science or industrialization, is their greatest need."[90] His disrespect was palpable in a story he liked to tell about why he allowed natives to pick all the fruit that they wanted from his orange trees. "You see, the good Lord has protected the trees. He made the Africans too lazy to pick them bare."[91]

In all his years in Africa, Schweitzer never attempted to learn an African dialect, never dined with natives, and never learned to treat them as equals or collaborators.[92] In a revealing passage in *More from the Primeval Forest,* Schweitzer rationalized his behavior:

> I daresay we should have had fewer difficulties with our savages if we could occasionally sit around the fire with them and show ourselves to them as men, and not merely as medicine men and custodians of law and order in the hospital. But there is no time for that. All three of us, we two doctors and nurse Kottmann, are so really overwhelmed with work that the humanity within us cannot come out properly. But we cannot help it. For the present we are condemned to the trying task of carrying on the struggle with sickness and pain, and to that everything else has to give way.[93]

Yet Schweitzer also acknowledged an alternative. To Michael Scott, a priest who began working in South Africa in 1943, and who tried to identify with those he served, Schweitzer said, "I helped Africa the easy way. You did it the hard way."[94] Ironically, much of Schweitzer's criticism of colonialists was equally applicable to himself. As he put it, these whites "may have come up to Africa full of idealism, but in the daily contest have become weary and hopeless, losing little by little what they once possessed of spiritualism. That it is so hard to keep oneself really humane, and so to be a standard bearer of civilization, that is the tragic element in the problem of the relations between white and coloured men in Equatorial Africa."[95]

At the time, Schweitzer's racism generally escaped public notice or criticism.[96] Indeed, *Time* magazine's 1949 profile claimed that his "36 years of selfless pioneering as a missionary to the natives of French Equatorial Africa are a bright highlight in the relations between the white race and the black."[97] That was far from the truth. Although such views were almost universal among European colonists in Africa, this does not excuse Schweitzer's own involvement in colonialism or the racist attitudes that he modeled. But even if his racist attitudes were typical of his times, many of his charitable actions were not. And as one biographer pointed out, these actions helped to improve the lives of thousands of patients who had almost no other access to medical services.[98] So too, a *New York Times* obituary noted that "Although Schweitzer's views on Africa were out of date, he did what no man had done before him—he healed thousands and he welded world attention on Africa's many plights."[99] Through his example, he inspired others to commit time, resources, and in some instances, their entire professional lives to improving the lives of millions desperately in need of assistance. However mixed his overall legacy, this example of selfless commitment was compelling by any measure. Schweitzer also both recognized and communicated the importance of role models in advancing the social good. As he himself put it, "Example is not the *main* thing in influencing others. It is the *only* thing."[100]

Mother Teresa

Mother Teresa was a Roman Catholic nun and missionary who has been described as the most decorated woman in the history of civilization.[101] She won the Nobel Peace Prize in 1979 and was canonized as a saint in 2016.[102] During her lifetime, she figured eighteen times in the yearly Gallup poll as one of the ten women Americans admired most, and in 1999 she ranked first in Gallup's List of Most Widely Admired People of the Twentieth Century.[103] Yet despite her iconic status, Mother Teresa also drew sharp criticism. Although widely revered for her charitable works, she was also widely condemned for her opposition to birth control and for the substandard medical conditions in institutions under her responsibility.

In 1910, Mother Teresa was born Anjeze (Agnes) Bojaxhiu to Albanian parents in Skopje, a small city now the capital of Macedonia. In her early years, Agnes was interested in stories of missionaries, and at age twelve, she announced that she wanted to become a nun.[104] By age seventeen, she had decided to become a missionary in India, after reading about the work of Yugoslavian priests who were working among the poor and sick in Bengal.[105] A year later, she left home to join the Sisters of Loreto at an Irish abbey, where she could learn English, the language that nuns spoke as teachers in India.[106] In 1929, she joined a convent in Darjeeling, where she became fluent in Bengali and taught in a local school. When she took her vows as a nun, she chose to be named after the patron saint of missionaries, Therese de Lisieux, although she adopted the Spanish spelling of Teresa because another nun had already chosen the same name.[107] Mother Teresa subsequently spent almost two decades as a teacher, and then headmistress, at the Loreto convent school in Entally, Calcutta.[108] She did not last in her position running the school, reportedly because of concerns about her effectiveness and image.[109] She was Albanian, which appeared to some constituencies as the wrong nationality for the head of a school serving wealthy British families.[110] After leaving that position, ill health caused her to move to the better climate of Darjeeling to recuperate. While en route, she experienced what she described as a "call within a call" from God to work among the poor in Calcutta.[111]

The need for such assistance was overwhelming. The Bengal famine of 1943 exacerbated poverty, and the partition of India and Pakistan created millions of refugees that the city was ill-equipped to accommodate. Housing, sanitation services, and healthcare were in critically short supply. As a consequence, Calcutta had what was then the lowest life expectancy in the world.[112] Yet despite the urgent need for assistance, it was highly irregular for a nun to provide it. Mother Teresa had to obtain consent from her Mother Superior, her Archbishop, and then the Vatican, which authorized the work for a year, renewable at the pleasure of the Archbishop.[113] That enabled her to become the first nun in the history of the Roman Catholic Church not to reside within the confines of a religious community.[114]

After rudimentary medical training, Mother Teresa embarked on her mission, equipped only with three saris and a five-rupee note.[115] Her first effort was a makeshift school, which began with no building, books, or even pencils. Students sat on the ground, and drew in the dirt.[116] What she lacked in resources, she made up for in faith, persistence, and extraordinary entrepreneurial ability. With funding from a parish priest, Mother Teresa was soon able to rent a room and purchase supplies. She then sent out thousands of begging letters and amassed a small cadre of volunteers. Her next effort was to establish a dispensary, stocked with medicines that she managed to obtain from local pharmacies.[117] Her technique was well illustrated by a visit to one pharmacist who said he couldn't possibly help. Mother Teresa responded by sitting on the floor and reciting rosaries. At the end of the day, he supplied what she needed.[118]

Not everyone in the Roman Catholic Church was pleased with her growing success. Some priests complained that it was unseemly for a nun to walk the streets in a sari rather than a habit, and to perform the tasks of a secular social worker. The Mother Provincial of the Loreto order pleaded with Mother Teresa to return to the convent. She refused, reasoning that "If the rich people can have the full service and devotion of so many nuns and priests, surely the poorest of the poor and the lowest of the low can have the love and devotion of us few."[119]

In 1949, a wealthy Roman Catholic man offered her rent-free living quarters in the second floor of his residence. This gave her a base from which to open more schools and dispensaries, and to collect large amounts of donations.[120] She also recruited more volunteers, whom she called sisters. With the assistance of local priests, she drew up a constitution for the Missionary Sisters of Charity. It required sisters to take vows of poverty, chastity, obedience, and service to the poorest of the poor.[121] Initially she had intended that she and her sisters would live and eat like those they served. But medical missionaries who advised her "said I was to feed my sisters well" to keep them healthy.[122] She attempted to do so. But living conditions remained at subsistence levels, and at times the sisters lacked fuel for cooking and had to eat raw wheat.[123] When advised that the sisters should have fans, Mother Teresa responded, "I do not want them to have fans. The poor whom they are to serve have no fans."[124] No task was too menial for any member of the group. One of the early sisters recalled being repelled by the state of the toilet, and then seeing Mother Teresa clean it herself.[125]

As the organization grew, the sisters expanded their range of activities. In 1952, Mother Teresa opened the first Home for the Dying, a hospice for the poor, in an abandoned Hindu temple. Patients received palliative care and the opportunity to die with dignity according to the rituals of their faith.[126] The conversion of the temple was controversial, and Mother Teresa responded with a characteristic mix of personal courage and pragmatic persuasion. When rumors surfaced that the dying were offered shelter to convert them to Catholicism, an angry mob hurled rocks at the home and made death threats. One day when stones came through the windows, Mother Teresa stepped out to confront the protestors. "Kill me," she told them. "And I'll be in heaven all the sooner. But do not disturb those inside. Let them die in peace."[127] The mob disbanded and protests died down when it became clear that the home was respecting religious traditions for the last rites of each patient. Sisters were seen reading the Koran over the deathbeds of unconscious Muslims.

Mother Teresa also addressed the needs of lepers. She jump-started her campaign by declaring a Leprosy Day on the date of Gandhi's assassination, and asking for donations in the name of the "father of modern India." Collection boxes were circulated with pictures of Gandhi and a request: "touch a leper with your compassion."[128] The campaign received widespread publicity and generous financial support. Mother Teresa first established mobile leprosy clinics, but soon determined that a permanent facility was also necessary. Finding a site proved

challenging, and Mother Teresa responded to mob violence at one potential location with a characteristic mix of persistence and pragmatism. "I don't think
God wants us to open a clinic here," she observed, and continued her search for
another site.[129] When she found one, she made sure that lepers learned a trade
that could put them on the path to self-sufficiency. They wove clothing to sell
in marketplaces throughout the world. Government officials then became concerned that lepers would flock to Calcutta, so it provided the Missionaries of
Charity with land in an adjoining state to create another leper colony. By 1975,
the Missionaries of Charity operated more than one hundred leper colonies
throughout the world.[130]

Mother Teresa also saw the need for a facility for orphans. In 1955 she opened
the Children's Home of the Immaculate Heart, and the concept spread. Her
fundraising skills were again on display when a group of European women collected clothes and toys for a Christmas celebration for Christian children. These
benefactors gathered together in a spirit of self-congratulation and waited for
Mother Teresa to thank them. She did, but then added that she also needed
clothes and presents for the Muslim children's annual festival of Ramadan, and
for the Hindu children's festival of light.[131]

Mother Teresa proved equally persuasive in Church circles. Vatican approval
was necessary for expansion, and Mother Teresa carefully cultivated a relationship
with the newly elected pope Paul VI. When he visited the Home for the Dying,
he found it spruced up for the occasion. His photograph had replaced the one of
Gandhi in the entrance and statues of saints were strategically placed throughout
the former Hindu temple. The pope blessed Mother Teresa and gave her his new
Lincoln Continental, which she promptly auctioned off for charity.[132] In 1965,
she received authorization to expand, and in 1966, she established a Missionary
Brothers of Charity. For the first time in the history of the Catholic church, an
order for men had evolved from an order for women. It had always been the other
way around.[133]

While other religious congregations suffered from a lack of applicants, the
Missionaries of Charity faced no shortages. Some of those who wished to help
were lay Catholics and non-Catholics, who became Coworkers, a term borrowed
from Gandhi. By 1990, the International Association of Coworkers was growing
at a faster rate than any charitable fund in the world.[134] From 1970 to 2002, a new
center opened somewhere every six months.[135] In 1985, Mother Teresa established
New York's first AIDS hospice in the rectory of a Greenwich Village church.[136]
Other homes opened in various American and African cities. Eventually the
Missionaries of Charity ran orphanages, soup kitchens, mobile clinics, homeless
shelters, and hospices in more than 130 countries.[137]

Such rapid growth presented obvious challenges, which were compounded by a lack of financial and management expertise within the organization. As Mother Teresa herself acknowledged, "I did not know that our work would grow so fast or go so far. . . . Humanly speaking, it is impossible, out of the question because none of us has got the experience. None of us has got the things that the world looks for. . . . God is using . . . [us—we] are just instruments in his hands."[138] To minimize accounting problems, the Missionaries refused to take any financial donations that required an audit, which excluded most government and foundation grants. Mother Teresa also imposed severe limits on fundraising activities. "People are beginning to doubt and so let us not give them the chance," she explained.[139] In 1975, which marked the twenty-fifth anniversary of the founding of the Missionaries of Charity, Mother Teresa gave instructions that the occasion was not to be used for fundraising or for spending money, even for the printing of brochures or pamphlets.[140] But the potential for financial scandal still loomed large, particularly in the Coworkers Association, and in 1993, she terminated it.

As her international influence spread, she often intervened in crisis situations. Her involvement mobilized aid from around the world. One of her requests resulted in five thousand tons of food within a week for the famine-stricken people of Ethiopia and Tanzania.[141] She traveled to assist radiation victims at Chernobyl and earthquake victims in Armenia.[142] Her personal courage was often on display. In war-torn Beirut in 1982, Mother Teresa learned that a number of mentally and physically disabled Muslim children were trapped without food and water in a hospital where shelling was heavy. Local authorities and church leaders warned that it would be suicidal to attempt a rescue. Mother Teresa went anyway, and snipers held their fire while a Red Cross van reached the children and transported them to a convent in East Beirut. After their arrival, she organized the supplies necessary for their care. One of the Red Cross officials involved characterized her as a "cross between a military commander and St Francis."[143] As another explained, "We didn't expect a saint to be so efficient."[144]

In other contexts, her diplomatic skills proved equally crucial. When Chinese officials told her that they had no poor in China needing her assistance because the government looked after the needy, Mother Teresa responded that her organization would simply like to bring "hope to the discouraged."[145] The government allowed it. Even in old age, her willingness to take on new challenges seemed unbounded. She traveled across the globe on a pass begged from the airlines. When they didn't respond to her initial requests for free travel, she offered to serve as an air hostess on flights on which she traveled. That produced the desired response.[146] When asked about her punishing travel schedule, she explained, "there will be plenty of time to rest in eternity. Here there is so much to do."[147]

In recognition of these efforts, Mother Teresa received the Nobel Peace Prize in 1979. True to form, she convinced the Nobel Committee to cancel the customary awards banquet and instead offer the money saved for those who really needed a meal. Others across Europe made further donations and she used the funds to feed two thousand poor people on Christmas Day.[148]

Not everyone believed that Mother Teresa's growing list of honors were well deserved. Her efforts attracted criticism on multiple grounds. One was her outspoken opposition to abortion and contraception, which critics believed endangered women's lives and women's control over their own destinies. In her lecture accepting the Nobel Peace Prize, Mother Teresa declared that "the greatest destroyer of peace today is abortion, because it is a direct . . . murder by the mother herself."[149] She made similar claims before a national Prayer Breakfast in Washington.[150] In her view, "the poorest country is the country that has to kill the unborn child to be able to have extra things and extra pleasures. They are afraid to feed one more child."[151]

Mother Teresa's condemnation of abortion made no exception for victims of rape. The implications of that position became clear on her trip to Bangladesh after that country's liberation from the Pakistanis in 1972. Three thousand naked rape survivors were found there in army bunkers. Their saris had been taken away so that they would not hang themselves. To women who were pregnant and wanted abortions, Mother Teresa responded that this would involve "murder" and that the shame would be with them for life. As she explained, "They will never forget that they [are] mothers [who] have killed their children."[152] In commenting on this explanation, Germaine Greer noted that "there is no room in Mother Teresa's universe for the moral priorities of others. There is no question of offering suffering women a choice."[153]

Mother Teresa's views on contraception attracted similar criticism. Her organization offered sex education classes that taught only the rhythm method, and her speeches included unsubstantiated claims of its effectiveness. In her Nobel Prize lecture, she asserted that 61,273 fewer children had been born because of the use of the rhythm method. Eighteen months later, while speaking in Washington, DC, she doubled the number.[154] Never did she disclose how she arrived at those figures. Nor did she make allowances for AIDS victims who wanted to use condoms, or for lepers, who wanted to take part in national sterilization programs because parents almost always infect their children.[155] When the first home for AIDS patients opened in India, Mother Teresa was asked what she could do to help prevent the spread of AIDS. Her response was "Nothing. It is God's will. They must die in peace with God."[156]

Christopher Hitchens offered a withering critique of these views on sex and reproductive issues in *The Missionary Position: Mother Teresa in Theory and*

Practice.[157] When he interviewed Mother Teresa on the subject, she showed him one of her organization's orphanages, and told him "See, this is how we fight abortion and contraception." Hitchens wryly commented later that "it is difficult to spend any time at all in Calcutta and conclude that what it most needs is a campaign against population control."[158]

Hitchens also lambasted Mother Teresa for substandard medical conditions in her facilities. He was in good company. In 1994, the British medical journal *Lancet* exposed inadequacies in the treatment offered at Calcutta's Home for the Dying. A doctor who had visited the home described misdiagnoses and the absence of pain management and medications.[159] Some patients assumed to be dying were actually suffering from malnutrition.[160] Other physicians documented dangerously unsanitary conditions and inadequately trained medical assistants.[161] Hitchens noted that the global income of the Missionaries of Charity was enough to operate "first class" clinics, but that instead it delivered "haphazard" care.[162] When Mother Teresa herself suffered from one of her many illnesses or heart attacks, she went to expensive facilities, while patients in her homes often lacked even rudimentary painkillers.[163]

Critics also charged Mother Teresa with befriending corrupt politicians and taking tainted money. She praised donor Jean-Claude Duvalier, a brutal Haitian dictator who lived a life of luxury while most of the nation lived in abject poverty. She wrote a letter seeking clemency for another donor, American millionaire Charles Keating, who looted the Lincoln Savings and Loan bank.[164]

Despite her own leadership role in religious and philanthropic circles, Mother Teresa was no advocate of women's rights. Nor did she engage poor people in activism on their own behalf. She infuriated feminists by constantly exhorting women to be homemakers and by opposing not only birth control but also the ordination of female priests.[165] She further irritated progressives by refusing to acknowledge, let alone address, the structural causes of poverty. On one of her visits to the United States, Mother Teresa met with a group of black men who told her about the absence of decent jobs, housing, and social services in their impoverished community. When asked what she was going to do about that, she responded, "First, we must learn to love one another."[166] On another occasion, Mother Teresa explained, "We all have a duty to serve God where we feel called. I feel called to help individuals, not interest myself in structures or institutions."[167] When a United State senator asked whether she ever got "discouraged when you can see the magnitude of the poverty and realize how little you can really do," she responded, "God has not called me to be successful. God has called me to be faithful."[168]

Yet in evaluating these criticisms, it bears note that Mother Teresa was not indifferent to the need for self-sufficiency among the poor. To her, the question was one of timing. To critics who suggested, metaphorically, that she should give the poor not fish but fishing rods with which to catch their own fish, she responded, "My God, you should see these people. They have not even the strength to lift a fishing rod, let alone use it to fish. Giving them fish, I help them to recover the strength for the fishing of tomorrow."[169] Many of her programs also supplied a rod. In response to horrific violence in Bangladesh in 1971, she established not only clinics but also training programs for widows and unmarriageable rape victims who needed job skills to survive. Her assistance helped impoverished women set up businesses selling puffed rice.[170] So too, as noted earlier, her leprosy colonies offered training and opportunities for paid work.

Moreover, her resilience and steadfast determination to do something to address horrendous conditions was an inspiration to others. When critics dismissed her efforts as small drops in an ocean of need, she told them, "I do not think the way you do. . . . I do not add up. I only subtract from the total number of poor or dying. . . . So we use ourselves to save what we can."[171] If there are poor in the world, she believed, it was not because God had made them poor but because "you and I do not share enough."[172] Simplistic though that message was, it encouraged thousands to share more.

Ultimately, it was this message that gave such resonance to her work. Her willingness to suffer personally from the deprivations of poverty inspired generosity in others. By her faith, sacrifice, and courage, she set an example that mobilized thousands of donors and volunteers to live up to their best sense of themselves. One need not share her views about poverty, reproductive rights, or other issues central to gender equality to admire her compassion and commitment. The United Nations General Assembly designated the anniversary of her death as the International Day of Charity, and it is a fitting tribute for a life committed to helping the poorest of the poor.[173]

Despite their different backgrounds, circumstances, and contributions, Jane Addams, Albert Schweitzer, and Mother Teresa shared many common qualities: courage, perseverance, empathy, altruism, integrity, and steadfast adherence to principle. All of them ignored the advice and practices of those around them to forge an unconventional path. All made enormous personal sacrifices in the service of others. All were inspired by reading about individuals who had made similar sacrifices. Albert Schweitzer stumbled on an article about missionaries in the Congo; Mother Teresa saw an account of Yugoslavian priests who were assisting impoverished Bengalis; Jane Addams read about the founders of Toynbee Hall, a settlement house for the London poor. These experiences testify to the power of narratives in shaping character and commitment to the common good. The hope underlying this chapter is that many readers will find similar inspiration for their own lives.

7

Profiles in Character

THE PURSUIT OF SOCIAL JUSTICE

AMONG OUR MOST inspiring role models are those who dedicate their lives to social justice. This chapter profiles four such individuals whose careers exemplify the qualities of character that leave enduring legacies. Ida Wells was one of America's first African American woman leaders; her activism helped achieve a national response to lynching. Mahatma Gandhi pioneered techniques of nonviolent resistance that helped win India's independence and provided the foundations for many other social justice movements around the world. Thurgood Marshall, as legal director for the National Association for the Advancement of Colored People (NAACP), crafted the litigation strategies that challenged racial discrimination during the early American civil rights movement. Nelson Mandela led the anti-apartheid campaign in South Africa, and after twenty-seven years in prison, emerged to form the coalition that made democracy in that nation possible. These individuals had different strengths and weaknesses. But they all demonstrated qualities of courage, commitment, and integrity that have improved the lives of millions around the world.

Ida B. Wells

Ida Wells was born a slave in 1862, in Holly Springs, Mississippi, just two months before President Lincoln issued the Emancipation Proclamation.[1] Her father was a carpenter, her mother a cook, and both continued to work at those jobs after the Civil War brought them freedom. Wells's father was a man of principle who lost his job when he refused to vote the way his white employer dictated.[2] Both parents believed strongly in the value of education, and Wells attended school until she was sixteen, when her mother, father, and one of her seven siblings died

of yellow fever. Wells was visiting grandparents at the time, and on learning of
the tragedy, she courageously insisted, against all medical advice, on immediately
returning home.[3] Once she was there, her father's fellow Masons came up with a
plan to divide and place the orphans among friends who would take them. Wells
resisted. Her mother had been separated from her family at auction, and both
she and her husband, Wells believed, would "turn over in their graves to know
their children had been scattered like that."[4] Wells agreed to care for them if the
Masons would help her find work. They did, and she got a job as a teacher in a
country elementary school nearby.

Her schedule was grueling. She spent the workweek at the school, while her
grandmother cared for the children at home. Wells returned on the weekends to
do the laundry, cleaning, and cooking for the next week.[5] During the summers,
she studied at the local university until a quarrel with the administration led to
her expulsion. Although at the time she was deeply resentful, she later acknowledged that her own "tempestuous, rebellious, hardheaded willfulness" was to
blame.[6] Her domestic arrangements throughout this period also caused problems.
Young women did not normally live without the protection of a father or husband. Rather than give Wells credit for her efforts to keep the family together,
some community members spread rumors that she wanted to live independently
in order to have illicit relationships with white men.[7]

After three years, Wells accepted an invitation to live with her aunt in
Memphis, where she could earn higher wages and be close to other family
members. She took three of her youngest siblings with her; her brothers stayed
behind as apprentice carpenters. She found a job outside the city and commuted
by train. In 1884, a railroad conductor ordered her to give up the first class seat
she had purchased for the ladies car and demanded that she move to the crowded
smoking car. She refused and bit the conductor when he attempted to drag her
from her seat. When he finally succeeded, she got off the train, rather than sit in
second class. White passengers cheered derisively as she turned to walk back to
Memphis.[8]

On her return, she hired a lawyer to sue the railroad. She won in the lower
court and refused to settle when the railroad appealed.[9] Although the law
allowed trains to segregate by race, it required them to offer opportunities for
first class accommodations to all passengers. In finding for Wells, the Tennessee
trial court noted that she was a person of "lady-like appearance and deportment,
a school teacher, and one who might be expected to object to traveling in the
company of rough or boisterous men." The local newspaper was less complimen-
tary and ran a story under the headline "A Darky Damsel Obtains a Verdict for
Damages . . . $500."[10] The Tennessee Supreme Court reversed the verdict on the
implausible ground that the two cars were in fact equal. In the court's view, Wells's

behavior on the train demonstrated that she was no ' "lady" but merely a "mulatto passenger," whose purpose was "to harass with a view to this suit." And she was held liable for court costs, a devastating blow given her own substantial legal fees and financial struggles as a sole breadwinner with a minimal salary.[11]

That unhappy outcome did have one redeeming byproduct. The editor of a black newspaper, *The Living Way,* asked her to write about the incident.[12] Wells had already been publishing columns as the editor of the Memphis *Lyceum* newspaper, and a few had been reprinted in *The Living Way.*[13] Unlike the vast majority of female journalists in that era, who confined their work to feminine subjects, Wells wrote on issues of general interest to the black community.[14] Among her best work was criticism of racism by white officials and white-dominated political parties.[15] For example, one column documented racial bias in the criminal justice system: a white city official who had stolen six thousand dollars of taxpayer money was pardoned after a fifteen-month sentence, while a black man who had stolen food, alcohol, and cigars worth about seven dollars was sentenced to eight years in prison.[16] Wells also underscored the responsibilities of black leaders to give back to their communities. In one 1885 column, she asked, "What material benefit is a 'leader' if he does not, to some extent, devote his time, talent and wealth to the alleviation of the poverty and misery and elevation of his people?"[17] However, she also wrote columns on "Women's Mission," and "The Model Woman," in which, according to her diary, she tried to suppress her "unfeminine anger."[18]

In 1889, Wells became an editor and part owner of the *Free Speech and Headlight,* which served the Memphis black community. This made her the first and only black woman in the country to achieve that status at a major city newspaper.[19] Her leadership also made for a grueling schedule, when combined with her full-time work as a teacher. However, that problem ended when the school district refused to renew her contract in retaliation for one of her columns. It had criticized the crowded and dilapidated conditions in black schools, and the practice of board members of awarding teaching jobs in return for "illicit" sexual favors.[20] Although Wells was not earning enough from journalism to afford losing her teaching position, she felt it was "right to strike a blow against a flaring evil, and I did not regret it."[21]

To make up for her lost income, Wells concentrated on boosting her paper's sales. She began seeking invitations to speak in nearby cities, where she could find new audiences. As a result, the newspaper's circulation increased 250 percent.[22] Her writing explored a wide range of issues until the 1892 murder of three black businessmen in Memphis focused her attention on lynching.

Although in contemporary usage, "lynching" conjures up hanging, its original meaning was much broader. The term originated during the Revolutionary War era, in a practice by a Virginia justice of the peace, Charles Lynch. He ordered whippings of suspected Tories and horse thieves who supplied them, all without formal trial proceedings.[23] The term "lynch law" evolved to describe any act of vigilante justice, including hanging, shooting, and burning at the stake, done with broad public approval.[24] Motivations for lynching varied in different regions and time periods.[25] In the post-Reconstruction South, such violence was targeted at blacks and served, as Wells put it, to teach the "lesson of subordination."[26]

The 1892 lynching that changed Well's life involved one of her friends, Thomas Moss. He was a polite and unassuming letter carrier who had used his savings to purchase the People's Grocery store in a black neighborhood just outside of Memphis. A white competitor, H. S. Barnett, was looking for an opportunity to destroy the business, and found one after a fight broke out near the store among a racially mixed group of boys playing marbles. Barnett entered the store looking for a suspected participant, and started another fight. Moss and two employees were arrested. After blacks held a meeting to strategize about responses, Barnett used rumors of unrest to persuade a judge to issue warrants for further arrests. He also spread rumors in the black community that a white mob was preparing to attack. When a sheriff's posse not wearing uniforms came to the grocery to make arrests, black neighbors mistook them for part of a mob and shot and wounded several officers. That sparked outrage; whites lynched Moss and his employees, and looted his store. Barret bought what was left at a fraction of its value.[27] In covering the incident, white newspapers caricatured Moss as a "turbulent, virulent negro"; he and his employees were presented as "desperados," motivated by "vicious and venomous rancor," part of a "nest of vipers" intent on slaying innocent whites.[28] The lynching was described as "one of the most orderly of its kind ever conducted.... There was no whooping, not even loud talking, not cursing, in fact nothing boisterous. Everything was done decently and in order."[29]

Wells was incensed. That incident, she later explained, "opened my eyes to what lynching really was. An excuse to get rid of Negroes who were acquiring wealth and property and thus keep the race terrorized and 'keep the nigger down.'"[30] Her first column after the lynching claimed that "there is only one thing left that we can do; save our money and leave a town which will neither protect our lives and property, nor give us a fair trial in the courts but [will] take us out and murder us in cold blood when accused by white persons."[31] Some four thousand to six thousand black residents agreed and left Memphis.

Wells then channeled her outrage into investigative journalism. She became the first American to research the causes of lynching and debunk conventional wisdom.[32] White-owned newspapers often claimed that interracial rapes were rising and that lynchings were a response to the "brutal passion of the Negro."[33] Even the *New York Times* declared in 1892 that the offense of rape was "one to which the African race was particularly prone."[34] But after compiling statistics from white-owned newspapers, Wells found that allegations of rape were present in only one-third of all reported lynchings, and in some of those cases, the relationships were consensual.[35] In one notorious example, an Arkansas mob insisted that a white woman claim that her black lover had raped her and that she light the bonfire that burned him to death.[36] Shortly after Moss's murder, Wells responded to a local newspaper's account of an interracial rape with an editorial claiming that "nobody in this section of the country believes the old threadbare lie that Negro men rape white women. If Southern white men are not careful, they will overreach themselves and public sentiment will have a reaction; a conclusion will then be reached which will be very damaging to the moral reputation of their women."[37]

Wells's implication that white women were sexually attracted to black men infuriated local whites. A local newspaper suggested that the "black wretch" who had authored such "foul lies should be . . . burned at a stake."[38] A mob organized by local businessmen trashed her newspaper's office and threatened any future publisher with death. Wells had the foresight to be out of town at a conference when the story broke. Her co-owner, however, received threats of castration and hanging, and was forced to flee the city; the paper's former owner was pistol whipped.[39] When white leaders vowed to kill Wells if she dared to return, and posted sentinels at the train station, she decided not to test their resolve.[40]

Wells relocated to New York, where her experience with mob violence gained widespread publicity. The editor of the *New York Age* hired her to write weekly articles and gave her partial ownership in return for the subscription list of the gutted Memphis paper.[41] In 1892, she published the first statistical study of lynching, later republished as a pamphlet, *Southern Horrors: Lynch Law in All Its Phases*.[42] Wells found that most victims were blacks who had run for political office, competed with whites in business, failed to pay debts, or were too "sassy."[43] The pamphlet also noted that rapes of black women by white men were rarely punished; mob retribution had more to do with race than sexual assault.[44] To combat lynching, Wells called for new strategies including self-defense and civil disobedience. Train and trolley car boycotts were also necessary, because the "appeal to the white man's pocket has ever been more effectual than all the appeals ever made to his conscience."[45] By the time of *Southern Horrors*, the number of African Americans lynched across the nation exceeded that of whites, even though blacks constituted less than 12 percent of the population.[46] Somebody must "show that the Afro-American race is more sinned against than sinning," wrote Wells, "And it seems to have fallen on me to do so."[47] At a time when few women were willing to even use the term "rape" in polite company, Wells's willingness to discuss its dynamics earned her a reputation as "dauntless."[48]

Wells's exposé was a bombshell. She began to lecture widely, at a time when female lecturers were rare and black female lecturers were rarer still.[49] Wells also published a follow-up pamphlet, *United States Atrocities: Lynch Law*, which situated the crime in a broader discussion of discrimination and debunked the romanticized view of frontier justice. Wells cited cases such as a Louisiana lynching in which the victims were the children of the man whom the mob really sought but had been unable to catch. She also described the pressure on white women in biracial relationships to fabricate claims of rape, and challenged the myth that lynchings were necessary to secure justice.[50] As Wells noted, "With judges, juries and prosecuting attorneys all Southern white men," blacks were unlikely to escape punishment for consensual relationships with white women.[51]

In 1893 and 1894, Wells took her anti-lynching campaign abroad, while serving as the only paid black correspondent for a daily paper.[52] In Great Britain, she gave over a hundred lectures, and occasionally addressed crowds of more than a thousand. There was widespread press coverage, which Wells made sure was mailed to prominent American politicians, newspapers, and clergy.[53] Not all the accounts were favorable, however. Some white newspapers denounced her as a "wench," "strumpet," "courtesan," and "notorious woman of ill repute," who was "raising money for her own personal use in the anti-lynching campaign."[54] At a time before professional civil rights advocates routinely appealed for financial support, the *New York Times* questioned whether her purpose in fundraising may "plausibly be supposed to have been an income rather than an outcome."[55] Even black leaders sometimes criticized her for "sowing scandal" and "polluting the minds of the innocent and pure."[56]

When condemned for her salacious coverage of lynchings, Wells responded:

> I see the *Memphis Daily Commercial* pays me the complement of calling me a "Negro Adventuress." If I am become an adventuress for simply stating facts, by what name must be those who furnish these facts? However revolting these lynchings, I did not perform a single one of them, nor could the wildest effort of my imagination . . . equal the reality. If the same zeal to excuse and conceal the facts were exercised to put a stop to these lynchings, there would be no need for me to relate . . . these tales of barbarity.[57]

Wells's efforts abroad had a significant impact. A widely publicized British Anti-Lynching Committee took up the cause and helped shame some American states into passing anti-lynching legislation.[58] The trip also gained her considerable public recognition in the United States, though much of it was critical. In commenting on her first public lecture after returning from Great Britain, the

New York Times reported a recent incident in which a "negro had made an assault upon a white woman for purposes of lust and plunder." The paper hoped
that "the circumstances of this fiendish crime may serve to convince the mulatress
missionary . . . just how her theory of negro outrages is, to say the least of it, in-
opportune."[59] Wells, however, remained unconvinced. In her lecture, she noted
that "black women have had to suffer far more at the hands of white men than
white women at the hands of black men. Every single report [of rape] which is
published should be investigated."[60] The *Times* responded that she was "slan-
derous and dirty-minded," that no "decent" colored woman had been raped by a
white man, and that no "reputable or respectable negro" had ever been lynched.[61]

The attacks took a toll. Some black as well as white Americans shied
away from association with Wells. Many were also put off by her assertions
about consensual relationships between white women and black men, which
could exacerbate racial tensions.[62] But, unfazed by criticism, Wells returned
to Chicago, where she helped set up an anti-lynching committee and fielded
speaking invitations from around the country. In 1895, she published *The Red
Record,* a hundred-page pamphlet describing lynching in the United States
since the Emancipation Proclamation.[63] By her estimate, more lynchings were
occurring each year than lawful executions.[64] The pamphlet included several
graphic photographs as well as descriptions of particularly brutal incidents
involving torture and mutilation.[65] Wells's efforts met with some success.
More states passed anti-lynching legislation, and such crimes began to decline
after 1892, the year that she started her campaign.[66] But failures to obtain adequate legal prohibitions in the South or at the national level gave continued
urgency to her activism.

In 1895, Wells married, and began a difficult decade of balancing work and
family responsibilities. She had been in no rush to find a husband, and wrote
in her diary after moving to Memphis, "I am an anomaly to myself as well as to
others. I do not wish to be married but I do wish for the society of gentlemen."[67]
She seemed, however, to have found an ideal partner in Ferdinand Barnett, a
black lawyer and founder of Chicago's first black newspaper, *The Conservator.*[68]
Wells had worked with Barnett on race-related issues, and he had advised her on
a potential libel suit against a white-owned newspaper for calling her a "black
harlot" and the mistress of her Memphis coeditor.[69] Just before the marriage,
Wells bought *The Conservator* from Barnett because he was about to become
Illinois's first black assistant state's attorney and needed to avoid conflicts of interest.[70] And, in another decision that was highly unusual at the time, she chose to
hyphenate her name.[71] In commenting on this unconventional start to domestic
life, one journalist noted that Wells-Barnett's "determination to marry a man
while still married to a cause" was sure to be a topic of national interest.[72]

Barnett had two sons from a previous marriage, and lived with his mother, so his wife immediately inherited substantial family responsibilities. This caused some tensions, and when the couple began having children of their own, the two teenage boys and their grandmother took up a separate residence. Wells-Barnett had ambivalent feelings toward domesticity. Although in a column on the "Model Girl," she had endorsed housekeeping as among women's "best accomplishments," she had little taste for it herself; her husband did much of the cooking, another highly unconventional arrangement in that era.[73] In her autobiography, Wells-Barnett speculated that her "early entrance into public life . . . had something to do with smothering the mother instinct."[74] Or perhaps after her early experience of caring for her brothers and sisters, "somehow I felt entitled to the vacation from days as nurse."[75] After the birth of her first child, she confessed that "although I tried to do my duty as mother toward my newborn and refused the suggestion not to nurse him, I looked forward to the time when I should have completely discharged my duty in that respect."[76] When her son was five months old, Wells-Barnett took him with her to a conference of an organization that became the National Association of Colored Women. It was such an unusual decision that the group dubbed him the "Baby of the Federation."[77] Shortly afterward, when organizers asked her to help campaign for a woman seeking statewide office, she agreed if they would arrange for childcare. In remarking on the arrangement, Wells-Barnett observed, "I honestly believe that I am the only woman in the United States who ever traveled through the country with a nursing baby to make political speeches."[78]

Over the next two decades, she continued to juggle personal and professional activities. In 1897, Wells-Barnett responded to an editorial in the *Chicago Times-Herald* claiming that one reason citizens resorted to lynching was because justice was delayed through legal technicalities. She countered with a letter to the editor pointing out the absence of evidence to back up that claim. Who benefited from delays, she asked rhetorically. "Poor men, criminals who are ignorant, penniless and friendless? Certainly not . . . . Appeals cost money, and plenty of it. . . . Let it be confessed with sorrow that many an innocent man has gone to prison or to his death because poverty stood between him and substantial justice."[79] Wells-Barnett also remained active in local civic activities. On her trip to Great Britain, she had been impressed with English women's organizations, and after her return, she helped establish several, including one that bore her name.[80] The Ida B. Wells club focused on racial conditions in Chicago, and in 1897, established the city's first black kindergarten. Childcare was an issue of particular importance for blacks, whose families had a high proportion of working mothers.

The kindergarten initiative was controversial and time-consuming, which may have contributed to her announcement after the birth of her second child that she was giving up public life. She resigned as editor of the *Conservator*, and as president of the Ida B. Wells Club in order to remain at home with her children.[81] Her resolve lasted three months. Then, in 1898, a particularly brutal lynching occurred in South Carolina. The victim, the first African American postmaster in a small city, had refused to give up his position even after whites boycotted the post office and then burned it to the ground. Finally, a mob set his house on fire and shot and killed him and his one-year-old infant. His other children were badly injured by bullet wounds but survived. Although some members of the mob were ultimately indicted, they were all acquitted.[82] Black protestors around the country demanded federal action and persuaded Wells-Barnett to join lobbying efforts in the capital. As she explained in her autobiography, it "seems that the needs of the world were so great that again I had to venture forth."[83] She spent five weeks in Washington, making speeches, raising money, and lobbying Congress.

Later that year, she visited Susan B. Anthony, who gave her some unsolicited advice. Anthony, who was unmarried, told Wells-Barnett that domesticity was not for women like her "who had a special call for special work." Motherhood gave her a "divided duty."[84] The exchange helped convince Wells-Barnett to re-enter public life, but the challenges that she confronted there continued to present tensions for her marriage. On one occasion, her political activity so alienated the governor that it almost cost her husband his job as assistant state's attorney. She also believed that her reputation was partly responsible for her husband's inability to attain his dream of becoming the city's first black municipal judge.[85] It didn't help when newspapers suggested that Ida wore the "trousers" in the family or identified Ferdinand simply as the "husband of the brilliant Ida B. Wells-Barnett."[86] The couple had two more children, and the demands of raising a family of four limited her professional activities. She avoided significant work outside the home until her youngest child was eight.[87]

As her family obligations eased, Wells-Barnett became more fully engaged in racial justice causes. She helped to found a number of national and local organizations, including the National Association for the Advancement of Colored People (NAACP), the National Association of Colored Women, and the Chicago Negro Fellowship League.[88] The League helped provide poor black men with employment, food, temporary housing, and back wages; Wells-Barnett supported its activities from her salary as the city's first black probation officer.[89] She fought segregation in the schools and in public transportation, campaigned for women's suffrage, and organized responses to race riots.[90] For example, in 1922, she traveled to Little Rock, Arkansas, following riots triggered by blacks' refusal to sell cotton at the reduced prices that white businessmen demanded. Twelve blacks were arrested, beaten, tortured, and sentenced to death after what Wells-Barnett labeled a "mockery of a trial."[91] She met with the prisoners, helped organize

protests, raised money for their defense, and threatened to launch an exodus of
black laborers if the men were executed.[92] After a new trial, the defendants were
acquitted.[93]

Not all of her efforts ended so happily. During the latter part of her life, Wells-
Barnett suffered a long series of slights and thwarted ambitions in black organizations, and also lost an election for the Illinois state legislature.[94] She was even
omitted in some histories of lynching and of notable black activists.[95] According
to a leading biography by Paula Giddings, part of the reason was Wells-Barnett's
reputation as a "difficult woman." She was, as Giddings, adds, "certainly that, even
when taking into account the double standard applied to assertive independent
women."[96] One of her "chronic difficulties was that her domineering style often
resulted in her being the issue rather than the principle she was trying to impart."[97]
Other accounts similarly note that her "militancy," "dominating" approach, and
lack of "diplomatic skills" cost her allies.[98] Another biographer chronicles how
Wells-Barnett's "prickly personality," "uncompromising self righteousness," and
"need to be the leader in movements in which she participated" often sabotaged
her efforts.[99] She did not "mince words or spare the feelings of those whom she
decided were do-nothings."[100] Nor did she hesitate to offend potential donors,
other civil rights leaders, or women whom she considered to have a "petty outlook on life."[101] Another African American newspaper editor claimed that she
had "delegated to herself the care and keeping of the entire colored population
of the United States," and that the black press should "resent this egotistical self-
appointed" spokesperson.[102]

Part of what made the style of Wells-Barnett so off-putting had to do with
gender. Some black men were uncomfortable with a female leader.[103] Although
other prominent blacks, including W. E. B. Du Bois, were described as arrogant, their conduct did not arouse the same hostility.[104] Women were under
greater pressure to be conciliatory team players, and that was not Wells-
Barnett's leadership style. In explaining her exclusion from top positions at the
NAACP, one of the association's officers noted that she was a "great fighter,
but . . . she had to play a lone hand."[105] Another NAACP officer complained
that after the Chicago riots in 1919, Wells-Barnett had "launched into a tirade"
against those who did not join her organization. She also had compromised
the association's efforts to establish a defense fund for rioters by raising money
on her own.[106] Similar criticisms occurred after the Arkansas riots, when Wells-
Barnett competed for credit and funds with the NAACP, which was defending
the rioters.[107] As one biographer noted, she had "no gift for compromise and
often departed in a huff from organizations that she helped create, her famous
temper flaring when negotiations did not go her way."[108] Even she acknowledged these shortcomings. In her diary, she entreated God "to help me better

to control my temper."[109] Her autobiography notes that "temper . . . has always been my besetting sin" and chronicles multiple examples.[110] Yet at the same time, the anger that compromised her effectiveness as an organizational leader also inspired her continued crusades for justice.[111]

It is hard to know how much of a role her personal shortcomings, as opposed to her race and gender, played in limiting her achievements. Many white women leaders of social reform organizations did not expect "to be criticized or challenged by a black woman," and her anger over both personal slights and matters of principle impeded cross-racial alliances.[112] In one celebrated incident, at a 1913 parade organized by the National American Woman Suffrage Association, the organization's leaders decided that all the black participants must march at the end rather than with their state delegations. Wells-Barnett, after having lost the vote over Illinois's compliance with that decision, simply defied it. As the state's delegation marched down Pennsylvania Avenue in the nation's capital, she stepped out from the crowd and joined the group's white members.[113]

The combination of racial and gender bias, coupled with Wells-Barnett's own limitations as a leader, marginalized her contributions later in life. When she died of kidney disease in 1931, at the age of sixty-eight, her death did not spark the public recognition that her achievements deserved.[114] Nor was she adequately recognized for decades after.[115] It took forty years to find a publisher for her autobiography, and it was not until the 1970s that her uncompromising militancy attracted newfound admiration among feminists and civil rights activists.[116] Many came to recognize that Wells-Barnett had, in the words of W. E. Du Bois, helped awaken "the conscience of the nation."[117] As one of her biographers noted, "few Americans before or after have more consistently refused to compromise with the evil of racial prejudice."[118] But the lack of public recognition in her own lifetime was a source of considerable frustration. Wells-Barnett opened her autobiography with an account of a twenty-five-year-old woman who had approached her out of ignorance of her achievements. As Wells-Barnett recalls, the young woman had been

[A]t a YWCA vesper service when the subject for discussion was Joan of Arc. Each person was asked to "tell of someone they knew who had traits of character resembling this French heroine and martyr. She was the only colored girl present, and . . . she named me [Wells-Barnett]. She was then asked to tell why she thought I deserved such mention. She said, 'Mrs. Barnett, I couldn't tell why I thought so. . . . I was dreadfully embarrassed. Won't you please tell me what it was you did, so the next time I am asked such a question I can give an intelligent answer?' "[119]

That ignorance is being slowly rectified. The newly opened National Memorial for Peace and Justice in Montgomery, Alabama, which commemorates the victims of lynching, has dedicated a space to her memory, and a movement has formed to build a monument in her honor on the South Side of Chicago.[120] Ida Wells-Barnett deserves a more prominent place in our historical memory. Of all those profiled in this and the preceding chapter, she confronted the most substantial barriers: the combined obstacles of race, class, and gender. Her steadfast courage and candor in the face of violence and vitriol helped force the nation to confront the horrific consequences of racial subordination. And her struggle to combine work and family at a time when society failed even to recognize this as a significant issue served as an example for generations to follow.

Mohandas Gandhi

Mohandas Gandhi was born in 1869 in the state of Porambandar, India. Admirers called him Mahatma, meaning "great souled one."[121] His father was the chief minister of the small state and Gandhi was the fourth child of his father's fourth and last wife.[122] As was then traditional for Hindu families, Gandhi was betrothed before he was old enough to understand its meaning. His first two fiancées died. A third married him when he was thirteen. Gandhi later wrote that he could "see no moral argument in support of such a preposterous early marriage as mine."[123] Nonetheless, the marriage lasted more than sixty years and produced four sons, as well as a daughter who died shortly after birth.

Gandhi's early childhood was marked by strong religious influences. His mother was extremely pious, and her prayers and fasting provided a lifelong example.[124] In his autobiography, Gandhi makes a full confession of the misdeeds of his youth, but, as George Orwell noted, "in fact there is not much to confess."[125] Gandhi recounts only a few forbidden cigarettes and mouthfuls of meat, a few coins pilfered from a maidservant, and two visits to a brothel that he left without "doing anything."[126]

Gandhi was an average student, but did well enough on exams to enter the region's only college. He suffered from headaches and homesickness, and performed poorly, so he departed after only a term.[127] Nonetheless, Gandhi was the best educated of his family, and was seen as the most likely son to succeed his father as chief minister. To prepare for that role, he traveled to London when he was nineteen to study for the bar, first at University College and then at Inner Temple. Initially, Gandhi tried hard to make himself into a proper English gentleman. He wore a top hat, and took lessons in dancing, French, and the violin. Disappointed with the results, he decided that "character" would have to suffice to make a gentlemen of him.[128] During his time in London, he became active in the Vegetarian Society and became interested in Christian as well as Hindu teachings.[129]

In 1891, Gandhi was called to the bar and then returned to India. His efforts to establish a law practice in Bombay failed because he was too shy to argue in court. After moving to Rajkot, where his family had relocated, he made a modest living doing petty legal work.[130] In 1893, at age twenty-four, he accepted a retainer from a Muslim law firm to work for a year in Natal, South Africa, representing primarily Muslim Indian traders.

There Gandhi encountered pervasive racism. Indians as well as blacks were subject to a wide array of social and legal discrimination. A defining moment came shortly after his arrival, when he was thrown off a train for refusing to leave the first class compartment even though he had a first class ticket; a white passenger had objected to sharing the compartment with an Indian.[131] Gandhi then suffered further discrimination on the journey. He was denied hotel rooms and beaten by a stagecoach driver when he refused to leave to make room for a European passenger. Those experiences left him resolved to "try, if possible, to root out the disease and suffer hardships in the process."[132] His first test came when he applied for admission to the Supreme Court of Natal, and the local law society opposed his application on the grounds of his color. Ultimately the court overruled the objection and Gandhi continued to practice law as well as to organize the Natal Indian Congress.[133]

As he was preparing to return home to India, the Natal government proposed a bill to deprive Indians of their right to elect members of the legislature. Friends convinced Gandhi to remain in South Africa and lead the opposition to the bill. He agreed to stay a month. He remained twenty years. As the leader of the country's Indian community, he argued that its members were equal citizens of the British empire and deserved equal rights. He was jailed and beaten as a consequence.[134] When he went back to India to fetch his family, he published a pamphlet describing the conditions of Indians in South Africa that was circulated to every newspaper and every party leader in the country.[135] That account enraged white South Africans. On his return, his ship was quarantined for twenty-three days in an effort to force him to turn around and go back to India. When he refused and disembarked, a mob pelted him with stones and bricks. He was saved by the wife of the police superintendent who stood between him and the crowd and shielded him with her parasol.[136]

In 1900, during the Boer War, Gandhi volunteered to lead an Indian ambulance corps in support of British forces. He wanted to demonstrate that Indians were capable of courageous front-line service, but because they were forbidden to use firearms, they could enlist only as stretcher-bearers and medical orderlies.[137] He and thirty-seven other Indians received a medal for their contributions.

Again, in 1906, when the British fought the Zulus in Natal, Gandhi organized Indians to serve in the ambulance corps. He hoped that their service would help legitimize their claims to full citizenship.[138] That effort fell short.

In 1906, the government of the Transvaal region promulgated a new policy compelling registration of the colony's Indian and Chinese populations.[139] Gandhi's response was nonviolent protest, which he called Satyagraha, meaning firmness in truth.[140] This strategy sought to convert the adversary by "suffering in one's own person."[141] Its aim was to arouse the conscience of the oppressor and build a sense of moral urgency and agency among the oppressed. Inspiration for this approach came from diverse sources, including Hindu and Jainist traditions of nonviolence, Henry David Thoreau's philosophy of civil disobedience, and British suffragists' protest tactics.[142] Satyagraha was not simply "passive resistance," which Gandhi thought implied weakness. Satyagraha came from strength, and required courage in pursuit of social transformation.

Gandhi applied this philosophy to the nationalist movement in India, as well as to his campaign in South Africa. His views on Indian nationalism were influenced by Tolstoy's *Letter to a Hindu,* which argued that a small clique of white colonialists could not rule a nation of three hundred million natives if they refused to cooperate. In 1910, Gandhi wrote his influential *Hind Swarajh,* calling for Indian home rule and expulsion of British authorities. Although the book was banned in India, its ideas spread.[143]

In South Africa, Gandhi urged Indians to strike, burn their registration cards, and engage in other forms of nonviolent resistance. For such activism, he was repeatedly jailed. He was also physically attacked by some of his own former supporters, who felt that he was not militant enough.[144] Over the course of his Satyagraha campaigns from 1907 to 1914, thousands of Indians and other Asians were imprisoned, flogged, or shot. In 1913, in response to a discriminatory tax, some fifty thousand workers went on strike. The government's repressive reaction and mass arrests sparked an international outcry. In the face of growing political and economic pressure, the country's leaders negotiated a compromise.[145]

During these Satyagraha campaigns, Gandhi transformed his personal life and developed his political philosophy. He renounced his profitable law practice, discarded his Western clothing, and took up a simpler, more religious way of living, characterized by self-discipline and self-restraint. The earth, he believed, "provides enough to satisfy every man's need but not . . . every man's greed."[146] At age thirty-six, he also took a vow of celibacy. Sex, he said, was "meant only for the purpose of creation."[147] The ideal man "will have no relish for sensual pleasures and will keep himself occupied with such activity as ennobles the soul."[148] As he further explained in his autobiography, "I should find myself unequal to the task [of service] if I were engaged in the pleasures of family life and in the propagation and rearing of children."[149]

It does not, however, appear that Gandhi was ever fully "engaged" in family life. By his own account, he was not a conscientious father. His efforts to educate his sons were "inadequate," and he refused to use his influence to enroll them in a proper school because other Indians lacked that privilege.[150] Never did he manage to treat his wife as an equal. In the early years of marriage, he demanded obedience and in one notorious episode, ordered her to empty the chamber pot of his law clerk.[151] To put his philosophy of a simpler and celibate life into practice, Gandhi founded two experimental communities, Phoenix and Tolstoy Farm. In these settings, he began his widely criticized practice of sleeping in close proximity to attractive young women in order to exercise sexual restraint.[152]

In assessing Gandhi's South African legacy, it is important to note what his actions did not achieve, or even aim to achieve. Gandhi challenged the country's discrimination against only Indians, not blacks. He believed in the "purity of race" and did not think that blacks and Indians should be forced to live in the same suburbs.[153] His goal, as one biographer put it, was not to "overturn the color bar but to get whites to accept Indians on their side of the line."[154] Still, his two decades in South Africa laid the foundations for his later achievements. Although his campaign of nonviolent resistance fell far short of ending all forms of racial discrimination, even against Indians, it charted a path for social progress.[155] It was successful enough that when Gandhi returned to India in 1914, the head of the South African government declared, "The saint has left our shores, I sincerely hope forever."[156]

Gandhi arrived in India in 1915 at age forty-five with an international reputation. He joined the Indian National Congress, and soon assumed a leadership role that helped transform the body from a party of relatively privileged Indians to the catalyst of a mass movement.[157] He fought discrimination against untouchables, the Hindu pariah caste that was subject to segregation and denial of basic human rights in all walks of life. Gandhi repeatedly told his followers that untouchability was a "heinous crime against humanity," and that as long as sixty million untouchables lacked such rights, India did not deserve freedom from colonial rule and would never win it.[158] That view proved highly unpopular, and when Gandhi accepted an untouchable family into the ashram he had founded, its financial support from affluent Indian donors dramatically declined.[159] His adherence to principle came at a substantial price because, as commentators sometimes ironically noted, it took the wealthy to keep Gandhi and his followers in poverty.

Also controversial was his effort to recruit combat troops for the British during World War I. He viewed voluntary enlistment as preferable to conscription, which might take place if Indians did not volunteer. No moral or political advantage would be gained if they served under compulsion.[160] However, the inconsistency of this position on the war effort with his position on nonviolence did not escape public attention.

Gandhi's anti-colonial activities in India began with protests against oppressive taxes, and evolved into a more general strategy of noncooperation with British rule. He believed that this tactic could be successful because colonial governance depended on local collaboration. By the turn of the twentieth century, only about four thousand of India's five hundred thousand civil servants were British.[161] In 1919, a massacre of unarmed Indians by British troops in the Punjab helped spark Gandhi's demand for an end to British rule.[162] His campaign of noncooperation called for a boycott of British-run elections, law courts, educational institutions, and honors. He even returned the medals he had won in the Boer War and Zulu uprising.[163] When this campaign strategy proved ineffective, he shifted tactics, and in 1921 called for a boycott of foreign cloth. The spinning wheel became for him a symbol of economic independence. Homespun cloth, he believed, should replace imported textiles from Britain. The boycott soon gained traction, and bonfires of British cotton burned throughout the country. However much to Gandhi's disappointment, these initiatives were sometimes accompanied by rioting and looting of shops.[164] "The movement of non-violent non-cooperation," he stressed, "does not aim at destroying the tyrant. . . . It is a movement of self-purification. It therefore seeks to convert the tyrant."[165]

In 1922, Gandhi was arrested on charges of conspiring to overthrow the government. He pled guilty and promised to repeat the offense, which led to a prison sentence of six years. His need for an appendectomy caused the British to release him after two years. The government never tried him again, although he was arrested and jailed on several further occasions. The consensus among authorities was apparently that he wielded more influence in prison than outside it.

After his release, Gandhi sought to broaden his movement's appeal by reaching out to Muslims.[166] In 1924, he started a twenty-one-day fast for Hindu-Muslim Friendship. He knew it might be fatal, given his weakened condition following the appendectomy, but he persisted.[167] These strategies captured public imagination. As one biographer noted, Gandhi was a "master of communication and symbol in a society where literacy was low and there were few modes of mass communication."[168] His piety, selfless lifestyle, and commitment to principle gave his efforts strong moral resonance.[169]

Gandhi's next major initiative was a refusal to pay taxes. His particular target was a salt tax, which had emerged as a symbol of colonial oppression due to Britain's monopoly of the salt trade. In 1930, he organized a twenty-four-day march to the sea, which ultimately enlisted several thousand participants. On reaching the beach, Gandhi and his fellow protestors collected saltwater in earthen jars. Evaporation of the water left them with salt, which evaded the tax. It was powerful political theater. In the words of Winston Churchill, then a prominent conservative British politician, "When Gandhi went to the seashore a year ago to make salt he was not looking for salt, he was looking for trouble."[170] He got it. Gandhi was again arrested, and within a few weeks, as many as sixty thousand Indians were imprisoned. A mass boycott of British goods followed, and drew international attention. *Time* magazine named him Man of the Year in a cover story titled "Saint Gandhi."[171]

Faced with rising protests and declining revenues, the British viceroy in India released Gandhi in 1931 and invited him to negotiate. Among British authorities, this was a controversial decision. Churchill declared that "it is alarming and also nauseating to see Mr Gandhi, a seditious Middle Temple lawyer, now posing as a fakir . . . striding half naked up the steps of the Vice-regal palace . . . to parley on equal terms with the representative of the King Emperor."[172] The negotiations however, proved constructive. In the Delhi Pact of 1931, the government agreed to release political prisoners and lift the ban on the Indian National Congress party; Gandhi agreed to call off the civil disobedience campaign.[173]

Gandhi then traveled to London to represent the Indian National Congress at a roundtable conference on Indian affairs. During the Conference, he lodged in the slums to identify himself with the poor rather than the privileged. He also took every opportunity to publicize Indian concerns with members of Parliament, church leaders, and other interested groups.[174] He even visited King George and Queen Mary at Buckingham Palace, wearing his usual loin cloth. When a journalist asked Gandhi if he thought himself underdressed, he replied, "the King had enough on for both of us."[175]

After he returned to India, he launched another civil disobedience campaign and in 1932 was again arrested. From jail, he announced that he would fast unto death unless the government improved its treatment of untouchables. His fast ended after six days when the government accepted his demands.[176] However, he quickly began another fast. Over objections of his doctors, he proclaimed that unless there was an improvement in Hindu attitudes toward untouchables, he would fast unto death.[177] As a consequence, many temples admitted untouchables, privileged Brahmins dined with pariah street cleaners, and citizens adopted resolutions promising to stop their discrimination. After copies of the resolutions accumulated in Gandhi's prison yard, he ended his fast. Although many of the habits of discrimination soon re-emerged, Gandhi had altered the terms of the debate and laid the foundations for further progress. As one historian noted, even though the fast "did not kill the curse of untouchability," its acceptability was no longer taken for granted. "While once it had been socially improper to consort with untouchables, it now became in many circles socially improper not to con- sort with them."[178] Gandhi paid a continuing price for that progress. In 1934, he was attacked by a mob that resented his efforts.[179] He was undeterred. In his view, "Hinduism has sinned in giving sanction to untouchability. It has degraded us. . . . What crimes for which we condemn the [British] Government as satanic, have not we been guilty of toward our untouchable brethren?"[180]

Gandhi also opposed discrimination against women and recruited them as partners in his protest activities.[181] He opposed practices such as purdah (the seclusion of women) and suttee (the self-immolation of widows), as well as gender inequalities in politics and education. In challenging conventional arguments for suttee, he noted that "If the wife has to prove her loyalty and undivided devotion to her husband so has the husband to prove his allegiance and devotion to his wife. . . . Yet we have never heard of a husband mounting the funeral pure of his deceased wife."[182] In Gandhi's view,

> Woman has been suppressed under custom and law, for which man was responsible, and in the shaping of which she had no hand. . . . Men have not realized this truth in its fullness in their behavior toward women. They have considered themselves to be lords and masters . . . instead of friends and coworkers. . . . Wives should not be dolls and objects of indulgence, but should be treated as honored comrades in common service.[183]

Although Gandhi had not always lived up to these principles in his own marriage, he at least publicly acknowledged that failure.[184] And his inclusion of women in his political efforts gave them a new self-confidence and dignity. Many defied purdah to participate in protests and boycotts, and some became active in campaigns to raise the status of untouchables.[185]

Gandhi was unique in his time for his focus not just on women's rights but also on women's empowerment. As he noted, "I hold radical views about the emancipation of women. . . . [T]he real advancement of women can only come by and through their own efforts."[186] By encouraging such efforts in his own campaigns, he helped lay the foundations for a feminist movement.[187] According to one scholar, he was the first public figure in India to see that "women had the potential of contributing significantly to the making of the nation. In fact he alone succeeded in galvanizing the traditional house-bound woman into a powerful instrument of political action and social reconstruction."[188]

There were, however, limits to Gandhi's egalitarianism. He accepted much of the caste system apart from untouchability, and forbade one of his sons from marrying a woman from a different caste, although he eventually came to support intermixing and intermarriage.[189] Some historians have argued that he could not have survived politically in India if he had launched an all-out assault on caste.[190] But Gandhi's tolerance for class-based distinctions extended beyond India. On his visit to England, when heads of upper-class families brought out their servants to greet him and obtain his autograph, he noted with approval the "loving family tie" between master and servant and viewed it as a model for India.[191]

As to Indian independence, however, Gandhi's views were more radical and uncompromising, and his campaign was ultimately successful. But the end of British rule in 1947 did not produce the unified nation that he had envisioned. A rise in Muslim nationalism and fighting between religious factions led to partition of the country into a Hindu-dominated India and a Muslim-dominated Pakistan. As a result, some ten to twelve million individuals were displaced, and half a million were killed in riots.[192] Gandhi was the only leader of the Indian Congress to hold out against partition, although once it occurred, he urged acceptance.[193] To promote peace, Gandhi went to Noakhali, which had experienced widespread Muslim attacks on Hindus that in turn had provoked riots elsewhere. At age seventy-seven, he spent five months trekking between villages, preaching reconciliation and lodging with peasants, preferably Muslims.[194] He then faced angry mobs in Calcutta. While Muslims distrusted Gandhi as a Hindu partisan, many Hindus faulted him for not being partisan enough.[195] After Gandhi took a wounded Muslim into his house and angry Hindus attacked it, he announced a fast unto death unless the killings stopped. Terrified of being held responsible for his death, Calcutta officials united in an effort to stop the violence.[196]

Following that modest success, Gandhi promptly departed for migrant camps outside of Delhi. Again he faced down an angry mob, this one of Muslim youths chanting "death to Gandhi."[197] His presence was a calming influence.[198] Throughout this period, he was, in the words of Lord Mountbatten, Britain's last Indian viceroy, a "one man boundary force."[199] He also continued his campaign on behalf of untouchables, and made a point of lodging in their quarters.[200]

The violence, however, persisted, and in 1948, Gandhi began what was to be his final fast. He demanded that Hindus and Muslims agree to live in peace, and that India, despite its financially precarious circumstances, make the restitution payments it had promised to Pakistan for lost territories.[201] As he approached death, India announced that it would make the payments. A vast procession of Hindus and Muslims marched toward his house, and 130 leaders met to discuss reconciliation.[202] Gandhi ended his fast. Two days later, in a still weakened state, he was walking to a prayer meeting when a militant Hindu nationalist shot and killed him.[203] It was the sixth attempt on his life, and it was successful partly because Gandhi refused to take precautions to protect himself.[204] The nation went into mourning. Over a million Hindus, Muslims, Sikhs, whites, and untouchables joined his funeral procession and a million more watched from rooftops. His birthday became a national holiday. Tragically, he achieved only in death the ceasefire that he had struggled to promote in life.[205]

At the time of his assassination, he was under consideration for a Nobel Peace Prize, and after his assassination, the Nobel Committee decided not to award the honor at all that year. The official explanation, that there was no "suitable living candidate," was a thinly veiled reference to Gandhi.[206] Although this prize eluded him, his principles and practices inspired other Nobel laureates and world leaders. By their own accounts, his disciples included Martin Luther King Jr., Nelson Mandela, the Dalai Lama, Aung San Sun Kyi, and Barack Obama. In assessing his legacy, Gandhi once wrote that "I have nothing new to teach the world. Truth and Nonviolence are as old as the hills. All I have done is to try experiments in both on as vast a scale as I could do."[207] But that was no small accomplishment. As one historian put it, "perhaps never before on so grand a scale has any man succeeded in shaping the course of history while using only the weapons of peace."[208] What made those weapons so uniquely powerful was Gandhi's own courage and selflessness in their deployment. "Even if the sacrifice demanded is my very life," Gandhi wrote, "I hope I may be prepared to give it."[209] He was, time and time again.

Yet Gandhi's qualities of character mattered in part because he was fortunate in his enemies. He believed in "arousing the world" through peaceful resistance, but as George Orwell pointed out, this is "only possible if the world gets a chance to hear what you are doing. It is difficult to see how Gandhi's methods could be applied in a country where opponents of the regime disappear in the middle of the night and are never heard of again."[210] In a 1938 meeting with India's former viceroy, Lord Halifax, Hitler offered a simple solution to Britain's colonial problem: "Shoot Gandhi."[211] That the authorities chose otherwise and treated him with solicitude, even in jail, was a tribute to what Gandhi himself termed the "British sense of fair play."[212]

Moreover, much of Gandhi's political success was attributable, ironically enough, not simply to his nonviolent methods but also to their potential for triggering violence by others. As historian Arthur Herman noted, his fasts became "potent weapons . . . because of fear that his death would set off riots all over India. It was violence, not nonviolence, that forced the British first to change course . . . and then finally to leave India."[213]

From the standpoint of character, however, what distinguished Gandhi was not simply his courageous commitment to nonviolence. It was also his selfless devotion to the common good. Gandhi believed that "a man must arrange his physical and cultural circumstances so that they may not hinder him in the service of humanity."[214] That entailed considerable personal sacrifice. Altogether, he spent almost seven years in Indian and South African prisons.[215] In much of his adult life, he had few creature comforts. In 1920, he declared that "in India, it must be held to be a crime to spend money on dinner and marriage parties . . . and other luxuries so long as millions of people are starving. . . . If India is one family, we should have the same feeling as we would in a private family."[216]

He also generalized those principles and insisted that all nations and all peoples must recognize the "primacy of self-sacrifice over self-interest."[217] Anticipating global environmental principles, he noted that if India's 300 million residents "took to similar economic exploitation" as the Western world, "it would strip the world bare like locusts."[218] Gandhi lived by those principles. In 1931, he reported to a customs official that his earthly possessions consisted of six spinning wheels, some prison dishes, a can of goat's milk, six homespun loincloths, "and my reputation which cannot be worth much."[219] He reportedly had fewer than ten possessions when he died; the "whole outfit," George Orwell noted, "could be purchased for about 5 pounds."[220]

None of this is to suggest that Gandhi was without flaws. Among them were blind spots concerning race and caste. Contemporary critics fault him for his ties to the Hindu elite and for failing to do more to dismantle the caste system, which still plagues Indian society.[221] Also problematic were his treatment of family members and sexual practices. After his wife's death, he slept naked with naked young women, including even his niece.[222] When people called him a "saint trying to be a politician," Gandhi responded that he was instead a "politician trying to be a saint."[223] That his efforts fell short should not detract from his accomplishments. His courage, sacrifices, selflessness, and integrity were an inspiration to millions, and significantly advanced social justice around the world.

In 1931, when Gandhi was in London arguing for India's independence, a small girl started to ask for his autograph. Then she hesitated, sizing up this strange-looking man in a loin cloth. Turning to her mother, she asked; "Mummy, is he really great?"[224] History leaves no doubt of the answer.

Thurgood Marshall

Thurgood Marshall was born in 1908 in a segregated middle-class neighborhood of Baltimore. It was a world of rampant racism; those who resisted encountered retaliation and violence. The year Marshall was born, eighty-nine blacks were lynched.[225] The indignities of discrimination were large and small. Blacks in Baltimore could not attend the same schools, ride the same trains, or use the same drinking fountains as whites. The downtown had no public restrooms for blacks, and Marshall recalled the humiliation of once not making it home in time.[226] The club where he worked to earn money for college had a sign that read "No Niggers or Dogs Allowed."[227]

Marshall's great-grandfather was a slave, his mother was a teacher, and his father was a railway porter and later a country club steward.[228] Although his father had not graduated from high school, he had a love of learning and an interest in the law. He passed these on to his son, who sometimes accompanied him to watch local court proceedings. The two argued about legal issues over dinner, and Marshall later attributed his interest in becoming a lawyer to these early debates.[229] His mother's dream was that he would become a dentist, which promised a secure livelihood in a city where most professional occupations were unavailable to blacks. His grandmother taught him to cook, on the theory that no one ever saw a "jobless Negro cook."[230]

Marshall himself had other aspirations. He excelled in debate, first in high school and then at Lincoln College, an all-black school in Pennsylvania. After marrying a University of Pennsylvania student, Vivian ("Buster") Burey, Marshall settled down to his studies, graduated with honors, and decided to go to law school. Because the University of Maryland wouldn't admit blacks, he enrolled at Howard University in Washington, DC. He needed to work his way through both college and law school; his mother pawned her wedding and engagement rings for his tuition, but it wasn't enough.[231] In an era before student loans, Marshall got part-time jobs as a waiter, bellhop, delivery boy, and assistant in the law school library.[232] During law school, that part-time work, together with his course load and commute from his parent's home in Baltimore, made for a brutal schedule. He was up at five and didn't finish studying until midnight.[233] "Isn't it nice," Marshall once commented, that "no one cares which 23 hours of the day I work."[234] He still managed to graduate first in his class.

His performance attracted the notice of a professor, William Hastie, and the dean, Charles Houston, who both tapped Marshall to work on civil rights cases.[235] Houston also invited Marshall to travel with him after graduation on a fact-finding tour for the NAACP concerning segregated schools in the South.[236] The conditions they found were appalling, and reinforced Marshall's interest in civil rights work.

That interest persisted, but was hard to reconcile with the financial realities of legal practice. Marshall hung out his shingle in 1933, in the midst of the Depression. No Baltimore firms would hire blacks, few landlords were willing to rent them office space, and few clients—black or white—wanted to trust their cases to a black attorney.[237] Marshall struggled to make a living, while also working as legal counsel for the Baltimore branch of the NAACP. His first major case involved the University of Maryland law school, which had denied admission to an honors graduate from Amherst college with the simple explanation, "the University does not accept Negro students."[238] Marshall and Houston filed suit in state court challenging the policy on constitutional grounds. In *Plessy v. Ferguson,* the US Supreme Court had held that states could segregate schools only if they provided substantially equal facilities for both races. Because Maryland had not done so, the state court of appeals directed the university to admit the plaintiff, Donald

Murray. Marshall, however, was not content with just a legal victory. He also wanted to ensure that the plaintiff graduated. To that end, he managed to find financial help for Murray, and convinced two white students to sit next to him in class when the dean tried to keep him segregated from the other students.[239]

While struggling to establish a paying legal practice, Marshall took on additional civil rights work. He lobbied for an anti-lynching bill and challenged discrimination in teachers' salaries. Throughout the South, black teachers earned about half of what whites did, and in Maryland, earned substantially less than white janitors.[240] Marshall also helped organize and defend a boycott of businesses that sold to black customers but would not hire black employees.[241] This work, however satisfying, did not pay the rent, and Marshall's secretary later joked that he "had a genius for ignoring cases that might earn him some money."[242] In 1936, when he was working almost exclusively on civil rights cases, and holding a part-time night job in a health clinic to make ends meet, Marshall asked the NAACP for a monthly retainer.[243] Charles Houston, who had become the organization's special counsel, instead invited Marshall to come to New York for six months to work out of the national office.[244] Marshall agreed, and two years later, when Houston returned to Washington, Marshall, at age thirty, became the legal director of the organization.

In 1939, in order to take advantage of tax exemptions available for nonprofits that did not engage in lobbying, the legal wing of the NAACP spun off into a separate organization, the NAACP Legal Defense and Education Fund, Inc. (Inc. Fund). Under Marshall's leadership, it became the model for public interest law firms generally, and Marshall himself became known as "Mr. Civil Rights."[245] He also exemplified the principles he was fighting for in his own workplace. He hired women legal staff during the 1940s, at a time when few others would, earning the reputation as one of the country's "first feminists."[246]

Over the next quarter century, Marshall criss-crossed the country, establishing a network of lawyers willing to challenge racial injustice. It was a difficult and dangerous life. He was on the road six to nine months every year, traveling an average of sixty thousand miles annually before jet planes or the interstate highway system. In preparing for trial with little staff assistance, Marshall frequently worked sixteen-hour days.[247] His cases led him into segregated regions with no restaurants or hotels that would serve blacks.[248] He picked his battles carefully, and put up with personal abuse and indignities because "I'm down here representing a client—the NAACP—and not myself."[249] On the road, he stayed with local residents, typically moving every night, sometimes every few hours, to evade hostile whites.[250]

On more than one occasion, he narrowly escaped lynching, and was often protected by armed black volunteers.[251] Police were sometimes part of the problem rather than the solution. In one case, he was chased at gunpoint by a local officer, who claimed, "you black son of a bitch, I've got you now."[252] In another instance, after being arrested on the pretext of drunk driving, and told to walk unaccompanied into a local magistrate's office, Marshall prudently refused and told the officers, "You aren't going to shoot me in the back while I'm 'escaping.' "[253] So too, while changing trains in Mississippi, Marshall was confronted by a man with a pistol who warned him that there was only one more train coming through that day and he had "better be on it because the sun is never going down on a live nigger in this town."[254] Marshall "wrapped up" his constitutional rights "and put 'em in my hip pocket! . . . And caught the next train out of there."[255] But mostly he stayed and fought, even in the face of hostility from those who were in theory "officers of the court." In one school desegregation case, the attorney for the state warned Marshall that "If you ever show your black ass in Clarendon County again, you'll be dead."[256]

Marshall's extraordinary courage and commitment helped change the landscape of American race relations. He successfully argued cases challenging discrimination in schools, housing, voting, public transportation, and police conduct.[257] Marshall often faced off against adversaries with vastly more resources, and the ability to exhaust plaintiffs literally and financially for extended intervals. One Alabama lawsuit involving discrimination in teacher salaries took nine years to resolve, partly because the school board retaliated against plaintiffs by not renewing their contracts, which forced Marshall to keep finding new clients.[258]

Marshall also traveled to Japan and Korea in 1950 and 1951 in response to frequent complaints about racial discrimination by the military. There, he encountered black soldiers sentenced to life imprisonment after court martials lasting as little as ten minutes.[259] Not only did he prepare a report documenting the extent of discrimination, he also confronted General MacArthur directly. In one famous exchange, Marshall asked MacArthur why there was not a single Negro on his headquarters or personal staff. MacArthur responded that none were qualified. Marshall then acerbically noted that there were also none in the military band, and added, "Now General, just between you and me, Goddammit, don't you tell me there's no Negro that can play a horn."[260]

Marshall's gift for using humor to make a point was legendary throughout his career. In another celebrated incident, Marshall was in London working on a constitution for Kenya when he had the opportunity to meet Prince Philip. While exchanging pleasantries, the Prince asked, "Would you care to hear my opinion of lawyers?" Marshall responded, "Only if you care to hear my opinion of princes."[261]

During the late 1940s and early 1950s, school segregation cases became an increasingly central part of the NAACP Inc. Fund's work. During Marshall's early years as director, his strategy was to target graduate and professional schools, on the theory that states could not show that black institutions offered comparable education in terms of reputation and facilities, and that it would be prohibitively expensive for them to try. In 1945, seventeen Southern states had no institutions that would admit black PhD candidates, and only two schools that were open to black medical and law students.[262] Some states offered racially segregated institutions that they ludicrously claimed were equal. Texas provided black students a basement room with a few boxes of books, which it presented as comparable to the University of Texas law school.[263] Marshall and his colleagues also believed that cases involving post-graduate programs would provoke less hostility than litigation targeting elementary and secondary schools, and that college-educated plaintiffs would seem deserving to conservative judges.

Still, the resistance was substantial, and even when the NAACP won in court, it faced defiance in enforcement. For example, after the Supreme Court required Oklahoma to provide equal access to legal education to black applicants, the regents responded by designating a roped-off area in the state capital as a makeshift law school and assigning three teachers to instruct the female plaintiff.[264] When Marshall objected, Oklahoma's law school admitted the plaintiff but required her to sit in the back of the class behind a wooden bar in a chair with a sign marked "colored."[265] In a follow-up case, when Oklahoma's graduate school of education was forced to accept a black student, it responded by relegating him to a special table in the cafeteria and a separate bench in the library. After the NAACP continued to challenge such discriminatory treatment, the Supreme Court finally found it unconstitutional but declined to revisit *Plessy v. Ferguson*'s doctrine of separate but equal.[266] Chief Justice Vinson, who wrote the opinion in the Oklahoma case, told a colleague that he didn't want anything in the decision that would "stir up feelings of anger and resentment in any portion of the country."[267]

Frustrated by the expense and delay of demonstrating that segregated institutions were in fact unequal on a case-by-case basis, Marshall in 1947 persuaded the NAACP Inc. Fund board to declare that the organization would now only pursue claims that segregation was inherently unequal.[268] It was a controversial decision. Many in the civil rights community feared that the Court was not ready to overturn *Plessy* and that a decision reaffirming separate but equal would set the movement back.[269] As Yale Law School professor John Franks put it, "a judge cannot be blamed if he shrinks from precipitating a race riot."[270] Commenting on the difficulties of reconciling factions within the civil rights movement, Marshall told a staff member, "the easy part of the job is fighting the white folks."[271]

Concerns about the Court's inclinations were well founded, but Marshall laid careful groundwork for a frontal challenge on segregation. The litigation that ultimately reached the Supreme Court in *Brown v. Board of Education* involved five consolidated cases coming from Kansas, South Carolina, Virginia, Delaware, and Washington, DC. Coordinating that litigation was a marathon effort. Among Marshall's accomplishments was an appendix to the *Brown* brief with a statement from thirty-two of the nation's most eminent experts in race relations who attested to the social and psychological damage of segregation. After the initial argument in *Brown* in 1953, the Court was sharply divided, and rather than deliver a splintered opinion, it set the cases for reargument. The Justices asked for additional briefing on several questions, including the history of the Fourteenth Amendment and strategies for implementing a desegregation order. While the case was pending, Chief Justice Vinson died, and his replacement was former California governor Earl Warren. That shift in leadership proved decisive. Unlike his predecessor, Warren was a supporter of integration. He was also a master politician, capable of forging consensus. The timing of Vinson's death and its implication for the *Brown* proceedings prompted Justice Frankfurter to tell a former clerk, "This is the first indication I have ever had that there is a God."[272]

After the Court issued its order for reargument, Marshall lost no time in putting out a desperate appeal for funds and assembling a team of two hundred experts to help prepare the brief. Work conditions were challenging. Everyone was on sweatshop schedules in a cramped and uncomfortable office space.[273] Historian John Hope Franklin recalled that "I have never seen a man work so long and so hard [as Marshall]. It was nothing for him to say at 1 am, 'How about a fifteen minute break?'"[274] Other colleagues noted Marshall's exceptional capacity to inspire others, reduce friction, and exercise sound strategic judgment.[275] It all paid off.

In 1954, the Court issued a unanimous opinion finding segregated schools unconstitutional.[276] Marshall was elated, although not unmindful of the challenges remaining. At a victory party following the decision, he cautioned staff, 'Don't any of you fool yourselves, it's just begun, the fight has just begun."[277] Still, he was confident of the ultimate outcome, and predicted in a *New York Times* interview that by the hundredth anniversary of the Emancipation Proclamation in 1963, all forms of segregation would be eliminated.[278] "I'm in a hurry," Marshall told one reporter. "I want to put myself out of business."[279] The Justices, however, had a somewhat more realistic assessment of the resistance that their decision was likely to provoke, and proceeded cautiously. They scheduled further argument on the remedy, and then issued a judgment that was not what Marshall had hoped for. Rather than set a date for compliance, the Court remanded the cases to the trial courts with instruction to ensure desegregation with "all deliberate speed."[280] Still, Marshall remained optimistic. Speaking with a friend two days after the ruling in *Brown* II, he predicted that "those white crackers were going to get tired of having Negro lawyers beating 'em every day in court. They're going to get tired of it."[281]

It was a rare, but stunning miscalculation. As historian Richard Kluger noted, those "crackers" reinterpreted "all deliberate speed" as "any conceivable delay."[282] The courts became embroiled in desegregation disputes over not just schools, but all aspects of public life—parks, hospitals, transportation, and recreational facilities. When they lost in the courts, opponents of desegregation took to the streets and to the legislatures. In some states, they sought to ban the NAACP entirely, and one such effort dragged on in legal proceedings for eight years.[283] Other jurisdictions passed statutes subsidizing private schools, repealing compulsory school attendance laws, and withdrawing funds from districts that tried to implement desegregation plans.[284] White Citizens' Councils formed to coordinate economic reprisals (such as denial of jobs, credit, and insurance) against any blacks who worked with civil rights groups.[285]

By the close of the decade, Marshall had argued seven more cases before the Supreme Court involving resistance to desegregation.[286] The most notorious involved schools in Little Rock, Arkansas, where defiance from the governor and riots by white residents finally forced President Eisenhower to send in a thousand troops. For an entire year, soldiers escorted nine brave black children to and from school every day, where they experienced constant harassment and abuse.[287] Marshall himself had armed guards as he challenged the schools' actions in court.[288] When the trial judge accepted delays in desegregation due to public unrest, Marshall successfully argued before the Supreme Court that this acquiescence put the "very survival of the Rule of Law" at risk. Giving in to "ruffians" would "subvert our entire constitutional framework."[289]

Massive resistance to integration overwhelmed Marshall and his understaffed office. "You can't take a breather," he noted. "If you do, the other guy will run you ragged."[290] The pace worsened as civil rights activists mounted protests of their own. Martin Luther King Jr., the Southern Christian Leadership Council, and the Student Nonviolent Coordinating Committee launched a series of boycotts, sit-ins, marches, and related activities. Marshall disagreed with civil disobedience that violated the law in the course of challenging it. In his view, "defiance of the law of the land in any form is dangerous to the country."[291] In a well-publicized speech that infuriated protestors, he explained, "I am a man of law, and in my book, anarchy is anarchy. It makes no difference who practices anarchy. It's bad, and punishable, and should be punished."[292] He told one of King's aides that in his view, the NAACP's job was "to get people out of jail, not get them in."[293]

Protestors who provoked their own arrests severely taxed the resources of the organization, which they expected to provide legal representation as well as to pay fines and legal expenses. From Marshall's vantage, King was "great as a leader," but "as an organizer he wasn't worth didly squat. . . . All he did was dump all his legal work on us, including the bills."[294] Marshall may also have felt some resentment about being displaced as the leader of the civil rights community. When the Supreme Court announced its ruling in favor of the NAACP in the Little Rock school desegregation case, a black cab driver turned to Marshall and asked, "Did you see what Martin Luther King did for us today?"[295] Still, Marshall put aside his personal reservations and came to the defense of protesters. His last legal argument before the Supreme Court defended students who had launched a sit-in at a segregated Louisiana restaurant.[296]

The rising militancy within the black community also took a personal toll. Black Muslims denounced Marshall as a "white nigger," and "half white son of a bitch"; their threats of violence once led the New York Police department to post an armed guard at his apartment.[297] In one confrontation, when a black activist told Marshall, "you are nothing but a tool of the Establishment," Marshall shot back, "Brother, I *am* the Establishment."[298]

By the early 1960s, Marshall was ready for a change. As he put it, "I've always felt the assault troops should never occupy the town. I figured after the school decisions, the assault was over for me. It was time to let newer minds take over."[299] Not only did Marshall feel that "I have outlived my usefulness," he wanted more time at home.[300] His first wife had died of lung cancer just after the *Brown* decision, and Marshall had remarried. He and his new wife "Cissy" (a former secretary at the NAACP Inc. Fund) had two young sons, and Marshall had no desire for a grueling travel schedule that would prevent spending time with them. When President Kennedy offered to appoint him to the bench, Marshall seized the opportunity. However, he wanted to be on an appellate court, and Kennedy initially offered only a trial court position. Marshall felt that he had too short a fuse to be a trial judge. So when Attorney General Robert Kennedy told him it was that or nothing, Marshall responded, "All I've ever had in my life is nothing. It's not new to me, so goodbye."[301] Kennedy relented, but then faced challenges in getting the nomination confirmed. The Chair of the Senate Judiciary committee was James Eastland from Mississippi, an ardent segregationist. Fortunately, although he opposed Marshall, Eastland was willing to trade. His college roommate, Harold Cox, wanted an appellate court appointment and Eastland reportedly told Robert Kennedy that if the president was "willing to give me . . . Cox, I will give him the nigger."[302] Kennedy agreed, but Eastland still delayed the hearing for almost a year and the process was contentious.

Marshall stoically soldiered through it, and when the Senate finally voted to confirm him, he became the second African American to sit on a federal court of appeals. His characteristic sense of humor was on display shortly after the appointment, when the judges convened to take a new picture with Marshall among them. The photographer blew a fuse and everyone was mingling in the dark when Marshall arrived for the photograph. The Chief Judge's secretary, who did not recognize him, announced with evident relief, "thank God, the electrician's arrived." To which Marshall reportedly responded, "Ma'am, you'd have to be crazy to think they'd let me in that union."[303]

The transition to life as an appellate judge was difficult. Marshall missed the celebrity, solidarity, and personal interaction of his former work, and he couldn't socialize with former colleagues because that might prevent him from hearing appeals of their civil rights cases. As one biographer put it, Marshall found it "hard to be alone sorting out minutia of the law."[304] Moreover, many details that he needed to master were in fields such as tax, securities, and commercial law, in which he had no background or interest.[305] He did, however, finally have enough time for family. As his former law clerk Owen Fiss recalled, Marshall was the only judge on the Second Circuit who drove his children to and from school each and every day—and enjoyed it.[306]

Despite the challenges, Marshall applied himself to his work and compiled a sufficiently impressive record that in 1965, President Lyndon Johnson offered him the position of solicitor general, the administration's advocate before the Supreme Court. Marshall accepted, and this time the confirmation process went smoothly, in part because Johnson threatened to cut off public project funding in the states of any senators who sought to block the nomination.[307] By all accounts, Johnson's plan was to prepare Marshall for appointment as the first black justice of the Supreme Court. According to one of his closest advisors, Johnson explained that he was making Marshall solicitor general so that "when somebody says, 'he doesn't have a lot of experience for the Supreme Court,' by God that son of a bitch will have prosecuted more cases before the Supreme Court than any lawyer in America. So how's anybody gonna turn him down?"[308]

Johnson further paved the way for Marshall's Supreme Court nomination by choosing Ramsey Clark as attorney general. This forced his father, Tom Clark, to retire from the Supreme Court to avoid conflicts of interest, and created the necessary vacancy.[309] In commenting on the nomination, the *New York Times* noted that there were possible candidates "whose judicial work had been far more outstanding than Mr. Marshall's record during his brief service on the Second Circuit. . . . But apart from the symbolism, Mr. Marshall brings to the Court a wealth of practical experience as a brilliant, forceful advocate."[310] Marshall's record spoke for itself. He had argued thirty-two cases before the Supreme Court and won twenty-seven.[311] Nonetheless, the hearings on Marshall's confirmation were ugly. On their final day, Senator Strom Thurmond posed a series of esoteric questions concerning the history of the Fourteenth Amendment that Marshall couldn't answer *Time* magazine labeled it a "hazing."[312]

Marshall served twenty-four years on the Supreme Court. Shortly after his arrival in 1967, its ideological composition began to shift. President Richard Nixon made four conservative appointments, including Chief Justice Warren Burger, and Marshall found himself in the minority on most issues that he cared about.[313] By the time of his retirement, he was known as the "great Dissenter"; he had written over eighteen hundred dissents, more than any of his colleagues.[314] He was also a great listener. As was true during his years as an advocate, he took care as a justice to understand and engage with his opponents' arguments. But he never lost sight of the unique perspective that he brought to the Court. As Yale law professor Paul Gewirtz noted, Marshall knew what it felt like to be "at risk" in the world and "he knew the difference law could make in all those places."[315] He believed that judges should not "close their eyes . . . to social realities."[316] In his view, law should be a vehicle for social justice, and he reminded his colleagues when their decisions fell short. In a tribute to Marshall on his retirement, Justice Byron White noted that Marshall "brought to the conference table years of experience in an area that was of vital importance to our work, experience that none of us could claim to match. He characteristically would tell us things that we knew but would rather forget; and he told us much that we did not know due to the limitations of our own experience."[317]

A case in point was Marshall's angry dissent In *United States v. Kras*, where the Court upheld the constitutionality of a $50 filing fee in bankruptcy cases.[318] In the majority's view, a poor person could simply pay the fee in weekly installments. Marshall rebuked his colleagues for failing to understand "how close to the margin of survival" many poor people are.[319] He concluded, "It is perfectly proper for judges to disagree about what the Constitution requires. But it is disgraceful for an interpretation of the Constitution to be premised upon unfounded assumptions about how people live."[320] Marshall had also seen so much racial bias in the criminal justice system firsthand that he did not believe that death penalties could be imposed in a fair and impartial manner. He dissented every time the Court upheld a death sentence or declined to hear a capital case.

Even when Marshall could not persuade his colleagues, his voice had influence. Justice O'Connor recalled the power of his stories, which were "constantly pushing and prodding us to respond not only to the persuasiveness of legal argument but also to the power of moral truth."[321] Justice Brennan similarly testified to Marshall's contributions in seeking to "close the gap between constitutional ideal and reality."[322]

Marshall also took advantage of opportunities to communicate his views more directly to the public. In one widely noted example, he refused to participate in a bicentennial reenactment of the drafting of the Constitution unless it was historically accurate. It would have to portray him in livery and knee britches, holding a tray.[323] That put an end to the proposed reenactment, but Marshall used other celebrations around the Constitution's anniversary to remind the nation of progress yet to be made. In an address republished in the *Harvard Law Review,* he pointed out that "We the people no longer enslave, but the credit does not belong to the Framers. It belongs to those who refused to acquiesce in outdated notions of 'liberty,' 'justice,' and 'equality,' and who strived to better them."[324]

Every attorney, Marshall believed, had an opportunity and obligation to continue that struggle. All lawyers, he told one law school audience, "have a duty to represent the public, to be social reformers in however small a way."[325] And the public had a duty as well, as he reminded his audience at a Baltimore ceremony commemorating a statue in his honor. "I just want to be sure," he told the crowd, "that when you see this statue, you won't think that's the end of it. I won't have it that way. There's too much work to be done."[326]

Marshall lived his own life according to that principle. His term on the Court was often frustrating as he struggled with poor health, social isolation, and the success of his conservative colleagues in rolling back progressive rulings that he had struggled so hard to achieve. Yet he never wavered in his determination to serve as what law professor Kathleen Sullivan described as the "conscience of the Court . . . [reminding it] of the human consequences of legal decisions."[327] Nor did he lose his sense of humor. In 1970, when Marshall was hospitalized with pneumonia, President Nixon asked to see his medical records. Marshall authorized their release but insisted on including in large bold letters on the front of the file, "Not Yet."[328] On other occasions, when asked about his plans for retirement, the justice responded that he intended to serve out the full term of his office, which, he noted, was for life. And he sometimes added with a twinkle, "I expect to die at 110, shot by a jealous husband."[329]

In fact, he stepped down at age eighty-three in the wake of further health problems. During many of his final years, he was frustrated with the Court's direction and with the opinions that conservative chief justices assigned him to write on esoteric and relatively unimportant issues. Critics, including at least one of his colleagues, felt that he was often inadequately prepared and overly reliant on his law clerks to draft such opinions.[330] But he soldiered on, unwilling to lose any opportunity to remind the Court and the country of its unfulfilled promises of social justice. Even in retirement, he took one last occasion before his death to focus public attention on this unfinished agenda. In 1992, in accepting the Liberty Medal, he noted, "The battle has not been won; we have barely begun. America can do better. . . . America has no choice but to do better to assure justice for all Americans, Afro and white, rich and poor, educated and illiterate. Our futures are bound together."[331] Marshall dedicated his life to that struggle. At his memorial service a year later, Chief Justice Rehnquist acknowledged Marshall's extraordinary contribution: "Inscribed above the front entrance to the Supreme Court building are the words 'Equal Justice Under Law.' Surely no one individual did more to make these words a reality than Thurgood Marshall."[332]

In a press conference announcing Marshall's retirement from the Court, a reporter asked how he would like to be remembered. Marshall responded, "He did what he could with what he had."[333] It was not a spontaneous quip. He gave a succession of law clerks the same answer.[334] I was fortunate to be among them. And the longer I have studied character, the more I have come to respect that aspiration and the life that it reflected. After his death, a reporter summed it up. "Not all great men are good men. Marshall was both."[335]

Nelson Mandela

Nelson Mandela was born in 1918 in a small village in segregated South Africa. His first name at birth was Rolihlahla, which, as he frequently and fondly pointed out, translates as "troublemaker."[336] His father was a local chief who was stripped of his position by a British magistrate, reportedly for corruption. According to his family, the real reason was retaliation for standing up to unreasonable demands.[337] Both of Mandela's parents were illiterate, but they wanted him to have a proper education. They sent him to a Methodist school, where he was baptized as a Christian and given the name Nelson by a teacher.[338] When Mandela was nine, his father died, and his mother entrusted his care to the chief of the Thembu region. Mandela and many of his friends later credited his leadership capacities to the lessons he learned in this royal household.[339]

During his early years, Mandela attended a mission school, a Methodist college, and then the University of Fort Hare, South Africa's only black university.[340] His involvement in student protests led to what he considered a dispute over principle with the administration, resulting in his expulsion.[341] To avoid an arranged marriage at home, Mandela then fled to Johannesburg. There, he eventually landed a job as a clerk in a law firm, run by a white partner sympathetic to the African National Congress (ANC). The Congress was the primary vehicle for the anti-apartheid movement, which was fighting a system that denied a vote to 80 percent of the country and enforced segregation in every aspect of life. To finish his undergraduate education, Mandela enrolled in a University of South Africa correspondence course.[342] After passing his BA exams, he began studying law at the University of Witwatersrand, where he was the only native African student. He became politically active and married a nurse, Evelyn Mase, who was also involved in the ANC.[343] They had four children before their divorce.

Mandela's growing political activism interfered with his studies, and he left the university without a law degree. He received one many years later, becoming one of only eighteen black lawyers in the country.[344] When he opened a law office with a fellow anti-apartheid activist, their partnership became the only black law firm in South Africa.[345] Unsurprisingly, it was popular with aggrieved blacks, particularly in cases of police brutality, and it was correspondingly unpopular with authorities. They denied the firm an office permit, forcing it to move to a remote location where its practice dwindled.[346] Mandela's political activism was similarly unpalatable, and he was several times banned from holding any elective office, attending meetings, or making public speeches.[347] The regime's brutal suppression of political dissent convinced Mandela and his colleagues in the ANC that they had no alternative to armed resistance. In 1956, Mandela, along with most of the ANC's high officials, were arrested and charged with treason. After extended delays and violent protests, the defendants were acquitted in 1961.[348] While the proceedings were pending, Mandela married a social worker, Winnie Madikizela, who also became active in ANC activities. The couple had two children.

Following his acquittal, Mandela went underground. Referred to as the "Black Pimpernel," Mandela traveled around the country, organizing ANC cells, strikes, and an armed wing of the ANC, known as MK, Umkhono we Sizwe, meaning "spear of the nation."[349] MK activists engaged in acts of sabotage that, as Mandela explained, "did not involve loss of life . . . [and therefore] offered the best hope for reconciliation among the races afterward."[350] Strategies included night bombings of military installations, power plants, telephone lines, and transport links. Activists also organized mass protests, which, in 1960, led the government to ban ANC activities.[351] The government also passed a Sabotage Act, which authorized the death penalty for even minor acts of destruction.[352] Mandela was undaunted, but with a warrant out for his arrest, he lived in constant danger. He seldom saw his family. As Winnie later complained, she was the most "unmarried married woman."[353] His now six children felt slighted as well. One of his daughters later told him, "you are a father to all our people, but you have never had the time to be a father to me."[354]

In 1962, after an international tour to raise money for anti-apartheid activities, Mandela was arrested on charges of inciting workers' strikes and leaving the country without permission. His strategy was to put the government on trial. He refused to call witnesses and turned his plea of mitigation into an indictment of the anti-apartheid regime. His conviction and sentence of five years in prison was a prelude to more serious charges. A police raid unearthed evidence that led to prosecution of Mandela and other ANC members for sabotage and conspiracy to overthrow the government.

Mandela and his codefendants admitted sabotage, but denied treason. His eloquent defense at trial established his reputation as the world leader of the anti-apartheid movement. As Mandela explained, his involvement in sabotage came only as a last resort after many years of tyranny and oppression:

> All lawful modes of expressing opposition to this principle [of white supremacy] had been closed by legislation, and we were placed in a position in which we had either to accept a permanent state of inferiority or defy the government. We chose to defy the law. . . . It was only when all else had failed, when all channels of peaceful protest had been barred to us, that the decision was made to embark on violent forms of political struggle. . . . We did so not because we desired such a course, but solely because the government had left us with no other choice.[355]

In another widely quoted passage from his trial defense, Mandela concluded:

> I have cherished the ideal of a democratic and free society in which all persons will live together in harmony and with equal opportunities. It is an ideal for which I hope to live and see realized. But, my lord, if it needs be, it is an ideal for which I am prepared to die.[356]

It took the trial judge no more than three minutes to find all conspirators except one guilty, and that defendant was immediately arrested on new offenses before he even left the courtroom. Mandela and his codefendants were sentenced to life imprisonment. The trial helped marshal support for the anti-apartheid movement. As the *Times of London* noted, "the verdict of history will be that the ultimate guilty party is the government in power."[357]

Mandela was forty-four when he entered prison; he would not leave until he was seventy-one. The conditions were brutal. In a sign of what was to come, the journey to Robben Island prison began with guards amusing themselves by urinating down air vents on the prisoners below deck.[358] The prison routine was one of hard labor at lime quarries, where the reflection and dust often caused serious eye damage. It took three years before authorities granted requests for sunglasses, and Mandela's eyes never recovered. Even after surgery, he could read only with difficulty.[359] He could send or receive a letter only once every six months, and authorities heavily censored the correspondence, or withheld it out of spite.[360] Solitary confinement and casual beatings were common.[361] The kitchen staff was corrupt, so food sometimes ran out. Although authorities claimed the meals were "balanced," Mandela noted that the balance was between "unpalatable and inedible."[362] The food was occasionally so full of dirt and insects that prisoners went hungry instead of eating.

Mandela quickly emerged as a leader, who honed his political skills by organizing resistance and settling disputes. He learned Afrikaans, the language of the dominant whites, and urged other prisoners to do the same.[363] As the number of ANC prisoners grew, reaching about one thousand by 1966, Mandela and his colleagues devised informal structures of communication and control. Messages were hidden in food and toilets, and alliances were formed with friendly guards who smuggled in newspapers and extra rations.[364] Mandela also helped organize a "University of Robben Island," in which prisoners lectured on their own areas of expertise and debated current issues.[365] Part of what earned Mandela a leadership role was his great capacity for empathy and his willingness to help with even the most menial and degrading tasks. When a flu epidemic hit the isolation section in 1974, Mandela, who escaped the outbreak, made the rounds each morning, emptying and cleaning the toilet buckets of his sick colleagues.[366]

What also generated widespread respect was his courage in standing up to prison authorities. During a tour that three judges made to inspect Robben Island, Mandela complained of the conduct of a particularly vindictive prison commander in his presence. The commander then warned Mandela that if he complained of beatings that he had not personally witnessed, "you will get yourself into trouble. You know what I mean?" Mandela turned to the judges and responded, "gentlemen, you can see for yourself the type of man we are dealing with as commanding officer. If he can threaten me here, in your presence, you can imagine what he does when you are not here."[367] Within months, the commander was transferred and conditions improved.

During the early 1980s, exiled ANC leaders decided that Mandela should be the human face of their public campaign. "Free Nelson Mandela" became a frequent protest chant, and even a pop chart anthem in Great Britain.[368] His picture circulated in many nations, which led Mandela to later claim that he was probably the world's best-known political prisoner even though many audiences had no real idea who he was. When "Free Mandela" posters went up in London, some young supporters reportedly thought "Free" was his Christian name.[369] The anti-apartheid movement slowly gained traction, and two thousand mayors in fifty-four countries signed a petition for Mandela's release.[370] He had become a "global icon," and the United Nations Security Council declared that freeing him was the only way to achieve "meaningful discussion of the future of the country."[371]

In response to this growing pressure, the government offered to release Mandela from prison seven times beginning in 1975 if he would agree to various restrictions, generally including bans on political activities. Mandela refused, which prolonged his imprisonment for sixteen years.[372] One of those offers came in 1985, after he was transferred to a prison outside Capetown. South African president P. W. Botha offered him freedom if he would renounce violence. Mandela again refused.[373] He released a statement expressing surprise at the condition because "I am not a violent man," but setting forth different terms for his release.

> Let [Botha] renounce violence. Let him say that he will dismantle apartheid. Let him unban the . . . African National Congress. . . . Let him guarantee free political activity so that people may decide who will govern them. I cherish my own freedom dearly, but I care even more for your freedom. . . . What freedom am I being offered while the organization of the people remains banned? . . . Only free men can negotiate. . . . I cannot and will not give any undertaking at a time when I and you, the people are not free.[374]

These were the first words heard from Mandela since his trial statement more than twenty years before. It was greeted with cheers at a mass rally, and pressure for his release continued to mount. Economic sanctions and boycotts of companies doing business in South Africa also made the antiapartheid regime more vulnerable.

In 1986, Mandela wrote a letter proposing secret negotiations, and the government agreed. It was a risky strategy for Mandela. ANC leaders would never have approved.[375] One of his most trusted colleagues felt that if any talks began, the government should initiate them. Mandela responded "what did it matter who initiated them? What mattered was what they achieved not how they started . . . not worry about who knocked on the door first."[376] Mandela subsequently got a message to the ANC leaders in exile, and, without disclosing any details about the negotiations, gained their authorization to maintain contact with the government.[377] Mandela's strategy paid off. South Africa's new president, Frederik Willem de Klerk, ultimately agreed to lift the ban on liberation organizations, to release some political prisoners, to repeal apartheid laws, and to grant Mandela an unconditional release.[378]

Following his release, Mandela's first statement to the crowds was a call to continue the struggle against apartheid. His first meeting with the press displayed a remarkable absence of rancor about his twenty-seven years in prison.[379] His message was one of hope and reconciliation. He understood Afrikaners' fear concerning their treatment in a post-apartheid regime, and emphasized that they were "fellow South Africans. We want them to feel safe and to know that we appreciate the contribution they made towards the development of this country."[380] Mandela believed that the rebuilding of the nation would be undermined by expressions of racial animosity. He also was convinced that nurturing resentment would ill serve those who had suffered most. When former American president Bill Clinton asked Mandela how he had felt at the time of his release, Mandela acknowledged that he had initially felt "anger and hatred and fear" toward those responsible for his imprisonment. But "I realized if I kept hating them, once I got in that car and got through the [prison] gate, I would still be in prison. So I let it go because I wanted to be free."[381]

Mandela's example was of profound importance. As observers later noted, "If Mandela had come out of prison and sent a different message . . . this country could be in flames."[382] By contrast, if he could emerge from his ordeal calling for reconciliation, how could others who had suffered less demand revenge and retribution? Mandela's absence of vindictiveness served to further bolster his international reputation. Following his release, he took a victory lap around the world. He met with many political leaders, addressed the US Congress, and was greeted by ecstatic crowds and a ticker tape parade in New York City.[383]

The years in prison had, however, taken a tremendous toll. Mandela suffered from tuberculosis and back pains as well as an eye ailment. His marriage had also disintegrated. Winnie had found a new lover, half her age, and she had no intention of giving him up. That affair, together with her misappropriation of ANC funds, led the couple to separate in 1992. In addition to his physical and marital difficulties, Mandela faced severe criticism from some ANC members, who suspected him of having been "bought off by the authorities."[384]

These personal challenges were compounded by the nation's political crisis. Mandela returned home from his international tour to a country racked by racial violence and economic chaos. As one biographer put it, Mandela "faced the most demanding task of his career, to negotiate a peaceful revolution without a violent backlash from the white right or the black left."[385] Both Mandela and de Klerk were arguing with their own parties as much as with each other, and also had to contend with militant Zulus and their charismatic leader Mangosuthu Buthelezi.[386] De Klerk was, as Mandela put it, a "gradualist," who did not initially want the end of white rule but rather a system of power-sharing based on group rights.[387] Mandela insisted on majority rule. In 1993, negotiations were disrupted by an Afrikaner's assassination of a beloved leader of black youth. The ANC announced a week-long campaign of mass protests, and Mandela went on national television appealing for calm. He shrewdly pointed out that it was only through an Afrikaner witness who had risked her life in coming forward that the police were able to apprehend the assassin.[388] And, he added, violence would trample on the values that the slain leader had stood for. "Those who commit such acts," Mandela argued, "serve only the interests of the assassins."[389] As a result, the protests remained relatively peaceful, which helped solidify Mandela's reputation as a leader. Negotiations resumed, and eventually secured an agreement between the warring factions that guaranteed free elections and a peaceful transition to a democratic state.

That compromise earned Mandela and de Klerk the 1993 Nobel Peace Prize. They were unlikely allies. Mandela despised de Klerk's tolerance of apartheid and indifference to racial violence. De Klerk felt that Mandela made "vicious and unwarranted" attacks on his record and integrity.[390] *Time* magazine, in awarding the two leaders its Men of the Year award, noted that "their negotiations at times resembled nothing so much as the conflict they were trying to resolve."[391] Their "mutual bitterness and resentments . . . [were] palpable. How could these two have agreed on anything—lunch, for instance—much less the remaking of a nation?"[392] But both were ultimately able to rise above their personal animosity. As Mandela noted, "I need him. Whether I like him or not is irrelevant."[393] It was Mandela's unique capacity to blend principle with pragmatism that helped forge the foundations for a sustainable democracy.

Mandela's character strengths also served him well in the subsequent battle with de Klerk for the presidency. As one biographer put it, Mandela's "exemplary lack of bitterness, his insistence on national reconciliation, and his willingness to compromise had earned him enduring respect among his adversaries. The white community would not vote for him, but they would accept a government under his presidency."[394] In a nationally televised debate between the two presidential rivals, Mandela won support by extending his hand at the close of his remarks and stating, "I think we are a shining example to the entire world of people drawn from different racial groups, who have a common loyalty, a common love, to their common country. . . . We are going to face the problems of this country together. I am proud to hold your hand for us to go forward."[395]

At age seventy-five, Mandela won the general election with 63 percent of the votes. Blacks lined up at the polls, sometimes waiting for as long as five hours, to cast their first presidential vote. As one voter observed, after waiting "nearly 350 years, 350 minutes is nothing."[396] An estimated billion viewers around the world watched Mandela's inauguration, which included three of his former prison warders as his personal guests.[397]

One person not in attendance was his only son, who was in Durban preparing for his law exam. That absence brought home the personal costs of Mandela's political commitments. In his autobiography, Mandela expressed no misgivings about his choices except those concerning his family:

> I was always prepared to face the hardships that affected me personally. But my family paid a terrible price, perhaps too dear a price for my commitment. . . . I did not in the beginning choose to place my people

above my family, but in attempting to serve my people, I found that I was prevented from fulfilling my obligations as a son, a brother, a father, and a husband. In that way, my commitment to my people, to the millions of South Africans I would never know or meet, was at the expense of the people I knew best and loved most.[398]

Yet on Mandela's ninetieth birthday, when asked by a CNN reporter if he regretted not spending more time with his family, Mandela answered no, because what he was doing was for the greater good of society.[399]

As president, Mandela faced enormous challenges. Apartheid had left a searing legacy of racial inequality and poverty. Blacks owned barely 2 percent of private sector assets. Half of all South African households were poor, and a third of the population was illiterate.[400] The economy was in dire straits, and the new government was saddled with crippling interest payments on debts incurred by the apartheid regime.[401] Accommodations to the white community met with harsh criticism from blacks.[402] But Mandela had seen the consequences of white flight in other post-colonial African nations, and he took pains to reassure Afrikaners that they would be protected and represented in the "Rainbow nation."[403] De Klerk served as Mandela's first deputy president, several other whites served as cabinet ministers, and Buthelezi was his minster of home affairs. Among Mandela's many gestures of goodwill was a lunch invitation to his former prosecutor, and a dinner invitation to the former commander of the Robben Island prison.[404]

Mandela also went out of his way to support rugby, an Afrikaner sport, and urged other blacks to do the same. Speaking before a black crowd, he wore a rugby supporter's cap, and asked his audience to "stand by them because they are our kind."[405] When South Africa won the 1995 World Cup, he walked onto the field wearing the team's green jersey.[406] As de Klerk later noted, that gesture "won the hearts of millions of white rugby fans."[407] In presenting the trophy, Mandela said "thanks for what you have done for South Africa." The team's captain responded, "Thanks for what you have done *to* South Africa."[408]

Another masterful stroke of bridge building was the Truth and Reconciliation Commission. The Commission was a compromise between blacks, who wanted trials and reparations, and Afrikaners, who opposed any such accountability. The compromise was for the Commission to offer amnesty from prosecution for those who made full disclosure of crimes carried out with a political objective. Much of the public doubted that the process would bring either truth or reconciliation, and predicted that few people would come forward. But in the end, over twenty-one thousand individuals testified. Although critics charged that white officials and ANC activists were often evasive, and that the process frequently inflamed rather than appeased, many found the findings cathartic. Most judged the Commission on the whole to be a success.[409] Part of the reason was that its condemnations did not spare even the highest level leaders, including de Klerk and Winnie Mandela.[410]

Mandela also achieved credit for bringing newfound respect for the rule of law. Speaking at the inauguration of the Constitutional Court in 1995, he proclaimed that on this court "hinges the future of our democracy."[411] Mandela helped solidify the court's legitimacy by publicly recognizing the supremacy of its rulings, even when it found his own actions unconstitutional. He also complied with a lower court order of dubious legality that compelled him to testify in public proceedings about the performance of official duties.[412] In commenting on those actions, one South African law professor noted, "Mandela was not a saint, but he could well be described as the patron saint of South Africa's democratic order."[413]

Not all of Mandela's presidential actions were, however, worthy of respect. He was tolerant of financial misconduct by some members of his government and party, including Winnie, whom he unwisely appointed deputy minister of arts. Not until she became openly disloyal to the government did he dismiss her and begin divorce proceedings.[414] Bishop Tutu famously charged that Mandela's government had stopped the gravy train only long enough to climb aboard.[415] When accused of cronyism, stifling dissent, and acting dictatorially, Mandela sometimes responded with just the kind of intolerance that opponents were criticizing.[416] He delegated most of the day-to-day decision-making to his deputy president, Thabo Mbeki, and made so many international junkets that critics sometimes sarcastically quipped, "This week President Mandela is paying a visit to South Africa."[417] De Klerk complained about Mandela's "tactic of papering over problems with charm and promises, without taking effective remedial action."[418] During Mandela's term in office, corruption, crime, poverty, and unemployment remained high, and he initially turned a blind eye to the AIDS crisis.[419] However, as he noted in 2002, in awarding the Nelson Mandela Prize for Health and Human rights to two HIV researchers, "At least I am willing to admit when I have made a mistake."[420] And he then threw his weight behind efforts to combat the disease.[421]

Moreover, whatever his political missteps, Mandela's personal life set a high standard. Accustomed to austerity, Mandela was free of greed and self-dealing. Although he lived part-time in official residences, he also maintained a modest house in Johannesburg where he made his own bed. He donated his Nobel Prize and a third of his salary to charity.[422] In his relations with staff, he went out of his way to show courtesy and respect, and often invited visiting dignitaries to shake hands with the woman who served them tea.[423] As de Klerk noted, Mandela had an "exceptional ability to make everyone with whom he came into contact feel special."[424] At parties, he might spend much of the evening in conversation with a constant stream of gardeners and domestic staff who wanted to greet him.[425] One biographer attributed such behavior to Mandela's strong desire to be liked and admired: "He wants you to come away from meeting him thinking that he is everything you had ever hoped for."[426]

After retirement as president, he capitalized on his iconic status to raise large funds for charities.[427] He remarried on his eightieth birthday, continued to travel, and finally managed to spend more time with family. At age eighty-five, in failing health, he announced that he was "retiring from retirement," and cut back on public events.[428] He died a decade later, and his funeral attracted dignitaries from around the world. In his remarks at Mandela's memorial service, President Barack Obama noted that the leader's great achievement was "to teach that reconciliation is not a matter of ignoring a cruel past, but a means of confronting it with inclusion and generosity and truth. He changed laws, but he also changed hearts."[429] One of those he changed was Obama himself, who credits Mandela's work with awakening his own responsibilities to others and setting him on the "improbable journey that finds me here today." Obama added that "while I will always fall short of [his] example, he makes me want to be a better man. He speaks to what's best inside us."[430]

In assessing Mandela's legacy, one biographer noted:

> Mandela's role in the transformation of South Africa from a country riven by racial division and violence to a fledgling democracy represented one of the supreme triumphs of the late twentieth century. Mandela's role in that transformation was vital to its success. . . . The generosity of spirit he showed after his prison ordeal had a profound impact on his white adversaries, earning him measures of trust and confidence which made a political settlement attainable. As president, he pursued the cause of national reconciliation with the same tenacity.[431]

Mandela's own assessment was more modest. He famously claimed that credit for the new South Africa belonged to the ANC. "I don't think there is much history can say about me. I just want to be remembered as part of that collective."[432] He was wrong about history.

Taken together, these lives reflect certain common themes. All of these leaders had firsthand experiences of injustice that crystalized their resolve. Wells and Gandhi were thrown out of first class train compartments and then witnessed far-reaching abuses. For Wells, it was the lynching of a friend; for Gandhi, it was proposed legislation denying voting rights to Indians. Marshall's conscience was aroused by being denied admission to Maryland's all-white law school and by witnessing the debilitating effects of school segregation. Mandela's activism was born less of any pivotal incidents than the cumulative brutality of apartheid.

In challenging such injustices, all three leaders displayed extraordinary courage, commitment, persistence, and personal sacrifice. Wells's columns cost her jobs as a teacher and newspaper editor, and exposed her to vitriolic criticism, and threats of lynching. Marshall was subject to similar threats and frequently needed armed guards. Gandhi and Mandela stood up to angry mobs, Mandela faced life imprisonment, and Gandhi was prepared for assassination or a fast until death. All of these individuals devoted their entire lives to the pursuit of social justice.

None were without flaws. Gandhi was tolerant of caste privilege and prejudice against blacks, and his treatment of his wife, children, and other female relatives with whom he slept raise serious concern. Mandela was intolerant of criticism and marginalized his family. Wells allowed her temper, self-righteousness, and domineering style to disrupt crucial alliances. Marshall was occasionally envious of rivals and, in his later years on the Supreme Court, was disengaged from some of his work. But they all far exceeded the self-description that Mandela himself offered: "not a saint . . . unless you think of a saint as a sinner who keeps on trying."[433] Whatever their shortcomings, these leaders left enduring legacies for our struggles toward social justice.

8

Conclusion

THURGOOD MARSHALL CARED about character. I was fortunate enough to observe that up close, beginning at our first meeting. Shortly after graduating from law school, I applied for one of his Supreme Court clerkships, and received an invitation for an interview. I was anxious beyond measure. Reading about his work during the nation's early civil rights campaigns was a large part of why I went to law school. I never prepared more for anything than that interview. I read every major decision Marshall had written over the last decade, and much of what commentators had said about them. I did not know then what I learned later. Marshall used a committee of former clerks, who had become leading practitioners and academics, to screen his applicants and prepare a short list for him to interview. If you were on that list, you were viewed as qualified. The interview was about something else. At mine, Marshall began by skimming my resume, and then noting, "It says here that you graduated Phi Beta Kappa at Yale. What do women do with those gold Phi Beta Kappa Keys?" That was not a question I had prepared for. But I didn't want to make something up, so I hedged. "Well, I'm not sure." He waited. All I could think of to add was that "I gave mine to my mother. I thought she deserved it at least as much as I did." Marshall chuckled, and that was pretty much the end of the interview. I sobbed in the ladies room afterward. It felt like I had come so close only to fail so miserably. But before I had time to leave the courthouse, I had a call from Marshall offering me a clerkship. That year, at a time when a number of Supreme Court justices were still hiring no female clerks, Marshall hired two.

Marshall's concerns about character have been widely shared, at least in principle. Americans claim that they care, as the preceding chapters documented. Ninety-nine percent of students agree that "it's important for me to be a person with good character," and 85 percent of parents want character education in schools.[1] Honesty and integrity are among the characteristics that the public ranks as most important in leaders.[2] Yet as prior discussion also reflected, there is a dispiriting disconnect between what Americans say and what they do when it comes to character-related decisions. Many character education programs lack adequate resources, teacher training, evaluation, and accountability. Millions of children participate in youth and sports organizations that claim to build character but have yet to demonstrate their effectiveness. And many of the individuals we choose as leaders fall short along dimensions of character. Only about a quarter of Americans think that elected officials are honest or that they put the interests of the country ahead of their own.[3] Only 8 percent of the public rates the ethical standards of members of Congress as high or very high.[4] Only 17 percent feel similarly about business executives.[5]

These are worrisome trends, not only because character-related traits affect leaders' performance in office but also because the significance (or lack of significance) we attach to those traits sends a powerful symbolic message. Who we choose for leadership positions shapes our own cultural character. What does it say about the nation's political priorities that integrity ranked only fourth among Democrats and sixth among Republicans and Independents who were asked about the relative importance of qualities in presidential candidates?[6] Less than a fifth of Americans considered President Trump honest and trustworthy, but almost half voted for him anyway.[7]

Our lack of confidence in the integrity of leaders should prompt a closer look at cultural values, and how we define success. In *The Road to Character*, *New York Times* columnist David Brooks distinguishes between what he calls "resume virtues" and "eulogy virtues."

> Resume virtues are the skills that contribute to external success; the eulogy virtues are the ones that exist at the core of your being—whether you are kind, brave, honest, or faithful. Most of us would say that the eulogy virtues are more important than the resume virtues, but I confess that for long stretches of my life I've spent more time thinking about the latter than the former. Our education system is certainly oriented around the resume virtues more than the eulogy ones. . . . Most of us have clearer strategies for how to achieve career success than we do for how to develop a profound character.[8]

Brooks is not alone. In one telling survey, Pew researchers asked young people age eighteen to twenty-five about their most important goals. Four-fifths said getting rich, half said being famous, and only a third said helping people who need help.[9] Those values are reflected in other measures of personal priorities. Only a quarter of Americans do volunteer work through or for an organization at least once a week, and their median contribution is only about an hour.[10] Two-thirds of the public think that Americans are selfish.[11] Even our use of terms such as "character," "virtue," and the "common good" has declined over the past century.[12] Few young Americans are absorbing advice along the lines that Albert Einstein offered: "Try not to become a man of success but rather try to become a man of value . . . [who] will give more than he receives."[13]

The materialism and self-interest driving contemporary culture are deeply rooted, and technology is making a bad situation worse. Social media provide individuals with more and more opportunities to inflate their self-image and to focus on "me" rather than "we."[14] The kind of attention that people once gave to the state of their souls now goes to the appearance of their bodies.[15] Young Americans focus on how to be hot, not how to be good.

These priorities are counterproductive for both individuals and society. Virtues are correlated with satisfaction, resilience, and physical well-being.[16] People who are motivated by intrinsic goals, such as personal growth and assisting others, are generally happier with their lives than those motivated primarily by extrinsic goals, such as wealth or fame.[17] Part of the reason is that material desires tend to increase as rapidly as they are satisfied. If self-worth is confused with net worth, individuals can become trapped on a "hedonic treadmill": the more they have, the more they need to have.[18] Money and status are positional goods; individuals' satisfaction depends on how they compare relative to others, and increases in wealth or status are readily offset by changes in reference groups.[19] By contrast, goals that transcend the self have the greatest impact on individuals' sense of fulfillment.[20] As one British military officer once put it, "you make a living by what you get. You make a life by what you give."[21]

Nurturing those deeper goals is critical not only for individual but also for societal well-being. People with exemplary moral character can make an enormous difference in the lives of others and in the pursuit of social justice. Despite their diverse backgrounds and challenges, Jane Addams, Albert Schweitzer, Mother Teresa, Ida Wells, Mahatma Gandhi, Thurgood Marshall, and Nelson Mandela all displayed crucial character traits: courage, empathy, perseverance, and sacrifice for the common good. Addams, Schweitzer, and Mother Teresa gave up lives of privilege and comfort to live among those who needed help most. Gandhi and Mandela gave up their freedom and, along with Wells and Marshall, faced threats of mob violence. None were without flaws, and their character weaknesses are no less instructive than their strengths. Schweitzer shared the racial prejudices of colonialists. Gandhi embraced class privilege and accepted discrimination against blacks. Wells let arrogance, self-righteousness, and temper undermine her effectiveness. Mandela neglected his family and was intolerant of criticism. Mother Teresa tolerated substandard medical care and held views on reproductive freedom that denied other women the capacity for self-determination that she herself exercised. But whatever their limitations, all were persons of vision, integrity, and principle. They braved hardship, hostility, and danger to promote the common good. Their achievements left a lasting legacy and provide a continuing inspiration.

The qualities that these individuals exemplified are also reflected in ways large and small by ordinary individuals. People display character in how they care for their families, friends, and communities, and how they respond to social needs and social injustices. Their character is the foundation for a purposeful life and a flourishing society. It deserves more effective development in our homes, our schools, our youth organizations, our laws, and our politics. We need to focus both on individuals and institutions, and on how personal character is shaped by cultural practices.

To that end, our concern should center on moral character, which includes qualities such as honesty, integrity, and empathy, as well as performance character, which includes qualities such as perseverance and self-control. Without performance traits, individuals lack the capacity to follow through on good intentions. But without moral foundations, individuals' other strengths may promote unethical or selfish ends. We should also nurture moral identity—the belief that morality is important to one's sense of self.

Development of these character traits needs to be a priority in all aspects of children's lives. That will require consistent messages from families, parents, teachers, coaches, and leaders of religious and secular youth organizations. Adults need to model and reward fairness, honesty, empathy, and mutual respect if they wish to foster those values in children. That effort needs to start with parents who set high expectations, and reinforce morally responsible actions. Role models who display altruism and treat others with empathy and compassion increase the likelihood that children will do so as well.

Because schools cannot avoid teaching values, they need to be more intentional and effective in their efforts. Part of their mission should be to create "communities of character," which reflect values such as honesty, integrity, altruism, and self-discipline. Although more innovation and evaluation is necessary to identify what interventions are most successful, the research available points to a number of strategies. Teachers need to promote a moral climate, model moral conduct, foster perseverance, involve students in resolving moral issues, integrate character concerns issues throughout the curricula, provide opportunities for service learning, and partner with parents, coaches, and youth leaders in these efforts. Each school should have a plan for character education that stakeholders can help shape, support, and assess. Higher education needs to do its part as well. Colleges should provide greater curricular and extracurricular opportunities for students to focus on character, ethics, and service.

So too, the law should reflect a more informed understanding of character. Legal standards play a much more critical role than is commonly assumed. Good moral character requirements define the kind of jobs and professional licenses people can hold, and whether they can become citizens or reside in the country legally. The law concerning character also affects judgments concerning culpability, punishment, and parole. Yet all too often, legal doctrine is out of touch with psychological research. The qualities that we associate with character are not static across time and situations. Character can evolve, and the law should become more wary of categorical pronouncements that individuals have it or they don't. Decisions about occupational licenses, citizenship, deportation, criminal sentences, and parole need to take into account a wider range of factors that bear on moral culpability and rehabilitation.

Educational, nonprofit, and media organizations also should do more to honor exemplary character and to withhold recognition from individuals whose conduct raises ethical concerns. In *The Common Good*, Robert Reich offers several examples. One is Alfred Taubman, who donated money to found the Taubman Center at Harvard's Kennedy School of Government, and who subsequently served a prison sentence for price-fixing. In refusing student requests to change the name, the Center Director claimed that "in the great scheme of things, Taubman['s] . . . conviction does not mean that his life has not been ethical, or one that Harvard doesn't want to associate with." Reich responds, "Hello? Taubman had just been convicted of price-fixing. His name was etched on Harvard's school of government, which is supposed to train students to work for the common good."[22] It is one thing for the law to recognize and reward rehabilitation; it is quite another to retain a felon's name on an institution dedicated to ethical leadership for no reason other than financial.

So too, in 2017, the Los Angeles Press Club honored Harvey Weinstein with its Truthteller Award for Contributions to the Public Discourse and Cultural Enlightenment of Our Society. The Club called him an example of "integrity and social responsibility" despite widespread rumors of his sexual abuses.[23] The only plausible explanation for that willful blindness was that so many Hollywood journalists were indebted to Weinstein for work as writers and consultants.[24] And until recent public outcry, many nonprofits accepted funding and named buildings after the Sackler family, despite its contribution to the opioid crisis.

Less egregious examples are common in award celebrations throughout the nation where we pretend to honor moral leadership but the real qualification is money. Some of that pretense may be inevitable for nonprofits struggling for survival, but we can surely do better in celebrating lives committed to the common good. We need more ways to honor those who, as Obama said of Mandela, "speak to what's best inside us."[25]

Finally, the public should give greater priority to character in selecting political leaders. Qualities of moral leadership are generally a better predictor of
presidential effectiveness than policy promises. Circumstances change, and new
information, constraints, or crises may require initiatives different than those
that candidates propose in seeking election. If we want more than 7 percent of
Americans to have a "a great deal of trust and confidence" in politicians, then
the public needs to select for qualities that earn such trust. We should demand
honesty, integrity, self-awareness, self-discipline, and commitment to democratic
principles and the common good.[26] If we are disappointed in the character of our
leaders, then at least part of the responsibility lies with the character of those who
elect them. As Congressman Barney Frank once pointed out, "everyone hates
Congress, everyone hates the media, everyone hates Washington. But let me tell
you something, the voters are no picnic either."[27]

This is not a modest agenda. And it is pushing against strong cultural forces
that too often reward wealth, power, and celebrity over qualities of moral character. But the stakes are too substantial for us to acquiesce in those priorities.
We must counter with a richer understanding of character and greater efforts to
pursue and honor lives that reflect it.

Notes

CHAPTER 1

1. Richard V. Reeves, The New Politics of Character, National Affairs 20 (Summer 2014): 111, 112.

2. Reeves, The New Politics of Character, 123 (quoting Wells).

3. Thomas Lickona, Character Matters: How to Help Our Children Develop Good Judgment, Integrity, and Other Essential Virtues (New York: Simon & Schuster, 2004) (quoting Adams).

4. James Davison Hunter and Carl Desportes Bowman, The Politics of Character: Survey of American Public Culture (Charlottesville: University of Virginia Institute for Advanced Studies in Culture, 2000), 2.

5. Henry Fielding, Joseph Andrews and Shamela (New York: Penguin Books, 1999), 39.

6. See discussion in chapter 2; Anne Colby and William Damon, Some Do Care: Contemporary Lives of Moral Commitment (New York: Free Press, 1992), 22. See also William Damon, The Path to Purpose: How Young People Find Their Calling in Life (New York: Free Press, 2008).

7. See chapter 5 and Gallup, Confidence in Institutions, June 1–15 (2016) (16 percent have confidence in the presidency, 15 percent in the Supreme Court, 6 percent in big business, and 4 percent in Congress).

8. Oxford English Dictionary (New York: Oxford University Press, 2016).

9. Taya R. Cohen, A. T. Panter, Nazli Turan, Lily Morse, and Yeonjeong Kim, Moral Character in the Workplace, Journal of Personality and Social Psychology 107 (2014): 943, 944; William Fleeson, Toward a Structure and Process-Integrated View of Personality? Traits as Density Distributions of States, Journal of Personality and Social Psychology 80 (2001): 1011.

10. Joel J. Kupperman, Character (New York: Oxford University Press, 1991), 5, 7–8.

11. Michael E. McCullough and C. R. Snyder, Classical Sources of Human Strength: Revisiting an Old Home and Building a New One, Journal of Social and Clinical Psychology 19 (2000): 4.

12. Daniel J. McKaughan, Character Traits and the Neuroscience of Social Behavior, in Christian B. Miller, R. Michael Furr, Angela Knobel, and William Fleeson eds., Character: New Directions from Philosophy, Psychology, and Theology (New York: Oxford University Press, 2015), 605, 618.

13. Hunter and Bowman, The Politics of Character, 24.

14. Thomas Lickona, Character Education: Seven Crucial Issues, Action in Teacher Education 20 (1999): 77, 78.

15. Christian B. Mille, Character and Moral Psychology (New York: Oxford University Press, 2014), 44, 120; Christian B. Miller, The Mixed Model of Character Traits and the Moral Domains of Resource Distribution and Theft, in Miller, Furr, Knobel, and Fleeson, Character: New Directions from Philosophy, Psychology, and Theology, 164, 169.

16. For discussion of incorruptible Nazis, see John M. Doris, Lack of Character: Personality and Moral Behavior (New York: Cambridge University Press, 2002), 18.

17. Character Education Partnership, Performance Values: Why They Matter and What Schools Can Do to Foster Their Development (Washington, DC: Character Education Partnership, April 2008).

18. Brent W. Roberts, Conscientiousness: A Primer, in Essays on Character and Opportunity, The Character and Opportunity Project, The Center on Children and Families (Brookings, 2014), 14; Brent W. Roberts, Nathan R. Kuncel, Rebecca R. Shiner, Avshalom Caspi, and Lewis R. Goldberg, The Power of Personality: The Comparative Validity of Personality Traits, Socioeconomic Status, and Cognitive Ability for Predicting Important Life Outcomes, Perspectives on Psychological Science 2 (2007): 313–345; Angela Lee Duckworth and Kelly M. Allred, Temperament in the Classroom, in Rebecca L. Shiner and Marcel Zentner eds., Handbook of Temperament (New York: Guilford Press, 2012), 627–644.

19. Walter Mischel, From Good Intentions to Willpower, in Peter M. Gollwitzer and John A. Bargh eds., The Psychology of Action: Linking Cognition and Motivation to Behavior (New York: Guilford Press, 1996), 197–218; Jonah Lehrer, Don't!, New Yorker, May 18, 2009, https://www.newyorker.com/magazine/2009/05/18/dont-2; Walter Mischel, Yuichi Shoda, and Philip K. Peake, The Nature of Adolescent Competencies Predicted by Preschool Delay of Gratification, Journal of Personality and Social Psychology 54 (1988): 687.

20. Terrie E. Moffit et al., A Gradient of Childhood Self-Control Predicts Health, Wealth, and Public Safety, Proceedings of the National Academy of Sciences 108 (February 2011).

21. Bill Puka, Altruism and Character, in Daniel K. Lapsley and Darcia Narváez eds., Moral Development, Self, and Identity (Mahwah, NJ: Lawrence Erlbaum, 2004), 61, 165.

22. Reeves, The New Politics of Character, 116 (quoting Adam Smith, The Theory of Moral Sentiments).

23. Sam A. Hardy and Gustavo Carlo, Moral Identity: What Is It, How Does It Develop, and Is It Linked to Moral Action?, Child Development Perspectives 5 (2011): 212.

24. Hardy and Carlo, Moral Identity, 215.

25. Colby and Damon, Some Do Care; Patrick J. Sweeney and Louis W. Fry, Character Development through Spiritual Leadership, Consulting Psychology Journal: Practice and Research 64 (2012): 89, 92; Augusto Blasi, The Development of Identity: Some Implications for Moral Functioning, in Gil G. Noam and Thomas E. Wren eds., The Moral Self (Cambridge, MA: MIT University Press, 1993), 99.

26. William Damon and Daniel Hart, Self-Understanding and Its Role in Social and Moral Development, in Marc H. Bornstein and Michael E. Lamb eds., Developmental Psychology: An Advanced Textbook (Mahwah, NJ: Lawrence Erlbaum, 4th ed., 1999), 421, 455.

27. Plato, The Republic, trans. Desmond Lee (London: Penguin Books, 1955), 119.

28. Plato, The Republic, 127.

29. Christopher Peterson and Martin E. P. Seligman, Character Strengths and Virtues: A Handbook of Classification (Washington, DC: Oxford University Press, 2004), 46–47.

30. Aristotle, The Nicomachean Ethics, trans. David Ross (New York: Oxford University Press, 2009), quoted in Nancy Sherman, The Fabric of Character: Aristotle's Theory of Virtue (Oxford: Oxford University Press, 1991), 177.

31. Aristotle, The Nicomachean Ethics, quoted in Sherman, The Fabric of Character, 179–180.

32. Kupperman, Character; Anthony Quinton, Character and Culture, The New Republic, October 17, 1983.

33. Orison Swett Marden, Character: The Grandest Thing in the World (New York: Thomas Y. Crowell, 1899), 34.

34. Warren I. Susman, "Personality" and the Making of Twentieth-Century Culture, in John Higham and Paul K. Conkin eds., New Directions in American Intellectual History (Baltimore: Johns Hopkins University Press, 1979), 212, 213–214.

35. Gertrude Himmelfarb, The De-moralization of Society: From Victorian Virtues to Modern Values (New York: Vintage Books, 1994), 50.

36. Susman, "Personality," 214; James Davidson Hunter, The Death of Character: Moral Education in an Age without Good or Evil (New York: Basic Books, 2000), 7–8.

37. Burt Clifford Bean, Power of Personality (Meriden: Pelton, 1920), 3, cited in Susman, "Personality," 218.

38. Orison Swett Marden, The Masterful Personality (New York: Thomas Y. Crowell, 1921).

39. David Riesman, Nathan Glaze, and Reuel Denney, The Lonely Crowd: A Study of the American Character (New Haven, CT: Yale University Press, 1950).

Notes to pages 6–8

40. Gordon W. Allport, Character and the "Culture of Personality," 1897–1937, History of Psychology 1 (1998): 58.
41. Gordon W. Allport, Personality: A Psychological Interpretation (New York: Henry Holt, 1937), 50–51; Gordon W. Allport, Personality and Character, The Psychological Bulletin 18 (1921): 441, 443.
42. David Brooks, The Road to Character (New York: Random House, 2015), 6–7, 258.
43. Alexander W. Astin, The Changing American College Student: Thirty-Year Trends, 1966–1996, Review of Higher Education 21 (1998): 115–135. See Brooks, The Road to Character, 257.
44. Christian Smith, Kari Christoffersen, Hilary Davidson, and Patricia Snell Herzog, Lost in Transition: The Dark Side of Emerging Adulthood (New York: Oxford University Press, 2011), 226–227.
45. David Brooks, What Is Your Purpose?, New York Times, May 5, 2015, A21.
46. Robert Reich, The Common Good (New York: Knopf, 2018), 4.
47. Hunter and Bowman, The Politics of Character, 3.
48. Christina Hoff Sommers and Fred Sommers, Vice and Virtue in Everyday Life (New York: Harcourt Brace Jovanovich, 1985); James D. Wallace, Virtues and Vices (Ithaca, NY: Cornell University Press, 1978); Alasdair MacIntyre, After Virtue: A Study in Moral Theory (Notre Dame, IN: University of Notre Dame Press, 1981); William F. May, Professional Ethics: Setting Terrain and Teacher, in Sidney Callahan and Sissela Bok eds., Ethics Teaching in Higher Education (New York: Springer US, 1980), 205.
49. Gilbert Harman, Moral Philosophy Meets Social Psychology: Virtue Ethics and the Fundamental Attribution Error, Proceedings of the Aristotelian Society 99 (1999): 315, 319.
50. Robert B. Louden, On Some Vices of Virtue Ethics, American Philosophical Quarterly 21 (1984): 227.
51. James Rachels and Stuart Rachels, The Elements of Moral Philosophy (New York: McGraw Hill Education, 2011), 178.
52. Peterson and Seligman, Character Strengths, 87.
53. Louden, On Some Vices of Virtue Ethics.
54. Geoffrey James Warnock, The Object of Morality (Ann Arbor, MI: Methuen Young Books, 1971), 276.
55. Gilbert Harman, Skepticism about Character Traits, Journal of Ethics 13 (2009): 235, 241.
56. Allport, Personality; David C. Funder, Explaining Traits, Psychological Inquiry 5 (1994): 125; Robert R. McCrae and Paul T. Costa Jr., The Stability of Personality: Observations and Evaluations, Current Directions in Psychological Science 6 (1994): 173.
57. Walter Mischel, Personality and Assessment (Mahwah, NJ: Lawrence Erlbaum, 1968), 147.

58. Kenneth S. Bowers, Situationism in Psychology: An Analysis and a Critique, Psychological Review 80 (1973): 307; Donald Robert Peterson, The Clinical Study of Social Behavior (Ann Arbor, MI: Appleton-Century-Crofts, 1968), 23; Brent W. Roberts and Eva M. Pomerantz, On Traits, Situations, and Their Integration: A Developmental Perspective, Personality and Social Psychology Review 8 (2004): 402; Gordon W. Allport, Traits Revisited, American Psychologist 21 (1966): 1, 9.

59. Doris, Lack of Character, 2; Mischel, Personality and Assessment, 146, 177. For a review of studies, see William Fleeson and Erik Noftle, The End of the Person-Situation Debate: An Emerging Synthesis in the Answer to the Consistency Question, Social and Personality Psychology Compass 2 (2008): 1667, 1669.

60. Lee Ross, Richard Nisbett, and Malcolm Gladwell, The Person and the Situation: Perspectives of Social Psychology (New York: McGraw-Hill, 1991); Harman, Moral Philosophy Meets Social Psychology, 315.

61. Stanley Milgram, Obedience to Authority: An Experimental View (New York: Harper & Row, 1974); Jerry M. Burger, Replicating Milgram: Would People Still Obey Today? The American Psychologist 64 (2009): 1

62. Milgram, Obedience to Authority; Roger Brown, Social Psychology (New York: Macmillan, 1986), 4.

63. Arthur G. Miller, The Obedience Experiments: A Case Study of Controversy in Social Science (New York: Praeger, 1986), 13, 21. For further details, see Doris, Lack of Character, 39–50.

64. Milgram, Obedience to Authority, 116–122.

65. Craig Haney, Curtis Banks, and Philip Zimbardo, Interpersonal Dynamics in a Simulated Prison, International Journal of Criminology and Penology 1 (1973): 69.

66. Bibb Latané and Judith Rodin, A Lady in Distress: Inhibiting Effects of Friends and Strangers on Bystander Intervention, Journal of Experimental Social Psychology 5 (1969): 189.

67. John M. Darley and C. Daniel Batson, "From Jerusalem to Jericho": A Study of Situational and Dispositional Variables in Helping Behavior, Journal of Personality and Social Psychology 27 (1973): 100.

68. Mischel, Personality and Assessment, 6.

69. Benoît Monin and Alexander H. Jordan, The Dynamic Moral Self: A Social Psychological Perspective, in Darcia Narváez and Daniel K. Lapsley eds., Personality, Identity, and Character: Explorations in Moral Psychology (New York: Cambridge University Press, 2009), 341, 347. For the limits of situationism, see John Sabini and Maury Silver, Lack of Character? Situationism Critiqued, Ethics 115 (2005): 535.

70. Norman S. Endler and David Magnusson, Toward an Interactional Psychology of Personality, Psychological Bulletin 83 (1976): 956; David C. Funder, Towards a Resolution of the Personality Triad: Persons, Situations, and Behaviors, Journal of Research in Personality 40 (2006): 21, 22; Fleeson and Noftle, The End of the

Person-Situation Debate; Wiebke Bleidorn, Moving Character beyond the Person-Situation Debate: The Stable and Dynamic Nature of Virtues in Everyday Life, in Miller, Furr, Knobel, and Fleeson, Character: New Directions from Philosophy, Psychology, and Theology, 129; Daniel Heller, Jennifer Komar, and Wonkyong Beth Lee, The Dynamics of Personality States, Goals, and Well-Being, Personality and Social Psychology Bulletin 33 (2007): 898.

71. For the genetic component, see Fleeson and Noftle, The End of the Person-Situation Debate, 1670.

72. Walter Mischel and Yuichi Shoda, A Cognitive-Affective System Theory of Personality: Reconceptualizing Situations, Dispositions, Dynamics, and Invariance in Personality Structure, Psychological Review 102 (1995): 246; Walter Mischel, Personality Coherence and Dispositions in a Cognitive-Affective Personality System (CAPS) Approach, in Daniel Cervone and Yuichi Shoda eds., The Coherence of Personality: Social-Cognitive Bases of Consistency, Variability, and Organization (New York: Guilford Press, 1999).

73. Mischel and Shoda, A Cognitive-Affective System Theory of Personality, 246.

74. Bleidorn, Moving Character beyond the Person-Situation Debate, 145.

75. Wiliam Fleeson, Toward a Structure-and Process-Integrated View of Personality: Traits as Density Distribution of States, Journal of Personality and Social Psychology 80 (2001): 1011. For discussion of the relative stability of self-regulatory traits, see Walter Mischel, Toward an Integrative Science of the Person, Annual Review of Psychology 55 (2004): 1, 17.

76. Angela Lee Duckworth and Eli Tsukayama, Domain Specificity in Self-Control, in Miller, Furr, Knobel, and Fleeson, Character: New Directions from Philosophy, Psychology, and Theology, 393, 397.

77. Ross, Nisbet, and Gladwell, The Person and the Situation, 18–20; Lee Ross and Donna Shestowsky, Contemporary Psychology's Challenges to Legal Theory and Practice, Northwestern University Law Review 97 (2003): 1081, 1095.

78. Gil G. Noam, Reconceptualizing Maturity: The Search for Deeper Meaning, in Gil G. Noam and Kurt W. Fischer eds., Development and Vulnerability in Close Relationships (Mahwah, NJ: Lawrence Erlbaum, 1996); Rick Weissbourd, Moral Teachers, Moral Students, Educational Leadership 60 (March 2003): 6.

79. Peterson and Seligman, Character Strengths, 27.

80. Adam Grant, Raising a Moral Child, New York Times, April 11, 2014.

81. Gustavo Carlo, The Development and Correlates of Prosocial Moral Behaviors, in Melanie Killen and Judith G. Smetana eds., Handbook of Moral Development (New York: Psychology Press, 2014), 208, 210.

82. Sheldon Berman, Children's Social Consciousness and the Development of Social Responsibility (New York: SUNY Press, 1997), 47.

83. Todd E. Jennings, Self-in-Connection as a Component of Human Rights Advocacy and Education, Journal of Moral Education 23 (1994): 285, quoted in Berman, Children's Social Consciousness, 57.

84. Gustavo Carlo, Lisa M. Pytlikzillig, Scott C. Roesch, and Richard A. Dienstbier, The Elusive Altruist: The Psychological Study of the Altruistic Personality, in Daniel K. Lapsley and Darcia Narváez eds., Personality Identity, and Character: Explorations in Moral Psychology (New York: Cambridge University Press, 2009), 275–276.

85. John F. Dovidio, Jane Allyn Pilliavin, David A. Schroeder, and Louis A. Penner, The Social Psychology of Prosocial Behavior (New York: Psychology Press, 2006), 265. See also Carlo, Pytlikzillig, Roesch, and Dienstbier, The Elusive Altruist, 288.

86. Matthias R. Mehl, Kathryn L. Bollich, Hohn M. Doris, and Simine Vazine, Character and Coherence: Testing the Stability of Naturalistically Observed Daily Moral Behavior, in Miller, Furr, Knobel, and Fleeson, Character: New Directions from Philosophy, Psychology, and Theology, 630, 643.

87. Elliot Aronson and Joshua Aronson, The Social Animal (New York: Worth, 2011); Carlo, Pytlikzillig, Roesch, and Dienstbier, The Elusive Altruist, 277; Miller, Character and Moral Psychology 209.

88. Darcia Narváez and Tonia Block, Developing Ethical Expertise and Moral Personalities, in Larry Nucci, Tobias Krettenauer, and Darcia Narváez eds., Handbook of Moral and Character Education (New York: Routledge, 2014), 140, 141; Lawrence Kohlberg, Essays on Moral Development: The Philosophy of Moral Development (New York: Harper & Row, 1981).

89. Narváez and Block, Developing Ethical Expertise, 141–142; Jonathan Haidt, The Emotional Dog and Its Rational Tail: A Social Intuitionist Approach to Moral Judgment, Psychological Review 108 (2001): 814.

90. Jonathan Haidt and Fredrik Bjorklund, Social Intuitionists Answer Six Questions about Morality, in Walter Sinnott-Armstrong ed., Moral Psychology, Volume 2: The Cognitive Science of Morality: Intuition and Diversity (Cambridge, MA: MIT University Press, 2008), 181. For an overview, see Augusto Blasi, The Moral Functioning of Mature Adults and the Possibility of Fair Moral Reasoning, in Darcia Narváez and Daniel K. Lapsley eds., Personality, Identity, and Character: Explorations in Moral Psychology (New York: Cambridge University Press, 2009), 396, 415.

91. Taya R. Cohen and A. T. Panter, Character Traits in the Workplace, in Miller, Furr, Knobel, and Fleeson, Character: New Directions from Philosophy, Psychology, and Theology, 150, 157.

92. David Gallardo-Pujol, Elizabet Orekhova, Verónica Benet-Martínez, and Mel Slater, Taking Evil into the Lab: Exploring the Frontiers of Morality and Individual Differences, in Miller, Furr, Knobel, and Fleeson, Character: New Directions from Philosophy, Psychology, and Theology, 652, 656–657.

93. Peterson and Seligman, Character Strengths, 51.

94. Christin-Melanie Vauclair, Marc Wilson, and Ronald Fischer, Cultural Conceptions of Morality: Examining Laypeople's Associations of Moral Character, Journal of Moral Education 43 (2014): 54, 61.

95. Geoffrey P. Goodwin, Jared Piazza, and Paul Rozin, Understanding the Importance and Perceived Structure of Moral Character, in Miller, Furr, Knobel, and Fleeson, Character: New Directions from Philosophy, Psychology, and Theology, 100, 107.

96. James Davison Hunter and Carl Desportes Bowman, The Politics of Character (Charlottesville: University of Virginia Institute for Advanced Studies in Culture, 2000), 13–19.

97. Thomas Lickona, a leading expert in character education, singles out ten: wisdom, justice, fortitude, self-control, love, a positive attitude, hard work, integrity, gratitude, and humility. Lickona, Character Matters, xxv.

98. Peterson and Seligman, Character Strengths, 15.

99. Peterson and Seligman, Character Strengths, 29–30.

100. Lickona, Character Matters, xxv.

101. Barry R. Schlenker, Marisa L. Miller, and Ryan M. Johnson, Moral Identity, Integrity and Personal Responsibility, in Darcia Narváez and Daniel K. Lapsley eds., Personality, Identity, and Character: Explorations in Moral Psychology (New York: Cambridge University Press, 2009), 324, 326.

102. Schlenker, Miller, and Johnson, Moral Identity, Integrity and Personal Responsibility, 328–329.

103. Schlenker, Miller, and Johnson, Moral Identity, Integrity and Personal Responsibility, 331.

104. Lehrer, Don't!

105. Geoffrey P. Goodwin, Jared Piazza, and Paul Rozin, Moral Character Predominates in Person Perception and Evaluation, Journal of Personality and Social Psychology 106 (2014): 148; Glenn D. Reeder and Michael D. Coovert, Revising an Impression of Morality, Social Cognition 4 (1986): 1.

106. Goodwin, Piazza and Rozin, Understanding Moral Character; Reeder and Coovert, Revising an Impression of Morality.

107. Doris, Lack of Character, 115.

108. Michel de Montaigne, Of the Inconsistency of Our Actions, reprinted in Elizabeth D. Samet, Leadership: Essential Writings by Our Greatest Thinkers (New York: W.W. Norton, 2015), 683, 685, 686.

109. Mark Snyder, The Influence of Individuals on Situations: Implications for Understanding the Links between Personality and Social Behavior, Journal of Personality 51 (1983): 497.

110. Angela Duckworth, Grit: The Power of Passion and Perseverance (New York: Simon & Schuster, 2016), 148.

CHAPTER 2

1. James Arthur, Traditional Approaches to Character Education in Britain and America, in Nucci, Narváez, and Krettenauer, Handbook of Moral and Character Education, 43.

2. Robert J. Nash, A Postmodern Reflection on Character Education: Coming of Age as a Moral Constructivist, in Daniel K. Lapsley and F. Clark Power eds., Character Psychology and Character Education (Notre Dame, IN: University of Notre Dame Press, 2005), 245, 250.

3. Ethics in Action, Josephson Institute Newsletter, October–December 1998, 1.

4. David Brooks, If It Feels Right . . . , New York Times, September 12, 2011; William Kilpatrick, Why Johnny Can't Tell Right from Wrong: And What We Can Do about It (New York: Simon and Schuster, 1993), 13; Smith, Christoffersen, Davidson, and Herzog, Lost in Transition, 238.

5. Christina Hoff Sommers, Teaching the Virtues, in Christina Sommers and Fred Sommers eds., Vice and Virtue in Everyday Life: Introductory Readings in Ethics (New York: Harcourt Brace, 4th ed., 1997), 679.

6. Ben Sasse, The Vanishing American Adult: Our Coming of Age Crisis—and How to Rebuild a Culture of Self-Reliance (New York: St. Martin's Press, 2017), 119–149.

7. William Damon and Anne Colby, Education and Moral Commitment, Journal of Moral Education 25 (1996): 31.

8. Christopher Peterson and Martin E. P. Seligman, Character Strengths and Virtues: A Handbook of Classification (Washington, DC: American Psychological Association, 2004), 5.

9. Rick Weissbourd et al., The Children We Mean to Raise: The Real Messages Adults are Sending about Values (Making Caring Common Project, Harvard Graduate School of Education, 2014), https://www.castilleja.org/uploaded/Administration/Kauffman/The_Children_We_Mean_to_Raise__The_Real_Messages_Adults_Are_Sending_About_Values.pdf.

10. Weissbourd et al., The Children We Mean to Raise; Emily Bazelon, Kids Value Achievement over Caring Because They Think Their Parents Do, XX Factor, Slate, June 25, 2014 (quoting Richard Weissbourd and Stepanie Jones), https://slate.com/human-interest/2014/06/making-caring-common-project-study-finds-that-students-value-achievement-over-caring-for-others.html.

11. James Davison Hunter, The Death of Character: Moral Education in an Age without Good or Evil (New York: Basic Books, 2000), 79.

12. Hunter, Death of Character, 9.

13. J. Phillip London, Character: The Ultimate Success Factor (Jacksonville, FL: Fortis, 2013), 1, 25.

14. For criminality, see James Q. Wilson, On Character: Essays by James Q. Wilson (Washington, DC: AEI Press, 1995), 43–45. For altruism, see Adam Grant, Raising a Moral Child, New York Times, April 11, 2014.

15. Wilson, On Character, 46–48.

16. Eric Schaps, Esther F. Schaeffer, and Sanford N. McDonnell, What's Right and Wrong in Character Education Today, Education Week, September 12, 2001, 40.

17. Thomas Lickona, Character Matters: How to Help Our Children Develop Good Judgment, Integrity, and Other Essential Virtues (New York: Simon & Schuster, 2004), xxiii–xxiv.

18. Paul Tough, Helping Children Succeed: What Works and Why (New York: Houghton Mifflin Harcourt, 2016), 51.

19. Mary Cable, The Little Darlings: A History of Child Rearing in America (New York: Charles Scribner's Sons, 1972), 172.

20. Cable, The Little Darlings, 10.

21. Craig A. Cunningham, A Certain and Reasoned Art: The Rise and Fall of Character Education in America, in Lapsley and Power, Character Psychology and Character Education, 166, 169–171; Cable, The Little Darlings, 184.

22. The Lost Wallet Experiment, Readers Digest (December, 1995) discussed in Lickona, Character Matters, 14–15.

23. Robert M.; Sapolsky, Behave: The Biology of Humans at Our Best and Worst (New York: Penguin, 2017), 207; Tom R. Tyler and Rick Trinkner, Why Children Follow Rules: Legal Socialization and the Development of Legitimacy (New York: Oxford University Press, 2017), 138–140; Diana Baumrind, Parenting Styles and Adolescent Development, in Jeanne Brooks-Gunn, Richard Lerner, and A. C. Petersen eds., The Encyclopedia of Adolescence (New York: Garland, 1989). See also Laurence Steinberg et al., Authoritative Parenting and Adolescent Adjustment across Varied Ecological Niches, Journal of Research on Adolescence 1 (1991): 19–36; Diana Baumrind, Authoritative Parenting for Character and Competence, in D. Streight ed., Parenting for Character: Five Experts, Five practices (Portland: CSEE Publications, 2008), 17–30.

24. Tyler and Trinkner, Why Children Follow Rules, 138–140; Piko and Balazs, Authoritative Parenting Style and Adolescent Smoking and Drinking, Addictive Behaviors 37 (2012): 353. Diane Baumrind, The Influence of Parenting Style on Adolescent Competence and Substance Use, Journal of Early Adolescence 11 (1991): 56; 1991, Hoeve et al., The Relationship between Parenting and Delinquency: A Meta-analysis, Journal of Abnormal and Child Psychology 37 (2009): 749; Hoeve et al., Trajectories of Delinquency and Parenting Styles, Journal of Abnormal Child Psychology 36 (2008): 223.

25. Tyler and Trinkner, Why Children Follow Rules 131–132; Elizabeth Thompson Gershoff, Corporal Punishment by Parents and Associated Child Behaviors and Experiences Psychological Bulletin 128 (2002): 539; Straus and Donnelly, Beating the Devil Out of Them: Corporal Punishment in American Families and Its Effects on Children (New Brunswick, NJ: Transaction, 2001).

26. Laurence Steinberg, Beyond the Classroom: Why School Reform Has Failed and What Parents Need to Do (New York: Simon & Schuster, 1997). For other research, see studies cited in Daniel Solomon, Marilyn S. Watson, and Victor A. Battistich, Teaching and Schooling Effects on Moral/Prosocial Development, in Virginia

Richardson ed., Handbook of Research on Teaching (Washington, DC: American Educational Research Association, 4th ed., 2001), 566, 569.

27. Lickona, Character Matters, xxiii–xxiv.

28. Kilpatrick, Why Johnny Can't Tell Right from Wrong, 259; Alfie Kohn, The Brighter Side of Human Nature: Altruism and Empathy in Everyday Life (New York: Basic Books, 1990), 91–92.

29. Samuel P. Oliner and Pearl M. Oliner, The Altruistic Personality: Rescuers of Jews in Nazi Europe (New York: The Free Press, 1988), 164–165.

30. Oliner and Oliner, The Altruistic Personality, 165.

31. E. Gil Clary and Jude Miller, Socialization and Situational Influences on Sustained Altruism, Child Development 57 (1986): 1358; David L. Rosenhan, Learning Theory and Prosocial Behavior, Journal of Social Issues 28 (1972): 151.

32. Rosenhan, Learning Theory.

33. Colby and Damon, Some Do Care, 141–142.

34. Kenneth Keniston, Young Radicals: Notes on Committed Youth (New York: HBJ College & School Division, 1968); David L. Rosenhan, Learning Theory and Prosocial Behavior, Journal of Social Issues 28 (1972): 151; Oliner and Oliner, The Altruistic Personality.

35. Bernard R. Brogan and Walter A. Brogan, The Formation of Character: A Necessary Goal for Success in Education, Educational Forum 63 (1999): 348; Nancy Eisenberg and Paul Henry Mussen, The Roots of Prosocial Behavior in Children (Cambridge: Cambridge University Press, 1989). For the role of imitation in social learning in general and character development in particular, see S. E. Oladipo, Moral Education of the Child: Whose Responsibility? Journal Social Science 20 (2009): 149, 151. For the impact of parental volunteering on teen volunteering, see Virginia A. Hodgkinson and Murray S. Weitzman, Giving and Volunteering in the United States (Washington, DC: The Independent Sector, 1992).

36. David Maraniss, Barak Obama: The Story (New York: Simon & Schuster, 2012), 515.

37. Joseph M. Hoedel, Role Models: Examples of Character and Leadership (Williamston, MI: Character Development Group, 2012), 85.

38. Alfie Kohn, Punished by Rewards: The Trouble with Gold Stars, Incentive Plans, A's, Praise, and Other Bribes (New York: Mariner Books, 2d ed., 1999), 240.

39. Damon, The Path to Purpose, 118.

40. Damon, The Path to Purpose, 83–97.

41. Sheldon Berman, Children's Social Consciousness and the Development of Social Responsibility (Albany: State University of New York Press, 1997), 85–87; Oladipo, Moral Education of the Child, 152; Marvin W. Berkowitz and John H. Grych, Fostering Goodness: Teaching Parents to Facilitate Children's Moral Development, Journal of Moral Education 27 (1998): 371; Oliner and Oliner, The Altruistic Personality, 249–250.

42. Berman, Children's Social Consciousness, 86–87.

43. Joan E. Grusec and Erica Redler, Attribution, Reinforcement and Altruism: A Developmental Analysis, Developmental Psychology 16 (1980): 525. See Adam Grant, Raising a Moral Child, New York Times, April 11, 2014.

44. Adam Grant, Originals: How Non-Conformists Move the World (New York Penguin 2016), 169; Christopher J. Bryan, Allison Master, and Gregory M. Walton, Helping versus Being a Helper: Invoking the Self to Increase Help in Young Children, Child Development 85 (2014): 1836; Christopher J. Bryan, Gabrielle S. Adams, and Benoit Monin, When Cheating Would Make You a Cheater: Implicating the Self Prevents Unethical Behavior, Journal of Experimental Psychology: General 142 (2013): 10001.

45. Berman, Children's Social Consciousness, 85–86; John Wilson, Volunteerism Research: A Review Essay, Nonprofit and Voluntary Sector Quarterly 4 (2012): 176, 182, 188; Jean M. Twenge and W. Keith Campbell, The Narcissism Epidemic: Living in the Age of Entitlement (New York: Atria Books, 2009), 294.

46. Norma Deitch Feshbach, Learning to Care: A Positive Approach to Child Training and Discipline, Journal of Clinical Child Psychology 12 (1983): 266; Kohn, Punished by Rewards, 242–244; Grant, Originals, 165.

47. Berman, Children's Social Consciousness, 91–102; Kohn, Punished by Rewards, 244.

48. Lickona, Character Matters, 36–49.

49. American Academy of Pediatrics, American Academy of Pediatrics Announces New Recommendations for Children's Media Use; Healthy Children, Family Media Plan, AAP, 2018, https://www.healthychildren.org/English/media/Pages/default.aspx.

50. Caroline Knorr, Build Character Strengths with Quality Media, Common Sense Media, March 4, 2016, https://www.commonsensemedia.org/blog/build-character-strengths-with-quality-media; Sierra Filucci, Raising a Good Person in a Digital World, CNN, September 9, 2016, https://www.cnn.com/2016/09/09/health/kids-character-digital-world/index.html.

51. American Academy of Pediatrics, Media Use in School-Aged Children and Adolescents, Council on Communications and Media 138 (2016).

52. Lickona, Character Matters, 49–59.

53. Kohn, Punished by Rewards, 249.

54. Kohn, Punished by Rewards, 35–45.

55. Kohn, Punished by Rewards.

56. Madeline Levine, The Price of Privilege: How Parental Pressure and Material Advantage Are Creating a Generation of Disconnected and Unhappy Kids (New York: Harper Perennial, 2008), 56; Wendy S. Gronick, The Psychology of Parental Control: How Well Meant Parenting Backfires (Mahwah, NJ: Lawrence Erlbaum, 2003); Kohn, Punished by Rewards; Grant, Raising a Moral Child.

57. Dan Kindlon, Too Much of a Good Thing: Raising Children of Character in an Indulgent Age (New York: Hyperion, 2001), 123.

58. Kindlon, Too Much of a Good Thing, xi.

59. Twenge and Campbell, The Narcissism Epidemic, 296.

60. Kindlon, Too Much of a Good Thing, 3–5.

61. Kindlon, Too Much of a Good Thing, 11.

62. Paul Tough, How Children Succeed: Grit, Curiosity, and Hidden Power of Character (New York: Houghton Mifflin Harcourt, 2012), 81–86. See also Weissbourd et al., The Children We Mean to Raise, 2.

63. William Deresiewicz, Excellent Sheep: The Miseducation of the American Elite and the Way to a Meaningful Life (New York: Free Press, 2014), 44.

64. Nicholas Lemann, The Big Test: The Secret History of the American Meritocracy (New York: Farrar, Straus & Giroux, 1999); Deresiewicz, Excellent Sheep, 33; Weissbourd et al., The Children We Mean to Raise, 10.

65. Levine, Price of Privilege, 10.

66. Weissbourd et al., The Children We Mean to Raise, 11. See also Lucia Ciciolla, Alexandria S. Curlee, Jason Karageorge, and Suniya S. Luthar, When Mothers and Fathers Are Seen as Disproportionately Valuing Achievements: Implications for Adjustment among Upper Middle Class Youth, Journal of Youth and Adolescence 46 (2017): 1057.

67. Madeline Levine, The Price of Privilege. See also Rachel Simmons, Enough as She Is: How to Help Girls Move beyond Impossible Standards of Success to Live Healthy, Happy, and Fulfilling Lives (New York: Harper Collins, 2018), x, 12, 211; Benoit Denizet-Lewis, The Kids Who Can't, New York Times Magazine, October 15, 2017, 40.

68. Suniya S. Luthar, Samuel H. Bankin, and Elizabeth J. Crossman, "I Can, Therefore I Must": Fragility in the Upper-Middle Classes," Development and Psychopathology 25 (2013): 1529, 1532.

69. Adam Grant, What Straight-A Students Get Wrong, New York Times, December 9, 2018, SR 2.

70. Gallup-Purdue Index, Press Release, It's Not "Where" You Go to College, But "How" You Go to College (May 6, 2014), https://www.purdue.edu/newsroom/releases/2014/Q2/gallup-purdue-index-releases-inaugural-findings-of-national-landmark-study.html.

71. Frank Bruni, Where You Go Is Not Who You'll Be: An Antidote to the College Admissions Mania (New York: Grand Central, 2016).

72. D. Michael Lindsay with M. G. Hager, A View from the Top: An Inside Look at How People in Power See and Shape the World (Hoboken, NJ: Wiley, 2014).

73. Bruni, Where You Go, 11 (quoting Anthony Carnevale).

74. Sapolsky, Behave, 193–197.

75. Richard V. Reeves, The New Politics of Character, National Affairs 20 (Summer 2014).

76. For an overview, see Tough, Helping Children Succeed, 35–42, 112–113.

77. Alan Wolfe, Moral Freedom: The Search for Virtue in a World of Choice (New York: W.W. Norton, 2002), 186.

78. Jacqueline L. Salmon, Non-Christians Learn Sunday School Values, Washington Post, June 21, 2008.

79. Frank Glenn Lankard, A History of the American Sunday School Curriculum (New York: The Abingdon Press, 1927), 62.

80. Anne M. Boylan, Sunday School: The Formation of an American Institution, 1790–1880 (New Haven, CT: Yale University Press, 1988), 133–134.

81. Charles Gallaudet Trumbull, The Nineteenth Century Sunday-School, in The Development of the Sunday-School, 1780–1905 (Boston: The Fort Hill Press, 1905), 10.

82. Jack L. Seymour, From Sunday School to Church School: Continuities in Protestant Church Education in the United States, 1860–1929 (Washington, DC: University Press of America, 1982), viii; Boylan, Sunday School, 27.

83. Hunter, Death of Character, 66–67.

84. Joe Maxwell, Will Sunday School Survive?, Christianity Today, December 9, 1988, 63.

85. Melissa Pandika, Has the Sun Set on Sunday School?, USA Today, March 22, 2015, https://www.usatoday.com/story/news/nation/2015/03/22/ozy-has-sun-set-on-sunday-school/25080073/; Bob Allen, Can Sunday School Be Saved?, Baptist News Global, January 6, 2012, https://baptistnews.com/article/can-sunday-school-be-saved/#.WfO_bltSxhE. Although precise data are unavailable about the impact of sex scandals on Sunday school enrollment, research shows a significant adverse affect on Catholic schools, and the trends are likely to be related. Ali Moghtaderi, Child Abuse Scandal Publicity and Catholic School Enrollment: Does the *Boston Globe* Coverage Matter?, Social Science Quarterly 99 (2017): 169; Angela K. Dills and Ray Hernandez-Julian, Negative Public and Catholic Schools, Economic Inquiry 50 (2012): 143.

86. Barna Group Research, Sunday School Is Changing in Under-the-Radar but Significant Ways, July 11, 2005, https://www.barna.com/research/sunday-school-is-changing-in-under-the-radar-but-significant-ways/.

87. For the role of Jewish Community Centers, see Barry Chazan, The Philosophy of Informal Jewish Education, in David Bryfman ed., Experience and Jewish Education (Los Angeles: Torah Aura Productions, 2014), 13, 15.

88. Pew Research Center, Importance of Religion in One's Life, http://www.pewforum.org/religious-landscape-study/importance-of-religion-in-ones-life/ (last visited February 14, 2019).

89. David M. Hansen, Reed W. Larson, and Jodi B. Dworkin, What Adolescents Learn in Organized Youth Activities: A Survey of Self-Reported Developmental Experiences, Journal of Research on Adolescence 13 (2003): 25, 46.

90. Charles Howard Hopkins, History of the Y.M.C.A in North America (New York: Association Press, 1951), 5; Laurence L. Doggett, History of the Young Men's Christian Association (New York: Association Press, 1922), 47.

91. YMCA Program Materials (New York, 1980), quoted in Hunter, Death of Character, 101.

92. Hunter, Death of Character, 57.

93. David I. MacLeod, Building Character in the American Boy: The Boy Scouts, YMCA, and Their Forerunners, 1870–1920 (Madison: University of Wisconsin Press, 2004), 137.

94. Juliette Lowe, Girls Scouts as an Educational Force, U.S. Department of the Interior, Bureau of Education Bulletin no. 33 (1919), 3.

95. David I. MacLeod, Act Your Age: Boyhood, Adolescence and the Rise of the Boy Scouts of America, Journal of Social History 16 (Winter 1982): 7.

96. MacLeod, Building Character, 50.

97. MacLeod, Building Character, 254.

98. Taylor Hosking, Why Do the Boy Scouts Want to Include Girls?, Atlantic, October 12, 2017.

99. https://www.scouti9ngnewsroom.org...bsa.../boty-scouts-of-america-tradtional-membership; https://www.girlscouts.org/en/about-girl-scouts/who-we-are/facts.html. (last visited February 16, 2019).

100. Hosking, Why Do the Boy Scouts Want to Include Girls?

101. Peterson and Seligman, Character Strengths and Virtues, 28.

102. America's Promise Alliance, http://www.americaspromise.org/our-history (last visited February 16, 2019).

103. Jessica Lynn Mullins, Character Education and 4-H Youth Development, Master's thesis, University of Kentucky (2011), http://uknowledge.uky.edu/cgi/viewcontent.cgi?article=1087&context=gradschool_theses.

104. Richard F. Catalano et al., Positive Youth Development in the United States: Research Findings on Evaluations of Positive Youth Development Programs, The ANNALS of the American Academy of Political and Social Science 591 (2004):98; Richard E. Catalano, John W. Toumbourou, and J. David Hawkins, Positive Youth Development in the United States: History, Efficacy, and Links to Moral and Character Education, in Nucci, Narváez, and Krettenauer, Handbook of Moral and Character Education, 432–435.

105. Peterson and Seligman, Character Strengths and Virtues, 642; Jacquelynne Eccles and Jennifer Appleton Gootman, eds., Community Programs to Promote Youth Development (Washington, DC: National Academy Press, 2002).

106. Keniston, Young Radicals; Colby and Damon, Some Do Care; Richard A. Hoehn, Up from Apathy: A Study of Moral Awareness and Social Involvement (Nashville, TN: Abingdon Press, 1986).

107. Daniel Frankl, Youth Sports: Innocence Lost, California State University, Los Angeles, School of Kinesiology and Nutritional Science (2007), http://www.kidsfirstsoccer.com/PDF/Youth-Sport-Innocence-Lost-Jan2007-FranklD.pdf.

108. Vern D. Seefeldt and Martha E. Ewing, Youth Sports in America: An Overview, President's Council on Physical Fitness and Sports Research Digest (PCPFS), 2007. Prior to the mid-1950s, organized sports experiences for youth occurred within youth organizations such as the Boy Scouts and Girl Scouts, And YMCAs and YWCAs.

109. F. Clark Power and Kristin K. Sheehan, Moral and Character Education through Sports, in Nucci, Narváez, and Krettenauer, Handbook of Moral and Character Education, 488, 491–492; Frankl, Youth Sports: Innocence Lost; Jennifer M. Beller and Sharon Kay Stoll, Moral Reasoning of High School Student Athletes and General Students: An Empirical Study versus Personal Testimony, Pediatric Exercise Science 7 (1995): 352; Brenda Jo Bredemeier, Moral Reasoning and the Perceived Legitimacy of Intentionally Injurious Sport Acts, Journal of Sport Psychology 7 (1985): 110; Brenda Jo Bredemeier, Divergence in Children's Moral Reasoning about Issues in Daily Life and Sport Specific Contexts, International Journal of Sport Psychology 26 (1995): 453.

110. See research summarized in Power and Sheehan, Moral and Character Education through Sports, 491; Robert K. Fullinwider, Sports, Youth and Character: A Critical Survey, Center for Information and Research on Civic Learning and Engagement (CIRCLE), Working Paper 44 (February, 2006). David Light Shields and Brenda Light Bredemeier, Can Sports Build Character?, in Lapsley and Power, Character Psychology and Character Education, 121, 124–125; Jennifer Beller, Positive Character Development in School Sport Programs, Educational Resource Information Center (ERIC) Digest (2002), http://files.eric.ed.gov/fulltext/ED477729.pdf; Brenda Light Bredemeier and David Light Shields, Sports and Character Development, President's Council on Physical Fitness and Sports Research Digest (PCPFS), March 2006; Beller and Sholl, Moral Reasoning of High School Student Athletes and General Students, 352.

111. Bruce C. Ogilvie and Thomas A. Tutko, Sport: If You Want to Build Character, Try Something Else, Psychology Today (October 1971): 63.

112. Bredemeier and Shields, Sports and Character Development, 4; Power and Sheehan, Moral and Character Education through Sports, 488, 489.

113. Twenge and Campbell, The Narcissism Epidemic, 294.

114. Jay Coakley, Sports in Society: Issues and Controversies (New York: McGraw-Hill Education, 9th ed., 2007).

115. David Light Shields, Brenda Light Fredemeier, Nicole M. LaVoi, and F. Clark Power, The Sports Behavior of Youth, Parents, and Coaches: The Good, the Bad, and the Ugly, Journal of Research in Character Education 3 (2005): 43.

116. Barry Svrluga, Little League Champs Lose Their Title, Washington Post, February 12, 2015, A1.

117. Glyn C. Roberts, Yngvar Ommundsen, Pierre-Nicolas Lemyre, and Blake W. Miller, Cheating in Sport, in Charles D. Spielberger ed., Encyclopedia of Applied Psychology (Amsterdam and New York: Elsevier Academic Press, 2004).

118. Anita L. Allen, The New Ethics: A Guided Tour of the Twenty-First Century Moral Landscape (New York: Miramax Books, 2004), 36.

119. Herb Appenzeller, Ethical Behavior in Sport (Durham, NC: Carolina Academic Press, 2011), 45.

120. F. Clark Power and Alesha D. Seroczynski, Coaching for Moral Development, Report to the LA '84 Foundation, 2013, discussed in Power and Sheehan, Moral and Character Education through Sport, 501–502.

121. Rick Weissbourd, Moral Teachers, Moral Students, Educational Leadership 60 (March, 2003): 6.

122. Richard H. Hersh, John P. Miller, and Glen D. Fielding, Models of Moral Education: An Appraisal (New York: Longman, 1980), 17 (quoting A Manual of the System of Discipline and Instruction of the Public School Society of New-York, New York: Egbert & King, 1850).

123. Douglas Sloan, The Teaching of Ethics in the American Undergraduate Curriculum, 1876–1976, in Daniel Callahan and Sissela Bok, Ethics Teaching in Higher Education (The Hastings Center Series in Ethics) (New York: Springer, 1980), 1, 2; The Teaching of Ethics in Higher Education: Reports from the Hastings Center (New York: Hastings Center, 1980), 17, 18.

124. Richard J. Storr, Academic Culture and the History of American Higher Education, Journal of General Education 5 (1950): 6, 13 (quoting Gilman).

125. Arthur, Traditional Approaches to Character Education, 47–48. See B. Edward McClellan, Moral Education in America: Schools and the Shaping of Character since Colonial Times to the Present (New York: Teacher's College Press, 1999); Craig A. Cunningham, A Certain and Reasoned Art, in Lapsley and Power, Character Psychology and Character Education.

126. For the rise in Catholic schools, and the later growth in fundamentalist Christian schools, see McClellan, Moral Education, 38–40, 94–97. For the later rise in Muslim schools, see Patricia Z. Salahuddin, Character Education in a Muslim School: A Case Study of a Comprehensive Muslim School's Curricula, Florida International University Unpublished Dissertation (2011): 53–54, http://digitalcommons.fiu.edu/cgi/viewcontent.cgi?article=1548&context=etd.

127. For the evolution and overlap of these different approaches, see Wolfgang Althof and Marvin W. Berkowitz, Moral Education and Character Education: Their Relationship and Roles in Citizenship Education, Journal of Moral Education 35 (2006): 495, 499–501.

128. Kilpatrick, Why Johnny Can't Tell Right from Wrong, 98.

129. W. J. Hutchins, Children's Code of Morals for Elementary Schools (Washington, DC: Character Education Institution, 1917); Sherry L. Field, Historical Perspective on Character Education, Educational Forum 60 (1996): 118; James

S. Laming, In Search of Effective Character Education, Educational Leadership 51 (November, 1993): 63.

130. Cunningham, A Certain and Reasoned Art, 169–171.

131. Hugh Hartshorne and Mark May, Studies in the Nature of Character: Studies in Deceit, vol. 1 (New York: Macmillan, 1928), 413.

132. Hugh Hartshorne and Mark May, Studies in the Nature of Character: Studies in Service and Self-Control, vol. 2 (New York: Macmillan, 1929), 273.

133. Hugh Hartshorn, Mark May, and Frank K. Shuttleworth, Studies in the Nature of Character: Studies in the Organization of Character, vol. 3 (New York: Macmillan, 1930), 173.

134. Hartshorne and May, Studies in the Nature of Character: Studies in Deceit, vol. 1; Hartshorne and May, Studies in the Nature of Character: Studies in Service and Self-Control, vol. 2; Hartshorne, May, and Shuttleworth, Studies in the Nature of Character: Studies in the Organization of Character, vol. 3.

135. Roger V. Burton, Generality of Honesty Reconsidered, Psychological Review 70 (1963): 481.

136. Gordon W. Allport, Personality, 52.

137. Hunter, Death of Character, 70.

138. William K. Frankena, Ethical Theory, in E. Richard Schlatter, Philosophy (New Jersey: Englewood Cliffs, 1964), 437–438; Kai Nielson, Problems of Ethics, in Paul Edwards ed., The Encyclopedia of Philosophy (1967), 117, 119; Sloan, The Teaching of Ethics in the American Undergraduate Curriculum, 39; McClellan, Moral Education, 65.

139. George Henry Moulds, The Decline and Fall of Philosophy, Liberal Education 50 (1964): 360, 361.

140. Philip E. Jacob, Changing Values in College (New York: Harper and Brothers, 1957).

141. H. Danner Clouser, The Teaching of Ethics in Higher Education: A Report by the Hastings Center (Hastings-on-Hudson, New York: Insitute of Society, Ethics and the Life Sciences, 1980), 19.

142. Hastings Center Staff, The Teaching of Ethics in American Higher Education: An Empirical Synopsis, in Callahan and Bok, Ethics Teaching in Higher Education, 153, 162. See also William F. May, Professional Ethics: Setting, Terrain and Teacher, in Callahan and Bok, Ethics Teaching in Higher Education, 205, 207.

143. Dale Moss, Why Can't Law Schools Teach Ethics, Student Lawyer, October 1991). See Hastings Center Staff, Teaching Ethics in American Higher Education, 164–165; Deborah L. Rhode, Professional Responsibility: Ethics by the Pervasive Method (New York: Aspen, 2d ed., 1998).

144. John Dewey, Human Nature and Conduct: An Introduction to Social Psychology (New York: Modern Library, 1922), 37; Hersh, Miller, and Fielding, Models of Moral Education, 21.

145. John Dewey, Teaching Ethics in the High School, Educational Theory 17 (July, 1967): 222.

146. John Dewey, Ethical Principles Underlying Education, reprinted in John Dewey and Reginald Archambault eds., John Dewey on Education: Selected Writings (Chicago: University of Chicago Press, 1964), 129.

147. John Dewey, Moral Principles in Education (Boston: Houghton Mifflin, 1909); John Dewey, Democracy and Education (New York: Macmillan, 1916); John Dewey, The School and Society (Chicago: University of Chicago Press, 1915).

148. John Dewey and Evelyn Dewey, Schools of Tomorrow (New York: E. P. Dutton, 1915), 199–200.

149. Hersh, Miller, and Fielding, Models of Moral Education, 22.

150. McClellan, Moral Education, 73–73; Field, Historical Perspective on Character Education, 120.

151. Hersh, Miller, and Fielding, Models of Moral Education, 23.

152. Jerome S. Bruner, "The Process of Education" Revisited, Phi Delta Kappan (September 1971): 21.

153. Hersh, Miller, and Fielding, Models of Moral Education.

154. Louis E. Raths, M. Harmin, and Sidney B. Simon, Values and Teaching: Working with Values in the Classroom (Columbus, OH: Charles E. Merrill, 1966).

155. Louis E. Raths, M. Harmin, and Sidney B. Simon, Values and Teaching: Working with Values in the Classroom (Columbus OH: Charles E. Merrill, 2d ed., 1978), 8–9 (quoting John Gardner).

156. Sidney B. Simon, Leland W. Howe, and Howard Kirschenbaum, Values Clarification (New York: Hart, rev. ed., 1978), back cover. See also Kilpatrick, Why Johnny Can't Tell Right from Wrong, 80.

157. Raths, Harmin, and Simon, Values and Teaching, 113.

158. Charles J. Sykes, Dumbing Down Our Kids: Why American Children Feel Good about Themselves But Can't Read, Write, or Add (New York: St. Martin's Griffin, 1995).

159. Sommers, Teaching the Virtues, 683–684.

160. Kilpatrick, Why Johnny Can't Tell Right from Wrong, 16–17.

161. Sommers, Teaching the Virtues, 683.

162. Alan L. Lockwood, The Effects of Values Clarification and Moral Development Curricula on School-Age Subjects: A Critical Review of Recent Research, Review of Educational Research 48 (1978): 325.

163. James S. Leming, Curricular Effectiveness in Moral/Values Education: A Review of Research, Journal of Moral Education 10 (1981): 147, 150.

164. Lawrence Kohlberg, Indoctrination versus Relativity in Value Education, Journal of Religion and Science 6 (1971): 285.

165. Cary J. Roseth, Character Education, Moral Education, and Moral-Character Education, in Lyn Corno and Eric M. Anderman, Handbook of Educational Psychology (New York: Routledge, 3d ed., 2015), 213, 217.

166. Carol Gilligan, In a Different Voice: Psychological Theory and Women's Development (Cambridge, MA: Harvard University Press, 1982).

167. Kilpatrick, Why Johnny Can't Tell Right from Wrong, 84–85.

168. Thomas Lickona, What Does Moral Psychology Have to Say to the Teacher of Ethics? in Callahan and Bok, Ethics Teaching in Higher Education, 103, 115.

169. Lickona, What Does Moral Psychology Have to Say to the Teacher of Ethics, 108; Laming, In Search of Effective Character Education, 65.

170. Edwin A. Delattre, Ethics and Education in America, Network News and Views (February 1991): 19–20; Kilpatrick, Why Johnny Can't Tell Right from Wrong, 88.

171. Delattre, Ethics and Education in America, 19–20; Kilpatrick, Why Johnny Can't Tell Right from Wrong, 88.

172. Lawrence Kohlberg, Moral Education Reappraised, The Humanist 38 (1978): 13, 15.

173. James Davison Hunter and Carl Desportes Bowman, The Politics of Character: Survey of American Political Culture (Charlottesville: Institute for Advanced Studies in Culture, University of Virginia, 2000), 3; Sonia L. Nazario, Schoolteachers Say It's Wrongheaded to Try to Teach Students What's Right, Wall Street Journal, April 6, 1990; A Study of Core Values and the Schools, Phi Delta Kappan, October 1996, discussed in Thomas Lickona, The Case for Character Education, Tikkun, January/February 1997: 26.

174. Poll Shows Most Prefer Values Taught at School, Fort Worth Star-Telegram, October 9, 1994, 8. See William J. Bennett, The Book of Virtues: A Treasury of Great Moral Stories (New York: Simon & Schuster, 1993).

175. Bonnidell Clouse, Character Education: Borrowing from the Past to Advance the Future, Contemporary Education 72 (2001): 23, 26; Andrew J. Milson, Creating a Curriculum for Character Development: A Case Study, Clearing House 74 (2000): 89 (noting forty-eight states had mandates or were developing them). For the thirty-six states that have laws requiring character education, see Character. org, http://character.org/more-resources/character-education-legislation (last visited February 16, 2019). For character education in other nations, including Canada, Korea, Japan, and China, see Larry Nucci, Darcia Narváez, and Tobias Krettenauer, Introduction and Overview, in Nucci, Narváez, and Krettenauer, Handbook of Moral and Character Education, 1.

176. Sense of Congress Regarding Good Character, Public Law No. 105–244 Section 863.

177. Brian H. Smith, School-Based Character Education in the United States, Childhood Education 89 (2013): 350, 352.

178. Mathew L. Davidson, Harness the Sun, Channel the Wind: The Art and Science of Effective Character Education, in Lapsley and Power, Character Psychology and Character Education, 218.

179. Character Counts Homepage, https://charactercounts.org/.

180. Character.org, http//www.exchange.character.org/.

181. Nazario, Schoolteachers Say It's Wrongheaded to Try to Teach Students What's Right, 1, 6.

182. Virginia General Assembly, S.B. 817, adopted April 4, 1999.

183. Thomas Jefferson Center for Character Education, How to Be Successful in Less than Ten Minutes a Day (Pasadena, CA: Jefferson Center for Character Education, 1991).

184. Thomas Jefferson Center for Character Education, How to Be Successful in Less than Ten Minutes a Day.

185. California Task Force on K-12 Civic Learning, Revitalizing K-12 Civic Learning in California: A Blueprint for Action (2014), 10; Paul Barnwell, Students' Broken Moral Compasses, Atlantic, July 25, 2016.

186. Lickona, The Case for Character Education, 24.

187. William J. Bennett, Moral Literacy and the Formation of Character, NASSP Bulletin, December 1988, 29.

188. Campbell, What Is Education's Impact on Civic and Social Engagement, in R. Desjardins and T. Schuller eds., Measuring the Effects of Education on Health and Civic/Social Engagement, Paris Organization for Economic Cooperation and Development, Center for Educational Research and Innovation (2006): 25–126; Judith Torney-Purta, Britt Wilkenfeld, and Carolyn Barber, How Adolescents in 27 Countries Understand, Support and Practice Human Rights, Journal of Social Issues 64 (2008): 857.

189. Josephson Institute of Ethics, 2012 Report Card on the Ethics of American Youth (Los Angeles: Josephson Institute of Ethics, 2012).

190. Lickona, The Case for Character Education, 24; Thomas Lickona, Educating for Character: A Comprehensive Approach, in Alex Molnar ed., The Construction of Children's Character (National Society for the Study of Education, Chicago: University of Chicago Press, 1997), 45.

191. Stephen L. Carter, Integrity (New York: Harper Perennial, 1996), 238.

192. Lickona, Educating for Character, 20–21.

193. Lickona, Educating for Character, 108.

194. Character Education Partnership, Performance Values: Why They Matter and What Schools Can Do to Foster Their Development (Washington, DC: Character Education Partnership, April 2008).

195. Mathew Davidson, Thomas Lickona, and Vladimir Khmelkov, Smart and Good Schools: A New Paradigm for High School Character Education, in Nucci, Narváez, and Krettenauer, Handbook of Moral and Character Education, 305. For the variation in definitions, see Roseth, Character Education, 213–215.

196. Tough, How Children Succeed; Angela Lee Duckworth, Christopher Peterson, Michael D. Mathews, and Dennis R. Kelly, Grit: Perseverance and Passion for Long-Term Goals, Journal of Personality and Social Psychology 92 (2007): 1087; Laura Pappano, "Grit" and the New Character Education, The Education Digest, May 2013, 4.

197. Davidson, Lickona and Khmelkov, Smart and Good Schools; K. Anders Ericsson, Neil Charness, Paul J. Feltovich, and Robert R. Hoffman, The Cambridge Handbook of Expertise and Expert Performance (Cambridge: Cambridge University Press, 2006); Angela Lee Duckworth, Grit: The Power of Passion and Perseverance (New York: Simon & Schuster, 2016), 34–42, 74–75; David Brooks, The Character Factory, New York Times, August 1, 2014.

198. Duckworth, Grit, 147.

199. Duckworth, Grit, 82.

200. Rebecca Mead, Learn Different, New Yorker, March 7, 2016, 43.

201. Terry Ehiorobo, Bullying in School: The Traumatic Effects of Bullying on Children (CPI April 2012), https://www.crisisprevention.com/Blog/April-2012/Bullying-in-School-The-Traumatic-Effects-of-Bullyi (48 percent report harassment); Josephson Institute of Ethics, 2012 Report Card on the Ethics of American Youth (Los Angeles: Josephson Institute of Ethics, 2012), 58 (49 percent report serious bullying or harassment); Steve Nish and David Gawkowski, Character Education and Bullying, Seen Magazine, http://www.seenmagazine.us/Articles-detail/ArticleID2343/ (last visited February 16, 2019); Samerer Hinduja and Justin W. Patchin, Cyberbullying: Identification, Prevention and Response (Cyberbullying Research Center), 3 (about a third of middle and high schoolers report having been cyberbullied); Caralee Adams, Cyberbullying: What Teachers and Schools Can Do, Scholastic, https://www.scholastic.com/teachers/articles/teaching-content/cyberbullying-what-teachers-and-schools-can-do/ (last visited February 16, 2019) (42 percent report having been bullied online); Alison DeNisco, Are Schools Doing Enough to Stop Bullying?, District Administration Magazine, September 9, 2013 (reporting findings by Pacer's National Bullying Prevention Center that one-third of school-aged children report bullying).

202. Human Rights Campaign, Post-Election Survey of Youth (2017), 2.

203. Southern Poverty Law Center, The Trump Effect: The Impact of the 2016 Presidential Election on Our Nation's Schools (Southern Poverty Law Center, 2017), 4.

204. Southern Poverty Law Center, The Trump Effect, 7–9.

205. Scott Grabel, Cyberbullying: The New Online Crime, https://www.ucps.k12.nc.us/ (last visited February 16, 2019); Jaana Juvonen, School Violence: Prevalence, Fears, and Prevention (Rand Corporation), https://www.rand.org/pubs/issue_papers/IP219/index2.html (last visited February 16, 2019); Richard Alan Spurling, The Bully-Free Zone Character Education Program: A Study of Impact on Five Western North Carolina Middle Schools (East Tennessee State University Electronic Theses and Dissertations, 2004), 24, http://dcetsu.eduetd/939.

206. Spurling, The Bully-Free Zone, 14, 26, 145; Bowman, Survey of Students Documents the Extent of Bullying, Education Week 20 (2001).

207. Juvonen, School Violence.

208. Adams, Cyberbullying; United States Department of Health and Human Services, Stopbullying.gov, Prevention at School, https://www.stopbullying.gov/prevention/at-school/index.html (last visited February 16, 2019); Ulrich Boser, How to Stop Bullying in Schools, U.S. News, February 27, 2018, https://www.usnews.com/opinion/knowledge-bank/articels/218-02-27.

209. Althof and Berkowitz, Moral Education and Character Education, 509–510; Anne Colby, Thomas Ehrlich, Elizabeth Beaumont, and Jason Stephens, Educating Citizens: Preparing America's Undergraduates for Lives of Moral and Civic Responsibility (San Francisco: Jossey-Bass and the Carnegie Foundation for the Advancement of Teaching, 2003), 13; Judith Torney-Purta and Susan Vermeer Lopez, Developing Citizenship Competencies from Kindergarten through Grade 12: A Background Paper for Policymakers and Educators (National Center for Learning and Citizenship, 2006), 7.

210. Robert Reich, The Common Good, 178.

211. Althof and Berkowitz, Moral Education and Character Education, 503; Benjamin R. Barber, Public Talk and Civic Acton: Education for Participation in a Strong Democracy, Social Education 53 (October 1989): 355; Charles C. Moskos, A Call to Civic Service: National Service for Country and Community (New York: Free Press, 1988), 9.

212. Reich, The Common Good, 179.

213. Schaps, Schaeffer, and McDonnell, What's Right and Wrong in Character Education Today.

214. Maurice J. Elias et al., The Complementary Perspectives of Social and Emotional Learning, Moral Education, and Character Education, in Nucci, Narváez, and Krettenauer, Handbook of Moral and Character Education, 272, 274–278.

215. Sommers, Teaching the Virtues; The Public Interest 111 (Spring, 1993): 10, 13; Bennett, Moral Literacy and the Formation of Character; Robert Coles, The Call of Stories: Teaching and the Moral Imagination (Boston: Houghton Mifflin, 1989); Lynne Cheney, The Importance of Stories, Academic Questions 4 (Spring 1991); Kevin Ryan and Karen E. Bohlin, Building Character in Schools: Practical Ways to Bring Moral Instruction to Life (Thousand Oaks, CA: Jossey-Bass, 1999).

216. Colin Greer and Herbert Kohl eds., A Call to Character: Family Treasury of Stories, Poems, Plays, Proverbs, and Fables to Guide the Development of Values for You and Your Children (New York: Harper Collins, 1995); Steven Barboza ed., The African-American Book of Values: Classic Moral Stories (New York: Doubleday, 1998).

217. Joel J. Kupperman, Character (New York: Oxford University Press, 1995), 173; John M. Doris, Lack of Character: Personality and Moral Behavior (New York: Cambridge University Press, 2002), 123.

218. See the discussion of the California Child Development Project later on in this chapter, and in Laming, In Search of Effective Character Education, 63, 68–69;

Developmental Studies Center, The Child Development Project: Description of Findings in Two Initial Districts and the First Phase of a Further Extension (Oakland, CA: Developmental Studies Center, 1993).

219. Mike Rose, Character Education: A Cautionary Note, in Essays on Character and Opportunity (Washington, DC: Brookings, 2014), 45, 46.

220. Laming, In Search of Effective Character Education, 63, 69.

221. Social and Character Development Research Consortium, Efficacy of School-Wide Programs to Promote Social and Character Development and Reduce Problem Behavior in Elementary School Children (Washington, DC: National Center for Education Research, Institute of Education Sciences, U.S. Department of Education, 2010). See Sarah D. Sparks, Character Education Found to Fall Short in Federal Study, Education Week, October 21, 2010.

222. Martin W. Berkowitz, Leading Schools of Character, in Alan M. Blankstein and Paul D. Houston eds., Leadership for Social Justice and Democracy in Our Schools (Thousand Oaks, CA: Corwin, 2011): 93; Marvin W. Berkowitz, Victor A. Battistich, and Melinda C. Bier, What Works in Character Education: What Is Known and What Needs to Be Known, in Nucci, Narváez, and Krettenauer, Handbook of Moral and Character Education, 414; Jacques S. Benninga, Marvin W. Berkowitz, Phyllis Kuehn, and Karen Smith, Character and Academics: What Good Schools Do, Phi Delta Kappan (February 2006): 448, 450. See Roseth, Character Education, 222.

223. Marvin W. Berkowitz and Melinda C. Bier, Research-Based Character Education, Annals of the American Academy of Political and Social Science 591 (2004): 72, 74–75. See also Marvin W. Berkowitz and Melinda C. Bier, What Works in Character Education: A Research-Driven Guide for Educators (Character Education Partnership, February 2005), 19.

224. Allen, The New Ethics, 74.

225. Alfie Kohn, How Not to Teach Values: A Critical Look at Character Education, Phi Delta Kappan 78 (February 1977): 428, 430.

226. Schaps, Schaeffer, and McDonnell, What's Right and Wrong in Character Education Today, 40.

227. Schaps, Schaeffer, and McDonnell, What's Right and Wrong in Character Education Today, 40.

228. David E. Purple, The Politics of Character Education, in Molnar, The Construction of Children's Character.

229. Kohlberg, Indoctrination versus Relativity in Value Education.

230. Smith, Christoffersen, Davidson, and Herzog, Lost in Transition, 63. See also Berman, Children's Social Consciousness, 185.

231. Davidson, Lickona, and Khmelkov, Smart and Good Schools, 290. Thomas Lickona and Matthew Davidson, Smart and Good High Schools: Integrating Excellence and Ethics for Success in School, Work, and Beyond (Cortland,

NY: Center for the 4th and 5th Rs and the Institute for Excellence and Ethics (2005).

232. Salahuddin, Character Education in a Muslim School, 41, 44, 141; Robert W. Howard, Preparing Moral Educators in an Era of Standards-Based Reform, Education Quarterly 32 (2005):43; Torney-Purta and Lopez, Developing Citizenship Competencies, 17; Sheryl O'Sullivan, The Soul of Teaching: Educating Teachers of Character, Action in Teacher Education 26 (2005): 3; Dorothy L. Prestwich, Character Education in America's Schools, School Community Journal 14 (2004): 139.

233. Civic Enterprises with Peter D. Hart Research Associates, The Missing Piece: A National Teacher Survey on How Social and Emotional Learning Can Empower Children and Transform Schools (Washington, DC: Civic Enterprises, 2013).

234. Character Education Partnership, Teachers as Educators of Character (Washington, DC: Character Education Partnership, 1999), 4; Emily Nielsen Jones, Kevin Ryan, and Karen Bohlin, Character Education and Teacher Education: How Are Prospective Teachers Being Prepared to Foster Good Character in Students? Action in Teacher Education 20 (1998): 11, 16–17.

235. Smith, Christoffersen, Davidson, and Herzog, Lost in Transition.

236. Smith, Christoffersen, Davidson, and Herzog, Lost in Transition, 21, 23.

237. Smith, Christoffersen, Davidson, and Herzog, Lost in Transition, 25, 23.

238. Smith, Christoffersen, Davidson, and Herzog, Lost in Transition, 21.

239. Smith, Christoffersen, Davidson, and Herzog, Lost in Transition, 48.

240. Smith, Christoffersen, Davidson, and Herzog, Lost in Transition, 48.

241. Smith, Christoffersen, Davidson, and Herzog, Lost in Transition, 41.

242. Smith, Christoffersen, Davidson, and Herzog, Lost in Transition, 53.

243. Smith, Christoffersen, Davidson, and Herzog, Lost in Transition, 36.

244. Smith, Christoffersen, Davidson, and Herzog, Lost in Transition, 205, 212.

245. Smith, Christoffersen, Davidson, and Herzog, Lost in Transition, 226–227.

246. Weissbourd et al., The Children We Mean to Raise, 12.

247. California Task Force on K–12 Civic Learning, Revitalizing K–12 Civic Learning in California: A Blueprint for Action (2014), 6.

248. Smith, Christoffersen, Davidson, and Herzog, Lost in Transition, 61, 238.

249. Aldous Huxley, Island (New York: Harper & Row, 1962).

250. Lickona, Character Matters, 262.

251. William Damon and Ann Colby, Education and Moral Commitment, Journal of Moral Education 25 (1996): 31.

252. Lickona, Character Matters, 267.

253. Character.org, Principles of Effective Character Education (2015).

254. DeRoche and Williams, Educating Hearts and Minds, 59.

255. Character.org, Principles of Effective Character Education, 181. See also Lickona, Educating for Character, 58.

256. Character.org, Principles of Effective Character Education, 6.

257. Developmental Studies Center, The Literature Project: Reading for Real (Oakland, CA: Developmental Studies Center, 1995); California Task Force on K–12 Civic Learning, revitalizing K–12 Civic Learning, 36.

258. DeRoche and Williams, Educating Hearts and Minds, 73; Weissbourd, Moral Teachers, Moral Students, 1; Damon and Colby, Education and Moral Commitment; F. Clark Power and Ann Higgins-D'Alessandro, The Just Community Approach to Moral Education and the Moral Atmosphere of the School, in Larry Nucci and Darci Narváez, Handbook of Moral and Character Education (New York: Routledge, 2008), 231; Lawrence Kohlberg, The Just Community Approach to Moral Education in Theory and Practice, in Marvin W. Berkowitz and Fritz Oser eds., Moral Education: Theory and Application (Hillsdale, NJ: L. Erlbaum, 1985); Fritz K. Oser, Toward a Theory of the Just Community Approach: Effects of Collective Moral, Civic, and Social Education, in Nucci, Narváez, and Krettenauer, Handbook of Moral and Character Education, 198, 204.

259. Thomas Lickona, Character Education: Seven Crucial Issues, Action in Teacher Education 20 (1999): 77; Roy F. Baumeister and Julie Juola Exline, Virtue, Personality, and Social Relations: Self-Control as the Moral Muscle, Journal of Personality 67 (1999): 1165, 1179.

260. Southern Poverty Law Center, The Trump Effect, 13.

261. Marilyn Watson, Developmental Discipline and Moral Education, in Nucci, Narváez, and Krettenauer, Handbook of Moral and Character Education, 159, 170; Kohn, Punished by Rewards, 108.

262. Elizabeth Campbell, Teaching Ethically as a Moral Condition of Professionalism, in Nucci, Narváez, and Krettenauer, Handbook of Moral and Character Education, 107; Darcia Narváez and Tonia Black, Developing Ethical Expertise and Moral Personalities, in Nucci, Narváez, and Krettenauer, Handbook of Moral and Character Education, 150; Benninga, Berkowitz, Kuehn, and Smith, Character and Academics, 451.

263. Marilyn Watson, The Child Development Project: Building Character by Building Community, Action in Teacher Education 20 (1998): 59l; Eric Schnaps, Victor Battistich, and Daniel Solomon, School as a Caring Community: A Key to Character Education, in Molnar, The Construction of Children's Character, 127, 137–138; Solomon, Watson, and Battistich, Teaching and Schooling Effects on Moral/Prosocial Development, 582.

264. Davidson, Lickona, and Khmelkov, Smart and Good Schools, 290, 301; Pappano, "Grit" and the New Character Education, 7–8; Angela Lee Duckworth, Don't Grade Schools on Grit, New York Times, March 27, 2016, SR5.

265. Tough, How Children Succeed, 93.

266. Pappano, "Grit" and the New Character Education, 8; Gavin Newsom, as Mayor of SF Commencement Address at San Francisco State University, New York Times, June 15, 2008, A16.

267. Tough, Helping Children Succeed, 84–85.

268. Tough, How Children Succeed; Duckworth, Don't Grade Schools on Grit.

269. Jonah Lehrer, Don't!, The New Yorker, May 18, 2009.

270. Simmons, Enough As She Is, 173.

271. Victor Battistich, Marilyn Watson, Daniel Solomon, and Judith Solomon, The Child Development Project: A Comprehensive Program for the Development of Prosocial Character; Laming, In Search of Effective Character Education, 68.

272. Hoehn, Up from Apathy, 100; Davidson, Harness the Sun, 231–232; Eric Schaps, Marilyn Watson, and Catherine Lewis, A Sense of Community Is Key to Effectiveness in Fostering Character Education, Journal of Staff Development 17 (1996): 42, 43.

273. Laming, In Search of Effective Character Education, 68–69; Developmental Studies Center, The Child Development Project: Description of Findings in Two Initial Districts and the First Phase of a Further Extension. See also Solomon, Watson, and Battistich, Teaching and School Effects on Moral/Prosocial Development, 594–596.

274. Tough, Helping Children Succeed, 71: California Task Force on K–12 Civic Learning, Revitalizing K–12 Civic Learning, 17, 33.

275. Tough, How Children Succeed, 77 (quoting Dominic Randolph).

276. Nat Hentoff, American Heroes: In and out of School (New York: Delacorte Press, 1987); A Holiday for Heroes, Newsweek, July 4, 1988; Sara Ensor, Purpose for Living (for ages 9 to 13). See Lickona, Educating for Character, 306–311.

277. This example is drawn from Mary Crossan, Gerard Seijts, and Jeffrey Gandz, Developing Leadership Character (New York: Routledge, 2015), 140–142.

278. Crossan, Seijts, and Gandz, Developing Leadership Character, 142.

279. Judith A. Boss, The Effect of Community Service Work on the Moral Development of College Ethics Students, Journal of Moral Education 23 (1994): 183; Judith A. Boss, Teaching Ethics through Community Service, Journal of Experiential Education (1995): 20.

280. For the poll, see Joan Schine, Beyond Test Scores and Standards: Service, Understanding and Citizenship, in Jeff Claus and Curtis Ogden eds., Service Learning for Youth Empowerment and Social Change (New York: Peter Lang, 1999), 15. For public service involvement see Daniel M. Hart, Kyle Matsuba, and Robert Atkins, The Moral and Civic Effects of Learning to Serve, in Nucci, Narváez, and Krettenauer, Handbook of Moral and Character Education, 456. For service learning, see Rebecca Skinner and Chris Chapman, Service-Learning and Community Service in K–12 Public Schools, National Center for Education Statistics (November 1999).

281. Shelley Billig, Research on K–12 School-Based Service-Learning: The Evidence Builds, Phi Delta Kappan (May 2000): 658; National Youth Leadership Council, K–12 Service Learning Standards for Quality Practice, (2009).

282. Jay W. Brandenberger, College, Character, and Social Responsibility: Moral Learning through Experience, in Lapsley and Power, Character Psychology and Character Education, 318–319.

283. Colby, Ehrich, Beaumont, and Stephens, Educating Citizens, 140.

284. Peter C. Scales et al., The Effects of Service Learning on Middle School Students Social Responsibility and Academic Success, Journal of Early Adolescence 20 (2000): 232; James S. Leming, Integrating a Structured Ethical Reflection Curriculum into High School Community Service Experiences: Impact on Students' Sociomoral Development, Adolescence 36 (2001): 33.

285. Hart, Matsuba, and Atkins, The Moral and Civic Effects of Learning to Serve, 459–460; Billig, Research on K-12 School-Based Service-Learning; Alexander W. Astin, Kimberly Misa, Lori J. Vogelgesang, and Erica Yamamura, Understanding the Effects of Service-Learning: A Study of Students and Faculty (The Higher Education Research Institute, Graduate School of Education and Information Studies, University of California, Los Angeles, 2006); Peterson and Seligman, Character Strengths and Virtues, 385; Billig, Research on K–12 School-Based Service-Learning, 658. See, generally, James Youniss and Miranda Yates, Promoting Identity Development: Ten Ideals for School-Based Service Learning Programs, in Claus and Ogden, Service Learning for Youth Empowerment and Social Change, 43; Solomon, Watson, and Battistich, Teaching and School Effects on Moral/Prosocial Development, 566, 592.

286. Christine I. Celio, Joseph Durlak, and Allison Dymnicki, A Meta-Analysis of the Impact of Service-Learning on Students, Journal of Experiential Education 34 (2011): 164; Conway, Amel, and Gerwien, Teaching and Learning in the Social Context: A Meta-analysis of Service Learning's Effects on Academic, Personal, Social and Citizenship Outcomes, Teaching of Psychology 36 (2009): 233; Greg Behr, Millie Finch, William Dobson, Stacey Abrams, and Coin Brown III eds., The Content of Our Character: Voices of Generation X (Durham, NC: Kenan Ethics Program, 1999), 16.

287. Judicial Council of California, More Civic Learning to Reach California Schools, February 3, 2017, https://newsroom.courts.ca.gov/news/more-civic-learning-to-reach-california-schools. Examples of partnership opportunities are described at http://www.powerofdemocracy.org/civic-learning/civic-learning-partnerships/.

288. James Youniss and Miranda Yates, Community Service and Social Responsibility in Youth (Chicago: University of Chicago Press, 1997).

289. Youniss and Yates, Community Service, 121, 126, 134.

290. Linda Sax and Alexander W. Astin, The Benefits of Service: Evidence from Undergraduates, Educational Record 78 (1997): 25, 28.

291. Gregory B. Markus, Jeffrey P. F. Howard, and David C. King, Integrating Community Service and Classroom Instruction Enhances Learning: Results from an Experiment, Educational Evaluation and Policy Analysis 15 (1993): 410.

292. Laurent A. Parks Daloz, Cheryl H. Keen, James P. Keen, and Sharon Daloz Parks, Common Fire: Leading Lives of Commitment in a Complex World (Boston: Beacon Press, 1996); Laurent A. Parks Daloz, Cheryl H. Keen, James P. Keen, and Sharon Daloz Parks, Lives of Commitment: Higher Education in the Life of the New Commons, Change 28 (May/June 1996): 11, 14.

293. Colby, Ehrich, Beaumont, and Stephens, Educating Citizens, 114; Arthur J. Schwartz, It's Not Too Late to Teach College Students about Values, Chronicle of Higher Education, June 9, 2000, A68.

294. Anne Colby, Fostering the Moral and Civic Development of College Students, in Nucci, Narváez, and Krettenauer, Handbook of Moral and Character Education, 368, 369.

295. Hastings Center Report, The Teaching of Ethics in Higher Education, 30, 61. See also the goals articulated by the Hastings Center Director in Daniel Callahan, Goals in the Teaching of Ethics, in Callahan and Bok, Ethics Teaching in Higher Education.

296. James J. F. Forest, Service Academies of the United States: Issues of Context, Curriculum, and Assessment, New Directions for Institutional Research 118 (Summer 2003): 79, 82.

297. United States Military Academy, Academic Program, Class of 2018 (Redbook) (September 2015): 13; United States Military Academy, West Point, Character Development Strategy (February 2015): 6.

298. United States Military Academy, West Point, William E. Simon Center for the Professional Military Ethic (January 2018), https://www.usma.edu/SCPME/SitePages/Home.aspx; United States Military Academy, Character Development Strategy, at 14.

299. United States Military Academy, Character Development Strategy, at 7–8.

300. Rhode, Professional Responsibility: Ethics by the Pervasive Method; May, Professional Ethics: Setting, Terrain and Teacher, in Callahan and Bok, Ethics Teaching in Higher Education, 205, 237; Susan Resneck Parr, The Teaching of Ethics in Undergraduate Nonethics Courses, in Callahan and Bok, Ethics Teaching in Higher Education, 191.

301. Damon, The Path to Purpose, 109; Smith, Christoffersen, Davidson, and Herzog, Lost in Transition.

302. Ernest T. Pascarella and Patrick T. Terenzini, Moral Development, in Ernest T. Pascarella and Patrick T. Terenzini eds., How College Affects Students: A Third Decade of Research, vol. 2 (San Francisco: Jossey-Bass, 2005), 345; Marcia Mentkowski & Associates, Learning That Lasts: Integrating Learning, Development, and Performance in College and Beyond (San Francisco: Jossey-Bass, 2000), 121; Muriel J. Bebeau, Promoting Ethical Development and Professionalism: Insights from Education Research in the Professions, University of St. Thomas Law Journal 5 (2008): 366, 384–385; John D. Bransford, M. Suzanne

Donovan, and James W. Pellegrino eds., How People Learn: Brain, Mind, Experience, and School (Washington, DC: National Research Council, National Academic Press, 2000), 51–78; James R. Rest, Why Does College Promote Development in Moral Judgement, Journal of Moral Education 17 (1988): 183; Anne Colby, Whose Values Anyway? in William Damon ed., Bringing in a New Era in Character Education (Stanford, CA: Hoover Institution Press, 2002), 163–164.

303. For undergraduate courses, see Colby, Ehrich, Beaumont, and Stephens, Educating Citizens, 172. For professional school courses, see Muriel J. Bebeau and Verna E. Monson, A Theoretical and Evidence-Based Approach for Designing Professional Ethics Education, in Nucci, Narváez, and Krettenauer, Handbook of Moral and Character Education, 507, 520.

CHAPTER 3

1. This chapter draws on Deborah L. Rhode, Virtue and the Law: The Good Moral Character Requirement in Occupational Licensing, Bar Regulation and Immigration Proceedings, Law and Social Inquiry 43 (2018): 1027.

2. Mathew Friedman, Just Facts: As Many Americans Have Criminal Records as College Diplomas (New York: Brennan Center for Justice, 2015); The Sentencing Project, Americans with Criminal Records (2015), http://www.sentencingproject. oprg/wp-content/uploads/2015/Americans-with-Criminal-Records-and-Opporunnity-Profilepdf.

3. Alexandra Natapoff, Punishment without Crime (New York: Basic Books, 2018),113–114 (quoting Willilams).

4. Natapoff, Punishment without Crime (quoting Williams).

5. Clyde Pharr et al., The Theodosian Code and Novels and the Sirmondian Constitutions (Princeton, NJ: Princeton University Press, 1952), 32.

6. Jennifer Lundquist, Devah Pager, and Eiko Strader, Does a Criminal Past Predict Worker Performance? Evidence from One of America's Largest Employers, Social Forces 96 (2018): 1039; Mike Vuolo, Sarah Lageson, and Christopher Uggen, Criminal Record Questions in the Era of "Ban the Box," Criminology and Public Policy 16 (2017): 139, 142; Christopher Uggen, Mike Vuolo, Sarah Lageson, Ebony Ruhland, and Hilary Whitham, The Edge of Stigma: An Experimental Audit of the Effects of Low-Level Criminal Records on Employment, Criminology 52 (2014): 627.

7. Lunquist, Pager, and Strader, Does a Criminal Past Predict Worker Performance?; Megan Denver, Justin T. Pickett, and Shawn D. Bushway, Criminal Records and Employment: A Survey of Experiences and Attitudes in the United States, Justice Quarterly (2017): 1, 5.

8. Sarah Shannon, Christopher Uggen, and Melissa Thompson, Growth in the U.S. Ex-Felon and Ex-Prisoner Population, 1948 to 2010, Paper Presented at

the Annual Meeting of the Population Association of America (Washington, DC: Population Association of America, April 2011), 11–12.

9. Binyamin Appelbaum, Out of Trouble, but Criminal Records Keep Men out of Work, New York Times, February 28, 2015. Mark Obbie, In Search of the Felon-Friendly Workplace, New York Times, June 26, 2016, B6. Some 13 million cases (excluding speeding offenses) are filed each year. Alexandra Natapoff, Punishment without Crime (New York:Basic Books, 2018), 41.

10. Vuolo, Lageson and Uggen, Criminal Record Questions, 141.

11. Justice Center, National Resource Center, What Works in Reentry Clearinghouse; Employment (The Council of State Governments), https:// whatworks.csgjusticecenter.org/. See Vuolo, Lageson, and Uggen, Criminal Record Questions, 158; Christopher Uggen and Sarah Shannon, Productive Addicts and Harm Reduction: How Work Reduces Crime—But Not Drug Use, Social Problems 61 (2014): 105.

12. Obbie, In Search of the Felon-Friendly Workplace, B6.

13. Tanzina Vega, Out of Prison and out of Work: Jobs out of Reach for Former Inmates, CNN, October 30, 2015, http://money.cnn.com/2015/10/30/news/economy/former-inmates-unemployed/.

14. Michelle Natividad Rodriguez and Beth Avery, Unlicensed and Untapped: Removing Barriers to State Occupational Licenses for People with Records (National Employment Law Project, April 2016), 8; Devah Pager, Marked: Race, Crime, and Finding Work in an Era of Mass Incaeration (Chicogo: University of Chiago Press, 2007), 67- 71, 90-91; Devah Pager, The Mark of a Criminal Record, American Journal of Sociology 108 (2003): 937.

15. Corinne Lathrop Gilb, Hidden Hierarchies: The Professions and Government (New York: Harper and Row, 1966), 60.

16. Walter Gellhorn, Individual Freedom and Governmental Restraints (Baton Rouge: Louisiana State University Press, 1956), 106.

17. Lawrence M. Friedman, Freedom of Contract and Occupational Licensing 1890–1910: A Legal and Social Study, California Law Review 53 (March 1965): 487, 500.

18. Gilb, Hidden Hierarchies, 61.

19. Gellhorn, Individual Freedom, 106; Walter Gellhorn, The Abuse of Occupational Licensing, University of Chicago Law Review 44 (1976): 6.

20. Gellhorn, The Abuse of Occupational Licensing, 13.

21. Gellhorn, Individual Freedom, 138.

22. Gellhorn, Individual Freedom, 128.

23. Ga. Code Ann. § 84–23125 (1975).

24. Gellhorn, Individual Freedom, 130.

25. Department of the Treasury et al., Occupational Licensing: A Framework for Policymakers, The White House Report (July 2015); Council on Licensure Enforcement and Regulation (CLEAR), CLEAR's Mission (2017), https:// www.clearhq.org/page-1720466; Patricia Cohen, Horse Rub? Where's Your

License?, New York Times, June 18, 2016, B1; Morris M. Kleiner, Licensing Occupations: Ensuring Quality or Restricting Competition? (Kalamazoo: W. E. Upjohn Institute for Employment Research, 2006), 148.

26. Kleiner, Licensing Occupations, 14; Lisa Riordan Seville, Got a Criminal Record? Please Go Away, The Crime Report, March 21, 2011; Department of the Treasury et al., Occupational Licensing, 4; Cohen, Horse Rub?, B5; Steve Patterson, In Federal Court, Attorneys Spar over St. Augustine Artist Restrictions, First Amendment, St. Augustine Record, August 21, 2015; Consumer Affairs and Business Regulation, 269 Code of Massachusetts Regulations (CMR) 3.00: Individual Licensure, https://www.mass.gov/regulations/269-CMR-3-individual-licensure.

27. W. Brad Johnson and Clark D. Campbell, Character and Fitness Requirements for Professional Psychologists: Are There Any?, Professional Psychology: Research and Practice 33 (2002): 1.

28. Larry Craddock, "Good Moral Character" as a Licensing Standard, Journal of the National Association of Administrative Law Judiciary 28 (2008): 450, 464–466.

29. Licensing Laws & Requirements, State of Iowa Alcoholic Beverages Division, June 21, 2017, https://abd.iowa.gov/licensing/licensing-laws-requirements.

30. Massage Permits, City of Santa Barbara, http://www.santabarbaraca.gov/business/license/massage.asp (last visited June 21, 2017).

31. Dittman v. California, 191 F.3d 1020, 1032 (9th Cir. 1999).

32. Disciplinary Actions Fiscal Year 2015–2016 California Board of Chiropractic Examiners, http://www.chiro.ca.gov/enforcement/actions.shtml (last visited February 17, 2019).

33. Cohen, Horse Rub?, B5 (number of statutes); Obbie, In Search of the Felon-Friendly Workplace, B6 (number of Americans with a record).

34. Department of the Treasury et al., Occupational Licensing, 5.

35. American Bar Association, National Inventory of the Collateral Consequences of Conviction (Justice Center: The Council of State Governments, 2016), https://niccc.csgjusticecenter.org/.

36. Bruce E. May, The Character Component of Occupational Licensing Laws: A Continuing Barrier to the Ex-felon's Employment Opportunities, North Dakota Law Review 71 (1995): 187, 193, 197.

37. Lahny R. Silva, In Search of a Second Chance: Channeling *BMW v. Gore* and Reconsidering Occupational Licensing Restrictions, Kansas Law Review 61 (2012): 495, 502; Sandra J. Mullings, Employment of Ex-offenders: The Time Has Come for a True Antidiscrimination Statute, Syracuse Law Review 64 (2014): 261, 267.

38. James W. Hunt et al., Laws, Licenses, and the Offenders' Right to Work: A Study of State Laws Restricting the Occupational Licensing of Former Offenders (Washington, DC: National Clearinghouse on Offender Employment Restrictions, 1974).

39. Fox Butterfield, Freed from Prison, but Still Paying a Penalty, New York Times, December 29, 2002.

40. Rodriguez and Avery, Unlicensed and Untapped, 1.

41. Craddock, "Good Moral Character," 455.

42. Glenn E. Martin, "Marching Upstream: Moving beyond Reentry Mania," in Mark Mauer and Kate Epstein eds., To Build a Better Criminal Justice System (New York: The Sentencing Project, 2013), 48.

43. Rodriguez and Avery, Unlicensed and Untapped, 13.

44. *In re* Kindschi, 319 P.2d 824 (Wash. 1958); Windham v. Bd. of Med. Quality Assurance, 104 Cal. App. 3d 461 (1980); Nadia N. Sawicki, Character, Competence, and the Principles of Medical Discipline, Journal of Health Care Law and Policy 13 (2010): 286, 305; Weissbuch v. Board of Med. Examiners, 41 Cal. App. 3d 924 (1974); McLaughlin v. Bd. of Med. Examiners, 35 Cal. App. 3d 1010 (1973).

45. Sawicki, Character, Competence, and the Principles of Medical Discipline, 301–304.

46. Sawicki, Character, Competence and the Principles of Medical Discipline, 305.

47. Equal Employment Opportunity Commission, Notice No. N-915, Policy Statement on the Issue of Conviction Records under Title VII of the Civil Rights Act of 1964 (February 4, 1987); EEOC Enforcement Guidance No. 915.002, Consideration of Arrest and Conviction Records in Employment Decisions under Title VII of the Civil Rights Act of 1964 (2012), http://www.eeoc.gov/laws/guidance/arrest_conviction.cfm.

48. Anthony C. Thompson, Releasing Prisoners, Redeeming Communities: Reentry, Race, and Politics (New York: New York University Press, 2008), 109.

49. Thompson, Releasing Prisoners, Redeeming Communities, 111; Fox Butterfield, Freed from Prison, but Still Paying a Penalty, New York Times, December 29, 2001, 18.

50. Megan Denver and Alec C. Ewald, Credentialing Decisions and Criminal Records: A Narrative Approach, Criminology 56 (2018) 715–749.

51. Denver and Ewald, Credentialing Decisions, 33.

52. Dick M. Carpenter II et al., License to Work: A National Study of Burdens from Occupational Licensing (Institute for Justice, 2012), http://ij.org/wp-content/uploads/2015/04/licensetowork1.pdf.

53. Rodriguez and Avery, Unlicensed and Untapped, 6.

54. Anton-Hermann Chroust, Rise of the Legal Profession in America (Norman: University of Oklahoma Press, 1965), 261.

55. Jerold S. Auerbach, Unequal Justice: Lawyers and Social Change in Modern America (New York: Oxford University Press, 1976).

56. Character Examination of Candidates, Bar Examiner 1 (1932): 63, 68.

57. Walter C. Douglas, The Pennsylvania System Governing Admission to the Bar, American Bar Association Report 54 (1929): 701, 703–705.

58. Douglas, The Pennsylvania System, 703–705. The rejection of the woman attorney was reversed by the state board.

59. An Answer to the Problem of the Bootlegger's Son, Bar Examiner 1 (1932): 100, 109.

60. Douglas, The Pennsylvania System, 703; Character Examination of Candidates, 65.

61. Corporation of Haverford College v. Reeher, 329 F. Supp. 1196, 1206 (E.D. Pa. 1971).

62. *In re* Higbie, 493 P.2d 97, 101–02 (Cal. 1972).

63. Deborah L. Rhode, Moral Character as a Professional Credential, Yale Law Journal 94 (1985): 552–553.

64. *In re* Wallace, 19 S.W.2d 625 (Mo. 1929).

65. *In re* Isserman, 140 A. 253 (N.J. 1928).

66. *Compare* Florida Bar v. Kay, 232 So. 2d 378, 379 (Fla. 1970), *cert. denied*, 400 U.S. 956 (1970), with *In re* Wood, 358 N.E.2d 128, 133 (Ind. 1976).

67. *In re* Summers, 325 U.S. 561 (1945) (conscientious objection); *In re* Anastaplo, 366 U.S. 82 (1961) (refusal to discuss possible Communist Party membership); Application of Patterson, 302 P.2d 227 (Or. 1956), (belief in communism), *vacated*, 353 U.S. 952 (1957); Application of Cassidy, 51 N.Y.S.2d 202 (N.Y. App. Div. 1944), (member of Christian Front organization), *aff'd*, 73 N.E.2d 41 (N.Y. 1947); Application of Stone, 288 P.2d 767, 771 (Wyo. 1955) (religious fanaticism), *cert. denied*, 352 U.S. 815 (1956).

68. David Ray Papke, The Watergate Lawyers All Passed the Character and Fitness Test, Columbia University Forum 2 (1973): 15, 18–19.

69. Harry Kalvin Jr. and Roscoe Steffen, The Bar Admission Cases: An Unfinished Debate between Justice Harlan and Justice Black, Legal Transition 21 (1961): 155, 178.

70. Rhode, Moral Character, 495.

71. Konigsberg v. State Bar of California, 353 U.S. 252, 263 (1957).

72. Schware v. Board of Bar Examiners of the State of New Mexico, 353 U.S. 232, 239 (1957).

73. Rhode, Moral Character, 538.

74. Rhode, Moral Character, 538 (quoting Secretary, New Mexico Board of Bar Examiners).

75. Rhode, Moral Character, 532.

76. Rhode, Moral Character, 539 (quoting Special Reporter, Montana, and Secretary of Maryland State Board of Law Examiners).

77. Rhode, Moral Character, 53 (quoting President, Missouri Board of Bar Examiners).

78. See Thomas Arthur Pobjecky, Beyond Rehabilitation: Permanent Exclusion from the Practice of Law, Bar Examiner 76 (February 2007): 6, 10.

79. For examples, see Deborah L. Rhode, David Luban, Scott L. Cummings, and Nora F. Engstrom, Legal Ethics (St. Paul: Foundation Press, 7th ed. 2016).

80. Aaron M. Clemens, Facing the Klieg Lights: Understanding the "Good Moral Character" Examination for Bar Applicants, Akron Law Review 40 (2007): 255, 277, 285, 287.

81. Application of Guberman, 363 P.2d 617, 619 (Cal. 1962); Rhode, Moral Character, 545 (quoting Michigan Character and Fitness Committee).

82. *In re* Glass, 58 Cal. 4th 500, 519 (2014).

83. *In re* Glass, 58 Cal. 4th 500, 526 (2014).

84. Tony Mauro, From Felony Conviction to Bar Exam, National Law Journal, October 6, 2014.

85. *In re* Bar Application of Simmons, Washington Supreme Court, April 5, 2018.

86. *In re* Bar Application of Simmons.

87. Josh Jacobs, Why It's Difficult for Former Inmates to Become Lawyers, Atlantic, November 16, 2017.

88. National Conference of Bar Examiners, Comprehensive Guide to Bar Admission Requirements, Chart One, 1 (2015).

89. Personal Responsibility and Work Opportunity Reconciliation Act of 1996, 8 U.S.C. § 1621.

90. *In re* Garcia, 315 P.3d 117 (Cal. 2014).

91. Dana Beth Solomon, Immigrant Lawyer Facing Big Challenges, San Francisco Daily Journal, January 7, 2015, A1. Garcia got his green card in 2015. See also Malcolm Maclachian, Lawyer Once Illegally in US Has Thriving Practice, San Francisco Daily Journal, March 29, 2017, A1.

92. Florida Board of Bar Examiners Re Question as to Whether Undocumented Immigrants Are Eligible for Admission to Florida Bar, 134 So. 3d 432 (Fla. 2014).

93. Alan Gomez, New Fight for Immigrants, USA Today, July 2, 2012, A3.

94. Leslie C. Levin, Christine Zozula, and Peter Siegelman, The Questionable Character of the Bar's Character and Fitness Inquiry, Law and Social Inquiry 40 (2015): 51, 54; Rhode, Moral Character, 516.

95. Joseph A. Volerio, The Impact of the Character and Fitness, Honesty and Financial Responsibility Requirements on Underprivileged Groups, Georgetown Journal of Legal Ethics 30 (2017): 1093, 1108–1112.

96. Karen Sloan and Tony Mauro, From Convict to Counsel: Clearing the Hurdles to Practice, National Law Journal, May 25, 2018.

97. See sources cited in Rhode, Moral Character, 559; David H. Kaye, Science in Evidence, LexisNexis, 1997, 272–274. For difficulties in predicting violence, see Min Yang et al., The Efficacy of Violence Prediction: A Meta-analytic Comparison of Nine Risk Assessment Tools, Psychological Bulletin, 136 (2010): 740.

98. Levin, Zozula, and Siegelman, The Questionable Character of the Bar's Character and Fitness Inquiry, 52.

99. Levin, Zozula, and Siegelman, The Questionable Character of the Bar's Character and Fitness Inquiry, 79.

100. Rhode, Moral Character, 549.

101. American Bar Association, Model Rules of Professional Conduct, Rule 8.4(b) (2015).

102. ABA Standards for Imposing Lawyer Sanctions (Chicago: American Bar Association, 2005), 26–28.

103. *In re* Lamb, 776 P.2d. 765, 769 (Cal. 1989).

104. Lorraine J. Bacchus, Gillian Mezey, and Susan Bewley, Domestic Violence: Prevalence in Pregnant Women and Associations with Physical and Psychological Health, European Journal of Obstetrics and Gynecology and Reproductive Biology 113 (2004): 6.

105. *In re* Boudreau, 815 So. 2d 76 (La. 2002).

106. *In re* Boudreau, 815 So. 2d 76 (La. 2002).

107. Kellyn O. McGee, Unnecessary Ambiguity: Relinquishing "Moral Turpitude" from Lawyer Discipline, Journal of the Legal Profession 41 (2017): 301, 319–320; Rhode, Luban, Cummings and Engstrom, Legal Ethics, 120–121; Brian K. Pinaire et al., Barred from the Bar: The Process, Politics, and Policy Implications of Discipline for Attorney Felony Offenders, Virginia Journal of Social Policy and the Law 13 (2006): 290, 319. For domestic violence, see Ignascio G. Camarena II, Comment, Domestically Violent Attorneys: Resuscitating and Transforming a Dusty, Old Punitive Approach to Attorney Discipline into a Viable Prescription for Rehabilitation, Golden Gate University Law Review 31 (2001): 155, 173.

108. See studies cited in Jennifer Lundquist, Devah Pager, and Eiko Strader, Does a Criminal Past Predict Worker Performance?; Denver, Pickett and Bushway, Criminal Records, 21; Sarah Esther Lageson, Mike Vuolo, and Christopher Uggen, Legal Ambiguity in Managerial Assessments of Criminal Records, Law and Social Inquiry 40 (2015): 175.

109. Denver, Pickett, and Bushway, Criminal Records, 14.

110. Lundquist, Pager, and Strader, Does a Criminal Past Predict Worker Performance?; Harry J. Holzer, Steven Raphael, and Michael A. Stoll, "Will Employers Hire Former Offenders? Employer Checks, Background Checks, and Their Determinants," in Mary Pattillo, David Weiman, and Bruce Weston eds., Imprisoning America: The Social Effects of Mass Incarceration (New York: Russell Sage Foundation, 2004), 205–210; Devah Pager, Marked: Race, Crime, and Finding Work in an Era of Mass Incarceration (Chicago: University of Chicago Press, 2007).

111. James Forman Jr., Locking Up Our Own: Crime and Punishment in Black America (New York: Farrar, Straus and Giroux, 2017), 188.

112. Foreman, Locking Up Our Own, 192.

113. Jim Dwyer, Shift on Marijuana Policy Was a Long Time Coming, and Too Late for One Man, New York Times, November 13, 2014.

114. Equal Employment Opportunity Commission, Enforcement Guidance on the Consideration of Arrest and Conviction Records in Employment Decision Under Title VII of the Civil Rights Act of 1964, April 25, 2012, 11, 16, http://www.eeoc.gov/laws/guidance/arrest_conviction.cfm.

115. National Employment Law Project, Ban the Box Is a Fair Chance for Workers with Records, Fact Sheet, April 2017. See also Appelbaum, Out of Trouble, but Criminal Records Keep Men out of Work.

116. Jennifer L. Doleac and Benjamin Hansen, Does "Ban the Box" Help or Hurt Low-Skilled Workers? Statistical Discrimination and Employment Outcomes When Criminal Histories Are Hidden (Cambridge: MA, National Bureau of Economic Research, Working Paper 22469, 2016); Vuolo, Lageson, and Uggen, Criminal Record Questions, 143, 152–155.

117. Lundquist, Pager, and Strader, Does a Criminal Past Predict Worker Performance?, 1039–1040.

118. American Civil Liberties Union, Back to Business: How Hiring Formerly Incarcerated Job Seekers Benefits Your Company (New York: American Civil Liberties Union), 45; A New Look at Job Applicants with Criminal Records, Society for Human Resource Management (October 22, 2013).

119. For examples, see American Civil Liberties Union (ACLU), Back to Business: How Hiring Formerly Incarcerated Job Seekers Benefits Your Company (Trone Private Sector and Education Advisory Council to the ACLU, 2017), 8, 10, 16.

120. ACLU, Back to Business, 9; Lundquist, Pager, and Strader, Does a Criminal Past Predict Worker Performance?

121. Pew Center of the States, State of Recidivism: The Revolving Door of America's Prisons (Pew Center, 2011), http://www.pewtrusts.org/~/media/legacy/uploadedfiles/pcs_assets/2011/pewstateofrecidivismpdf.pdf. See Domenic Calabro, Locked Up, Then Locked Out: Removing Barriers to Employment for Persons with Criminal Records (Florida Tax Watch, 2016), http://www.floridatrend.clom/publicd/userfiles/news/pdfs/reemployment2015Final.pdf, and ACLU, Back to Business, 10.

122. David DeSteno and Piercarlo Valdesolo, Out of Character: Surprising Truths about the Liar, Cheat, Sinner (and Saint) Lurking in All of Us (New York: Crown Publishing, 2011), 57.

123. The poll was by Public Opinion Strategies. Holly Harris, The American People Have Spoken: Reform our Criminal Justice System, The Hill, February 11, 2018.

124. Morris M. Kleiner, The Hamilton Project, Reforming Occupational Licensing Policies (Washington, DC: The Brookings Institution, 2015), 3.

125. Kleiner, The Hamilton Project, 3 (summarizing recommendations of Kleiner).

126. Kleiner, The Hamilton Project, 4–5 (summarizing recommendations of Kleiner).

127. Cohen, Horse Rub?, B5.

128. Minnesota Statute Annotated Section 147.02 (West, 1989). Maine deleted good moral character from its medical licensing statute in 1983. Maine Revised Statute Annotated Title 32 § 3271 (West, 1991).

129. Rodriguez and Avery, Unlicensed and Untapped, 31–32.

130. Rodriguez and Avery, Unlicensed and Untapped, 31–32.

131. New York Correction Law § 752 (McKinney, 1998); New York Executive Law § 296 (McKinney, 1998).

132. New York Correction Law § 752.

133. Soto-Lopez v. N.Y. City Civil Service Comm'n, 713 F. Supp. 677 (S.D.N.Y. 1989).

134. El v. Se. Pa. Transp. Auth., 479 F.3d 232 (3d Cir. 2007).

135. 479 F.3d. at 248.

136. Alfred Blumstein and Kiminori Nakamura, "Redemption" in an Era of Widespread Criminal Background Checks, National Institute of Justice Journal 263 (2009): 10.

137. Blumstein and Nakamura, "Redemption" in an Era of Widespread Criminal Background Checks, 12.

138. Subrmamanian, Moreno, and Gebreselassie, Relief in Sight, 13–18, 25.

139. Joseph A. Volerio, The Impact of the Character and Fitness Honesty and Financial Responsibility Requirements on Underprivileged Groups, Georgetown Journal of Legal Ethics 30 (2017): 1093, 1112.

140. ACLU, Back to Business, 14–15.

141. Rule of Naturalization, 1 Annals of Congress 114 (1790).

142. Naturalization Bill, 4 Annals of Congress 1026 (1794).

143. Albert S. Persichetti, Good Moral Character as a Requirement for Naturalization, Temple Law Quarterly 22 (1948): 182, 185.

144. *Compare* United States *ex rel.* Iorio v. Day, 34 F.2d 920, 921 (2d Cir. 1929) (conduct), with Petitions of Naturalization of F-G-and E-E-G, 137 F. Supp. 782 (S.D.N.Y. 1956) (convictions).

145. For traffic offenses, compare *In re* Capozzi, 289 N.Y.S. 869, 873 (Sup. Ct. Onondaga County, 1936) (traffic violations, "no matter how numerous, do not reflect on moral character"), with Petition of Donath, 39 Cornell Law Quarterly 478 (D. N.J. 1953) (numerous speeding violations justify postponing granting of the petition). For sexual behavior, see Petitions of Naturalization of F-G-and E-E-G, 137 F. Supp. 782 (adultery); *In re* Schmidt, 289 N.Y.S.2d 89 (Sup. Ct. Duchess County 1968) (homosexuality).

146. Petitions of Naturalization of F-G-and E-E-G, 137 F. Supp. at 785.

147. Lisa H. Newton, On Coherence in the Law: A Study of the "Good Moral Character" Requirement in the Naturalization Statute, Temple Law Quarterly 46 (1972): 40, 70.

148. Albert S. Persichetti, Good Moral Character as a Requirement for Naturalization, Temple Law Quarterly 22 (1948): 182, 193.

149. For an account of Lennon's troubles, see Bill Ong Hing, The Failure of Prosecutorial Discretion and the Deportation of Oscar Martinez—Part I, Bender's Immigration Bulletin, October 15, 2013, at 33–36.

150. Hing, The Failure of Prosecutorial Discretion, 35 n. 266.

151. Lennon v. INS, 527 F.2d 187, 189–90 (2d Cir. 1975).

152. 8 U.S.C. §§ 1255, 1375c (2008); Dana Leigh Marks and Denise Noonan Slavin, A View through the Looking Glass: How Crimes Appear from the Immigration Court Perspective, Fordham Urban Law Journal 39 (2012): 91, 109.

153. Immigrant Legal Resource Center, Naturalization and U.S. Citizenship: The Essential Legal Guide (San Francisco: Immigrant Legal Resource Center 2014), Sections 6.2 and 6.3.

154. Immigrant Legal Resource Center, Naturalization and U.S. Citizenship, Section 6.2.

155. Pub. L. No. 100–690, 102 Stat. 4181, 8 U.S.C. § 1101(a) (2014); Pub L. 101–649 § 501(a), 104 Stat. 4978, 5048 (1990).

156. Kevin Lapp, Reforming the Good Moral Character Requirement for U.S. Citizenship, Indiana Law Journal 87 (2012): 1571, 1591.

157. Rachel E. Rosenbloom, U.S. Must Rethink Deportation Laws, Albany Times Union, March 29, 2007, A13 (describing case of a former child refugee who was deported for urinating in public); United States v. Pacheco, 225 F.3d 148, 149 (2d Cir. 2000). In the college drug case, the judge determined not to report the defendant, but that did not prevent his deportation many years later. Adriane Menses, The Deportation of Lawful Permanent Residents for Old and Minor Crimes: Restoring Judicial Review, Ending Retroactivity, and Recognizing Deportation as Punishment, Scholar 14 (2012): 767, 850. For related problems, see Natalie Liem, Mean What You Say, Say What You Mean: Defining the Aggravated Felony Deportation Grounds to Target More than Aggravated Felons, Florida Law Review 51 (2007): 1071.

158. Menses, The Deportation of Lawful Permanent Residents, 775.

159. INA § 237(a).

160. 8 U.S.C. § 1182(a)(9)(A)(i) (2013).

161. Rubén G. Rumbaut and Walter A. Ewing, The Myth of Immigrant Criminality and the Paradox of Assimilation: Incarceration Rates among Native and Foreign-Born Men, Immigration Policy Center, American Immigration Law Foundation, 2007. Though undocumented immigrants have higher crime rates than immigrants in the United States legally, they have far lower crime rates than U.S. citizens. See Richard Pérez-Peña, Contrary to Trump's Claims, Immigrants Are Less Likely to Commit Crimes, New York Times, January 26, 2017.

162. Meribah Knight, Deportation's Brief Adios and Prolonged Anguish, New York Times, May 8, 2010; Menses, The Deportation of Lawful Permanent Residents for Old and Minor Crimes, 847.

163. U.S. Immigration and Customs Enforcement, Deportation of Aliens Claiming U.S.-Born Children, First Half, Calendar Year 2015, Department of Homeland Security, August 1, 2016; U.S. Immigration and Customs Enforcement, Deportation of Aliens Claiming U.S.-Born Children, Second Half, Calendar Year 2015, Department of Homeland Security, August 1, 2016

164. 8 U.S.C. § 1182; INA § 237 (a)(2)(A)(ii) (2006); Menses, The Deportation of Lawful Permanent Residents for Old and Minor Crimes, 799.

165. Menses, The Deportation of Lawful Permanent Residents for Old and Minor Crimes, 800. See also Marks and Slavin, A View through the Looking Glass, 102–103.

166. Jordan v. De George, 341 U.S. 223, 235 (1951) (Jackson, J., dissenting).

167. 8 C.F.R. § 316.10(b)(3); Faddah v INS, 553 F.2d 491, 496 (5th Cir. 1977); Grunbaum v. District Director, CIS, No. 10–10147, 2012 WL 2359966, at 5–6 (E.D. Mich. May 21, 2012); Lapp, Reforming the Good Moral Character Requirement, 1610.

168. Lapp, Reforming the Good Moral Character Requirement, 1601; Nina Bernstein, After Governor's Pardon, an Immigrant Is Sworn in as a Citizen, New York Times, May 29, 2010, A20.

169. Lapp, Reforming the Good Moral Character Requirement, 1613; Judith Bernstein-Baker, Citizenship in a Restrictionist Era: The Mixed Messages of Federal Policies, Temple Political and Civil Rights Law Review 16 (2007): 367, 376.

170. Lapp, Reforming the Good Moral Character Requirement, 1613.

171. George Saunders, Trump Days, The New Yorker, July 11 and 18, 2016, 57.

172. Saunders, Trump Days, 57.

173. Time Staff, Here's Donald Trump's Presidential Announcement Speech, TIME, June 16, 2015, http://time.com/3923128/donald-trump-announcement-speech/.

174. Donald J. Trump Statement on Preventing Muslim Immigration, Donald Trump for President, Inc., December 7, 2015, http://www.academia.edu/29787743/DONALD_J._TRUMP_STATEMENT_ON_PREVENTING_MUSLIM_IMMIGRATION.

175. Jeremy Diamond, Trump Orders Construction of Border Wall, Boosts Deportation Force, CNN, January 25, 2017, http://www.cnn.com/2017/01/25/politics/donald-trump-build-wall-immigration-executive-orders/.

176. For various accounts of Trump's language, see Aaron Blake, The Trump "Shithole Countries" Flap Takes an Even More Ridiculous Turn, Washington Post, January 16, 2018; Andrew Prokop, The "Shithouse Defense" Explained: How Trump's Allies Are Trying to Dig Him Out of His Shithole, Vox, January 16, 2018; Chris Cillizza, Why No One Should Believe Trump's "Shithole Countries" Denial, CNN, January 12, 2018, https://www.vox.com/2018/1/16/16897016/trump-shitholle-shithouse-countries.

177. President Donald J. Trump, Executive Order: Protecting the Nation from Foreign Terrorist Entry into the United States, The White House, January 27, 2017; Glenn Kessler, Trump's Claim That Obama First "Identified" the 7 Countries in His Travel Ban, Washington Post, February 7, 2017, https://www.washingtonpost.com/news/fact-checker/wp/2017/02/07/trumps-claim-that-obama-first-identified-the-seven-countries-in-his-travel-ban/?utm_term=.77f17c3a2d1c.

178. Glenn Thrush, Trump's Revised Travel Ban Spares Iraqis, New York Times, March 6, 2017.

179. Federal court decisions are collected in Litigation Documents and Resources Related to Trump Executive Order on Immigration, Lawfare, 2017, https://lawfareblog.com/litigation-documents-resources-related-trump-executive-order-immigration; President Donald J. Trump, Executive Order: Protecting the Nation from Foreign Terrorist Entry into the United States, March 6, 2017.

180. Trump v. Hawaii, No. 17-965, 585 U.S. ___ (June 26, 2018).

181. Trump, Executive Order: Protecting the Nation.

182. President Donald J. Trump, Executive Order: Enhancing Public Safety in the Interior of the United States, Section 5, January 25, 2017.

183. Vivan Yee, As Arrests Surge, Immigrants Fear even Driving, New York Times, November 26, 2017, A1; Natapoff, Punishment without Crime, 32.

184. Haley Sweetland Edwards, No One Is Safe: How Trump's Immigration Policy Is Splitting Families Apart, Time, March 8, 2018.

185. Edwards, No One Is Safe.

186. Michael Krasny, Forum, NPR February 28, 2018, https://www.npr.org/podcasts432307980/forum (quoting Oakland Mayor Libby Schaaf).

187. Joshua Brisblatt, Data Shows Prosecutorial Discretion Grinds to a Halt in Immigration Courts, American Immigration Council Immigration Impact (July 24, 2017).

188. Nicholas Kristof, Mr. Trump, How Is This Man a Danger?, New York Times, February 11, 2018.

189. Chris Oberhotz, Lawrence Chemistry Professor Facing Deportation Gets Immigration Hearing, KCTV Kansas City, August 14, 2018 https://www.kctv5.com/news/lawrence-chemistry-professor-facing-deportation-gets-immigration-hearing/article_a137215b-ec20-5bea-84c9-0612c971e697.html.

190. Miriam Jordan, Breaking Up Immigrant Families: A Look at the Latest Border Tactic, New York Times, May 12, 2018; Julianne Hing, For Trump, Cruelty Is the Point, Nation, April 9, 2018, 12.

191. Violence, Development, and Migration Waves: Evidence from Central American Child Migrant Apprehensions—Working Paper 459 (Washington, DC: Center for Global Development, 2017), https://www.cgdev.org/publication/violence-development-and-migration-waves-evidence-central-american-child-migrant; Hing, For Trump, Cruelty Is the Point, 14; Julie M. Linton, Marsha Griffin, and Alan J. Shapiro, Detention of Immigrant Children, American Academy of Pediatrics Policy Statement Pediatrics 139 (April 2017):1, 2.

192. Lipton, Griffin, and Shapiro, Detention of Immigrant Children. See also Julie Hirschfield Davis and Michael D. Shear, Border Policy Had Been Seen as Inhumane, New York Times, June 17, 2018.

193. Nicole Goodkind, UN Calls on Trump Administration to Stop Separating Immigrant Children from Parents, Newsweek, June, 2018.

194. Michael D. Shear, Abby Goodnough, and Maggie Haberman, Trump Retreats on Separating Families, but Thousands May Remain Apart, New York Times, June 20, 2018; Michael D. Shear, Julie Hirschfeld Davis, Thomas Kaplan, and Robert Pear, Federal Judge in California Halts Splitting of Migrant Families at Border, New York Times, June 26, 2018.

195. Sonia Nozario, Don't Put Families in Cages, New York Times, June 24, 2018.

196. Hing, For Trump, Cruelty Is the Point, 14; Wendy Cervantes and Hannah Matthews, Our Children's Fear: Immigration Policy's Effects on Young Children (CLASP, March 2018).

197. Cervantes and Mathews, Our Children's Fear; Natapoff, Punishment without Crime, 33.

198. Leila Schochet, Trump's Immigration Policies Are Harming American Children, Center for American Progress, July 31, 2017, 2; Jennifer Medina, Too Scared to Report Abuse, for Fear of Being Deported, New York Times, April 30, 2017, 1, 21.

199. Schochet, Trump's Immigration Policies, 11; Edwards, No One Is Safe, National Scientific Council on the Developing Child, Persistent Fear and Anxiety Can Affect Young Children's Learning and Development, Working Paper 9 (Harvard University Center on the Developing Child, 2010).

200. John F. Kennedy, A Nation of Immigrants (New York: Harper Perennial, 2008), 50.

201. Human Rights Watch, US: Deportation Splits Families (New York: Human Rights Watch, 2009).

202. Lapp, Reforming the Good Moral Character Requirement, 1630–1631.

203. Under the Rehabilitation of Offenders Act, criminal convictions can become "spent," that is, ignored, after a specified rehabilitation period, typically three to ten years. The length of the rehabilitation period depends on the sentence given and the age at the time of conviction. Lapp, Reforming the Good Moral Character Requirement, 1634; Home Office UK Border Agency, Guide: Naturalization as a British Citizen—A Guide for Applicants (2010), 15.

204. Ann Sherlock, Deportation of Aliens and Article 8 ECHR, European Law Review 23 (1998): 62; Melissa Cook, Banished for Minor Crimes: The Aggravated Felony Provision of the Immigration and Nationality Act as a Human Rights Violation, Boston College Third World Law Journal 23 (2003): 293, 316.

205. Cook, Banished for Minor Crimes, 319.

206. President George W. Bush, State of the Union Address, January 20, 2004.

CHAPTER 4

1. A version of this chapter, titled Character in Criminal Justice Proceedings, is forthcoming in the American Journal of Criminal Law. John F. Pfaff, The War on Drugs and Prison Growth: Limited Importance, and Limited Legislative Options, Harvard Journal on Legislation 52 (2015): 173.

2. Michelle Ye Hee Lee, Yes, U.S. Locks People Up at a Higher Rate than Any Other Country, Washington Post, July 5, 2015.

3. H. Richard Uviller, Evidence of Character to Prove Conduct: Illusion, Illogic, and Injustice in the Courtroom, University of Pennsylvania Law Review 130 (1982): 845.

4. Peter Arenella, Character, Choice, and Moral Agency: The Relevance of Character to Our Moral Culpability Judgments, Social Philosophy and Policy 7 (1990): 59, 74.

5. Federal Rules of Evidence, Rule 404. Forty-one states have evidence codes patterned after the Federal Rules of Evidence, and the remaining states also recognize the prohibition on using character evidence. Edward J. Imwinkelried, Reshaping the "Grotesque" Doctrine of Character Evidence: The Reform Implications of the Most Recent Psychological Research, Southwestern University Law Review 36 (2008): 741, 743 n.19.

6. For the absence of a definition, see David P. Leonard, Character and Motive in Evidence Law, Loyola of Los Angeles Law Review 34 (2001): 439, 450; Barrett J. Anderson, Recognizing Character: A New Perspective on Character Evidence, Yale Law Journal 121 (2012): 1912, 1919. For treatise descriptions, see John Henry Wigmore, Evidence, Volume 1A, Section 52 (Boston: Peter Tillers rev. ed. 1983), 1148 ("actual moral or psychical disposition"); Charles Tilford McCormick et al., McCormick on Evidence, Volume 1, Section 195 (Eagan: West Publishing, John William Strong, 4th ed., 1992), 185.

7. Roger C. Park, Character at the Crossroads, Hastings Law Journal 49 (1998): 717, 745; David P. Leonard, In Defense of the Character Evidence Prohibition: Foundations of the Rule against Trial by Character, Indiana Law Review 73 (1998): 1161, 1184.

8. Janice Nadler and Mary-Hunter Morris McDonnell, Moral Character, Motive, and the Psychology of Blame, Cornell Law Review 97 (2012): 255, 279–281.

9. Janice Nadler, Blaming as a Social Process: The Influence of Character and Moral Emotion on Blame, Law and Contemporary Problems 75 (2012): 1, 18, 28.

10. Dowling v. United States, 493 U.S. 342, 361–62 (1990) (Brennan, J., dissenting).

11. United States v. Foskey, 636 F.2d 517, 523 (D.C. Cir. 1980) (quoting United States v. Myers, 550 F.2d 1036, 1044 (5th Cir. 1977)).

12. See Park, Character at the Crossroads, 748; Federal Rules of Evidence, 412–415.

13. John M. Doris, Lack of Character: Personality and Moral Behavior (Cambridge: Cambridge University Press, 2002), 93; Lee Ross and Donna Shestowsky, Contemporary Psychology's Challenges to Legal Theory and Practice, Northwestern University Law Review 97 (2003): 1081, 1087, 1092–1093); Robert G. Lawson, Credibility and Character: A Different Look at an Interminable Problem, Notre Dame Law Review 50 (1975): 758, 778.

14. David J. Schneider, Albert H. Hastorf, and Phoebe Ellsworth, Person Perception (Boston: Addison-Wesley, 2nd ed., 1979), 231–240.

15. Gordon W. Allport, Personality, 521.

16. See studies reviewed in Miguel Angel Méndez, California's New Law on Character Evidence: Evidence Code Section 352 and the Impact of Recent Psychological Studies, UCLA Law Review 31 (1983-1984): 1003, 1045–1046.

17. Charles Lord, Lee Ross, and Mark R. Lepper, Biased Assimilation and Attitude Polarization: The Effects of Prior Theories on Subsequently Considered Evidence, Journal of Personality and Social Psychology 37 (1979): 2098, 2099.

18. See Miguel A. Méndez, The Law of Evidence and the Search for a Stable Personality, Emory Law Journal 45 (1996): 221, 223.

19. Leonard, In Defense of the Character Evidence Prohibition, 1186.

20. Federal Rules of Evidence, Rule 404(b).

21. For an early case admitting evidence of prior receipt of stolen property to show knowledge, see People v. Rando, 3 Park. Crim. 335 (N.Y. Sup. Ct. 1857).

22. Uviller, Evidence of Character to Prove Conduct.

23. Mike Redmayne, Character in the Criminal Trial (Oxford: Oxford University Press, 2015), 58–59.

24. Federal Rules of Evidence, Rule 609.

25. See chapter 1; Susan Marlene Davies, Evidence of Character to Prove Conduct: A Reassessment of Relevancy, Criminal Law Bulletin 27 (1991): 504, 520–521; Richard Friedman, Character Impeachment Evidence: Psycho-Bayesian [!?] Analysis and a Proposed Overhaul, UCLA Law Review 38 (1991): 637, 655–664.

26. Theodore Eisenberg and Valerie P. Hans, Taking a Stand on Taking the Stand: The Effect of a Prior Criminal Record on the Decision to Testify and on Trial Outcomes, Cornell Law Review 94 (2009): 1353, 1357, 1380–1385; Nadler and McDonnell, Moral Character, 269.

27. For the disregard of instructions, see Kerri L. Pickel, Inducing Jurors to Disregard Inadmissible Evidence: A Legal Explanation Does Not Help, Law and Human Behavior 19 (1995): 407; Roselle L. Wissler, and Michael J. Saks, On the Inefficacy of Limiting Instructions: When Jurors Use Prior Conviction Evidence to Decide on Guilt, Law and Human Behavior 9 (1985): 37. See also Redmayne, Character in the Criminal Trial, 60–63.

28. Uviller, Evidence of Character to Prove Conduct, 869 n. 85 (noting one study in which 98 percent of criminal attorneys believed that juries were unable to follow an instruction to consider prior convictions for the purpose of evaluating the defendant's credibility rather than his guilt).

29. Friedman, Character Impeachment Evidence, 632.

30. Friedman, Character Impeachment Evidence, 668. James E. Beaver and Steven L. Marques, A Proposal to Modify the Rule on Criminal Conviction Impeachment, Temple Law Quarterly 58 (1985): 585, 609.

31. John Thibaut and Laurens Walker, Procedural Justice: A Psychological Analysis (Hillsdale: Lawrence Erlbaum Associates, 1975); Tom R. Tyler, Procedural Justice, Legitimacy, and the Effective Rule of Law, Crime and Justice Review of Research

30 (2003): 283; Tom R. Tyler, Psychological Perspectives on Legitimacy and Legitimation, Annual Review of Psychology 57 (2006): 375.

32. Federal Rules of Evidence, 413–415.

33. Karen M. Fingar, And Justice for All: The Admissibility of Uncharged Sexual Misconduct Evidence under the Recent Amendment to the Federal Rules of Evidence, Southern California Review of Law and Women's Studies 5 (1996): 501, 505; Larry The and Irene Sage, Alleged Assaults by Smith Described: Accounts by 3 Women Are Similar to Charges in Palm Beach Rape Case, Boston Globe, July 24, 1991, 1; Paul Richter Jury Acquits Smith of Rape at Kennedy Estate, Los Angeles Times, December 12, 1991, A1.

34. Edward J. Imwinkelried, Uncharged Misconduct Evidence (Evidence Series) (New York: West Group, 1998), 5.

35. 137 Congressional Record Section 3240 (Daily Record, March 13, 1991).

36. The Severity of Crime, Bureau of Justice Statistics Bulletin (January 1984). For similar findings, see Edward J. Imwinkelried, Undertaking the Task of Reforming the American Character Evidence Prohibition: The Importance of Getting the Experiment Off on the Right Foot, Fordham Urban Law Journal 22 (1995): 284, 297.

37. See 140 Congressional Record S12,990 (Daily Edition, September 20, 1994) (statement of Senator Dole). For the difficulties encountered by rape complainants, see Deborah L. Rhode, What Women Want: An Agenda for the Women's Movement (New York: Oxford University Press, 2015), 121–127.

38. Imwinkelried, Reshaping the "Grotesque" Doctrine of Character Evidence, 743.

39. Katharine K. Baker, Once a Rapist? Motivational Evidence and Relevancy in Rape Law, Harvard Law Review 110 (1997): 563, 596.

40. Imwinkelried, Undertaking the Task of Reforming the American Character Evidence Prohibition, 297–298, 301; Park, Character at the Crossroads, 759.

41. U.S. Bureau of Justice Statistics, Recidivism of Sex Offenders Released from Prison in 1994 (Washington, DC: Department of Justice, 2003); U.S. Bureau of Justice, Recidivism of Prisoners Released in 1994 (Washington, DC: U.S. Department of Justice, 2002), 9.

42. Park, Character at the Crossroads, 762–764.

43. Marnie E. Rice, Vernon L. Quinsey, and Grant T. Harris, Sexual Recidivism among Child Molesters Released from a Maximum Security Psychiatric Institution, Journal of Consulting and Clinical Psychology 59 (1991): 381.

44. A. Nicholas Groth, Robert E. Longo, and J. Bradley McFadin, Undetected Recidivism among Rapists and Child Molesters, Crime and Delinquency 28 (1982): 450, 453–458. There was a 65 percent recidivism rate for the rapists and a 37 percent recidivism rate for the child molesters.

45. Graham Bowley, Now That He's Been Convicted, What Comes Next?, New York Times, April 28, 2018, A18.

46. Attorneys used the same defense in the retrial. Graham Bowley and Jon Hurdle, In Bill Cosby's Case, Who's the Con Artist? Both Sides Close by Pointing Fingers, New York Times, April 24, 2018.

47. Timothy Williams, Why Cosby Verdict Is Probably Less Breakthrough than Anomaly, New York Times, April 28, 2018, A18. The admissibility of such evidence is subject to appeal. Sherry F. Colb, Bill Cosby and the Rule against Character Evidence, Verdict, January 15, 2016.

48. Park, Character at the Crossroads, 775; Davies, Evidence of Character to Prove Conduct, 535–56; Uviller, Evidence of Character to Prove Conduct, 889.

49. Davies, Evidence of Character to Prove Conduct, 534.

50. Court Rules, Judicial Conference of the United States, Report of the Judicial Conference on the Admission of Character Evidence in Certain Sexual Misconduct Cases, 159 F.R.D. 51, 54–55 (1995). See Imwinkelried, Reshaping the "Grotesque" Doctrine of Character Evidence, 765; Andrew E. Taslitz, Patriarchal Stories I: Cultural Rape Narratives in the Courtroom, Southern California Review of Law and Women's Studies 5 (1996): 387, 496.

51. George P. Fletcher, Rethinking Criminal Law (New York: Oxford University Press, 1978).

52. Marc Miller, Purposes at Sentencing, Southern California Law Review 66 (1992): 413, 456.

53. Jeffrie G. Murphy, Does Kant Have a Theory of Criminal Punishment?, Columbia Law Review 87 (1987): 509, 530–531.

54. Immanuel Kant, The Penal Law and the Law of Pardon, in The Metaphysical Elements of Justice (1787; Indianapolis: Library Press, Bobbs Merrill, 1965 ed., trans. J. Ladd), 100.

55. Fletcher, Rethinking Criminal Law, 800. Robert Nozick, Philosophical Explanations (Cambridge, MA: Harvard University Press, 1983), 381.

56. Benjamin B. Sendor, Relevance of Conduct and Character to Guilt and Punishment, Notre Dame Journal of Law, Ethics, and Public Policy 10 (2012): 99, 127–128.

57. Sendor, Relevance of Conduct, 128–129.

58. Sendor, Relevance of Conduct, 129.

59. The poll was by Public Opinion Strategies. Harris, The American People Have Spoken.

60. John M. Darley, Kevin M. Carlsmith, and Paul H. Robinson, Incapacitation and Just Deserts as Motives for Punishment, Law and Human Behavior 24 (2000): 659, 676.

61. Darley, Carlsmith, and Robinson, Incapacitation and Just Deserts as Motives for Punishment, 676.

62. Daniel P. Mears and Joshua C. Cochran, Prisoner Reentry in the Era of Mass Incarceration (Thousand Oaks, CA: Sage, 2014), 52.

63. James Forman Jr., Exporting Harshness: How the War on Crime Helped Make the War on Terror Possible, New York University Review of Law & Social Change 33 (2009): 331, 374 (quoting Pete Wilson and Nelson Rockefeller).

64. Alan Jenkins, A Visionary Criminal Justice System: Our Unprecedented Opportunity, in Marc Mauer and Kate Eptstein eds., The Sentencing Project, To Build a Better Criminal Justice System: 25 Experts Envision the Next 25 Years of Reform (New York: The Sentencing Project, 2012), 14.

65. Rachel E. Barkow and Kathleen M. O'Neill, Delegating Punitive Power: The Political Economy of Sentencing Commission and Guideline Formation, Texas Law Review 84 (2006): 1973, 1980–1982.

66. Frances T. Cullen, Bonnie S. Fisher, and Brandon K. Applegate, Public Opinion about Punishment and Corrections, Crime and Justice 27 (2000): 1, 8, 50.

67. For the quote, see Michael Tonry, Malign Neglect: Race, Crime and Punishment in America (New York: Oxford University Press, 1995), 6. For the studies of stereotypes and punitive policies, see Jon Hurwitz and Mark Peffley, Public Perceptions of Race and Crime: The Role of Racial Stereotypes, American Journal of Political Science 41 (1997): 375, 393; Mears and Cochran, Prisoner Reentry, 56.

68. Todd Clear, The "Iron Law" of Prison Populations: Reducing Prison Admissions and Length of Stay to End Mass Incarceration, in Mauer and Eptstein, To Build a Better Criminal Justice System, 56, 57; Sonja B. Starr and M. Marit Rehavi, Racial Disparity in Federal Criminal Sentences, Journal of Political Economy 122 (2014): 1320, 1351.

69. Melissa S. Kearney et al., Ten Economic Facts about Crime and Incarceration in the United States (Washington DC: Hamilton Project, May, 2014), 4.

70. Mears and Cochran, Prisoner Reentry, 65.

71. Mears and Cochran, Prisoner Reentry, 54.

72. Paul Butler, Let's Get Free: A Hip Hop Theory of Justice (New York: New Press, 2009), 27.

73. The Sentencing Project, Report of the Sentencing Project to the United Nations Human Rights Committee Regarding Racial Disparities in the United States Criminal Justice System (August, 2013), 16.

74. Bordenkircher v. Hayes, 434 U.S. 357 (1978).

75. Samuel R. Wiseman, Fixing Bail, George Washington Law Review 84 (2016): 417, 428–431.

76. Will Dobbie, Jacob Goldin, and Crystal S. Yang, The Effects of Pre-Trial Detention on Conviction, Future Crime, and Employment: Evidence from Randomly Assigned Judges, American Economic Review 108 (2018): 201; Megan Stevenson and Sandra G. Mayson, Bail Reform: New Directions for Pretrial Detention and Release, University of Pennsylvania Law School, Legal Scholarship Repository (2017); Paul Heaton, Sandra Mayson, and Megan Stevenson, The Downstream

Consequences of Misdemeanor Pretrial Detention, Stanford Law Review 69 (2017): 711.

77. 3 Days Count: Commonsense Pretrial, Pretrial Justice Institute, https://www. pretrial.org/what-we-do/plan-and-implement/3dayscount-for-state-level-change/ (last visited February 17, 2019); Lauryn P. Gouldin, Disentangling Flight Risk from Dangerousness, BYU Law Review (2016): 837; Crystal S. Yang, Toward an Optimal Bail System, New York University Law Review 92 (2017): 1399, 1401.

78. Shaila Dawn, When Bail Is out of Defendant's Reach, Other Costs Mount, New York Times, June 10, 2015; Gouldin, Disentangling Flight Risk, 864; Insha Rahman, Against the Odds: Experimenting with Alternative Forms of Bail in New York City's Criminal Courts (New York: Vera Institute of Justice, 2017); Michael R. Jones, Unsecured Bonds: The as Effective and Most Efficient Pretrial Release Option (Washington, DC: Pretrial Justice Institute, 2013); Stevenson and Mayson, Bail Reform; Heaton, Mayson, and Stevenson, Downstream Consequences.

79. Lee, Yes, U.S. Locks People Up at a Higher Rate than Any Other Country; Peter Wagner and Alison Walsh, Prison Policy Initiative, States of Incarceration: The Global Context 2016, (2016).

80. Greg Berman and Julian Adler, Start Here: A Road Map to Reducing Mass Incarceration (New York: The New Press, 2018), 3; Michale D. McLauglin et al., The Economic Burden of Incarceration in the U.S. (St. Louis, MO: Concordance Institute for Advancing Social Justice, Washington University, 2016), https:// joinnia.com/wp-content/uploads/2017/02/The-Economic-Burden-of-Incarceration-in-the-US-2016.pdf.

81. Rehavi and Starr, Racial Disparity, 1320.

82. Rehavi and Starr, Racial Disparity, 1325.

83. William J. Stuntz, The Pathological Politics of Criminal Law, Michigan Law Review 100 (2001): 505, 586. Albert W. Alschuler, The Failure of Sentencing Guidelines: A Plea for Less Aggregation, University of Chicago Law Review 58 (1991): 901; Michael Tonry, The Failure of the U.S. Sentencing Commission's Guidelines, Crime and Delinquency 39 (1993): 131; Tamasak Wicharaya, Simple Theory, Hard Reality: The Impact of Sentencing Reforms on Courts, Prisons, and Crime (Albany: State University of New York Press, 995), 161.

84. United States v. Booker, 543 U.S. 220 (2005); Nancy Gertner, A Short History of American Sentencing: Too Little Law, Too Much Law, or Just Right, Journal of Criminal Law and Criminology 100 (2010): 691, 702–706.

85. Paul H. Robinson, Sean E. Jackowitz, and Daniel M. Bartels, Extralegal Punishment Factors: A Study of Forgiveness, Hardship, and Good Deeds, Apology, Remorse, and Other Such Discretionary Factors in Assessing Criminal Punishment, Vanderbilt Law Review 65 (2012): 737, 10.

86. United States v. Takai, 941 F.2d 738, 744 (9th Cir. 1991).

87. Carissa Byrne Hessick, Why Are Only Bad Acts Good Sentencing Factors?, Boston University Law Review 88 (2008): 1109, 1128–1129; U.S. Sentencing Guidelines Manual Section 5H1.11 (2004).

88. Lockett v. Ohio 438 U.S. 586 (1978); Harmelin v. Michigan, 501 U.S. 957, 994–95 (1991). See Hessick, Why Are Only Bad Acts Good Sentencing Factors?, 1126–1127.

89. Hessick, Why Are Only Bad Acts Good Sentencing Factors?, 1117–1118.

90. Alabama Sentencing Commission, Presumptive and Voluntary Sentencing Standards Manual (2013) 25.

91. Illinois Constitution 1970, Article I, Section 11; People v. Calhoun, 935 N.E.2d 663, 683 (Ill. Dist. Ct. App. 2010).

92. People v. Adkins, 242 N.E.2d 258, 260 (Ill. 1968).

93. Andrew Ashworth, Sentencing and Criminal Justice (Oxford: Butterworths, 3d ed., 2000), 72–73, 151; Andrew von Hirsch, Desert and Previous Convictions in Sentencing, Minnesota Law Review 65 (1981): 591, 609.

94. Jeffrie G. Murphy, Remorse, Apology and Mercy, Ohio State Journal of Criminal Law 4 (2007): 423, 437.

95. Lisa Belkin, Texas Judge Eases Sentence for Killer of 2 Homosexuals, New York Times, December 17, 1988, at 8.

96. Davidson v. State, 558 N.E.2d 1077 (Ind. 1990).

97. For mixed findings, see Stephen Rosoff, Henry Pontell, and Robert Tillman, Profit without Honor: White Collar Crime and the Looting of America (4th ed., Upper Saddle River, NJ: Prentice Hall, 2006), 407. For suggestions that white collar offenders no longer receive lenient treatment, see Samuel W. Buell, Is the White Collar Offender Privileged?, Duke Law Journal 63 (2014): 823. For increasing government pressure on organizations to identify white collar offenders, see Matt Apuzzo and Ben Protess, Justice Department Sets Sights on Wall Street Executives, New York Times, September 15, 2018. For data documenting shorter sentences for white collar offenders, see Katie A. Fredericks, Rima E. McComas, and Georgie Ann Weatherby, White Collar Crime: Recidivism, Deterrence, and Social Impact, Forensic Research and Criminology International Journal 2 (2016): 00039; Petter Gottschalk and Torbjørn Rundmo, Crime: The Amount and Disparity of Sentencing—A Comparison of Corporate and Occupational White Collar Criminals, International Journal of Law, Crime, and Justice 42 (2014): 175, 177; Sean Maddan, Richard D. Hartley, Jeffery T. Walker, and J. Mitchell Miler, Sympathy for the Devil: An Exploration of Federal Judicial Discretion in the Processing of White-Collar Offenders, American Journal of Criminal Justice 37 (2012): 4.

98. Maddan, Hartley, Walker, and Miler, Sympathy for the Devil, 15.

99. Robert Tillman and Henry N. Pontell, Is Justice "Collar-Blind?": Punishing Medicaid Provider Fraud, Criminology 30 (1992): 547.

100. Adam Brandolph, White-Collar Criminals Often Avoid Prison Terms, Trib Live, January 19, 2014, http://triblive.com/news/allegheny/5431279-74/collar-jail-criminals.

101. Peter J. Henning, The Challenge of Sentencing White-Collar Defendants, New York Times, February 25, 2013.

102. Robinson, Jackowitz, and Bartels, Extralegal Punishment Factors, 56, 64.

103. Redmayne, Character in the Criminal Trial, 275; Julian V. Roberts and Andrew von Hirsch, The Recidivist Premium: For and Against, in Andrew Ashworth, Andrew von Hirsch, and Julian V. Roberts, Principled Sentencing: Readings on Theory and Policy (Oxford and Portland: Hart, 3d ed., 2009), 148, 150–151, 155.

104. Roberts and von Hirscch, The Recidivist Premium, 153–156.

105. Barbara A. Hudson, Justice and Difference, in Ashworth, von Hirsch, and Roberts, Principled Sentencing: Readings on Theory and Policy, 367.

106. Lockyer v. Andrade, 538 U.S. 63 (2003).

107. Robert J. Sampson and John H. Laub, A Life-Course View of the Development of Crime, Annals of the American Academy of Political and Social Science 602 (2005): 12, 17.

108. Sampson and Laub, Life-Course View, 21.

109. Wiemond Wu, Crocodiles in the Judge's Bathtub? Why California Should End Unregulated Judicial Recall, University of Pacific Law Review 49 (2018): 699, 720–721.

110. Kate Berry, How Judicial Elections Impact Criminal Cases (New York: Brennan Center for Justice, 2015), 9.

111. Nicole Gonzalez Van Cleve, Crook County: Racism and Injustice in America's Largest Criminal Court (Stanford, CA: Stanford University Press, 2016), 120.

112. Kristan Conley, Kevin Sheehan, and Bruce Golding, Biker Thug Caught Prison Break from Soft Judge, New York Post, October 6, 2013.

113. Liam Stack, Light Sentence for Brock Turner in Stanford Rape Cases Draws Outrage, New York Times, June 6, 2016; Mark Joseph Stern, This Is How Mass Incarceration Happens, Slate (January 16, 2018), https://slate.com/news-and-politiocs/2018/01/the-dangeruos-miosguided-campaign-to-recall-the-judge-who-sentenced-brock-turner.html.

114. For the funds raised, see Julia Ioffe, When the Punishment Feels Like a Crime, Huffington Post, June 1, 2018.

115. Stern, This Is How Mass Incarceration Happens.

116. Ioffe, When the Punishment Feels Like a Crime (quoting prosecutor Jeff Rosen).

117. Megan McArdle, The Cost of a Judicial Recall, Washington Post, June 12, 2018.

118. Raymond Paternoster, How Much Do We Really Know about Criminal Deterrence?, Journal of Criminal Law and Criminology 100 (2010): 765, 818; Daniel S. Nagin, Deterrence in the Twenty-First Century, Crime and Justice 42 (2013): 199, 252; Anthony N. Doob and Cheryl Marie Webster, Sentence Severity

and Crime: Accepting the Null Hypothesis, Crime and Justice 30 (2003):143, 187; Richard L. Lippke, The Ethics of Plea Bargaining (New York: Oxford University Press, 2011), 139. Steven N. Durlauf and Daniel S. Nagin, Imprisonment and Crime: Can Both Be Reduced?, Criminology and Public Policy 10 (2011): 13, 27–31.

119. Carlton Gunn and Myra Sun, Sometimes the Cure Is Worse than the Disease: The One-Way White Collar Sentencing Ratchet, Human Rights 38 (2015): 9, 12; Peter J. Henning, Is Deterrence Relevant in Sentencing White-Collar Criminals?, Wayne State Law Review 61 (2015): 27, 41.

120. Paul H. Robinson and Jon M. Darley, The Role of Deterrence in the Formulation of Criminal Law Rules: At Its Worst When Doing Its Best, Georgetown Law Journal 91 (2003): 949, 954–956; Andrew Von Hirsch, Anthony E. Bottoms, Elizabeth Burney, and Per-Olot Wikström, Deterrent Sentencing as a Crime Prevention Strategy, in Ashworth, von Hirsch, and Roberts, Principled Sentencing: Readings on Theory and Policy, 57, 61–62; Paternoster, How Much Do We Really Know about Criminal Deterrence?, 810; Dan Waldorf and Sheigla Murphy, Perceived Risks and Criminal Justice Pressures on Middle Class Cocaine Sellers, Journal of Drug Issues 25 (1995): 11.

121. David A. Anderson, The Deterrence Hypothesis and Picking Pockets at the Pickpocket's Hanging, American Law and Economic Review 4 (2002): 295, 308; Anthony N. Doob and Cheryl M. Webster, Offender's Thought Process, in Ashworth, von Hirsch, and Roberts, Principled Sentencing: Readings on Theory and Policy; Steven D. Levitt, Why Do Increased Arrest Rates Appear to Reduce Crime: Deterrence, Incapacitation, or Measurement Error?, Economic Inquiry 36 (1998): 353, 355; Robinson and Darley, The Role of Deterrence, 460; Paternoster, How Much Do We Really Know about Criminal Deterrence?, 805.

122. Kenneth D. Tunnell, Choosing Crime: Close Your Eyes and Take Your Chances, in Barry W. Hancock and Paul M. Sharp eds., Criminal Justice in America: Theory, Practice and Policy (Englewood Cliffs, NJ: Prentice Hall, 1996), 43.

123. For an overview of studies, see Doob and Webster, Offender's Thought Process, 71–74.

124. Waldorf and Murphy, Perceived Risks and Criminal Justice Pressures on Middle Class Cocaine Sellers, 11.

125. Edward J. Latessa, Shelley J. Listwan, and Deborah Koetzle, What Works (and Doesn't) in Reducing Recidivism (New York: Routledge, 2014), 9, 202, 207; Francis T. Cullen and Karen E. Gilbert, Reaffirming Rehabilitation (Cincinnati: Anderson, 2013), 188.

126. United Nations Office on Drugs and Crime, Prison Reform and Alternatives to Imprisonment, Concept Note, February 2011, at 8, https://www.unodc.org/ documents/justice-and-prison-reform/UNODC_Prison_reform_concept_ note.pdf; see also United Nations Office on Drugs and Crime, Why Promote Prison Reform?, https://www.unodc.org/unodc/en/justice-and-prison-reform/

prison-reform-and-alternatives-to-imprisonment.html (last visited February 16, 2019).

127. Lee, Yes, U.S. Locks People Up at a Higher Rate than Any Other Country.

128. Jeffrie Murphy, Repentance, Punishment, and Mercy, in Amitai Etzioni and David Carney eds., Repentance: A Comparative Perspective (Lanham, MD: Rowman & Littlefield, 1997), 157.

129. Susan A. Bandes, Remorse and Demeanour in the Courtroom: Cognitive Science and the Evaluation of Contrition, in Jill Hunter, Paul Roberts, Simon N. M. Young, and David Dixon eds., The Integrity of Criminal Process: From Theory into Practice (Oxford: Hart, 2016), 321.

130. Stephanos Bibas and Richard A. Bierschbach, Integrating Remorse and Apology into Criminal Procedure, Yale Law Journal 114 (2004): 85, 93–94.

131. Michael Proeve and Steven Tudor, Remorse: Psychological and Jurisprudential Perspectives (London and New York: Routledge, 2010), 82–83.

132. Steven P. Garvey, Aggravation and Mitigation in Capital Cases: What Do Jurors Think?, Columbia Law Review 98 (1998): 1538, 1560–1561; Scott E. Sunby, The Capital Jury and Absolution: The Intersection of Trial Strategy, Remorse and the Death Penalty, Cornell Law Review 83 (1998): 1557, 1560; Theodore Eisenberg, Stephen P. Garvey, and Martin T. Wells, But Was He Sorry? The Role of Remorse in Capital Sentencing, Cornell Law Review 83 (1998): 1599 1631–1636.

133. U.S. Sentencing Commission Guidelines Manual Section 3E1.1 (2016); Bibas and Bierschbach, Integrating Remorse and Apology, 93 and n. 19. Stanton Wheeler, Kenneth Mann, and Austin Sarat, Sitting in Judgment: The Sentencing of White-Collar Criminals (New Haven, CT: Yale University Press, 1988), 115–118.

134. Mark W. Bennett and Ira P. Robbins, Last Words: A Survey and Analysis of Federal Judges' Views on Allocution in Sentencing, Alabama Law Review 65 (2014): 735, 758.

135. People v. Gandy, 591 N.E.2d 45, 63 (Ill. App. 5th Dist. 1992); Linger v. State, 508 N.E.2d 56, 64 (Ind. App. 4th Dist. 1987); Bryan H. Ward, Sentencing without Remorse, Loyola University Chicago Law Journal 38 (2006): 131, 161, n. 48.

136. United States v. Beserra, 967 F.2d 254, 256 (7th Cir. 1992).

137. Nicole Bronnimann, Remorse in Parole Hearings: An Elusive Concept with Concrete Consequences (unpublished student paper, 2018); Susan Bandes, Remorse and Criminal Justice, Emotion Review 8 (2016): 14, 17.

138. Bandes, Remorse and Demeanour in the Courtroom; Proeve and Tudor, Remorse: Psychological and Jurisprudential Perspectives, 90.

139. United States v. Royer, 895 F.2d 28, 30 (1st Cir. 1990).

140. Ward, Sentencing without Remorse, 133–34.

141. Payne v. State, 838 N.E.2d 503, 509 (Ind. App. 2005).

142. Rocksheng Zhong, Judging Remorse, New York University Review of Law and Social Change 39 (2015): 133, 158–159.

143. Zhong, Judging Remorse, 148.

144. Wheeler, Sitting in Judgment, 117.

145. Ward, Sentencing without Remorse, 159. For a case overturning a sentence, see Brown v. State, 934 P.2d 245 (Nev. 1997).

146. Van Cleve, Crook County, 81, 112.

147. Bandes, Remorse and Demeanour in the Courtroom.

148. Bandes, Remorse and Criminal Justice, 17.

149. Lippke, The Ethics of Plea Bargaining, 98.

150. Lippke, The Ethics of Plea Bargaining, 98, 117–118.

151. Bibas and Bierschbach, Integrating Remorse and Apology, 98, 106.

152. Martha-Grace Duncan, "So Young and So Untender": Remorseless Children and the Expectations of the Law, Columbia Law Review 102 (2002): 1469, 1499.

153. Riggins v. Nevada, 504 U.S. 127 (1992); Bandes, Remorse and Demeanour in the Courtroom, 318.

154. Barnes v. State, 634 N.E.2d 46, 49–50 (Ind. 1994).

155. Ronald S. Everett and Barbara C. Nienstedt, Race, Remorse, and Sentence Reduction: Is Saying You're Sorry Enough?, Justice Quarterly (1999): 99.

156. Bennett and Robbins, Last Words, 768, 770.

157. Lippke, The Ethics of Plea Bargaining, 117–118.

158. David Alan Sklansky, The Problems with Prosecutors, Annual Review of Criminology 1 (2017): 451.

159. David K. Shipler, Rights at Risk: The Limits of Liberty in Modern America (New York: Alfred A. Knopf, 2012), 115.

160. Alexandra Natapoff, Punishment without Crime (New York:Basic Books, 2018),10-11; Aditi Juneja, A Holistic Framework to Aid Responsible Plea-Bargaining by Prosecutors, New York University Law Journal Law and Liberty 11 (2017): 600, 624–625.

161. Emily Yoffe, Innocence Is Irrelevant, Atlantic, September, 2017.

162. Fred R. Shapiro ed., The Yale Book of Quotations (New Haven, CT: Yale University Press, 2006), 111 (quoting Lenny Bruce).

163. See sources cited in Anthony C. Thompson, Retooling and Coordinating the Approach to Prosecutorial Misconduct, Rutgers University Law Review 69 (2017): 623, 642.

164. David Alan Sklansky, The Nature and Function of Prosecutorial Power, Journal of Criminal Law and Criminology, 106 (2016): 473, 515.

165. Ronald F. Wright, Beyond Prosecutor Elections, Southern Methodist University Law Review 67 (2014): 593, 596; Marc L. Miller and Ronald F. Wright, The Black Box, Iowa Law Review 94 (2008): 125.

166. Michael J. Ellis, The Origins of the Elected Prosecutor, Yale Law Journal 121 (2012): 1539.

167. Wright, Beyond Prosecutor Elections, 600–601. The figures have not substantially changed over the last decade. Ronald F. Wright, How Prosecutor Elections Fail Us, Ohio State Journal of Criminal Law 6 (2009): 581, 592–595.

168. Wright, How Prosecutor Elections Fail Us, 583, 600–604. See also Sklansky, Prosecutorial Power, 517.

169. Wendy Sawyer and Alex Clark, New Data: The Rise of the Prosecutor Politician, Prison Policy Initiative, July 13, 2017.

170. Adam Gopnik, Rattling the Cage, New Yorker, April 10, 2017.

171. Butler, Let's Get Free, 105.

172. Sklansky, The Problems with Prosecutors, 4.8; Van Cleve, Crook County, 70.

173. Van Cleve, Crook County, 70.

174. Van Cleve, Crook County, 71.

175. Ronald F. Weight and Kay L. Levine, The Cure for Young Prosecutors' Syndrome, Arizona Law Review 56 (2014): 1065, 1068, 1082.

176. Wright and Levine, The Cure for Young Prosecutor's Syndrome, 1084–1085.

177. Jay Sterling Silver, Fixing the Conflict of Interest at the Core of Police Brutality Cases, Washington Post, December 4, 2014.

178. Van Cleve, Crook County, 72; Keith A. Findley and Michael S. Scott, The Multiple Dimensions of Tunnel Vision in Criminal Cases, Wisconsin Law Review (2006): 327, 329; Alex Kozinski, Criminal Law 2.0, Georgetown Law Journal Annotated Review of Criminal Procedure (2015): 1, xxiii.

179. APR Panelists Examine Why Prosecutors Are Largely Ignored by Disciplinary Offices, ABa /BNA Lawyers Manual on Professional Conduct (2006), 90; for other studies, see Deborah L. Rhode, David Luban, Scott L. Cummings, and Nora Freeman Engstrom, Legal Ethics (New York: Foundation Press, 7th ed., 2017), 448.

180. Nina Morrison, What Happens When Prosecutors Break the Law, New York Times, June 18, 2018.

181. Connick v. Thompson, 563 U.S. 51 (2011).

182. Connick v. Thompson, 563 U.S. 51 (2011).

183. John Thompson, The Prosecution Rests, But I Can't, New York Times, April 9, 2011.

184. Joan Petersilia, When Prisoners Come Home: Parole and Prisoner Reentry (New York: Oxford University Press, 2003), 58.

185. Petersilia, When Prisoners Come Home, 63; Joan Petersilia and Jimmy Threatt, Release from Prison, in Kent R. Kerley ed., The Encyclopedia of Corrections (New York: John Wiley and Sons, 2017), 3.

186. James Q. Wilson, Thinking about Crime (New York: Basic Books, 1975), 173.

187. Petersilia and Threatt, Release from Prison, 4.

188. Petersilia and Threatt, Release from Prison, 4.

189. American Civil Liberties Union, False Hope: How Parole Systems Fail Youth Serving Extreme Sentences (New York: ACLU Foundation, 2016), 4; Susan C. Kinnevy and Joel Caplan, Center for Research on Youth and Social Policy, Findings from the APAI International Survey of Releasing Authorities (University of Pennsylvania, 2008), 38.

190. ACLU, False Hope, 5.

191. ACLU, False Hope, 2.

192. ACLU, False Hope, 2.

193. New York Forgets Its Juvenile Lifers, New York Times, March 24, 2018.

194. ACLU False Hope, 2–3.

195. ACLU, False Hope, 10.

196. ACLU, False Hope, 6.

197. ACLU, False Hope, 7.

198. ACLU, False Hope, 4.

199. Mears and Cochran, Prisoner Reentry, 31.

200. Latessa, Listwan, and Koetzle, What Works (and Doesn't) in Reducing Recidivism, 231.

201. Loïc Wacquant, Class, Race & Hyperincarceration in Revanchist America, in Alexander Papachristou, Blind Goddess: A Reader on Race and Justice (New York: New Press, 2011), 32.

202. Clear, The "Iron Law" of Prison Populations, 57.

203. Juleyka Lantigua-Williams, Can a Notorious New York City Jail Be Closed?, The Atlantic, April 26, 2016 (quoting Martin).

204. Mark W. Bennett, The Implicit Racial Bias in Sentencing: The Next Frontier, Yale Law Journal Forum (2017): 391, 396; Mark W. Bennett and Victoria C. Plaut, Looking Criminal and the Presumption of Dangerousness: Afrocentric Facial Features, Skin Tone, and Criminal Justice, UC Davis Law Review 51 (2018): 745, 748–749, 795; Jerry Kang et al., Implicit Bias in the Courtroom, UCLA Law Review 59 (2012): 1124, 1131, 1151; Andrew Kahn and Chris Kirk, What It's Like to Be Black in the Criminal Justice System, Slate, http://www.slate.com/articles/news_and_politics/crime/2015/08/racial_disparities_in_the_criminal_justice_system_eight_charts_illustrating.html (last visited February 16, 2019); Jawjeong Wu, Racial/Ethnic Discrimination and Prosecution: A Meta-Analysis, Criminal Justice and Behavior 43 (2016): 437, 450 (finding minority offenders face greater odds of being fully charged and prosecuted).

205. Ashley Nellis, The Color of Justice: Racial and Ethnic Disparity in State Prisons (The Sentencing Project, 2016), https://www.sentencingproject.org/wp-content/uploads/2016/06/the-color-of-justice-racial-and-ethnic-disparity-in-state-prisons.pdf.

206. The Sentencing Project, Report of the Sentencing Project to the United Nations Human Rights Committee Regarding Racial Disparities in the United States Criminal Justice System (August, 2013), 1; Rehavi and Starr, Racial Disparity, 1320; Justin Murray: Re-Imagining Criminal Prosecution: Toward a Color-Conscious Professional Ethic for Prosecutors, American Criminal Law Review 49 (2012): 1541, 1543.

207. Wacquant, Class, Race, and Hyperincarceration, 36.

208. Sentencing Project, Race and the Criminal Justice System, 3; Colleen Walsh, The Costs of Inequality: Goal of Justice, But Reality of Unfairness, U.S. News, March 1, 2016.

209. Sentencing Project, Race and the Criminal Justice System, 8. See also Besiki Luka Kutateladze and Nacy R. Andigloro, Prosecution and Racial Justice in New York County: Technical Report (2014): 118, 130; Aditi Juneja, A Holistic Framework to Aid Responsible Plea-Bargaining by Prosecutors, New York University Journal of Law and Liberty 11 (2017): 600, 628.

210. The quote comes from Remarks of Stephen B. Bright, Georgetown University Law Center Commencement, May 17, 2015, https://www.schr.org/files/post?bright%20-%20Geortetown%20commencement%remarks%205-17-2015.pdf. For a similar claim, see Stevenson, Just Mercy, 300.

211. For arrests, see The Center for Constitutional Rights, Stop-Question-Frisk Analysis, in Papachristou, Blind Goddess, 57, 59; Bob Herbert, The Shame of New York, New York Times, October 30, 2010. For pretrial bail and detention, see Bennett and Plaut, Looking Criminal, 748, and in Ian Ayres and Joel Waldfogel, A Market Test for Race Discrimination in Bail Setting, Stanford Law Review 456 (1994): 987, 992. For sentences, see Carlos Berdejó, Criminalizing Race: Racial Disparities in Plea-Bargaining, Boston College Law Review 59 (2018): 1187, 1191; 1195–1196; United States Sentencing Commission, Demographic Differences in Sentencing, November 14, 2017, https://www.ussc.gov/research-reports/demographic-differences-sentencing; Rehavi and Starr, Racial Disparity, 1320. For findings of differences in rates of incarceration, see David S. Abrams, Marianne Bertrand, and Sendhil Mullainathan, Do Judges Vary in Their Treatment of Race?, Journal of Legal Studies 41 (2012): 347; Darrell Steffensmeier and Stephen Demuth, Ethnicity and Judges' Sentencing Decisions: Hispanic-Black-White, Comparisons Criminology 39 (2001): 145, 160.

212. American Civil Liberties Union, The War on Marijuana in Black and White (New York: American Civili Liberties Union, 2013), 47–48, 58; Natapoff, Punishment without Crime,152–153.

213. Bob Herbert, The Shame of New York, and Center for Constitutional Rights, Stop-and-Frisk, 59.

214. David Cole, No Equal Justice: Race and Class in the American Criminal Justice System (New York: New Press, 1999), 36.

215. For New York police explanations, see The Center for Constitutional Rights, Stop-Question-Frisk Analysis, 57, 59; Bob Herbert, The Shame of New York. For Nashville police explanations, see Yoffe, Innocence is Irrelevant.

216. David C. Baldus et al., Racial Discrimination and the Death Penalty in the Post-*Furman* Era: An Empirical and Legal Overview, with Recent Findings from Philadelphia, Cornell Law Review 83 (1998): 1638.

217. Samuel R. Sommers and Phoebe C. Ellsworth, White Juror Bias: An Investigation of Prejudice against Black Defendants in the American Courtroom, Psychology, Public Policy, and Law 7, (2001): 201, 217–219.

218. Sommers and Ellsworth, White Juror Bias, 209.

219. For the IAT and data about its findings see PROJECT IMPLICIT, http://projetimplicit.org, and Brian A. Nosek, Pervasiveness and Correlates of Implicit Attitudes and Stereotypes, European Review of Social Psychology 18 (2007): 1.

220. Anthony G. Greenwald et al., Understanding and Using the Implicit Association Test: Meta-Analysis of Predictive Validity, Journal of Personality and Social Psychology 97 (2009): 17; Kang et al., Implicit Bias in the Courtroom, 1131.

221. Keith Payne et al., How to Think about "Implicit Bias," Scientific American, March 27, 2108; Justin D. Levinson et al., Implicit Racial Bias: A Social Science Overview, in Justin D. Levinson and Robert J. Smith, Implicit Racial Bias across the Law (New York: Cambridge University Press, 2012), 9; Wu, Racial/Ethnic Discrimination and Prosecution, 439.

222. Nellis, The Color of Justice, 19; Bennett and Plaut, Looking Criminal, 774; Natapoff, Punishment without Crime, 156-157; ACLU Campaign for Smart Justice, Selling Off Our Freedom: How Insurance Corporations Have Taken Over Our Bail System, May 2017, 18; David Arnold, Will Dobbie, and Crystal Yang, Racial Bias in Bail Decisions, Quarterly Journal of Economics (forthcoming); Mark W. Bennett, The Implicit Racial Bias in Sentencing: The Next Frontier, Yale Law Journal 126 (2017): 391; Jennifer L. Eberhardt et al., Looking Deathworthy: Perceived Stereotypicality of Black Defendants Predicts Capital-Sentencing Outcomes, Psychological Science 17 (2006): 383.

223. Bennet, Implicit Bias, 403; Murray, Re-Imagining Criminal Prosecution, 1562; Bennett and Plaut, Looking Dangerous, 786 and n. 272.

224. Robert J. Smith, Justine D. Levinson, and Zoë Robinson, Implicit White Favoritism in the Criminal Justice System, Alabama Law Review 66 (2015): 871, 873–875; Justin D. Levinson and Danielle Young, Different Shades of Bias: Skin Tone, Implicit Racial Bias, and Judgments of Ambiguous Evidence, West Virginia Law Review 112 (201): 307, 337–339.

225. Matteo Forgiarini, Marcello Gallucci, and Angelo Maravita, Racism and the Empathy for Pain on Our Skin, Frontiers Psychology 2 (2011): 1; L. Song Richardson, Systemic Triage: Implicit Racial Bias in the Criminal Courtroom, Yale Law Journal 126 (2017): 862, 883–884.

226. James D. Johnson et al., Rodney King and O.J. Revisited: The Impact of Race and Defendant Empathy Induction on Judicial Decisions, Journal of Applied Social Psychology 32 (2002): 1208, 1215.

227. Van Cleve, Crook County, 66.

228. Even after the fair Sentencing Act of 2010 reduced the quantity disparity, it re-
     mains 18 to 1. Kara Gotsch, Breakthrough in U.S. Drug Sentencing Reform: The
     Fair Sentencing Act and the Unfinished Reform Agenda (2011), 9.

229. Richardson, Systemic Triage, 880–882; Van Cleve, Crook County.

230. Richardson, Systemic Triage, 882.

231. Bennett, Implicit Bias, 396–397, 404; Jeffrey J. Rachlinski et al., Does
     Unconscious Racial Bias Affect Trial Judges?, Notre Dame Law Review 84
     (2009): 1195, 1225.

232. Eric Luis Uhlmann and Geffrey L. Cohen, "I Think It, Therefore It's True": Effects
     of Self-Perceived Objectivity on Hiring Discrimination, Organizational Behavior
     and Human Decision Processes 104 (2007): 207.

233. Michelle Alexander, The Fire This Time, in Papachristou, Blind Goddess, 275

234. Bandes, Remorse and Demeanour in the Courtroom, 323.

235. Bandes, Remorse and Demeanour in the Courtroom, 324–325.

236. Devin G. Poe, Joseph Price, and Justin Wolfers, Awareness Reduces Racial Bias
     (National Bureau of Economic Research Working paper 19765, 2014); Emily
     Pronin, Perception and Misperception of Bias in Human Judgment, Trends in
     Cognitive Science 11 (2007): 37, 39; Nellis, The Color of Justice, 29; Emily Pronin
     and Matthew B. Kugler, Valuing Thoughts, Ignoring Behavior: The Introspection
     Illusion as a Source of the Bias Blind Spot, Journal of Experimental Social
     Psychology 43 (2007): 565.

237. Kang et al., Implicit Bias, 1186. See also Pamela M. Casey et al., Helping Courts
     Address Implicit Bias: Resources for Education (National Center for State
     Courts, 2012), http://citeseerx.ist.psu.edu/viewdoc/download?doi=10.1.1.259.10
     89&rep=rep1&type=pdf.

238. Richardson, Systemic Triage, 878.

239. Rachlinski et al., Does Unconscious Racial Bias Affect Trial Judges?, 1230.

240. Besike Kutateladze, Whitney Tymas, and Mary Crowley, Race and Prosecution in
     Manhattan (New York: Vera Institute of Justice, 2014).

241. Michael Tonry, Doing Less Harm, in Michael Tonry, Punishing Race: A
     Continuing American Dilemma (New York: Oxford University Press, 2011), 257;
     Michelle Alexander, The Fire This Time, 264, 267.

242. Lissa Griffin and Ellen Yaroshefsky, Ministers of Justice and Mass Incarceration,
     Georgetown Journal of Legal Ethics 30 (2017): 301, 303–304.

243. James S. Gavin, Juror Sentiment on Just Punishment: Do the Federal Sentence
     Guidelines Reflect Community Values?, Harvard Law and Policy Review 4
     (2010): 173, 187–188.

244. Eva S. Nilsen, Indecent Standards: The Case of *U.S. versus Weldon Angelos*, Roger
     Williams University Law Review 11 (2006): 543.

245. Snitch (PBS Video 1999).

246. Justin McCarthy, Americans' Views Shift on Toughness of Justice System (Gallup, October 20, 2016), http://news.gallup.com/poll/196568/americans-views-shift-toughness-justice-system.aspx.

247. Jenkins, A Visionary Criminal Justice System, 14.

248. Harris, The American People Have Spoken; Mears and Cochran, Prisoner Reentry, 52–53.

249. German Lopez, Want to End Mass Incarceration? This Poll Should Worry You, Vox, September 7, 2016, https://www.vox.com/2016/9/7/12814504/mass-incarceration-poll.

250. Juneja, A Holistic Framework, 618, Fred C. Zacharias, Justice in Plea Bargaining, William and Mary Law Review 39 (1998): 1121; Alliance for Safety and Justice, Crime Survivors Speak: The First-Ever National Survey of Victims' Views on Safety and Justice (2016), 24–25.

251. Alliance for Safety and Justice, Crime Survivors Speak, 5, 25.

252. Mears and Cochran, Prisoner Reentry; Juneja, A Holistic Framework, 613; Lynne M. Vieraitis, Tomislav V. Kovandzic, and Thomas B. Marvell, The Criminogenic Effects of Imprisonment: Evidence from State Panel Data, 1974–2002, Criminology and Public Policy 6 (2007): 589.

253. Dina R. Rose and Todd R. Clear, Incarceration, Social Capital, and Crime: Implications for Social Disorganization Theory, Criminology 36 (1998): 441, 465; Murray, Re-Imagining Criminal Prosecution, 1565–1566.

254. Murray, Re-Imagining Criminal Prosecution, 1565; Bruce Western, Punishment and Inequality in America (New York: Russell Sage Foundation, 2006), 129, 136, Jeffrey Fagan and Tracy L. Meares, Punishment, Deterrence and Social Control: The Paradox of Punishment in Minority Communities, Ohio State Journal of Criminal Law 6 (2008): 173, 200. Bruce Western and Becky Pettit, Incarceration and Social Inequality, in Papachristou, Blind Goddess, 223; Todd R. Clear, Death by a Thousand Little Cuts, in Todd R. Clear, Imprisoning Communities: How Mass Incarceration Makes Disadvantaged Neighborhoods Worse (New York: Oxford University Press, 2009).

255. Western and Pettit, Incarceration and Social Inequality, 220, 221.

256. Western and Pettit, Incarceration and Social Inequality, 222; Kearney et al., Ten Economic Facts, 15; Clear, Death by a Thousand Little Cuts.

257. Elizabeth Ann Carson, Prisoners in 2016 (Washington, DC: US Department of Justice, 2018), 113.

258. Greg Berman and Julian Adler, Start Here: A Road Map to Reducing Mass Incarceration (New York: The New Press, 2018), 28

259. Lauren-Brooke Eisen et al., How Many Americans Are Unnecessarily Incarcerated? (New York: Brennan Center for Justice, 2016), 7–8 (40 percent); Seema Gajwani, Retire the Leeches: The Promise of Evidence-Based Solutions, in

Mauer and Epstein, To Build a Better Criminal Justice System, 44 (33 percent of federal inmates).

260. Seema Gajwani, Retire the Leeches: The Promise of Evidence-Based Solutions, in Mauer and Epstein, To Build a Better Criminal Justice System, 44; Berman and Adler, Start Here,70.

261. Bill Keller, Nine Lessons about Criminal Justice Reform: What Washington Can Learn from the States, Address before the Ninth Circuit Judicial Project San Francisco, July 17, 2017, https://www.themarshallproject.org/2017/07/19/nine-lessons-about-criminal-justice-reform.

262. Greg Berman, Alternatives to Incarceration Are Cutting Prison Numbers, Costs and Crime, The Guardian, July 4, 2013.

263. Center for Court Innovation and NPC Research, Testing the Cost Savings of Judicial Diversion (New York: Center for Court Innovation, March 2013), iv–v.

264. Emily Galvin, How Treatment Courts Can Reduce Crime, Atlantic, September 29, 2015; Adam Benforado, Unfair: The New Science of Criminal Injustice (New York: Broadway Books, 2015), 281.

265. Douglas B. Marlowe, Research Update on Adult Drug Courts, National Association of Drug Court Professionals (NADCP), Need to Know (December, 2010), 1; Benforado, Unfair, 281. See also Shelli B. Rossman et al., The Multi-site Adult Drug Court Evaluation: Executive Summary, Urban Institute, Justice Policy Center, 2011), 5.

266. Keller, Nine Lessons. See also Berman and Adler, Start Here, 122–127.

267. Insha Rahman, Against the Odds; Stevenson and Mayson, Bail Reform; Wiseman, Fixing Bail; Yang, Toward an Optimal Bail System.

268. Tom R. Tyler and Rick Trinkner, Why Children Follow Rules, 116–117; Elizabeth S. Scott and Lawrence Steinberg, Rethinking Juvenile Justice (Cambridge, MA: Harvard University Press, 2008), 44–50; Lawrence Steinberg, Age of Opportunity: Lessons from the New Science of Adolescence (Boston: Houghton Mifflin Harcourt, 2014); Richard J. Bonnie and Elizabeth S. Scott, The Teenage Brain: Adolescent Brain Research and the Law, Current Directions in Psychological Science 22 (2013): 158.

269. Tyler and Trinkner, Why Children Follow Rules,121; Scott and Steinberg, Rethinking Juvenile Justice, 53–54.

270. Scott and Steinberg, Rethinking Juvenile Justice, 208–210.

271. Tyler and Trinkner, Why Children Follow Rules, 203; David Huizinga, Karl Schumann, Beate Ehret, and Amanda Elliott, The Effects of Juvenile Justice System Processing on Subsequent Delinquent and Criminal Behavior: A Cross-National Study (Washington DC: National Institute of Justice 2003).

272. Charles M. Borduin et al., Multisytemic Treatment of Serious Juvenile Offenders: Long Term Prevention of Criminality and Violence, Journal of Consulting and Clinical Psychology 63 (1995): 569, 572; Paul Gendreau,

Francis T. Cullen, and James Bonta, Intensive Rehabilitation Supervision: The Next Generation in Community Corrections?, in Joan Petersilia, Community Corrections: Probation, Parole and Intermediate Sanctions (New York: Oxford University Press, 1998): 198, 201–204.

273. Andrew von Hirsch, Andrew Ashworth, and Clifford Shearing, Specifying Aims and Limits for Restorative Justice: A "Making Amends" Model, in Ashworth, von Hirsch, and Roberts, Principled Sentencing: Readings on Theory and Policy, 211; Gerry Johnstone, Restorative Justice: An Alternative to Punishment or an Alternative Form of Punishment?, in Ashworth, von Hirsch, and Roberts, Principled Sentencing: Readings on Theory and Policy, 209; Gabrielle Maxwell and Allison Morris, The Role of Shame, Guilt and Remorse in Restorative Justice Processes for Young People, in Elmar G. M. Weitekamp and Hans-Jürgen Kerner eds., Restorative Justice: Theoretical Foundations (London and New York: Routledge, 2002), 267, 269, 280; Tyler and Trinkner, Why Children Follow Rules, 205.

274. Stephanos Bibas and Richard A. Bierschbach, Integrating Remorse and Apology into Criminal Procedure, Yale Law Journal 114 (2004): 85, 116–117; Lawrence W. Sherman and Heather Strang, Restorative Justice: The Evidence (London: The Smith Institute, 2007). See, generally, Andrea von Hirsch et al., Restorative Justice and Criminal Justice: Competing or Reconcilable Paradigms (Oxford: Hart, 2003).

275. Jeremy Travis, Summoning the Superheroes: Harnessing Science and Passion to Create a More Effective and Humane Response to Crime: Twenty-Fifth Anniversary Keynote Address, in Mauer and Epstein, To Build a Better Criminal Justice System, 5.

276. Bart Lubow, Juvenile Justice in 25 Years: A System That Passes the "My Child" Test, in Mauer and Epstein, To Build a Better Criminal Justice System, 34–35.

277. Michael Torny, Individualizing Punishments, in Ashworth, von Hirsch, and Roberts, Principled Sentencing: Readings on Theory and Policy, 354, 355–356.

278. Nicholas Fandos, Senate Passes Biparitsan Criminal Justice Bill, New York Times, December 18, 2018.

279. Murray, Re-Imagining Criminal Prosecution, 1593.

280. Inger H. Chandler, Conviction Integrity Review Units: Owning the Past, Changing the Future, Criminal Justice Magazine (Summer, 2016), 14–15; John Hollway, Conviction Review Units: A National Perspective, University of Pennsylvania Law School, Public Law and Legal Theory Research Paper No. 15–41 (2016), http://ssrn.com/abstract=2707809; Barry C. Scheck, Conviction Integrity Units Revisited, Ohio State Journal of Criminal Law 14 (2017): 705, 707–712.

281. Josie Duffy Rice, Do Conviction Integrity Units Work?, The Appeal, March 22, 2018, https://theappeal.org/do-conviction-integrity-units-work-a718bbc75bc7/;

Scheck, Conviction Integrity Units Revisited, 710–711. For support of more such units, see Kozinski, Criminal Law 2.0, xxxi.

282. Harris, The American People Have Spoken; ACLU, Americans Overwhelmingly Support Prosecutorial Reform, Poll Finds (American Civil Liberties Union, December 12, 2017, https://www.aclu.org/news/americans-overwhelmingly-support-prosecutorial-reform.

283. Wright, Beyond Prosecutor Elections, 611–615; ACLU Massachusetts, Press Release, Poll: Mass. Voters Think Criminal Justice System Is Biased, July 12, 2017, https://aclum.org/uncategorized/poll-mass-voters-think-criminal-justice-system-is-biased/; Jennifer Gonnerman, Acts of Conviction, The New Yorker, October 29, 2018, 31; Sklansky, Problems with Prosecutors, 2.13.

284. American Law Institute Model Penal Code Proposed Official Draft (Philadelphia: American Law Institute, 1962).

285. Vincent Southerland, With AI and Criminal Justice, The Devil Is in the Data (New York: Center on Race, Inequality and the Law, New York University Law School, April 9, 2018): For concerns about fairness, see ACLU False Hope, 11–13; Michelle Alexander, The Newest Jim Crow, New York Times, November 11, 2018.

286. Petersilia and Threatt, Release from Prison, 8; Mears and Cochran, Prisoner Reentry, 166.

287. Council of State Governments, National Inventory of Collateral Consequences of Convictions (Council of State Governments, 2019), https://niccc.csgjusticecenter.org/ (last visited on February 16, 2019).

288. Mears and Cochran, Prisoner Reentry, 134–140 and discussion in chapter 3.

289. Sue Halpern, Sister Sympathy, New York Times Magazine, May 9, 1993 (quoting Prejean).

290. The Opportunity Agenda, An Overview of Public Opinion and Discourse on Criminal Justice Issues, 22; Harris, The American People Have Spoken.

291. The speech was delivered on August 28, 1963, at the March on Washington for Jobs and Freedom. It is available at https://okra.stanford.edu/media/audio/630828000.mp3.

CHAPTER 5

1. Alexander Hamilton, Federalist Paper 68, in Clinton Rossiter ed., The Federalist Papers (New York: Merton, 1961), 414.

2. Robert E. Denton, Moral Leadership and the American Presidency (Lanham, MD: Rowman and Littlefield, 2005), 2.

3. Rasmussen Report, October 19, 2016, http://www.rasmussenreports.com/public_content/politics/elections/election_2016/voters_rate_a_candidate_s_policies_more_important_than_character. For discussion, see Theodore Bunker, Poll: Voters Rate Candidate's Policies More Important than Character, Newsmax, October 19, 2016, https://www.newsmax.com/t/newsmax/article/754289.

4. James Davison Hunter, The Politics of Character (Charlottesville: Institute for Advanced Studies in Culture, University of Virginia, 2000), 9; Rasmussen Report.

5. Campaign 2016, October 10–13, 2016, PollingReport.com, http://www.pollingreport.com/wh16.htm.

6. Campaign 2016, October 10–14, 2016, August 5–8, 2016, June 10–13, 2016, PollingReport.com, http://www.pollingreport.com/wh16.htm.

7. Mark Blumenthal, The Underpinnings of Donald Trump's Approval Rating, Huffington Post, February 11, 2017, https://www.huffingtonpost.com/entry/the-underpinnings-of-donald-trumps-approval-rating_us_589e4206e4b080bf74f03c20.

8. Martin P. Wattenberg, The Declining Relevance of Candidate Personal Attributes in Presidential Elections, Presidential Studies Quarterly 46 (2016): 125, 137.

9. Denton, Moral Leadership, 11.

10. Robert L. Shogan, The Double Edge Sword: How Character Makes and Ruins Politicians from Washington to Clinton (Boulder, CO: Westview Press, 1999), 217.

11. Wattenberg, The Declining Relevance, 138.

12. Donald R. Kinder, Presidential Character Revisited, in Richard R. Lau and David O. Sears eds., Political Cognition (Hillsdale, NJ: Lawrence Erlbaum, 1986), 253.

13. Stanley A. Renshon, The Psychological Assessment of Presidential Candidates (New York: New York University Press, 1996), 7.

14. Renshon, Psychological Assessment, 17.

15. Marc J. Hetherington, Meri T. Long, and Thomas J. Rudolph, Revising the Myth: New Evidence of a Polarized Electorate, Public Opinion Quarterly 80, Issue S1 (March 2016): 23.

16. James P. Pfiffner, The Character Factor: How We Judge America's Presidents (College Station: Texas A & M University Press, 2004), 6.

17. George Friedman, Character, Policy and the Selection of Leaders, Geopolitical Weekly, September 4, 2012, https://worldview.stratfor.com/article/character-policy-and-selection-leaders.

18. For discussion of the public's desire for adaptability, see Stanley A. Renshon, High Hopes: The Clinton Presidency and the Politics of Ambition (New York: New York University Press, 1996), 35–36.

19. Julie Ray, World's Approval of U.S. Leadership Drops to New Low, Gallup, January 18, 2018.

20. Richard Wike, Bruce Stokes, Jacob Poushter, and Janell Fetterolf, U.S. Image Suffers as Publics around World Question Trump's Leadership (Pew Research Center, June 26, 2017).

21. William J. Bennett, The Death of Outrage: Bill Clinton and the Assault on American Ideals (New York: Free Press, 1998), 42.

22. James David Barber, The Presidential Character: Predicting Performance in the White House (Englewood Cliffs, NJ: Prentice Hall, 3d ed., 1985), 2; Robert

E. Denton, Moral Leadership and the American Presidency (Lanham, MD: Roman & Littlefield, 2005), 43; Richard Waterman, Gilbert K. St. Clair, and Robert Wright, The Image Is Everything Presidency (Boulder, CO: Westview Press, 1999).

23. Donald R. Kinder, Presidential Character Revisited, in Lao and Sears, Political Cognition, 233, 235.

24. Robert N. Bellah, The Meaning of Reputation in American Society, California Law Review 74 (1986): 743, 746. Richard Posner, An Affair of State (Cambridge, MA: Harvard University Press, 1999), 148; J. Patrick Dobel, Judging the Private Lives of Public Officials, Administration and Society 30 (May 1998): 115–142.

25. Peggy Noonan, Ronald Reagan, in Robert A. Wilson ed., Character above All (New York: Simon, 1995), 202.

26. Denton, Moral Leadership, 21.

27. Hunter, Politics of Character, 10, 57, Table 19.

28. Smith, Christoffersen, Davidson, and Herzog, Lost in Transition, 203.

29. Fred I. Greenstein, The Presidential Difference: Leadership Style from FDR to Barack Obama (Princeton, NJ: Princeton University Press, 3d ed. 2009), 3.

30. Renshon, The Psychological Assessment, 29, 124–125.

31. Renshon, Psychological Assessment, 31–32.

32. Mathew Nussbaum, Trump Touts His Temperament while Clinton Laughs, Politico, September 26, 2016, https://www.politico.com/story/2016/09/trump-clinton-no-stamina-look-228740.

33. Psychology Today Editorial Staff, Shrinks Battle over Diagnosing Donald Trump, Psychology Today, January 31, 2017.

34. Evan Osnos, Endgames, New Yorker, May 8, 2107, 39.

35. Fred Greenstein, Foreword, in Alexander L. George and Juliette L. George eds., Presidential Personality and Performance (Boulder, CO: Westview, 1998), ix–x.

36. Dennis Thompson, Restoring Responsibility: Ethics in Government, Business, and Healthcare (New York: Cambridge University Press, 2004), 237.

37. Reinhold Niebuhr, Moral Man and Immoral Society (New York: Charles Scribners, 1932), xi–22.

38. Renshon, Psychological Assessment, 5.

39. Barry R. Schlenker, Marissa Miller, and Ryan M. Johnson, Moral Identity, Integrity and Personal Responsibility, in Darcia Narváez and Daniel K. Lapsley eds., Personality, Identity, and Character: Explorations in Moral Psychology, (New York: Cambridge University Press, 2009), 328–329.

40. Schlenker, Miller, and Johnson, Moral Identity, 331.

41. Bernard Williams, Politics and Moral Character, in Stuart Hampshire ed., Public and Private Morality (Cambridge: Cambridge University Press, 1978), 62.

42. Dennis Thompson, Constitutional Character: Virtues and Vices in Presidential Leadership, Presidential Studies Quarterly 40 (2010): 23, 24. For the commitment to public over personal interests, see Robert Dalleck, Can Clinton Still Govern?, Washington Post, October 5, 1998, 22.

43. James Bryce, The American Commonwealth, Volume 1 (New York: Maximilian, 2d ed., 1891), 74–75.

44. James N. Druckman and Lawrence R. Jacobs, Who Governs? Presidents, Public Opinion, and Manipulation (Chicago: University of Chicago Press, 2015), 76.

45. Hunter, Politics of Character, 10.

46. Pew Research Center, Beyond Distrust: How Americans View Their Government, August 27–October 4, 2016, November 23, 2015, http://www.people-press.org/2015/11/23/beyond-distrust-how-americans-view-their-government/.

47. Hunter, Politics of Character, 85, Table 78.

48. Gallup, Trust in Government, January 10, 2017, http://news.gallup.com/poll/5392/trust-government.aspx.

49. Richard Reeves, President Kennedy: Profile of Power (New York: Simon & Schuster, 1994), 92.

50. Deborah L. Rhode, Women in Leadership (New York: Oxford University Press, 2016), 39; Jennifer L. Lawless and Richard L. Fox, Men Rule: The Continued Underrepresentation of Women in U.S. Politics (Washington, DC: Women and Politics Institute, 2012), ii.

51. Renshon, High Hopes, 40.

52. Alexander L. George, Assessing Presidential Character, in Alexander L. George and Juliette L. George eds., Presidential Personality and Performance (Boulder, CO: Westview Press), 152.

53. George, Assessing Presidential Character, 175.

54. Joseph A. Califano Jr., The Triumph and Tragedy of Lyndon Johnson (New York: Simon and Schuster, 1991), 10.

55. Todd S. Purdum, Facets of Clinton, New York Times, May 19, 1996.

56. Anthony Brant, Lies, Lies, Lies, The Atlantic, November 1977 (quoting Montaigne).

57. Thomas L. Carson, Lying and Deception: Theory and Practice (New York: Oxford University Press, 2010), 209.

58. Madison Letter to W. T. Barry, August 4, 1822, in Gaillard Hunt ed., The Writings of James Madison, vol. 9 (New York: G. P. Putnam's Sons, 1910), 103.

59. John M. Orman, Presidential Secrecy and Deception: Beyond the Power to Persuade (Santa Barbara, CA: Praeger, 1980), 39–40.

60. Plato, Republic, Volume I, Books 1–5, ed. and trans. Christopher Emlyn-Jones and William Preddy (Cambridge, MA: Harvard University Press, 2013), 485.

61. Niccolo Machiavelli, The Prince, ed. and trans. Peter Bondanella (New York: Oxford University Press, 2005), 177.

62. David Abrahamsen, Nixon v. Nixon—A Psychological Inquest (New York: Farrar, Straus & Giroux, 1976), 195 (quoting anonymous friend).

63. Richard M. Nixon, Leaders (New York: Warner Books, 1982), 324.

64. Carl M. Canon, Untruth and Consequences, The Atlantic, January/February 2007 (quoting Wilentz).

65. Thompson, Constitutional Character, 34.

66. James P. Pfiffner, The Contemporary Presidency: Presidential Lies, Presidential Studies Quarterly 29 (1999): 903, 904. See also Sissela Bok, Lying: Moral Choice in Private and Public Life (New York: Vintage, 1979), 31.

67. Larry Schwartz, The 7 Biggest Liars in Presidential History, Alternet, February 7, 2016, http://www.alternet.org/print/culture/7-biggest-liars-presidential-history.

68. Schwartz, The 7 Biggest Liars.

69. Walter LaFeber, The American Age (New York: Norton, 1989), 381–382. See also Robert Dallek, Franklin D. Roosevelt and American Foreign Policy, 1932–1945 (New York: Oxford University Press, 1979), 285.

70. Franklin D. Roosevelt, Fireside Chat, September 11, 1941.

71. Dallek, Franklin D. Roosevelt and American Foreign Policy, 289; Bok, Lying, 179–180; Eric Alterman, When Presidents Lie (New York: Viking, 2004), 21.

72. Pfiffner, Contemporary Presidency, 909.

73. Stephen Ambrose, Eisenhower, The President (New York: Simon and Schuster, 1984), 509. See also Pfiffner, The Contemporary Presidency, 909.

74. Carl M. Cannon, Untruth and Consequences, The Atlantic January/February 2007, 65.

75. Stewart Alsop and Charles Bartlett, In Time of Crisis, Saturday Evening Post, December 8, 1962, 15.

76. Alterman, When Presidents Lie, 97.

77. The Lessons of the Cuban Missile Crisis, Time, September 27, 1982.

78. Alterman, When Presidents Lie, 128.

79. Alterman, When Presidents Lie, 132–133.

80. Alterman, When Presidents Lie, 133–134.

81. Alterman, When Presidents Lie, 135.

82. Dennis F. Thompson, Political Ethics and Public Office (Cambridge, MA: Harvard University Press, 1987), 25.

83. James David Barber, The Presidential Character: Predicting Performance in the White House (Englewood Cliffs, NJ: Prentice Hall, 3d ed., 1985) 26; David Wise, The Politics of Lying (New York: Vintage, 1973), 65.

84. Alterman, When Presidents Lie, 184.

85. Alterman, When Presidents Lie, 169–173.

86. Doris Kearns Goodwin, Lyndon Johnson and the American Dream (New York; St. Martins, 1991), 252–253.

87. Fredrik Logevall, Why Lyndon Johnson Dropped Out, New York Times, March 25, 2018, SR 7; Michael Beschloss, Presidents of War (New York: Crown, 2018), 505.

88. David Halberstam, LBJ and Presidential Machismo, in Jeffrey Kimball ed., To Reason Why: The Debate about the Causes of U.S. Involvement in the Vietnam War (Philadelphia: Temple University Press, 1990), 201.

89. Jeremi Suri, The Impossible Presidency: The Rise and Fall of America's Highest Office (New York: Basic Books, 2017), 221 (quoting Johnson).

90. Alterman, When Presidents Lie, 161.

91. Alterman, When Presidents Lie, 187–189.

92. Joseph C. Goulden, Truth Is the First Casualty: The Gulf of Tonkin Affair (Chicago: Rand McNally, 1969), 160. For a slightly different version of the quote, see Barber, Presidential Character, 29, and Beschloss, Presidents of War 520.

93. Anthony Austin, The President's War (New York: Lippincott, 1971), 30 (quoting Kenneth O'Donnell).

94. Alterman, When Presidents Lie, 216.

95. Pfiffner, Contemporary Presidency, 912.

96. Dallek, Flawed Giant, 121

97. Beschloss, Presidents of War, 577–578.

98. Beschloss, Presidents of War, 578.

99. Alterman, When Presidents Lie, 236.

100. Pfiffner, Contemporary Presidency, 913; William Shawcross, Sideshow: Kissinger, Nixon, and the Destruction of Cambodia (New York: Touchstone, 1987), 228.

101. Richard Nixon, RN: The Memoirs of Richard Nixon (New York: Grosset and Dunlap, 1978), 382.

102. John A. Farrell, Tricky Dick's Vietnam Treachery, New York Times, January 1, 2017; John A. Farrell, Richard Nixon: The Life (New York: Penguin Random House, 2017).

103. Bruce Fein, Lies, Damned Lies, and Presidential Statements about War, Huffington Post, October 14, 2015, http://www.huffingtonpost.com/bruce-fein/lies-damned-lies-and-press_b_8296074.html.

104. Pfiffner, The Character Factor, 128.

105. United States Senate Report 216, Report of the Congressional Committees Investigating the Iran-Contra Affair, 280, https://archive.org/details/reportofcongress87unit (last visited February 17, 2019).

106. Pfiffner, The Character Factor, 58 (quoting Washington Post, July 16, 1987, A15).

107. Suri, The Impossible Presidency, 257; Malcolm Byrne, Iran-Contra: Reagan's Scandal and the Unchecked Abuse of Presidential Power (Lawrence: University of Kansas Press, 2014), 3, 40.

108. Bob Spitz, Reagan: An American Journey (New York: Penguin Press, 2018), 675 (quoting George Shultz). See also Pfiffner, Contemporary Presidency, 915; George Shultz, Turmoil and Triumph: My Years as Secretary of State (New York: Scribner, 1993), 1133.

109. Pfiffner, Contemporary Presidency, 915 (quoting Walsh).

110. Schwartz, 7 Biggest Liars.

111. Spitz, Reagan, 698–699 (quoting Reagan).

112. George H. W. Bush and Victor Gold, Looking Forward (New York: Doubleday, 1987), 240.

113. Shultz, Turmoil and Triumph, 809.

114. Pfiffner, Presidential Lies, 908; Shultz, Turmoil and Triumph, 809.

115. Greg Grandin, Poppy's Bloody Legacy, Nation, December 2018, 4.
116. Frank Rich, The Greatest Story Ever Sold: The Decline and Fall of Truth from 9/11 to Katrina (New York: Penguin, 2016), 58–61; Eric Alterman and Mark Green, The Book on Bush: How George W. (Mis)Leads America (New York: Viking, 2004), 266–322; Dana Milbank, For Bush, Facts Are Malleable, Washington Post, October 22, 2002; Barton Gelman and Walter Pincus, Depiction of Threat Outgrew Supporting Evidence, Washington Post, August 10, 2003; Eric Alterman, Bush Lies, Media Swallows, The Nation, November 7, 2002.
117. Rich, Greatest Story Ever Sold, 58.
118. George W. Bush, Address to the Nation, March 17, 2003, http://www.presidency. ucsb.edu/ws/index.php?pid=63713andst=andst1.
119. Rich, Greatest Story Ever Sold, 58.
120. Cannon, Untruth and Consequences; Rich, Greatest Story Ever Sold, 219.
121. Rich, Greatest Story Ever Sold, 61, 68. For the lack of intelligence supporting the link, see Rich, Greatest Story Ever Sold, 188.
122. The 9/11 Commission, The 9/11 Commission Report, https://www.9-11commission.gov/report/911Report.pdf; Murray Waas, What Bush Was Told about Iraq, National Journal, March 2, 2006.
123. Beschloss, Presidents of War, 583.
124. George W. Bush, Decision Points (New York: Crown, 2010), 262.
125. James Risen, CIA Aides Feel Pressure in Preparing Iraqi Reports, New York Times, March 23, 2003.
126. Senate Select Committee on Intelligence, 108th Congress, US Senate, Report on the Intelligence Community's Prewar Intelligence Assessments on Iraq, July 7, 2004. For other evidence of the lack of pressure, see James Agresti, Did Bush Lie about Weapons of Mass Destruction?, CNS, February 18, 2016, https://www.cnsnews. com/commentary/james-agresti/did-bush-lie-about-weapons-mass-destruction.
127. Rich, Greatest Story Ever Sold, 97.
128. Todd S. Purum and Patrick E. Tyler, Top Republicans Break with Bush on Iraq Strategy, New York Times, August 16, 2002 (quoting Richard Perle). For the political payoffs, see Rich, Greatest Story Ever Sold, 215–217.
129. Rich, Greatest Story Ever Sold, 62.
130. Dana Millbank and Dana Priest, Warning in Iraq Report Unread, Washington Post, July 19, 2003.
131. Cannon, Untruth and Consequences (quoting David Corn, The Lies of George W. Bush).
132. Rich, Greatest Story Ever Sold, 111.
133. For cost estimates, see, https://www.nationalpriorities.org/campaigns/cost-war-iraq/?gclid=CKPR9ZSM4coCFQeTfgodhscK3g (last visited February 17, 2019).

134. Rich, Greatest Story Ever Sold, 176, 196.

135. Fawn M. Brodie, Richard Nixon: The Shaping of His Character (New York: W. W. Norton, 1981), 26 (quoting Nixon).

136. Stanley I. Kutler, Abuse of Power: The New Nixon Tapes (New York: Free Press, 1997), 514, 33.

137. Pfiiffner, Contemporary Presidency, 909; Stanley I. Kutler, The Wars of Watergate (New York: Knopf, 1990), 347.

138. Larry Berman, The New American Presidency (Boston: Houghton Mifflin, 1987), 189 (quoting White House transcripts).

139. For a list of lawyers and offenses, see Kathleen Clark, The Legacy of Watergate for Legal Ethics Instruction, Hastings Law Journal 51 (1999): 673, 678–682; Robert Pack, The Lawyers of Watergate, Washington Lawyer, (July/August 1999): 25.

140. Brodie, Richard Nixon, 516.

141. Richard Nixon, In the Arena: A Memoir of Victory, Defeat, and Renewal (New York: Simon & Schuster, 1990), 36, 40.

142. Brodie, Richard Nixon, 503.

143. Schwartz, 7 Biggest Lies.

144. George W. Bush, Decision Points (New York: Crown, 2010), 257; Cannon, Untruth and Consequences.

145. Marc Thiessen, Obama's Dishonest Presidency, Washington Post, November 4, 2013; Peter Baker, Obama: The Call of History (New York: Calloway, 2017), 166.

146. Juliet Eilperin, President Obama Apologizes to Americans Who Are Losing Their Health Insurance, Washington Post, November 7, 2013.

147. Robert Costa and Amy Goldstein, Trump Vows "Insurance for Everybody" in Obamacare Replacement Plan, Washington Post, January 15, 2017. For excerpts of Trump's promises, see The Daily Show with Trevor Noah, March 15, 2017, http://www.cc.com/video-clips/pv7c2y/the-daily-show-with-trevor-noah-health-care-in-america-should-we-just-let-poor-people-die.

148. Congressional Budget Office, American Health Care Act, March 13, 2017.

149. Glenn Kessler and Meg Kelly, President Trump Has Made More than 2000 False or Misleading Claims over 355 days, Washington Post, January 10, 2018.

150. David Greenberg, Are Clinton and Trump the Biggest Liars Ever to Run for President?, Politico, July/August 2016, https://www.politico.com/magazine/story/2016/07/2016-donald-trump-hillary-clinton-us-history-presidents-liars-dishonest-fabulists-214024; The Mendacity Index: Ronald Reagan, Washington Monthly, September, 2003.

151. Bob Spitz, Reagan, 8, 477 (quoting Ken Khachigian).

152. Dom Bonafede, The Press and the Hollywood Presidency, Washington Journalism Review, January/February 1981; Barber, The Presidential Character, 493.

153. Greenberg, Are Clinton and Trump the Biggest Liars?

154. Rachel Black and Alteta Sprague, The Welfare Queen Is a Lie, The Atlantic, September 20, 2016; Guy Demby, The Truth behind the Lies of the Original Welfare Queen, NPR, December 20, 2013.

155. Rachel Martin, Listen: The Making of Clinton and Trump, NPR, September 1, 2016, http://www.npr.org/20126/09/01/492013444/the-making-of-clinton-and-trump.

156. The Choice, New Yorker, October 31, 2016, 32.

157. Rubén G. Rumbaut and Walter A. Ewing, The Myth of Immigrant Criminality and the Paradox of Assimilation: Incarceration Rates among Native and Foreign—Born Men (American Immigration Law Foundation, 2007). See chapter 4 of this book for a discussion of lower crime rates among immigrants than US citizens, as well as studies summarized in Associated Press, Calvin Woodward and Colleen Long, AP FACT CHECK: Trump and the Disputed Border Crisis, Associated Press, January 9, 2019.

158. Nicholas Kristof, Trump's Five Craziest Arguments about the Shtudown, New York Times, January 12, 2019; Woodward and Long, AP FACT CHECK; Salvador Rizzo, Fact-Checking President Trump's Oval Office Address on Immigration, Washington Post, January 9, 2019.

159. Don P. McAdams, The Mind of Donald Trump, The Atlantic, June, 2016.

160. Nicholas Kristof, Clinton's Fibs vs. Trump's Huge Lies, New York Times, August 7, 2016.

161. Kristof, Clinton's Fibs vs. Trump's Huge Lies.

162. Kessler and Kelly, President Trump Has Made More than 2000 False or Misleading Claims.

163. David Leonhardt, Ian Prasad Philbrick, and Stuart A. Thompson, Trump's Lies vs. Obama's, New York Times, December 14, 2017.

164. Eric Boehlert, Trump's Deep Character Flaws Will Define His Presidency: Media Should Focus Attention There, Media Matters, January 26, 2017, https://www.mediamatters.org/blog/2017/01/26/trump-s-deep-character-flaws-will-define-his-presidency-media-should-focus-attention-there/215139.

165. Michael D'Antonio, Never Enough: Donald Trump and the Pursuit of Success (New York: St. Martin's Press, 2015), 216.

166. Greenberg, Are Clinton and Trump the Biggest Liars?; E. J. Dionne Jr., Norman J. Ornstein, and Thomas E. Mann, One Nation after Trump: A Guide for the Perplexed, the Disillusioned, the Desperate, and the Not-Yet Deported (New York: St. Martin's Press, 2017), 63; David Frum, Trumpocracy: The Corruption of the American Republic (New York: Harper Collins, 2018), 80–81, 108.

167. Igor Bobic, The First 100 Lies: The Trump Team's Flurry of Falsehoods, Huffington Post, February 28, 2017, https://www.huffingtonpost.com/entry/donald-trump-administration-lies-100_us_58ac7a0fe4b02a1e7dac3ca6; Peter Baker and Steven Erlanger, Trump Offers No Apology for Claim on British Spying, New York Times, March 17, 2017; Kevin Johnson, FBI's Comey Says Obama Did Not Order

Wiretapping of Trump's New York Office, USA Today, March 29, 2017; Ryan Struyk, What We Know about Trump's Unsubstantiated Wiretapping Allegations against Obama, ABC, http://abcnews.go.com/Politics/trumps-unsubstantiated-wiretapping-allegations-obama/story?id=45948238.

168. Baker and Erlanger, Trump Offers No Apology.

169. Baker and Erlanger, Trump Offers No Apology (quoting Tim Farron).

170. David Folkenflik, When the White House Can't Be Believed, NPR, June 20, 2018, https://www.npr.org/2018/06/621876079.

171. Frum, Trumpocracy, 73.

172. Maria Konnikova, Trump's Lies vs. Your Brain, Politico Magazine, January/February, 2017.

173. Peter Baker, When Fiction Is a Fact of Life for the President, New York Times, March 18, 2018 (quoting Trump).

174. Nicholas Kristof, Is Trump Obstructing Justice?, New York Times, May 14, 2017.

175. James Comey, A Higher Loyalty (New York: Flat Iron, 2018), xi.

176. Michael Sherer, Can Trump Handle the Truth?, Time, April 3, 2017, 37.

177. Mike Mariani, In Trump's Amerika, Vanity Fair, April 2017, 100.

178. Barak Obama, 16th Annual Mandela Annual Lecture, Nelson Mandela Annual Lecture 2018: Obama's full speech, https://www.nelsonmandela.org/news/entry/nelson-mandela-annual-lecture-2018-obamas-full-speech Time, July 30, 2018, 4.

179. Konnikova, Trump's Lies.

180. Konnikova, Trump's Lies.

181. Konnikova, Trump's Lies; James Pfiffner, Trump's Lies Corrode Democracy, Brookings, April 23, 2018.

182. Dionne, Ornstein, and Mann, One Nation after Trump, 62.

183. Donald J. Trump with Kate Bohner, Trump: The Art of the Comeback (New York: Random House, 1997), 186.

184. Sherer, Can Trump Handle the Truth?, 39.

185. Bella M. DePaulo, Deborah A. Kashy, Susan E. Kkirkendol, Melissa M. Wyer, and Jennifer M. Epstein, Lying in Everyday Life, Journal of Personality and Social Psychology 70 (1996): 979, 986, 991.

186. T. Harry Williams, Huey Long: A Biography (New York: Alfred A. Knopf, 1969), 3.

187. For claims by Kennedy, Johnson, and Clinton, see Cannon, Untruth and Consequences. For the claim by Nixon, see Brodie, Nixon, 27. For the claim by Trump, see Julie Hirshfield Davis and Mathew Rosenberg, With False Claims, Trump Attacks Media on Turnout and Intelligence Rift, New York Times, January 21, 2017; Lori Robinson and Robert Farber, Fact Check: The Controversy over Trump's Inauguration Crowd Size, USA Today, January 24, 2017; and Kristof, Clinton's Fibs vs. Trump's Huge Lies.

188. John Dean, Worse than Watergate: The Secret Presidency of George W. Bush (Boston, Little Brown, 2004), 25.

189. George W. Bush, Decision Points (New York: Crown, 2010), 76.

190. James B. Stewart, Blood Sport: The President and His Adversaries (New York: Simon and Schuster, 1996), 318–319. For his lies to aids about the draft, see George Stephanopoulos, All Too Human: A Political Education (Boston: Little Brown, 1999), 269. For the nickname, see Denton, Moral Leadership, 68; Floyd Brown, "Slick Willie": Why America Cannot Trust Bill Clinton (New York: Mass Market Paperback, 1992). For extramarital affairs and marijuana use, see Denton, Moral Leadership, 68; Pfiffner, The Character Factor, 158; David Maraniss, First in His Class (New York: Simon and Schuster, 1995), 153–154; Renshon, High Hopes, 9; Bill Clinton, My Life (New York: Alfred A. Knopf, 2004), 404; Catalina Camia, Bill Clinton, I Told the Truth about Smoking Pot, USA Today, December 4, 2013.

191. Stewart, Blood Sport, 421.

192. Stewart, Blood Sport, 432.

193. John Dean, Worse than Watergate, 14–15.

194. Robert Shogan, The Double Edged Sword: How Character Makes and Ruins Presidents (Boulder, CO: Westview Press, 1999), 76.

195. Geoffrey C. Ward, A First-Class Temperament: The Emergence of Franklin D. Roosevelt (New York: Harper and Row, 1989), 781.

196. Cannon, Untruth and Consequences.

197. Richard Reeves, President Kennedy: Profile of Power (New York: Simon and Schuster, 1993), 24, 86.

198. Reeves, President Kennedy, 24

199. Robert Dallek, The Medical Ordeals of JFK, The Atlantic, December 2002, 60, 49.

200. Reeves, President Kennedy, 84.

201. See Deborah L. Rhode, Adultery: Sexual Infidelity and the Law (Cambridge, MA: Harvard University Press, 2016), 127–158.

202. Prior to the election of Donald Trump, a historical survey reported seventeen. Robert P. Watson, Affairs of State: The Untold History of Presidential Love, Sex, and Scandal, 1789–1900 (Lanham, MD: Rowman & Littlefield, 2012), 39. Trump's extramarital affairs have been widely reported. Howard Kurtz, Marla Has Her Say about Ivana, Washington Post, July 25, 1990. He has also boasted about his relationships with married women. See Deborah L. Rhode, Why Is Adultery Still a Crime?, Los Angeles Times, May 2, 2016, http://www.latimes.com/opinion/op-ed/la-oe-rhode-decriminalize-adultery-20160429-story.html (quoting Trump).

203. Robert Dallek, Lone Star Rising: Lyndon Johnson and His Times, 1908–1960 (New York: Oxford University Press, 1991), 189; Pamela Druckerman, Our Ready Embrace of Those Cheating Pols, Washington Post, July 15, 2007, B1.

204. Matt Bai, All the Truth Is Out: The Week Politics Went Tabloid (New York: Knopf, 2014), 29.

205. E. J. Dionne Jr., David Johnston, Wayne King, and Jon Nordheimer, Courting Danger: The Fall of Gary Hart, New York Times, May 9, 1987.

206. Ken Gormley, The Death of American Virtue: Clinton vs. Starr (New York: Crown, 2010), 10.

207. Denton, Moral Leadership, 69.

208. Paul Grey, Lies, Lies, Lies, Time, October 5, 1992, 34.

209. See Clinton, My Life, 385. Clinton later acknowledged the affair. Clinton, My Life, 387.

210. Denton, Moral Leadership, 11.

211. Shogun, The Doubled Edged Sword, 225.

212. Clinton Hires Attorney to Fend Off Sex Suit, Capital, May 5, 1994, A2. See Richard Lacayo, Jones v. The President, Time, May 16, 1994, 45.

213. Jeffrey Toobin, A Vast Conspiracy: The Real Story of the Sex Scandal That Nearly Brought Down a President (New York: Random House, 2012), 180.

214. Toobin, A Vast Conspiracy, 244.

215. Joseph R. Blaney and William L. Benoit, The Clinton Scandals and the Politics of Image Restoration (Westport, CT: Praeger, 2001), 85.

216. Deborah L. Rhode, Conflicts of Commitment: Legal Ethics in the Impeachment Context, Stanford Law Review 52 (2000): 269, 318.

217. Don Van Natta Jr., It Depends on What Your Definition of Linguistic Trend Is, New York Times, October 17, 1999, A27.

218. Maureen Dowd, Liberties; The Wizard of Is, New York Times, Sept 16, 1998, 24.

219. Peter Baker and Juliet Eilperin, Debate on Impeachment Opens, Washington Post, December 11, 1998, at A1 (quoting David Shippers).

220. For excerpts, see Peter Baker, The Breach: Inside the Impeachment and Trial of William Jefferson Clinton (New York: Scribner, 2012), 34; James Bennet, Testing of a President: The Overview: Clinton Admits Lewinsky Liaison to Jury: Tells Nation "It Was Wrong" but Private, New York Times, August 18, 1998, A1.

221. Baker, The Breach, 34.

222. Joseph R. Blaney and William L. Benoit, The Clinton Scandals and the Politics of Image Restoration (Westport, CT: Praeger, 2001), 99; CNN USA Today/Gallup Poll, August 17, 1998; Molly W. Sonner and Clyde Wilcox, Forging and Forgetting: Public Support for Bill Clinton during the Lewinsky Scandal, Political Science and Politics 32 (1999): 554, 557.

223. See CNN USA Today/Gallup Poll, Aug 17, 1998; Sonner and Wilcox, Forging and Forgetting, 556. For denial of character, see Hunter, The Politics of Character, vol. 3, at 8.

224. Robert Busby, Defending the American Presidency (New York: Palgrave Macmillan, 2001), 210.

225. See studies cited in Deborah L. Rhode, Adultery: Infidelity and the Law (Cambridge, MA: Harvard University Press, 2015), 146; Busby, Defending the American Presidency, 176.

226. Laura Kipnis, Against Love: A Polemic (New York: Pantheon, 2003).

227. Donald Trump with Kate Bohner, Trump: The Art of the Comeback (New York Times: Times Books, 1997), 116.

228. Daniel Victor, "Access Hollywood" Reminds Trump: "The Tape Is Very Real," New York Times, November 28, 2017.

229. Jelani Cobb, State of Resistance, New Yorker, February 12 and 19, 2018, 27; Jessica Estepa, Meet 19 Women Who Claim Affairs with Trump or Accuse Him of Unwanted Sexual Advances, USA Today, March 20, 2018.

230. For conflicting statements from Trump and his lawyer and spokespersons about the porn star payments, see Karen Yourish, Conflicting Statements about the Payment to Stormy Daniels, New York Times, May 3, 2018.

231. PRRI/Brookings Survey, October 19, 2016, https://www.prri.org/research/prri-brookings-oct-19-poll-politics-election-double-digit-lead-trump/; Sarah Posner, Amazing Disgrace, New Republic, March 20, 2017 (noting that 81 percent of evangelicals voted for Trump).

232. Charles M. Blow, Where Trump Succeeded, New York Times, June 3, 2018.

233. Thomas Nagel, The Shredding of Public Privacy, The New Republic, August 14, 1998, 15.

234. Bai, All the Truth Is Out, 23.

235. Emily Price, Trump Defends Rob Porter following Spousal Abuse Allegations, Fortune, February 9, 2018; Donald Trump's Guide to Presidential Etiquette, New York Times, May 27, 2018; John Greenberg, Timeline: Rob Porter, Domestic Abuse and the White House, PolitiFact, February 14, 2018, http://www.politifact.com/truth-o-meter/article/2018/feb/14/timeline-rob-porter-domestic-abuse-and-white-house/.

236. Renshon, Psychological Assessment, 385.

237. Geoffrey C. Ward, A First-Class Temperament: The Emergence of FDR (New York: Harper & Row, 1989), xv; Greenstein, The Presidential Difference, 77.

238. A Letter from GOP National Security Officials Opposing Donald Trump, New York Times, August 8, 2016.

239. Colby and Damon, Some Do Care, 198–199.

240. Greenstein, Presidential Difference, 68.

241. Jonathan Alter, The Promise (New York: Simon and Schuster, 2010), 149; David Remnick, The Bridge: The Life and Rise of Barack Obama (New York; Vintage, 2011), 206 (quoting Christopher Edley).

242. Malcolm Gladwell, Cocksure, New Yorker, July 27, 2009, 25.

243. Gladwell, Cocksure, 28; Alter, The Promise, 218.

244. David Garrow, Rising Star: The Making of Barack Obama (New York: William Morrow, 2017), 1073, 1077; Dana Milbank, Is This the End of the White House Insufferable Insularity?, Washington Post, March 29, 2015; Charles Lipson, Downward Spiral of Obama's Presidency, Chicago Tribune, June 17, 2014.

245. Remnick, The Bridge, 324; Baker, Obama, 99 (quoting Mitch McConnell on Obama's condescension).

246. Margaret Carlson, Smart President Fails Test at Ground Zero, Bloomberg, August 18, 2010; Remnick, The Bridge, 265.

247. Evan Thomas, A Long Time Coming (New York: Public Affairs, 2009), 187.

248. Barber, Presidential Character, 373.

249. Pfiffner, Character Factor, 82; Jam Joboe Russell, Lady Bird: A Biography of Mrs. Johnson (New York: Taylor Trade, 2004), 280 (quoting George Reedy claiming, "No one could express a doubt about anything, No one could tell Lyndon Johnson to go soak his head").

250. David Kaiser, American Tragedy: Kennedy, Johnson, and the Origins of the Vietnam War (Cambridge, MA: Harvard University Press, 2002), 407; Alterman, When Presidents Lie, 180–181.

251. Alterman, When Presidents Lie, 180–181.

252. Richard Greene, Is Donald Trump Mentally Ill? 3 Professors of Psychiatry Ask President Obama to Conduct a Full Medical and Neuropsychiatric Evaluation, Huffington Post, December 17, 2016, https://www.huffingtonpost.com/richard-greene/is-donald-trump-mentally_b_13693174.html.

253. Donald Trump's First-Week Scorecard: Character over Content, Financial Times, January 27, 2017; Josh Greenman, Twitter Tirades Are the Least of Trump's Character Problems, New York Daily News, January 19, 2017.

254. Don P. McAdams, The Mind of Donald Trump, The Atlantic, June, 2016; Michael Grynbaum, Trump Calls the News Media the "Enemy of the American People," New York Times, February 17, 2017.

255. Michael D. Shear and Katie Benner, Trump's War on the Justice System Threatens to Erode Trust in the Law, New York Times, August 25, 2018 (quoting former prosecutor Christopher Hunter).

256. Maggie Haberman and Glenn Thrush, Trump, Saying He Is Treated "Unfairly" Signals a Fight, New York Times, May 17, 2017. See also Frum, Trumpocracy, 121.

257. Evan Osnos, Only the Best People, New Yorker, May 21, 2018, 58.

258. Mark Landler and Glenn Thrush, Trump Denies Any Collusion between His Campaign and Russia, New York Times, May 18, 2017; Michael D. Shear, Comey's Memoir Offers Visceral Details on a President Untethered to Truth, New York Times, April 12, 2018.

259. McAdams, Mind of Donald Trump; David Cay Johnston, It's Even Worse than You Think (New York: Simon & Schuster, 2018), 232 (quoting Trump).

260. John Fund, Trump's Fatal Flaw, National Review, September 2, 2016; Evan Osnos, Endgames, 34.

261. Fund, Trump's Fatal Flaw.

262. Tara Palmeri, How Trump's Campaign Staffers Tried to Keep Him off Twitter, Politico, https://www.politico.com/story/2017/02/trump-twitter-staffer-235263.

263. Osnos, Endgames, 37 (quoting Christopher Rudd); Palmeri, How Trump Campaign Staffers Tried to Keep Him off Twitter.

264. Johnston, It's Even Worse than You Think, 7 (quoting Trump).

265. Palmeri, How Trump Campaign Staffers Tried to Keep Him off Twitter.

266. Bob Woodward, Fear: Trump in the White House (New York: Simon & Schuster, 2018), 220, 223.

267. Woodward, Fear, 211.

268. Woodward, Fear, xix, xxii; I Am Part of the Resistance inside the Trump Administration, New York Times, September 5, 2018.

269. Osnos, Endgames (quoting Blair).

270. Wike, Stokes, Pouster, and Fetterolf, U.S. Image Suffers.

271. Mark Singer, Trump vs. Trump, New Yorker, July 11 and 18, 2016, 27; see also Trump with Bohner, The Art of the Comeback, 191.

272. Woodward, Fear, 339.

273. Julie Hirschfeld Davis, Trump Again Falsely Blames Democrats for His Separation Tactic, New York Times, June 16, 2018; Glenn Kessler, Fact-Checking President Trump's USA Today Op Ed on "Medicare for-All," Washington Post, October 10, 2018; Louis Jacobson, Donald Trump's Pants on Fire Claim about Democrats, Pre-Existing Conditions, Politicfact, October 5, 2018, https: www.politifact.com/truth-o-meter/statements/2018/oct/05/donald-trumps-pants-fire-claim-about-democrats-prexisting-conditions.

274. Maureen Dowd, Trump vs. Press: Crazy, Stupid Love, New York Times, February 26, 2017, SR 9N.

275. Doris Kearns Goodwin, Teddy vs. Trump, Vanity Fair, November 2018, 76 (quoting Trump).

276. President Trump Says He Is Thankful for Himself This Thanksgiving, ABC7 Chicago, November 23, 2018, https://abc7chicago.com/politics/trump-thankful-for-himself-this-thanksgiving/4747330/.

277. Dowd, Trump vs. Press, SR 9N.

278. Brodie, Richard Nixon, 517.

279. Nixon, RM: The Memoirs of Richard Nixo, 245–246; Greenstein, The Presidential Difference, 210.

280. Brodie, Richard Nixon, 24, 424–425; Robert Haldeman with Joseph Di Mona, The Ends of Power (New York: Quadrangle Books, 1978), 74–75.

281. Brodie, Richard Nixon, 236.

282. Renshon, High Hopes, 100–101; Meredith L. Oakley, On the Make: The Rise of Bill Clinton (Washington, DC: Regnery, 1994), 4–5.

283. Stephanopoulos, All Too Human, 286–288.

284. Dick Morris, Behind the Oval Office (Los Angeles: Renaissance, 1999), xxiv.

285. Stephen J. Wayne, Presidential Personality: The Clinton Legacy, in Mark J. Rozell and Clyde Wilcox, eds., The Clinton Scandal (Washington, DC: Georgetown University Press, 2000), 217–218.

286. Renshon, High Hopes, 107.

287. Elizabeth Drew, On the Edge: The Clinton Presidency (New York: Simon and Schuster, 1994), 48.

288. Jann S. Wenner and William Greider, President Clinton: The Rolling Stone Interview, Rolling Stone, December 9, 1993, 81.

289. Randall B. Woods, LBJ: Architect of American Ambition (Cambridge, MA: Harvard University Press, 2007), 440, 442 (quoting Johnson).

290. Drew, On the Edge, 97–98.

291. Drew, On the Edge, 134–135.

292. Drew, On the Edge, 291.

293. Gail Sheehy, Character: America's Search for Leadership (New York: William Morrow, 1988), 281.

294. Spitz, Reagan, 582 (quoting Stu Spencer).

295. Greenstein, Presidential Difference, 150–151.

296. Sheehy, Character, 278

297. Spitz, Reagan, 736.

298. Noonan, Ronald Reagan, 218.

299. Michael D. Shear, Obama at Night: 7 Almonds and Solitude, New York Times, January 1, 2007; Alter, The Promise, 215.

300. Garrow, Rising Star, 1068; Lipson, Downward Spiral of Obama's Presidency.

301. Garrow, Rising Star, 1064.

302. Garrow, Rising Star, 1071 (quoting Washington Post reporter Paul Kane).

303. Fund, Trump's Fatal Flaw.

304. Fund, Trump's Fatal Flaw.

305. Robert Pear, Pushing for Vote on Health Care Bill, Trump Seems Unclear on Its Details, New York Times, May 1, 2017.

306. Johnston, It's Even Worse than You Think, 261 (quoting Trump).

307. Philip Bump, Trump Used to Have a Slightly Different Opinion of Presidents Playing Golf, Washington Post, February 20, 2017.

308. Dan Merica, Trump, Critic of Obama's Golfing, Regularly Hits the Links, CNN, March 20, 2017, https://www.cnn.com/2017/03/19/politics/trump-golf-weekends; Erin McCann, Trump Criticized Obama for Golfing. Now He Spends Weekends on the Links, New York Times, February 12, 2017.

309. Julie Hirschfeld Davis, Was Trump Golfing? White House Shrouds Time at His Clubs in Mystery, New York Times, March 19, 2017; Dan Merica, Trump, Critic of Obama's Golfing Regularly Hits the Links, CNN, March 20, 2017, http://www.cnn.com/2017/03/19/politics/trump-golf-weekends/.

310. Joe Zimmerman, Not a Good Look for Golf, New York Times, February 18, 2018.

311. Bump, Donald Trump's Golfing; Mark Landler, Trump Uses His Tee Times for a Mix of Diplomacy and Recreation, New York Times, February 17, 2017; Davis, Was Trump Golfing?

312. Lauren Carroll, How Much Do Donald Trump's Trips to Mar-a-Lago Cost?, Politifact, April 18, 2017, https://www.politifact.com/truth-o-meter/statements/2017/apr/18/center-american-progress-action-fund/how-much-do-donald-trumps-trips-mar-lago-cost/.

313. Donald Trump's Guide to Presidential Etiquette, New York Times, May 27, 2018.

314. Jane Mayer, Donald Trump's Ghostwriter Tells All, The New Yorker, July 25, 2016.

315. Louise Nelson, Trump: "I Don't Need Daily Briefings," Politico, December 12, 2016, http://www.politico.com/story/2016/12/trump-briefings-232479; Don Gonyea, What Exactly Is the "President's Daily Brief," and Why Is It Important?, NPR, December 13, 2016, http://www.npr.org/2016/12/13/505348507/what-exactly-is-the-presidents-daily-brief-and-why-is-it-important.

316. John Wagner, It's about the Attitude: Trump Says He Doesn't Have to Prepare Much for His Summit with North Korea's Leader, Washington Post, June 7, 2018 (quoting Trump).

317. Ashley Dejean, Exclusive: Classified Memo Tells Intelligence Analysts to Keep Trump's Daily Brief Short, Mother Jones, February 16, 2017; Michel Kruse, Donald Trump's Shortest Attribute Isn't His Fingers, Politico, September 8, 2016, http://www.politico.com/magazine/story/2016/09/donald-trump-attention-span-214223.

318. Johnson, It's Worse than You Think, 6.

319. Steve Haller and Jeff Mason, Embroiled in Controversies, Trump Seeks Boost on Foreign Trip, Reuters, May 18, 2017.

320. John Walcott, "Willful Ignorance": Inside President Trump's Troubled Intelligence Briefings, Time, February 18–19, 2019, 40.

321. Dejean, Exclusive: Classified Memo; Gabby Morrongiello, Trump Wants "as Little as Possible" in Intel Briefs, The Examiner, January 18, 2017, https://www.washingtonexaminer.com/trump-wants-as-little-as-possible-in-intel-briefs.

322. For Obama's briefings, which included dissenting views, see Dejean, Exclusive: Classified Memo.

323. Evan Osnos, Endgames, 44 (quoting William Kristol).

324. Marc Risher, Trusting His Brain and Gut, Trump Forgoes Heavy Reading, Washington Post, July 18, 2016.

325. The 2018 AP news interview in which Trump made these claims is available at https://www.apnews.com/a28cc17d27524050b37f4d91e087955e.

326. Johnston, It's Worse than You Think, 8, 41.

327. Comey, A Higher Loyalty, 237 (quoting Trump).

328. Matthew Nussbaum, Trump Touts His Temperament while Clinton Laughs, Politico, September 26, 2016, http://www.politico.com/story/2016/09/trump-clinton-no-stamina-look-228740.

329. Nussbaum, Trump Touts His Temperament.

330. Stephen Hess, Presidents and the Presidency (Washington, DC: Brookings, 1995), 39–45. See also Thomas Cronin and Michael A. Genovese, The Paradoxes of the American Presidency (New York: Oxford University Press 1998), 38.

331. Jon Meacham, Transcript of Obama Interview, Newsweek, September 1, 2008, 32.

332. ABC World News, November 1, 2007, quoted in Stephen J. Wayne, Personality and Politics: Obama for and against Himself (Washington, DC: CQ Press, 2012), 23.

333. J. Patrick Dobel, Managerial Leadership and the Ethical Importance of Legacy, in Denis Saint-Martin and Fred Thompson eds., Public Ethics and Governance: Standards and Practices in Comparative Perspective (Oxford: Elsevior, JAI Press, 2006), 201.

334. Renshon, Psychological Assessment, 187.

335. Renshon, High Hopes, 124.

336. Renshon, Psychological Assessment, 228.

337. Renshon, High Hopes, 41.

338. David Brooks, Goodness and Power, New York Times, April 28, 2015.

339. See, for example, Harold D. Lasswell, Psychopathology and Politics (Chicago: University of Chicago Press, 1930), 75.

340. Shogan, The Double-Edged Sword, 51 (quoting Herndon).

341. Shogan, The Double-Edged Sword, 51 (quoting Herndon).

342. Elihu Root, Lincoln as a Leader of Men, in Robert Bacon and James B. Scott eds., Men and Policies: Addresses by Elihu Root (Cambridge, MA: Harvard University Press, 1924), 75.

343. Doris Kearns Goodwin, Barack Obama and Doris Kearns Goodwin: The Ultimate Exit Interview, Vanity Fair Magazine, November (quoting Obama).

344. Cathleen Falsani, Obama Interview, Chicago Sun Times, March 27, 2004.

345. Sheryl Gay Stolberg, Obama Pushes Agenda despite Political Risks, New York Times, July 15, 2010.

346. Garrow, Rising Star, 1060; Randall Kennedy, The Persistence of the Color Line: Racial Politics and the Obama Presidency (New York: Pantheon Books, 2011), 22–24.

347. Kennedy, The Persistence of the Color Line, 273.

348. Garrow, Rising Star, 1065 (quoting Sheila Jaggar).

349. Peter Baker, Obama: The Call of History (New York: Callaway, 2017), 281 (quoting David Brooks).

350. Brodie, Richard Nixon, 377.

351. Richard Nixon, In the Arena: A Memoir of Victory, Defeat, and Renewal (New York: Simon & Schuster, 1990), 41.

352. Michael A. Genovese and Iwan W. Morgan, Introduction: Remembering Watergate, in Michael A. Genovese and Iwan W. Morgan eds., Watergate Remembered: The Legacy for American Politics (New York: Palgrave Macmillan, 2012), 13 (quoting Colson).

353. Paul Greenberg, No Surprises (Washington, DC: Brassey's, 1996), 23.

354. Renshon, High Hopes, 55.

355. Clinton, My Life, 63.

356. David Maraniss, Clinton's Life Shaped by Early Turmoil, Washington Post, January 26, 1992, A1, A17.

357. Clinton, My Life, 7.

358. Wayne, The Presidential Personality, 215. See also Michael Kelly, A Man Who Wants to Be Liked, New York Times, November 4, 1992, A1.

359. Drew, On the Edge, 233, 237–238.

360. Dick Morris, Behind the Oval Office (New York: Random House, 1997), 16.

361. Joel Brinkley, As Governor, Clinton Remade Arkansas in His Own Image, New York Times, May 31, 1992, A16.

362. Bob Woodward, The Agenda: Inside the Clinton White House (New York: Simon & Schuster, 2005), 225.

363. Wayne, The Presidential Personality, 230.

364. Elizabeth Drew, Showdown (New York: Simon & Schuster, 1996), 237 (quoting David Obey).

365. Renshon, High Hopes, 66, quoting Rudi Moore Jr., They're Killing Me out Here, in Ernest Dumas ed., The Clintons of Arkansas: An Introduction by Those Who Know Them Best (Fayetteville: University of Arkansas Press, 1993), 89.

366. Drew, On the Edge, 126.

367. Toobin, A Vast Conspiracy, 244.

368. Nixon, Leaders, 334.

369. Denton, Moral Leadership, 79; Louise Fisher, When Presidential Power Backfires: Clinton's Uses of Clemency, Presidential Studies Quarterly 32 (2002): 585, 586–599.

370. Editorial: Arkansas Secrets, New York Times, March 31, 1994, A20.

371. Clinton, My Life, 941.

372. Oakley, On the Make, 197; Renshon, High Hopes, 267; Renshon, Psychological Assessment, 297.

373. Renshon, Psychological Assessment, 305.

374. Drew, On the Edge, 113 (quoting Mark Gearan); Renshon, High Hopes, 270 (quoting Mark Gearan).

375. Renshon, High Hopes, 271.

376. Renshon, High Hopes, 268.

377. David Mendell, Obama: From Promise to Power (New York: Harper Collins, 2007), 103–104 (quoting Obama).

378. Stanley A. Renshon, Barack Obama and the Politics of Redemption (New York: Routledge, 2012), 177, 179.

379. Renshon, Barack Obama, 193.

380. Transcript, President Obama, CBS 60 Minutes, September 11, 2009, quoted in Renshon, Barack Obama, 193.

381. Renshon, Barack Obama, 246 (quoting Obama); Maureen Dowd, Can the Dude Abide?, New York Times, October 31, 2010, WK 9 (quoting Obama).

382. Resnhon, Barack Obama, 42; Jonathan Marin and Carol E. Lee, Obama to GOP: I Won, Politico, January 23, 2009.

383. Baker, Obama, 99 (quoting Mitch McConnell).

384. Shogan, Double-Edged Sword, 122.

385. Robert Dallek, Lyndon Johnson, in Robert A. Wilson ed., Character above All: Ten Presidents from FDR to George Bush (New York: Simon & Schuster, 1995), 112.

386. Robert Dallek, Flawed Giant: Lyndon Johnson and His Times (New York: Oxford University Press, 1999), 112 (quoting Senator Richard Russell of Georgia).

387. Dallek, Flawed Giant, 114 (quoting Andrew Young).

388. Dallek, Flawed Giant, 120.

389. Pfiffner, The Character Factor, 154. See also John A. Andrew III, Lyndon Johnson and the Great Society (Chicago: Ivan R. Dee, 1999).

390. Hendrik Hertzberg, Jimmy Carter, in Wilson, Character above All, 189.

391. Suri, The Impossible Presidency, 222.

392. Josh Greenman, Twitter Tirades Are the Least of Trump's Character Problems, New York Daily News, January 19, 2017; McAdams, The Mind of Donald Trump.

393. Frank Bruni, Me, Me, Me, Me, Me, New York Times, February 5, 2017, SR 3.

394. Chris Cillizza, That Time Donald Trump Held a Listening Session on Black History Month and Did Most of the Talking, Washington Post, February 1, 2017.

395. Bruni, Me, Me, Me, Me, Me.

396. Bruni, Me, Me, Me, Me, Me.

397. Bruni, Me, Me, Me, Me, Me.

398. Saunders, Trump Days, 50 (quoting Trump).

399. Francisco Alvarado and David A. Fahrenthold, At One Trump Golf Resort, Fake Time Magazine Covers Are Taken off the Wall, Washington Post, June 29, 2017.

400. Frank Bruni, Burying Humility, New York Times, January 22, 2017.

401. Jill Lepore, It Was Never Thus, New Yorker, September 3, 2018, 16.

402. Michael D'Antonio, Never Enough: Donald Trump and the Pursuit of Success (New York: St. Martin's Press, 2015), 241.

403. Johnston, It's Even Worse than You Think, 5.

404. Craig Froehle, I Finally Figured Out What Bothers Me Most about Donald Trump, December 17, 2016, https://medium.com/@Craig/i-finally-figured-out-what-bothers-me-most-about-donald-trump-fa20b523f45b#.4hvi2tz5e.

405. David Leonhardt, The People vs. Donald J. Trump, New York Times, January 6, 2019, SR2.

406. The Editorial Board, Pick Your Favorite Ethics Offender in Trumpland, New York Times, April 1, 2017.

407. The Editorial Board, Pick Your Favorite Ethics Offender.

408. Frum, Trumpocracy, 67–68; and Frank Bruni, Beware the Former Trumpers, New York Times, April 1, 2018.

409. Dionne, Ornstein, and Mann, One Nation after Trump, 85–86; Evan Osnos, Only the Best People; Nicholas Fandos, Government Ethics Chief Reigns, Casting Uncertainty over Agency, New York Times, July 6, 2017; Philip Bump, All the Reasons EPA Administrator Scott Pruitt Is under Fire (as of Now), Washington Post, April 5, 2018.

410. Julie Turkewitz and Coral Davenport, Leader of Interior Dept. Resigns under Cloud of Ethics Inquiries, New York Times, December 16, 2018, A1.

411. New York Times editorial (June 2017), quoted in Robert Reich, The Common Good, 119.

412. Frum, Trumpocracy, xvi.

413. https://www.cnn.com/videos/politics/2018/01/15/trump-says-least-racist-person-orig-alee.cnn/video/playlists/donald-trump-and-race/ (last visited February 17, 2019).

414. German Lopez, Donald Trump's Long History of Racism, Vox, January 14, 2018, https://www.lvox.com/2016/7/25/12270880/donald-trump-racism-history.

415. Lopez, Donald Trump's Long History. For discussion of the "shithole" characterization, see chapter 4 of this book.

416. Campaign 2016, PollingReport.com, http://www.pollingreport.com/wh16.htm (last visited February 17, 2019).

417. South Asian Americans Leading Together (SAALT), Communities on Fire (SAALT, 2018), http://salt.org/category/blog/hate-crimes (documenting a 45 percent rise in hate crimes and xenophobic political rhetoric against South Asians, predominantly Muslims); Southern Poverty Law Center, The Trump Effect: The Impact of the 2016 Presidential Election on Our Nation's Schools (Southern Poverty Law Center, 2017); Darryl Johnson, Report in Hate Violence Tied to 2016 Presidential Election (Southern Poverty Law Center, March 1, 2018), https://www.splcenter.org/hatewatch/2018/03/01/report-rise-hate-violence-tied-2016-presidential-election.

418. For the accused mail bomber's support for Trump, see Alan Blinder and William K. Rashbaum, Mail Bomb Suspect Had a List of 100 Potential Targets, Officials Say, New York Times, October 29, 2018. For Trump's tweet blaming the media, see John Wagner, Trump Renews Attacks on Media as "the True Enemy of the People," Washington Post, October 29, 2018.

419. NBC Maris Poll, November 2018, https://www.npr.org/2018/11/01/662730647/poll-nearly-4-in-5-voters-concerned-incivility-will-lead-to-violence. For experts, see Southern Poverty Law Center, The Trump Effect; Johnson, Hate Violence; and publications by the Dangerous Speech Project, https://Dangerousspeech.org.

420. Abraham Lincoln, First Inaugural Address, quoted in Robert Meacham, The Soul of America: The Battle for Our Better Angels (New York: Random House, 2018), 31.

421. Frank Newport, Americans Evaluate Trump's Character across 13 Dimensions (Gallup, June 25, 2018).

422. Steven Levitsky and Daniel Ziblatt, How Democracies Die (New York: Crown, 2018).

423. Steven Litvitsky and Daniel Ziblatt, Why Autocrats Love Emergencies, New York Times, January 13, 2019.

424. Reich, The Common Good, 161–162.

425. Michael Kranish and Marc Fisher, Trump Revealed: An American Journey of Ambition, Ego, Money and Power (New York: Scribner, 2016), 157.

426. Johnstone, It's Even Worse than You Think, 259.

427. Peter Baker and Ceilia Kang, Trump Threatens NBC over Nuclear Weapons Report, New York Times, October 11, 2017.

428. Baker and Kang, Trump Threatens NBC.

429. Frum, Trumpocracy, 122.

430. Dionne, Ornstein, and Mann, One Nation after Trump, 62.

431. Art Swift, Americans Trust in Mass Media Sinks to New Low (Gallup, September 14, 2016), https://news.gallup.com/poll/195542/americans-trust-mass-media-sinks-new-low.aspx.

432. Confidence in Institutions, Gallup Historical Trends, June 2016, http://www.gallup.com/poll/1597/confidence-institutions.aspx.

433. Nathaniel Persily, Can Democracy Survive the Internet?, Journal of Democracy 28 (2017): 63, 72. See Frum, Trumpocracy, xv, and Suri, Impossible Presidency, 221–222.

434. Thomas E. Patterson, News Coverage of the 2016 General Election: How the Press Failed the Voters (Cambridge, MA: Harvard Kennedy School Shorenstein Center on Media Politics and Public Policy, in Conjunction with Media Tenor, December 2016), 3.

435. Asawn Suebsaeng, Trump Aides Are Confounded by His Hospital Lie: He's Just, You Know, Doing His Thing, Daily Beast, September 28, 2017, https://www.thedailybeast.com/trump-aides-are-confounded-by-his-hospital-lie-hes-just-you-know-doing-his-thing.

436. Johnston, It's Even Worse than You Think, 41.

437. Roberto Stefan Foa and Yascha Mounk, The Democratic Disconnect, Journal of Democracy 27 (July 2016): 5, 8–9.

438. Meacham, The Soul of America, 13 (quoting Adams).

439. Charles Barsotti, New Yorker, October 21, 1972, 39, available in New Yorker Album of Drawings 1925–1975 (New York: Viking Press, 1975), http://www.the-new-yorker-album-of-drawings-1925-1975-cartoon-nion-s-no-dope.pdf.

440. Renshon, Psychological Assessment, 380.

441. Johnston, It's Worse than You Think, 233 (quoting Trump).

442. Jeremy W. Peters, As Critics Assail Trump, His Supporters Dig in Deeper, New York Times, June 23, 2018.

443. Suri, The Impossible Presidency, ix.

444. Meacham, The Soul of America, 14 (quoting Roosevelt).

445. Confidence in Institutions, Gallup Historical Trends, June 2016, http://www.gallup.com/poll/1597/confidence-institutions.aspx.

CHAPTER 6

1. See discussion in chapter 2 of this book and Christian B. Miller, Character and Moral Psychology, 229.

2. Colby and Damon, Some Do Care, 3.

3. Jane Addams, Twenty Years at Hull House: With Autobiographical Notes (New York: Macmillan, 2010), 11.

4. Louise W. Knight, Citizen: Jane Addams and the Struggle for Democracy (Chicago: University of Chicago Press, 2005), 22–25.

5. Knight, Citizen, 68.

6. Knight, Citizen, 2–3. See also Allen F. Davis, American Heroine: The Life and Legend of Jane Addams (Chicago: Oxford University Press, 1973).

7. Louise W. Knight, Jane Addams: Spirit in Action (New York: W. W. Norton, 2010), 52.

8. Knight, Jane Addams, 57–59.

9. Knight, Citizen, 166–174.

10. Knight, Citizen, 179–180.

11. Victoria Bissell Brown, The Education of Jane Addams (Philadelphia: University of Pennsylvania Press, 2004), 264, 266 (quoting Addams).

12. William Damon and Ann Colby, The Power of Ideals: The Real Story of Moral Choice (New York: Oxford University Press, 2015), 5, 34.

13. Jane Addams: A Foe of War and Need, New York Times, May 22, 1935.

14. Knight, Jane Addams, 253.

15. Knight, Citizen, 182.

16. Addams, Twenty Years at Hull House, 179.

17. Addams, Twenty Years at Hull House, 166–167.

18. Knight, Citizen, 225, 238, 279.

19. Knight, Jane Addams, 73.

20. Robert Wuthnow, Acts of Compassion: Caring for Others and Helping Ourselves (Princeton, NJ: Princeton University Press, 1991), 3–4. Jane Addams's account of her visit to Tolstoy is chronicled in Addams, Twenty Years at Hull House, 186–199.

21. Wuthnow, Acts of Compassion, 249.

22. Jane Addams, Trade Unions and Public Duty, American Journal of Sociology 4 (1899): 448, 450.

23. Eileen Maura McGurty, Trashy Women: Gender and the Politics of Garbage in Chicago, 1890–1917, Historical Geography 26 (1998): 27–43.

24. Knight, Citizen, 209–210.

25. Knight, Citizen, 264–265.
26. Brown, The Education of Jane Addams, 280.
27. Knight, Jane Addams, 88 (quoting Addams).
28. Knight, Jane Addams, 88.
29. Knight, Jane Addams, 152; Knight, Citizen, 379–381, 389–390.
30. Knight, Jane Addams, 142.
31. Knight, Jane Addams, 159.
32. Jill Conway, Jane Addams: An American Heroine, Daedalus 93 (Spring 1964): 761, 776.
33. Knight, Jane Addams, 162 (quoting St. Louis Republic).
34. Knight, Jane Addams, 227.
35. Knight, Jane Addams, 217–218.
36. Obituary, Jane Addams: A Foe of War and Need, New York Times, May 22, 1935.
37. Addams, quoted in Mary Louise Degen, The History of the Woman's Peace Party (B. Franklin 1939), 223; Knight, Jane Addams, 227.
38. Knight, Jane Addams, 257.
39. Jane Addams: A Foe of War and Need.
40. James Weber Linn, Interpretation of Life, Religious Education 32 (1937): 217, 221.
41. Albert Schweitzer, Out of My Life and Thought: An Autobiography, trans. Antje Bultmann Lemke (New York: Henry Holt, 1933, 1990 ed.), 2; George Marshall and David Poling, Schweitzer: A Biography (New York: Doubleday, 1971), 14.
42. Schweitzer, Out of My Life, 24–28; Reuters, Albert Schweitzer, 90, Dies at His Hospital, New York Times, September 6, 1965.
43. Albert Schweitzer, J. S. Bach, trans. Ernest Newman (London: Breitkopf & Hartel, 1911); Albert Schweitzer, The Quest of the Historical Jesus, trans. William Montgomery (London: A. & C. Black, 1910).
44. Reuters, Albert Schweitzer, 90, Dies at His Hospital.
45. Schweitzer, Out of My Life, 83–84.
46. Schweitzer, Out of My Life, 92.
47. James Brabazon, Albert Schweitzer: A Biography (New York: G. P. Putnam Sons, 1975), 172.
48. Schweitzer, Out of My Life, 86; Brabazon, Albert Schweitzer, 202.
49. Reuters, Albert Schweitzer, 90, Dies at His Hospital.
50. Religion: Reverence for Life, Time, July 11, 1949.
51. Religion: Reverence for Life.
52. Brabazon, Albert Schweitzer, 221; Schweitzer, Out of My Life, 112–113.
53. Brabazon, Albert Schweitzer, 224.
54. Schweitzer, Out of My Life, 115; Brabazon, Albert Schweitzer, 224.
55. Reuters, Albert Schweitzer, 90, Dies at His Hospital.
56. Schweitzer, Out of My Life, 137.
57. Marshall and Poling, Schweitzer, 115.

58. Albert Schweitzer, On the Edge of the Primeval Forest, trans. Charles Thomas Campion (London: A. & C. Black, 1922; New York Macmillan, 1948), 37.

59. Brabazon, Albert Schweitzer, 363–364.

60. Brabazon, Albert Schweitzer, 366; Religion: Reverence for Life, Time.

61. Marshall and Poling, Schweitzer, 302.

62. Brabazon, Albert Schweitzer, 288–289.

63. Brabazon, Albert Schweitzer, 294–295.

64. Erica Anderson, Albert Schweitzer, The Schweitzer Album: A Portrait in Words and Pictures (New York: Harper & Row, 1965), 40.

65. Reuters, Albert Schweitzer, 90, Dies at His Hospital (quoting Schweitzer).

66. Reuters, Albert Schweitzer, 90, Dies at His Hospital (quoting Schweitzer).

67. Anderson and Schweitzer, The Schweitzer Album, 146.

68. Words to Live By, This Week Magazine, November 29, 1950.

69. Brabazon, Albert Schweitzer, 344.

70. Brabazon, Albert Schweitzer, 345.

71. Brabazon, Albert Schweitzer, 383.

72. Brabazon, Albert Schweitzer, 387.

73. Brabazon, Albert Schweitzer, 388–389.

74. Brabazon, Albert Schweitzer, 397.

75. Religion: Reverence for Life, Time, June 11, 1949; "The Greatest Man in the World"—That Is What Some People Call Albert Schweitzer, Jungle Philosopher, Life, October 6, 1947, reprinted in Gwen Grant Mellon and Rhena Schweitzer Miller, Brothers in Spirit: The Correspondence of Albert Schweitzer and William Larimer Mellon Jr., trans. Jeanette Q. Byers (Syracuse, NY: Syracuse University Press, 1996).

76. Brabazon, Albert Schweitzer, 394.

77. Marshall and Polling, Schweitzer, 257; Brabazon, Albert Schweitzer, 431.

78. Brabazon, Albert Schweitzer, 432.

79. Brabazon, Albert Schweitzer, 483, 488.

80. Brabazon, Albert Schweitzer, 500.

81. Brabazon, Albert Schweitzer, 507.

82. Albert Schweitzer, Peace or Atomic War (New York: Henry Holt, 1958).

83. Reuters, Albert Schweitzer, 90, Dies at His Hospital.

84. John Gunther, Inside Africa (New York: Harper and Brothers, 1955), 698.

85. Brabazon, Albert Schweitzer, 433.

86. Brabazon, Albert Schweitzer, 371.

87. Schweitzer, On the Edge of the Primeval Forest, 51.

88. Brabazon, Albert Schweitzer, 371, 372; Gunther, Inside Africa, 709.

89. Brabazon, Albert Schweitzer, 433.

90. Reuters, Albert Schweitzer, 90, Dies at His Hospital.

91. Reuters, Albert Schweitzer, 90, Dies at His Hospital.

92. Reuters, Albert Schweitzer, 90, Dies at His Hospital.

93. Albert Schweitzer, More from the Primeval Forest, trans. Charles Thomas Campion (London: A. & C. Black, 1931), 53.

94. Brabazon, Albert Schweitzer, 375.

95. Schweitzer, On the Edge of the Primeval Forest, 97–98.

96. Brabazon, Albert Schweitzer, 374.

97. Religion: Reverence for Life, Time, July 11, 1949.

98. Brabazon, Albert Schweitzer, 413.

99. Reuters, Albert Schweitzer, 90, Dies at His Hospital.

100. Albert Schweitzer, Thoughts for Our Times ed. Erica Anderson (New York: Pilgrim Press, 1975).

101. Paul Williams, Critical Lives: Mother Teresa (Indianapolis, Alpha, 2002), 134.

102. Elizabetta Povoledo, Pope Francis Approves Sainthood for Mother Teresa, New York Times, March 15, 2016; Christopher Wells, Mother Teresa, Four Others, to Be Canonized, Vatican News Release, March 15, 2016.

103. Frank Newport, David W. Moore, and Lydia Saad, Most Admired Men and Women: 1948–1998, Gallup Organization, December 13, 1999; Frank Newport, Mother Teresa Voted by American People as Most Admired Person of the Century, Gallup, December 31, 1999.

104. Williams, Critical Lives: Mother Teresa, 20, 23; Jose Luis Gonzalez-Balado and Janet N. Playfoot, Mother Teresa: My Life for the Poor (New York: Ballantine, 1985), 1.

105. Kathryn Spink, Mother Teresa: A Complete Authorized Biography (San Francisco: Harper San Francisco, 1997), 9.

106. Joan Graff Clucas, Mother Teresa (New York: Chelsea House, 1988), 28–29.

107. Meg Greene, Mother Teresa: A Biography (Westport, CT: Greenwood Press, 2004), 25.

108. Clucas, Mother Teresa, 32; Greene, Mother Teresa, 25.

109. Spink, Mother Teresa, 21.

110. Williams, Critical Lives: Mother Teresa, 43.

111. Spink, Mother Teresa, 22.

112. Williams, Critical Lives: Mother Teresa, 49–50.

113. Spink, Mother Teresa, 28–30.

114. Williams, Critical Lives: Mother Teresa, 57–58.

115. Navin Chawla, Mother Teresa (London: Sinclair Stevenson, 1992), xv.

116. Chawla, Mother Teresa, 34–35.

117. Chawla, Mother Teresa, 41.

118. Williams, Critical Lives: Mother Teresa, 54–55.

119. Williams, Critical Lives: Mother Teresa, 57.

120. Williams, Critical Lives: Mother Teresa, 57–58.

121. Williams, Critical Lives: Mother Teresa, 61.

122. Gonzalez-Balado and Playfoot, Mother Teresa, 14 (quoting Mother Teresa).
123. Spink, Mother Teresa, 47.
124. Eric Pace, Mother Teresa, Hope of the Despairing, Dies at 87, New York Times, September 6, 1997.
125. Spink, Mother Teresa, 48.
126. Spink, Mother Teresa, 55.
127. The quotes are combined from Williams, Critical Lives: Mother Teresa, 69–70, and Chawla, Mother Teresa, 190.
128. Williams, Critical Lives: Mother Teresa, 82–83.
129. Williams, Critical Lives: Mother Teresa, 84.
130. Williams, Critical Lives: Mother Teresa, 87.
131. Spink, Mother Teresa, 123.
132. Williams, Critical Lives: Mother Teresa, 94–95.
133. Williams, Critical Lives: Mother Teresa, 99.
134. Williams, Critical Lives: Mother Teresa, 110–113.
135. Williams, Critical Lives: Mother Teresa, 97.
136. Spink, Mother Teresa, 204, 210.
137. Elizabetta Povoledo, With Mother Teresa Set to Be Canonized, Her Work Lives On in the Streets, New York Times, September 1, 2016 (claiming 139 countries); Sewell Chan, Pope Francis Clears Mother Teresa's Path to Sainthood, New York Times, December 18, 2015 (claiming more than 130 countries).
138. Spink, Mother Teresa, 235.
139. Spink, Mother Teresa, 135.
140. Spink, Mother Teresa, 147.
141. Spink, Mother Teresa, 257.
142. Kenneth J. Cooper, Mother Teresa Laid to Rest after Multi-Faith Tribute, Washington Post, September 14, 1997.
143. Spink, Mother Teresa, 189. See also Clucas, Mother Teresa, 17.
144. Pace, Mother Teresa, Hope of the Despairing.
145. Spink, Mother Teresa, 199.
146. Chawla, Mother Teresa, 132.
147. Spink, Mother Teresa, 218.
148. Chawla, Mother Teresa, 187, 206.
149. Mother Teresa, Nobel Lecture, Nobel Prize, December 11, 1979, https://www.nobelprize.org/nobel_prizes/peace/laureates/1979/teresa-lecture.html.
150. Williams, Critical Lives: Mother Teresa, 6.
151. Gonzalez-Balado and Playfoot, Mother Teresa, 63. For a similar quote see Chawla, Mother Teresa, 124.
152. Gonzalez-Balado and Playfoot, Mother Teresa, 68 (quoting Mother Teresa).
153. Germaine Greer, Independent Magazine, September 22, 1972.
154. Williams, Critical Lives: Mother Teresa, 77–79.

155. Williams, Critical Lives: Mother Teresa, 87.

156. Williams, Critical Lives: Mother Teresa, 145.

157. Christopher Hitchens, The Missionary Position: Mother Teresa in Theory and Practice (New York, Verso, 1995), 24.

158. Hitchens, The Missionary Position, 24.

159. Robin Fox, Mother Teresa's Care for the Dying, Lancet 344, no. 8929 (1994): 807, 808.

160. Williams, Critical Lives: Mother Teresa, 71–72.

161. Kai Schultz, A Critic's Lonely Quest: Revealing the Whole Truth about Mother Teresa, New York Times, August 26, 2016.

162. Hitchens, The Missionary Position, 43.

163. Christopher Hitchens, Mommie Dearest, Slate, October 20, 2003; Williams, Critical Lives: Mother Teresa, 209.

164. Hitchens, Mommie Dearest; Hitchens, The Missionary Position, 5; Williams, Critical Lives: Mother Teresa, 181, 184.

165. Spink, Mother Teresa, 248–249.

166. Hitchens, The Missionary Position, 11.

167. Spink, Mother Teresa, 246, 247.

168. Spink, Mother Teresa, 245.

169. Spink, Mother Teresa, 246, 247.

170. Spink, Mother Teresa, 89.

171. Spink, Mother Teresa, 87.

172. Spink, Mother Teresa, 86.

173. Charity Contributes to the Promotion of Dialogue, Solidarity, and Mutual Understanding among People, International Day of Charity, United Nations, September 5, 2013.

CHAPTER 7

1. James West Davidson, "They Say": Ida B. Wells and the Reconstruction of Race (New York: Oxford University Press, 2008), 13; Linda O. McMurry, To Keep the Waters Troubled: The Life of Ida B. Wells (New York: Oxford University Press, 1998), 4; Paula J. Giddings, Ida: A Sword among Lions: Ida B. Wells and the Campaign against Lynching (New York: HarperCollins, 2008), 11.

2. Ida B. Wells and Alfreda M. Duster eds., Crusade for Justice: The Autobiography of Ida B. Wells (Chicago: University of Chicago Press, 1970), 8; Mia Bay, To Tell the Truth Freely: The Life of Ida B. Wells (New York: Hill and Wang, 2009), 20.

3. Bay, To Tell the Truth Freely, 30.

4. Wells, Crusade for Justice, 16; McMurry, To Keep the Waters Troubled, 16.

5. Wells, Crusade for Justice, 17; McMurry, To Keep the Waters Troubled, 17.

6. McMurry, To Keep the Waters Troubled, 13; Davidson, "They Say," 50.

7. Wells, Crusade for Justice, 17; McMurry, To Keep the Waters Troubled, 16.

8. Wells, Crusade for Justice, 18–19; McMurry, To Keep the Waters Troubled, 26; Bay, To Tell the Truth Freely, 49.

9. Wells, Crusade for Justice, 61–63; Bay, To Tell the Truth Freely, 53.

10. Wells, Crusade for Justice, 19.

11. The Chesapeake, Ohio and Southwestern Railroad Company v. Ida B. Wells, quoted in Davidson, "They Say," 109; Wells, Crusade for Justice, 20; Bay, To Tell the Truth Freely, 55.

12. Davidson, "They Say," 100; Sarah L. Silkey, Black Woman Reformer: Ida B. Wells, Lynching and Transatlantic Activism (Athens: University of Georgia Press, 2015), 49–52.

13. Wells, Crusade for Justice, 24; Giddings, Ida, 75–76.

14. Giddings, Ida, 78.

15. Giddings, Ida, 81–83.

16. McMurry, To Keep the Waters Troubled, 128.

17. McMurry, To Keep the Waters Troubled, 107 (quoting Wells).

18. Davidson, "They Say," 103; Giddings, Ida, 85.

19. Giddings, Ida, 154–155; Bay, To Tell the Truth Freely, 45.

20. Wells, Crusade for Justice, 36. See Davidson, "They Say," 115, 118; Silkey, Black Woman Reformer, 52; Giddings, Ida, 167.

21. Wells, Crusade for Justice, 37.

22. Davidson, "They Say," 122.

23. Philip Dray, At the Hands of Persons Unknown: The Lynching of Black America (New York: Modern Library, 2003), 21.

24. Bay, To Tell the Truth Freely, 96.

25. McMurry, To Keep the Waters Troubled, 145.

26. McMurry, To Keep the Waters Troubled, 161 (quoting Wells).

27. Davidson, "They Say," 148. For coverage of the incident, see also Bay, To Tell the Truth Freely, 82–85; McMurry, To Keep the Waters Troubled, 130–135.

28. Davidson, "They Say," 138; Bay, To Tell the Truth Truly, 85.

29. Memphis Appeal Avalanche, quoted in Davidson, "They Say," 134; McMurry, To Keep the Waters Troubled, 134.

30. Wells, Crusade for Justice, 64.

31. Wells, Crusade for Justice, 52.

32. Bay, To Tell the Truth Freely, 103.

33. Davidson, "They Say," 154 (quoting Memphis Commercial).

34. Mob Law in Arkansas, New York Times, February 23, 1892, 4.

35. McMurray, To Keep the Waters Troubled, 143–146.

36. Davidson, "They Say," 162.

37. Giddings, Ida, 2.

38. Wells, Crusade for Justice, 66.

39. Giddings, Ida, 1; McMurry, To Keep the Waters Troubled, 148.

40. Wells-Barnett, United States Atrocities: Lynch Law (London: "Lux" Newspaper and Publishing Co., 1892), 1–3; McMurry, To Keep the Waters Troubled, 146–149; Wells, Crusade for Justice, 61–67.
41. Wells, Crusade for Justice, 63; Davidson, "They Say," 160.
42. Ida B. Wells, Southern Horrors: Lynch Law in All Its Phases, reprinted in The Selected Works of Ida B. Wells-Barnett, compiled by Trudier Harris (New York: Oxford University Press, 1991), 14, http://www.gutenberg.org/files/14975/14975-h/14975-h.htm.
43. Wells, Southern Horrors, 30; Davidson, "They Say," 161.
44. Wells, Southern Horrors, 26–28.
45. Wells, Southern Horrors, 42.
46. Giddings, Ida, 2–3. For the percentage of blacks in the population, see U.S. Bureau of the Census, Historical Census Statistics on Population Totals by Race, 1790 to 1990, Table 1 (Washington, DC: Bureau of the Census, 2002). .
47. Wells, Southern Horror, 1.
48. Giddings, Ida, 229.
49. Bay, To Tell the Truth Freely, 110; McMurry, To Keep the Waters Troubled, 170.
50. Wells-Barnett, United States Atrocities, 8–9, 10–13, 19–21, https://digitalcollections.nypl.org/collections/united-states-atrocities-lynch-law#/?tab=about.
51. Wells-Barnett, United States Atrocities, 19.
52. Wells, Crusade for Justice, 125.
53. Davidson, "They Say," 164–166.
54. Giddings, Ida, 245; Silkey, Black Woman Reformer, 126; McMurry, To Keep the Waters Troubled, 214.
55. Giddings, Ida, 316.
56. McMurry, To Keep the Waters Troubled, 153.
57. Wells, Crusade for Justice 187.
58. Bay, To Tell the Truth Freely, 6, 192, 198.
59. New York Times, Editorial, no title, July 27, 1894.
60. Giddings, Ida, 317.
61. British Anti-Lynchers, New York Times, August 2, 1894; Giddings, Ida, 318. See also Bay, To Tell the Truth Freely, 199.
62. Silkey, Black Woman Reformer, 149; Wells, Crusade for Justice, 220–223.
63. Ida B. Wells-Barnett, The Red Record: Tabulated Statistics and Alleged Causes of Lynching in the United States, reprinted in The Selected Works of Ida B. Wells-Barnett, compiled by Trudier Harris (New York: Oxford University Press, 1991), 138, 141.
64. Wells-Barnett, The Red Record, 150; Duster, Introduction to Wells, Crusade for Justice, xix.
65. Wells-Barnett, The Red Record, 157–171.
66. Giddings, Ida, 348.

67. Bay, To Tell the Truth Freely, 59 (quoting Wells); McMurry, To Keep the Waters Troubled, 56.

68. Giddings, Ida, 345–346.

69. Bay, To Tell the Truth Freely, 139; McMurry, To Keep the Waters Troubled, 183, 238.

70. Bay, To Tell the Truth Freely, 217.

71. Giddings, Ida, 353, 355, 358.

72. Giddings, Ida, 358.

73. Bay, To Tell the Truth Freely, 72, 218; McMurry, To Keep the Waters Troubled, 239.

74. Wells, Crusade for Justice, 251.

75. Wells, Crusade for Justice, 251.

76. Wells, Crusade for Justice, 248.

77. Giddings, Ida, 372, 375–376.

78. Wells, Crusade for Justice, 244–245.

79. Letter to the Editor, Chicago Times Herald, November 21, 1897.

80. Duster, Introduction to Wells, Crusade for Justice, xix.

81. Giddings, Ida, 383.

82. Giddings, Ida, 385, 413.

83. Wells, Crusade for Justice, 252.

84. Wells, Crusade for Justice, 255.

85. Giddings, Ida, 621.

86. McMurry, To Keep the Waters Troubled, 239 (quoting Blanche K. Bruce); Giddings, Ida, 396.

87. Duster, Introduction to Wells, Crusade for Justice, xxiii; Wells, Crusade for Justice, 251.

88. Wells, Crusade for Justice, 327, Davidson, "They Say," 168.

89. Wells, Crusade for Justice, 327, 297–306, 333, 410; Bay, To Speak the Truth Freely, 288–289; McMurry, To Keep the Waters Troubled, 293–298.

90. Wells, Crusade for Justice, 274–78, 345, 383–404; Davidson, "They Say," 168; Giddings, Ida, 444–445, 562–563; Bay, To Speak the Truth Freely, 293, 300–301; McMurry, To Keep the Waters Troubled, 303.

91. Wells, Crusade for Justice, 399.

92. Wells, Crusade for Justice, 398–404.

93. Wells, Crusade for Justice, 404. It is, however not clear how much credit goes to Wells-Barnett as opposed to the NAACP, which was responsible for the men's defense. See Bay, To Speak the Truth Freely, 313.

94. Davidson, "They Say," 169; Bay, To Speak the Truth Freely, 223, 228, 265, 273, 321, 327; Giddings, Ida, 416, 439–440, 476–78, 493–494, 501, 540, 632.

95. Giddings, Ida, 6, 301, 636.

96. Giddings, Ida, 6.

97. Giddings, Ida, 534.

98. Richard Lingeman, O Pioneer!, New York Times Sunday Book Review, May 18, 2008; Bay, To Tell the Truth Freely, 230.

99. McMurry, To Keep the Waters Troubled, 243, 329.
100. Duster, Introduction to Wells, Crusade for Justice, xxvii.
101. Giddings, Ida, 509; McMurry, To Keep the Waters Troubled, 289, 307. Wells-Barnett made the "petty outlook" comment to Susan B. Anthony in explaining why she didn't think women's suffrage would accomplish what supporters hoped.
102. McMurry, To Keep the Waters Troubled, 232 (quoting Blanche K. Bruce).
103. McMurry, To Keep the Waters Troubled, 295.
104. Bay, To Tell the Truth Freely, 9.
105. Giddings, Ida (quoting Mary White Ovington), 478.
106. Walter White, A Man Called White: The Autobiography of Walter White (New York: Viking Press, 1948), 45–46.
107. Giddings, Ida, 609.
108. Bay, To Tell the Truth Freely, 9.
109. McMurry, To Keep the Waters Troubled, 69.
110. Wells, Crusade for Justice, 286.
111. McMurry, To Keep the Waters Troubled, 333.
112. Bay, To Speak the Truth Freely, 264.
113. Illinois Women Feature Parade, Chicago Tribune, March 4, 1913; Illinois Women Participants in Suffrage Parade, Chicago Tribune, March 4, 1913.
114. Duster, Introduction to Wells, Crusade for Justice, xxix–xxx; Giddings, Ida, 658.
115. Giddings, Ida, 7; Bay, To Tell the Truth Freely, 11; McMurry, To Keep the Waters Troubled, xvi.
116. McMurry, To Keep the Waters Troubled, 338.
117. McMurry, To Keep the Waters Troubled, 338 (quoting Du Bois).
118. McMurry, To Keep the Waters Troubled, 339.
119. Wells, Crusade for Justice, 3.
120. Patricia J Williams, Exciting Dissatisfaction, May 28, 2018, 10.
121. Mohandas K. Gandhi: The Indian Leader at Home and Abroad, New York Times, January 31, 1948.
122. Louis Fischer, The Life of Mahatma Gandhi (New York: Harper and Brothers, 1950), 13.
123. Mohandas K. Gandhi: The Indian Leader at Home and Abroad.
124. Ramachandra Guha, Gandhi before India (New York: Vintage Books, 2013), 23.
125. George Orwell, Reflections on Gandhi, in George Orwell, A Collection of Essays (New York: Doubleday Anchor Books, 1954), 177, 182.
126. Orwell, Reflections on Gandhi, 182 (quoting Gandhi).
127. Guha, Gandhi before India, 32.
128. Mohandas K. Gandhi, Autobiography: The Story of My Experiments with Truth (New York: Dover, 1983), 50; Kathryn Tidrick, Gandhi: A Political and Spiritual Life (London: I. B. Tauris, 2006), 4.

129. Judith M. Brown, Gandhi, Mohandas Karamchand [known as Mahatma Gandhi] (1869–1948), Oxford Dictionary of National Biography (New York: Oxford University Press, 2004).
130. Brown, Gandhi.
131. Gandhi, Autobiography, 91–97.
132. Mahatma Gandhi, with Preface by Eknath Easwaran, Louis Fischer ed., The Essential Gandhi: An Anthology of His Writings on His Life, Work, and Ideas (New York: Vintage Spiritual Classics, 2nd ed. 2002), 32. See also Gandhi, Autobiography, 97.
133. Gandhi, The Essential Gandhi, 33–34
134. Gandhi, The Essential Gandhi, 337–338; Brown, Gandhi.
135. Gandhi, The Essential Gandhi, 40–41.
136. Gandhi, The Essential Gandhi, 45.
137. Arthur Herman, Gandhi and Churchill: The Epic Rivalry That Destroyed an Empire and Forged Our Age (New York: Bantam Books, 2008), 118.
138. Herman, Gandhi and Churchill, 137.
139. Gandhi, The Essential Gandhi, 50.
140. Tidrick, Gandhi, 81
141. Mohandas K. Gandhi, Satyagraha in South Africa (Ahmedabad, Gujarat; Navajivan Publishing House, 2008), 106.
142. Herman, Gandhi and Churchill, 153–154.
143. Herman, Gandhi and Churchill, 178.
144. Herman, Gandhi and Churchill, 158.
145. Ugo Caruso, "The Struggle of Right against Might": An Introduction to the Figure of Mahatma Gandhi, in Eva Pföstl ed., Between Ethics and Politics: Gandhi Today (New Delhi: Routledge, 2014), 8; Caruso, The Struggle of Right against Might, 20–21.
146. Satinder Dhiman, Gandhi and Leadership: New Horizons in Exemplary Leadership (New York: Palgrave Macmillan, 2015), 169.
147. Tidrick, Gandhi, 278.
148. Gandhi, The Essential Gandhi, 62.
149. Gandhi, Autobiography, 289.
150. Herman, Gandhi and Churchill, 116.
151. Herman, Gandhi and Churchill, 115.
152. Tidrick, Gandhi, 97.
153. Herman, Gandhi and Churchill, 131 (quoting Gandhi). For critiques of Gandhi's South African work, see Ashwin Desai and Goolam Vahed, The South African Gandhi: The Stretcher-Bearer of Empire (Stanford, CA: Stanford University Press, 2015).
154. Herman, Gandhi and Churchill, 131.
155. Mohandas K. Gandhi: The Indian Leader at Home and Abroad.

156. Tidrick, Gandhi, 103 (quoting Smuts); Herman, Gandhi and Churchill, 197 (quoting Smuts).

157. Pankaj Mishra, The Great Protestor, New Yorker (October 22, 2018), 83.

158. Gandhi, The Caste System, Young India, December 8, 1920, quoted in Ramachandra Guha, Gandhi: The Years That Changed the World, 1914–1948 (New York: Alfred A. Knopf, 2018), 119; W. H. Roberts, A Review of the Gandhi Movement in India, Political Science Quarterly 38 (1923): 227, 243.

159. Tidrick, Gandhi, 108–109.

160. Tidrick, Gandhi, 130.

161. Tidrick, Gandhi, 158.

162. Parekh, Gandhi, 13.

163. Brown, Gandhi.

164. Mohandas K. Gandhi: The Indian Leader at Home and Abroad; Roberts, A Review of the Gandhi Movement, 237.

165. Gandhi, The Essential Gandhi, 174.

166. Roberts, A Review of the Gandhi Movement, 229.

167. Gandhi, The Essential Gandhi, 182.

168. Brown, Gandhi; Roberts, A Review of the Gandhi Movement, 230.

169. Tidrick, Gandhi, 193.

170. Herman, Gandhi and Churchill, 361 (quoting Churchill).

171. Saint Gandhi: Man of the Year, 1930, Time, January 5, 1931.

172. Herman, Gandhi and Churchill, 359 (quoting Churchill).

173. Mohandas K. Gandhi: The Indian Leader at Home and Abroad.

174. Brown, Gandhi.

175. Bhikhu Parekh, Gandhi: A Very Short Introduction (New York: Oxford University Press, 1997), 16–17.

176. Tidrick, Gandhi, 258; Mohandas K. Gandhi: The Indian Leader at Home and Abroad.

177. Mohandas K. Gandhi: The Indian Leader at Home and Abroad; Gandhi, The Essential Gandhi, 241.

178. Gandhi, The Essential Gandhi, 244.

179. Mohandas K. Gandhi: The Indian Leader at Home and Abroad.

180. Gandhi, The Essential Gandhi, 119.

181. Lyn Norvell, Gandhi and the Indian Women's Movement, British Library Journal 23 (1997): 12.

182. Gandhi, A Twentieth Century Sati, Young India, May 21, 1931, quoted in Guha, Gandhi, 373.

183. Gandhi, The Essential Gandhi, 262–263.

184. Guha, Gandhi, 275, 277.

185. Bina Kumari Sarma, Gandhian Movement and Women's Awakening in Orissa, Indian Historical Review 21 (1994): 78, 85–92.

186. Norvell, Gandhi and the Indian Women's Movement, 12 (quoting Gandhi).
187. Sarma, Gandhian Movement and Women's Awakening, 78.
188. Sarma, Gandhian Movement and Women's Awakening, 78–79.
189. Robert Payne, The Life and Death of Mahatma Gandhi (New York: E. P. Dutton, 1969), 452; Herman, Gandhi and Churchill, 298; Arundhati Roy, The Doctor and the Saint: Caste, Race and Annihilation of Caste, the Debate between B. R. Ambedkar and M. K. Gandhi (London: Haymarket Books, 2017). For his later views, see Guha, Gandhi, 429–430, 722.
190. Tidrick, Gandhi, 110.
191. Tidrick, Gandhi, 111.
192. Barbara D. Metcalf and Thomas R. Metcalf, A Concise History of Modern India (New York: Cambridge University Press, 2006), 221–222.
193. Tidrick, Gandhi, 308–309.
194. Gandhi, The Essential Gandhi, 313; Tidrick, Gandhi, 309.
195. Herman, Gandhi and Churchill, 572.
196. Herman, Gandhi and Churchill, 573.
197. Herman, Gandhi and Churchill, 574.
198. Gandhi, The Essential Gandhi, 314–318.
199. Tidrick, Gandhi, 318–319.
200. Tidrick, Gandhi, 310.
201. Mahatma Gandhi, History, http://www.history.co.uk/biographies/mahatma-gandhi (last visited February 17, 2019); Tidrick, Gandhi, 323.
202. Herman, Gandhi and Churchill, 579.
203. Herman, Gandhi and Churchill, 582.
204. Pyarelal, Mahatma Gandhhi: The Last Phase,vol. 10 (Ahmedabad: Navajivan Publishing House), 575; Caruso, The Struggle of Right against Might, 39.
205. Herman, Gandhi and Churchill, 587; Judith M. Brown, Modern India: The Origins of an Asian Democracy (New York: Oxford University Press, 1985), 337.
206. Oyvind Tonnesson, Mahatma Gandhi, the Missing Laureate, Nobelprize.org, 1998–2000.
207. Dhiman, Gandhi and Leadership, 119.
208. Robert Payne, The Life and Death of Mahatma Gandhi, 16.
209. Gandhi, Autobiography, ix.
210. Orwell, Reflections on Gandhi.
211. Herman, Gandhi and Churchill, 447 (quoting Hitler).
212. Herman, Gandhi and Churchill, 447 (quoting Gandhi).
213. Herman, Gandhi and Churchill, 554.
214. Nirmal Kumar Bose, Selections from Gandhi: Encyclopedia of Gandhi's Thoughts (Ahmedabad: Navajivan Publishing House, 1950), 49 (quoting Harijan).
215. Gandhi, The Essential Gandhi, 306.
216. Gandhi, The Essential Gandhi, 141.
217. Mishra, The Great Protestor, 84.

218. Mishra, The Great Protestor, 84 (quoting Gandhi).

219. Gandhi, The Essential Gandhi, 268.

220. Orwell, Reflections on Gandhi.

221. Jeffrey Gettleman, Where Gandhi's Halo Is No Longer So Bright, New York Times, January 27, 2019.

222. Tidrick, Gandhi, 303–305, 315.

223. Dhiman, Gandhi and Leadership, 5.

224. Yogesh Chadha, Gandhi: A Life (New York: John Wiley & Sons, 1997), 1.

225. Allen Day Grimshaw, Racial Violence in the United States (Berlin: Walter de Gruyter, 1969), 58.

226. Charles L. Zeldon, Thurgood Marshall: Race, Rights, and the Struggle for a More Perfect Union (New York: Routledge, 2013), 12; Michael D. Davis and Hunter R. Clark, Thurgood Marshall: Warrior at the Bar, Rebel on the Bench (New York: Birch Lane Press, 1992), 41; Susan Low Bloch, Remembering Justice Thurgood Marshall: Thoughts from His Clerks, Georgetown Journal on Fighting Poverty 1 (1993): 8.

227. Juan Williams, Thurgood Marshall: American Revolutionary (New York: Random House, 1998), 44.

228. Zeldon, Thurgood Marshall, 13–14; Linda Greenhouse, Thurgood Marshall, Civil Rights Hero, Dies at 84, New York Times, January 25, 1993; Howard Ball, A Defiant Life: Thurgood Marshall and the Persistence of Racism in America (New York: Crown, 1998), 15.

229. Zeldon, Thurgood Marshall, 14; Larry S. Gibson, Young Thurgood: The Making of a Supreme Court Justice (Amherst, NY: Prometheus Books, 2012), 327.

230. Davis and Clark, Thurgood Marshall, 39; Richard Kluger, Simple Justice (New York: Vintage, 1975), 177.

231. Sources differ over whether she pawned her rings for college or law school tuition. For law school, see Zeldon, Thurgood Marshall, 18; Greenhouse, Thurgood Marshall; Kluger, Simple Justice, 179. For college, see Davis and Clark, Thurgood Marshall, 42.

232. Ball, A Defiant Life, 45.

233. Williams, Thurgood Marshall, 53, 56; Davis and Clark, Thurgood Marshall, 48; Kluger, Simple Justice, 180.

234. Gibson, Young Thurgood, 330.

235. Ball, A Defiant Life, 47.

236. Williams, Thurgood Marshall, 58–59.

237. Williams, Thurgood Marshall, 60; Gibson, Young Thurgood, 27; Kluger, Simple Justice, 182.

238. Zeldon, Thurgood Marshall, 27.

239. Zeldon, Thurgood Marshall, 29. See also Randall W. Bland, Private Pressure on Public Law: The Legal Career of Justice Thurgood Marshall, 1934–1991 (Lanham, MD: University Press of America, 1993), 10.

240. Kluger, Simple Justice, 214.

241. Davis and Clark, Thurgood Marshall, 76; Gibson, Young Thurgood, 156.

242. Zeldon, Thurgood Marshall, 27.

243. Gibson, Young Thurgood, 227.

244. Mark V. Tushnet, The NAACP's Legal Strategy against Segregated Education, 1925–1950 (Chapel Hill: University of North Carolina Press, 1987), 46; Greenhouse, Thurgood Marshall.

245. Greenhouse, Thurgood Marshall; Kluger, Simple Justice, 272.

246. Gilbert King, Devil in the Grove (New York: Harper Collins, 2010), 46 (quoting Evelynn Cunningham).

247. Ball, A Defiant Life, 71.

248. Davis and Clark, 21, 103; Zeldon, Thurgood Marshall, 39; Mark V. Tushnet, Lawyer Thurgood Marshall, Stanford Law Review 44 (1992): 1277, 1281.

249. Williams, Thurgood Marshall, 163 (quoting Marshall).

250. Williams, Thurgood Marshall, 106.

251. Williams, Thurgood Marshall, 127, 141; King, Devil in the Grove, 5, 20.

252. Williams, Thurgood Marshall, 104.

253. Zeldon, Thurgood Marshall, 41–42; Kluger, Simple Justice, 225–226; Bland, Private Pressure, 40.

254. Williams, Thurgood Marshall, 107. See also Davis and Clark, Thurgood Marshall, 108.

255. Kluger, Simple Justice, 224.

256. Williams, Thurgood Marshall, 203; Kluger, Simple Justice, 534.

257. Ball, A Defiant life, 72–91; Bland, Private Pressure, 37–60.

258. Ball, A Defiant Life, 77.

259. Ball, A Defiant Life, 109.

260. Williams, Thurgood Marshall, 172 (quoting Marshall); Davis and Clark, Thurgood Marshall, 128 (quoting Marshall).

261. Williams, Thurgood Marshall, 286.

262. Ball, A Defiant Life, 73. See Kluger, Simple Justice, 257.

263. King, Devil in the Grove, 186. The NAACP brought a successful challenge in Sweatt v. Painter, 339 U.S. 629 (1950).

264. Bland, Private Pressure, 61; Kluger, Simple Justice, 259; Sipuel v. Board of Regents of the University of Oklahoma, 332 U.S. 631 (1948).

265. Ball, A Defiant Life, 74.

266. The case was McLauren v. Oklahoma, 339 U.S. 637 (1950). See Ball A Defiant Life, 75.

267. Ball, A Defiant Life, 75 (quoting Vinson).

268. Ball, A Defiant Life, 93; Zeldon, Thurgood Marshall, 70.

269. Zeldon, Thurgood Marshall, 68.

270. Kluger, Simple Justice, 535 (quoting John Frank).

271. Ball, A Defiant Life, 93 (quoting Marshall).

272. Kluger, Simple Justice, 656 (quoting Frankfurter).

273. Kluger, Simple Justice, 618.

274. Davis and Clark, Thurgood Marshall, 23 (quoting Franklin); Kluger, Simple Justice, 636 (quoting Franklin).

275. Kluger, Simple Justice, 642.

276. Brown v. Board of Education, 347 U.S. 483 (1954).

277. Zeldon, Thurgood Marshall, 86.

278. Kluger, Simple Justice, 714.

279. Williams, Thurgood Marshall, 231.

280. Brown v. Board of Education, 349 U.S. 294 (1955).

281. Kluger, Simple Justice, 747 (quoting Marshall).

282. Kluger, Simple Justice, 753.

283. Zeldon, Thurgood Marshall, 102.

284. Bland, Private Pressure on Public Law, 106–111.

285. Ball, A Defiant Life, 142–144; Davis and Clark, Thurgood Marshall, 185.

286. Davis and Clark, Thurgood Marshall, 197.

287. Zeldon, Thurgood Marshall, 105.

288. Williams, Thurgood Marshall, 263.

289. Excerpts from Oral Argument in Little Rock School Case, New York Times, September 12, 1958, A12–13.

290. Ball, A Defiant Life, 150 (quoting Marshall).

291. Thurgood Marshall, Brainwashing with a Vengeance, Address to the Virginia State Conference of NAACP Branches, Charlottesville, VA, October 9, 1955 (NAACP papers, Part II A 536, Folder 6).

292. Ball, A Defiant Life, 209 (quoting Marshall); Williams, Thurgood Marshall, 344 (quoting Marshall).

293. Davis and Clark, Thurgood Marshall, 214.

294. Zelden, Thurgood Marshall, 119 (quoting Marshall).

295. Mark V. Tushnet, The Meritocratic Egalitarianism of Thurgood Marshall, Howard Law Journal 52 (2009): 691, 707.

296. Ball, A Defiant Life, 174. The case was Garner v. Louisiana, 368 U.S. 157 (1961).

297. Williams, Thurgood Marshall, 278; Davis and Clark, Thurgood Marshall, 249.

298. Rebecca L. Brown, Deep and Wide: Justice Marshall's Contribution to Constitutional Law, Howard Law Journal 52 (2009): 637, 638.

299. Davis and Clark, Thurgood Marshall, 235 (quoting Marshall).

300. Ball, A Defiant Life, 174 (quoting Marshall); Zelden, Thurgood Marshall, 123 (quoting Marshall).

301. Zelden, Thurgood Marshall, 127 (quoting Marshall).

302. Davis and Clark, Thurgood Marshall, 235 (quoting Eastland); Ball, A Defiant Life, 175 (quoting Eastland).

303. Deborah L. Rhode, Letting the Law Catch Up, Stanford Law Review 44 (1992): 1259, 1265 (quoting Marshall). For similar versions of this story, see Williams, Thurgood Marshall, 304; Zelden, Thurgood Marshall, 133; and Ralph K. Winter, TM's Legacy, Yale Law Journal 101 (1991): 25, 29.

304. Williams, Thurgood Marshall, 105–106. See also Zelden, Thurgood Marshall, 132.

305. Zelden, Thurgood Marshall, 131.

306. Owen Fiss, Pillars of Justice: Lawyers and the Liberal Tradition (Cambridge, MA: Harvard University Press, 2017), 27,

307. Zelden, Thurgood Marshall, 137.

308. Carl T. Rowan, Dream Makers, Dream Breakers: The World of Justice Thurgood Marshall (Boston: Little Brown and Co., 1993), 287–288.

309. Ball, A Defiant Life, 193–194.

310. Marshall to the Court, New York Times, June 14, 1967, 46.

311. Bland, Private Pressure, 23; Andrew Rosenthal, Marshall Retires from High Court; Blow to Liberals, New York Times, June 28, 1991, A1, A13.

312. Kite Flying and Other Games, Time Magazine, July 28, 1967, 22; Ball, A Defiant Life, 196.

313. Ball, A Defiant Life, 200.

314. Owen Fiss, Pillars of Justice: Lawyers and the Liberal Tradition (Cambridge, MA: Harvard University Press, 2017), 25; Davis and Clark, Thurgood Marshall, 373.

315. Paul Gewirtz, Thurgood Marshall, in Roger Goldman with David Gallen eds., Thurgood Marshall: Justice for All (New York: Carroll & Graff, 1992), 109.

316. City of Richmond v. J. A. Croson Co., 488 U.S. 469, 558 (1989) (Marshall, J., dissenting).

317. Byron R. White, A Tribute to Justice Thurgood Marshall, Stanford Law Review 44 (1992): 1215–1216.

318. United States v. Kras, 409 U.S. 434 (1973).

319. Kras, 409 U.S. at 459–460 (Marshall, J., dissenting).

320. Kras, 409 U.S. at 460.

321. Sandra Day O'Connor, Thurgood Marshall: The Influence of a Raconteur, Stanford Law Review 44 (1992): 1217–1218.

322. William J. Brennan Jr., A Tribute to Justice Thurgood Marshall, Harvard Law Review 105 (1991): 23–24.

323. Davis and Clark, Thurgood Marshall, 370; Rhode, Letting the Law Catch Up, 1264; Haley Sweetland Edwards, A Voice for the Voiceless, Time, Special Edition, 2017, 60.

324. Thurgood Marshall, Reflections on the Bicentennial of the United States Constitution, Harvard Law Review 101 (1987): 1, 5.

325. Thurgood Marshall, Law and the Quest for Equality, Washington University Law Review (1967): 1, 7.

326. Dale Russakoff, Tribute to Marshall: City of Baltimore Dedicates a Statue to 1st Native Son on High Court, Washington Post, May 17, 1980, at C1.

327. Greenhouse, Thurgood Marshall (quoting Kathleen Sullivan).

328. Williams, Thurgood Marshall, 347–348.

329. Fiss, Pillars of Justice, 27 (quoting Marshall).

330. For discussion of the criticisms of Justice Powell and other justices' law clerks, see Bob Woodward and Scott Armstrong, The Brethren: Inside the Supreme Court (New York: Simon & Schuster, 1979), 197, 258.

331. Davis and Clark, Thurgood Marshall, 379 (quoting Marshall).

332. Nat Hentoff, Thurgood Marshall and the Chief, Village Voice, March 9, 1993 (quoting Rehnquist); Williams, Thurgood Marshall, 397 (quoting Rehnquist).

333. Excerpts from Marshall News Conference, Los Angeles Times, June 29, 1991, A23.

334. Janet Cooper Alexander, TM, Stanford Law Review 44 (1992): 1231, 1233.

335. Stuart Taylor, Glimpses of the Least Pretentious of Men, Legal Times, February 8, 1993, 36.

336. Bill Keller, Nelson Mandela, South Africa's Liberator as Prisoner and President, Dies at 95, New York Times, December 5, 2013; Nelson Mandela, Long Walk to Freedom: The Autobiography of Nelson Mandela (Boston: Little, Brown and Co., 1994), 3.

337. Mandela, Long Walk, 6 (insubordination); Anthony Sampson, Mandela: The Authorized Biography (London: HarperCollins, 1999), 4 (insubordination). Court records suggest the explanation was corruption. David James Smith, Young Mandela: The Revolutionary Years (London: Weidenfeld & Nicolson, 2010), 21–22; Joanne B. Ciulla, Essay: Searching for Mandela: The Saint as a Sinner Who Keeps on Trying, in Donna Ladkin and Chellie Spiller, Authentic Leadership: Clashes, Convergences, and Coalescences (Cheltenham, UK: Edward Elgar, 2013), 163.

338. Mandela, Long Walk, 3.

339. Keller, Nelson Mandela.

340. Mandela, Long Walk, 27–45; Sampson, Mandela, 17–21; Smith, Young Mandela, 31–34.

341. Sampson, Mandela, 26–27; Smith, Young Mandela, 34–35; Martin Meredith, Mandela: A Biography (New York: Public Affairs, 2010), 19–20; Robert Mnookin, Bargaining with the Devil: When to Negotiate: When to Fight (New York: Simon and Schuster, 2010), 112.

342. Mandela, Long Walk, 100; Sampson, Mandela, 34; Smith, Young Mandela, 44.

343. Sampson, Mandela, 35–37.

344. Mnookin, Bargaining with the Devil, 113.

345. Corrections, New York Times, December 24, 2013; Keller, Nelson Mandela; Mandela, Long Walk, 130.

346. Mandela, Long Walk, 131–132; Sampson, Mandela, 77–78.

347. Sampson, Mandela, 80.

348. Lamb, Mandela, 63; Mandela, Long Walk, 377–380; Sampson, Mandela, 143; Smith, Young Mandela, 178.

349. Mandela, Long Walk, 231–246; Sampson, Mandela, 151.

350. Mandela, Long Walk, 246.

351. A Brief History of the African National Congress, https://www.sahistory.org.za/topic/african-national-congress-timeline-1960-1969 (last visited February 17, 2019).

352. Sampson, Mandela, 169.

353. Smith, Young Mandela, 181.

354. Sampson, Mandela, 448.

355. Meredith, Mandela, 261–262.

356. Lamb, Mandela, 76; Keller, Mandela.

357. Meredith, Mandela, 268, 271.

358. Keller, Nelson Mandela.

359. Sampson, Mandela, 207.

360. Mandela, Long Walk, 348–349; Sampson, Mandela, 205; Meredith, Mandela, 283.

361. Tom Lodge, Mandela: A Critical Life (New York: Oxford University Press, 2006), 122; Meredith, Mandela, 239.

362. Mandela, Long Walk, 343–344.

363. Keller, Mandela.

364. Keller, Mandela.

365. Sampson, Mandela, 236–241; 288–294; Meredith, Mandela, 292–295.

366. Meredith, Mandela, 312.

367. Meredith, Mandela, 310.

368. Keller, Mandela.

369. Keller, Mandela.

370. Lamb, Mandela, 91.

371. F. W. de Klerk, The Last Trek: A New Beginning (London: Macmillan, 1998), 157; Meredith, Mandela, 339.

372. Ciulla, Essay: Searching for Mandela, 155.

373. Lamb, Mandela, 147,

374. Meredith, Mandela, 352.

375. John Kane, The Politics of Moral Capital (Cambridge: Cambridge University Press), 137.

376. Mandela, Long Walk, 406.

377. Mnookin, Bargaining with the Devil, 121.

378. Meredith, Mandela, 397; Kane, The Politics of Moral Capital, 138.

379. For his statement to the crowds, see de Klerk, The Last Trek, 169–170.

380. Mandela, Long Walk, 495. See also Meredith, Mandela, 402.

381. Tahman Bradley, Bill Clinton Invokes the "Bad Dreams" of a Former P.O.W., AP News, July 6, 2008.

382. Sampson, Mandela, 533 (quoting Graca Machel).

383. Meredith, Mandela, 410; Lodge, Mandela, 198.

384. Mandela, Long Walk, 498–499. See also Meredith, Mandela, 405–407.

385. Sampson, Mandela, 457.

386. Mandela, Long Walk, 501.

387. Mandela, Long Walk, 503.

388. Sampson, Mandela, 469.

389. Meredith, Mandela, 478.

390. de Klerk, The Last Trek, 223–224, 300–301, 332, 352.

391. Lance Morrow, To Conquer the Past, Time, January 3, 1994, at 36.

392. Paul Gray, Nelson Mandela and F. W. de Klerk, Time, January 3, 1994, at 54.

393. Meredith, Mandela, 494.

394. Meredith, Mandela, 493.

395. Mandela, Long Walk, 537–538; Sampson, Mandela, 489; Meredith, Mandela, 501.

396. Sampson, Mandela, 490.

397. Sampson, Mandela, 492; Meredith, Mandela, 514.

398. Mandela, Long Walk, 542–543.

399. Robyn Curnow, Mandela Talks with CNN, July 18, 2008, discussed in Ciulla, Essay: Searching for Mandela, 155.

400. Meredith, Mandela, 518–519.

401. Sampson, Mandela, 515.

402. Lamb, Mandela, 213.

403. Sampson, Mandela, 495–496; Meredith, Mandela, 574–575; Lodge, Mandela, 213.

404. Sampson, Mandela, 523–524.

405. Meredith, Mandela, 535–526.

406. Keller, Mandela. See also Lodge, Mandela, 212; Sampson, Mandela, 524.

407. de Klerk, The Last Trek, 346.

408. Meredith, Mandela, 526.

409. Keller, Mandela.

410. Meredith, Mandela, 561–564.

411. Pierre de Vos, To Call Mandela a Saint Is to Dishonor His Memory, Daily Maverick, December 6, 2013, https://www.dailymaverick.co.za/opinionista/2013-12-06-to-call-mandela-a-saint-is-to-dishonour-his-memory/#.WnjSJq6nFhE.

412. The order was later criticized by the Supreme Court. de Vos, To Call Mandela a Saint.

413. de Vos, To Call Mandela a Saint.

414. Sampson, Mandela, 499.

415. Kane, The Politics of Moral Capital, 145.

416. Meredith, Mandela, 546–548. For criticisms, see also de Klerk, The Last Trek, 350, 353–54, and Kane, The Politics of Moral Capital, 140.

417. Sampson, Mandela, 565, 584.

418. de Klerk, The Last Trek, 352.

419. Lodge, Mandela, 206; Meredith, Mandela, 565–571: Sampson, Mandela, 510, 573.
420. Meredith, Mandela, 585.
421. Lodge, Mandela, 219–220; Meredith, Mandela, 584–586.
422. Lodge, Mandela, 209.
423. Keller, Mandela.
424. de Klerk, The Last Trek, 346.
425. Meredith, Mandela, 482.
426. Richard Stengel, Nelson Mandela: Portrait of an Extraordinary Man (New York: Virgin, 2012), 1. See also Ciulla, Essay: Searching for Mandela, 168.
427. Meredith, Mandela, 577.
428. John Battersby, Afterword: Living Legend, Living Statue, in Sampson, Mandela, 598; Meredith Mandela, 593.
429. Remarks by President Obama at Memorial Service for Former South African President Nelson Mandela, December 10, 2013 (Washington, DC: White House Press Office).
430. Remarks by President Obama.
431. Meredith, Mandela, 573.
432. Alexander Abad-Santosabby and Ohlheisersara Morrison, Nelson Mandela, "The Epicenter of Our Time," Has Died, Atlantic, December 5, 2013 (quoting Mandela).
433. Remarks by Obama (quoting Mandela), also quoted in Hope Is a Powerful Weapon: Letters from Prison, New York Times, July 8, 2018.

CHAPTER 8

1. Josephson Institute Center for Youth Ethics, 2012 Report Card on the Ethics of American Youth (Los Angeles: Josephson Institute of Ethics, 2012); James Davison Hunter, The Politics of Character: Survey of American Public Culture (Charlottesville: Institute for Advanced Studies in Culture, University of Virginia, 2000), 3.
2. For leaders, see James M. Kouzes and Barry Z. Posner, The Leadership Challenge (San Francisco: Jossey Bass, 2007), 226 (honesty); Warren Bennis, On Becoming a Leader (Philadelphia: Warren Bennis, 1994), 40–41 (integrity, trust); Mihaly Csikszentmihalyi, Good Business: Leadership, Flow, and the Making of Meaning (New York: Viking, 1st ed., 2003), 157 (integrity); Robert Hogan and Robert B. Kaiser, What We Know about Leadership, Review of General Psychology 9 (2005): 169, 172 (integrity); Robert W. Cullen, The Leading Lawyer: A Guide to Practicing Law and Leadership (Eagen, MN: Thomas Reuters/West, 2010), 34–41 (integrity); Montgomery Van Wart, Dynamics of Leadership in Public Service: Theory and Practice (New York: Taylor and Francis, 2005), 112–114 (integrity and an ethic of public service). For presidents, Democrats ranked honesty first, and Republicans second. Stefan Hankin and Rasto Ivanic, What Voters

Most Want: Honesty or Intelligence?, Washington Monthly, October 19, 2015, https://washingtonmonthly.com/2015/10/19/what-voters-most-want-honesty-or-intelligence/.

3. Pew Research Center, Beyond Distrust: How Americans View Their Government, Pew, November 23, 2015 (29 percent think elected officials are honest, 22 percent think they put country first), http://www.people-press.org/20-15/11/23/beyond-distrust-how-americans-view-their-government/.

4. Gallup, Honesty/Ethics in Professions, http://www.gallup.com/poll/1654/honesty-ethics-professions.aspx (last visited February 17, 2019).

5. Gallup, Honesty/Ethics in Professions; Harris Interactive, The Harris Poll Annual Confidence Index Rises 10 Points, Business Wire, March 5, 2009, http://www.businesswire.com/news/home/20090305005071/en/Harris-Poll%C2%AE-Annual-Confidence-Index-Rises-10.

6. Stefan Hankin and Rasto Ivanic, What Voters Most Want.

7. Julia Manchester, Poll: Just 13 Percent of America Consider Trump Honest and Trustworthy, The Hill, May 17, 2018; Mark Blumenthal, The Underpinnings of Donald Trump's Approval Rating, Huffington Post, February 11, 2017, https://www.huffingtonpost.com/entry/the-underpinnings-of-donald-trumps-approval-rating_us_589e4206e4b080bf74f03c20.

8. Brooks, The Road to Character, xi.

9. See Twenge and Campbell, The Narcissism Epidemic, 253.

10. U.S. Department of Labor, Volunteering in the United States, 2015, Bureau of Labor Statistics News Release, February 25, 2016.

11. Pew Research Center, Beyond Distrust.

12. Pelin Kesebir and Selin Kesebir, The Cultural Salience of Moral Character and Virtue Declined in Twentieth Century America, Journal of Positive Psychology 7 (2012): 471; Brooks, The Road to Character, 258.

13. William Miller, Death of a Genius: His Fourth Dimension, Time, Overtakes Einstein, Life, May 2, 1955, https://quoteinvestigator.com/2017/11/20/value.

14. Twenge and Campbell, The Narcissism Epidemic, 270. See also Craig Kielburger and Marc Kielburger, Me to We, https://www.metowe.com/ (last visited February 17, 2019).

15. Diane Barthel, Putting on Appearances: Gender and Advertising (Philadelphia: Temple University Press, 1988), 137 (quoting Baudrillard). See also Deborah L. Rhode, The Beauty Bias (New York: Oxford University Press, 2010), 160.

16. Maria Luisa Martinez-Marti and Willibald Ruch, Character Strengths Predict Resilience over and above Positive Affect, Self-Efficacy, Optimism, Social Support, Self-Esteem and Life Satisfaction, Journal of Positive Psychology 12 (2017): 110, 111; Nansook Park, Christopher Peterson, and Martin E. P. Seligman, Strengths of Character and Well Being, Journal of Social and Clinical Psychology, 23 (2004): 603; Christopher Peterson, Nansook Park, and Martin E. P. Seligman, Greater Strengths of Character and Recovery from Illness, Journal of Positive Psychology 1 (2006): 17; William Damon, The Path to Purpose, 29.

17. Christopher P. Niemiec, Richard M. Ryan, and Edward L. Deci, The Path Taken: Consequences of Attaining Intrinsic and Extrinsic Aspirations in Post-College Life, Journal of Research in Personality 73, no. 3 (2009): 291; Tim Kasser, The High Price of Mateialism (Cambridge, MA: MIT Press, 2002); Helga Dittmar, Rod Bond, Megan Hurst, and Tim Kasser, The Relationship between Materialism and Personal Well-Being: A Meta-Analysis, Journal of Peronality and Social Psychology 107 (2014): 879, 912–915; Luthar, Bankin, and Crossman, "I Can, Therefore I Must," 1537.

18. Martin E. P. Seligman, Authentic Happiness: Using the New Positive Psychology to Realize Your Potential for Lasting Fulfillment (New York: Free Press, 2002), 49; Ed Diener, Richard E. Lucas, and Christie Napa Scollon, Beyond the Hedonic Treadmill: Revising the Adaptation Theory of Well-Being, American Psychologist 61 (2006): 305.

19. Robert H. Frank, How Not to Buy Happiness, Daedalus 133 (2004): 69, 69–71; David G. Myers, The Pursuit of Happiness: What Makes a Person Happy—and Why? (New York: W. Morrow, 1992), 39.

20. Jonathan Haidt, The Happiness Hypothesis: Finding Modern Truth in Ancient Wisdom (New York: Basic Books, 2006), 53.

21. Chaim Stern, Day by Day: Reflections on the Themes of the Torah from Literature, Philosophy, and Religious Thought (1998), 171 (quoting Sir Norman MacEwan).

22. Reich, The Common Good, 137–138.

23. Reich, The Common Good, 153

24. Reich, The Common Good, 153 (quoting Rebecca Traister).

25. Remarks by President Obama.

26. Gallup, Trust in Government, January 10, 2017, http://news.gallup.com/poll/5392/trust-government.aspx.

27. Mark Leibovich, This Town: Two Parties and a Funeral—Plus Plenty of Valet Parking!—in America's Gilded Capital (New York: Blue Rider Press, 2013), 277.

Index